the WILD COAST 3

the WILD COAST

3

COAST

A KAYAKING, HIKING
AND RECREATION
GUIDE FOR B.C.'S
SOUTH COAST
AND EAST
VANCOUVER ISLAND

by John Kimantas

whitecap

All recommendations are made without guarantee on the part of the author or Whitecap Books Ltd. The author and publisher disclaim any liability in connection with the use of this information. For additional information, please contact Whitecap Books, 351 Lynn Avenue, North Vancouver, British Columbia, Canada V7J 2C4. Visit our website at **www.whitecap.ca**.

Edited by Elaine Jones
Proofread by Joan E. Templeton
Cover by Jesse Marchand & Jacqui Thomas
Interior design by Jacqui Thomas
Typeset by Diane Yee, Enthusiastic Elephant Illustration & Design
Photography and maps by John Kimantas (**www.thewildcoast.ca**)
Author photo by Leanne Chetcuti

Printed and bound in China

LIBRARY AND ARCHIVES CANADA CATALOGUING IN PUBLICATION

Kimantas, John
     The wild coast III : a kayaking, hiking and recreation guide for BC's
     south coast and east Vancouver Island / John Kimantas, author.

Includes index.
ISBN 1-55285-842-1
ISBN 978-1-55285-842-4

1. Kayaking—British Columbia—Pacific Coast—Guidebooks.
2. Kayaking—British Columbia—Vancouver Island—Guidebooks.
3. Hiking—British Columbia—Pacific Coast—Guidebooks. 4. Hiking—British Columbia—Vancouver Island—Guidebooks. 5. Outdoor recreation—British Columbia—Pacific Coast—Guidebooks. 6. Outdoor recreation—British Columbia—Vancouver Island—Guidebooks. I. Title. II. Title: Wild coast three.

GV776.15.B7K553 2007   797.122'4'09711   C2006-905004-X

The publisher acknowledges the financial support of the Government of Canada through the Canada Book Fund (CBF) and the Province of British Columbia through the Book Publishing Tax Credit.

Contents

Acknowledgements

Thanks to the government agencies and organizations that contributed information: B.C. Parks, Parks Canada, Integrated Land Management Bureau, B.C. Geological Survey, B.C. Ministry of Environment, B.C. Conservation Data Centre, Nature Canada, Environment Canada Weather Office, Islands Trust and regional districts of Mount Waddington, Comox-Strathcona, Powell River and Sunshine Coast.

My appreciation to the many people who contributed information by means of interviews, conversations and even email questionnaires, both government and public. A tip of the hat to Laurie Reid of Pedals and Paddles in Sechelt for the lift across Sechelt Peninsula.

Huge thanks to Leanne Chetcuti for repeatedly driving across Vancouver Island and even the Sunshine Coast to pick me up and drop me off during my 2006 explorations of the south coast.

Thanks to Lou Pescarmona and Seaward Kayaks for graciously lending a kayak for the 2006 trip along the south coast. 'Twas a grim day when the kayak rack detached from my car, spilling the borrowed kayak onto the Island Highway at 117 km per hour. The hull was cracked in several places, which I was forced to repair (poorly) with some emergency epoxy. Lou took it all in stride. Sorry I broke your kayak, Lou, but it still performed well. See **www.seawardkayaks.com**.

Loughborough Inlet.

Introduction

A FEW YEARS AGO I WAS CHATTING WITH MY FATHER, FRANK, ABOUT MY weekend kayaking adventures around Vancouver Island when he suggested I write about them. I agreed it was a good idea. In theory. But not as another I-went-here, I-did-this book about travelling the B.C. coast. Despite a few efforts by writers to keep up the spirit of adventure, the coast really hasn't been exotic since *The Curve of Time*. It's no longer the K2 of marine travel. Rather, it's our backyard, a known quantity, travelled safely by thousands every year.

As I spread out in my travels, though, I quickly realized B.C. is essentially still wild and unexplored for kayaking. There are established routes along the coast, but venture outside those and you're in a kayaking wilderness. So my task pretty much wrote itself: kayak the points beyond the main routes and stretch the limits of what we know. I wrote the first volume on a whim, taking a summer off work to run the outer Vancouver Island coast. Happily, when Whitecap Books became involved, publisher Robert McCullough quickly saw the potential for extending the series to cover the rest of B.C. And in doing so I was able to complete what had become a personal ambition: to kayak the coast to Alaska. And so *Volume 2* was born after a 3,400-km (2,100-mile) trip from Port Hardy to the Alaskan border and back (plus most places between) in 2005.

Research for the third volume allowed yet a third full summer of kayaking. Another 78 days were spent on the water in 2006, covering another 3,000 km (1,900 miles), bringing the research for this series to well over 10,000 km (6,000 miles).

The third volume of *The Wild Coast* completes a kayaking perspective of the entire B.C. coast outside the Queen Charlotte Islands—or at least complete enough to be able to travel from the southern tip of Vancouver Island to the Alaskan border with kayaking information about each step of the way.

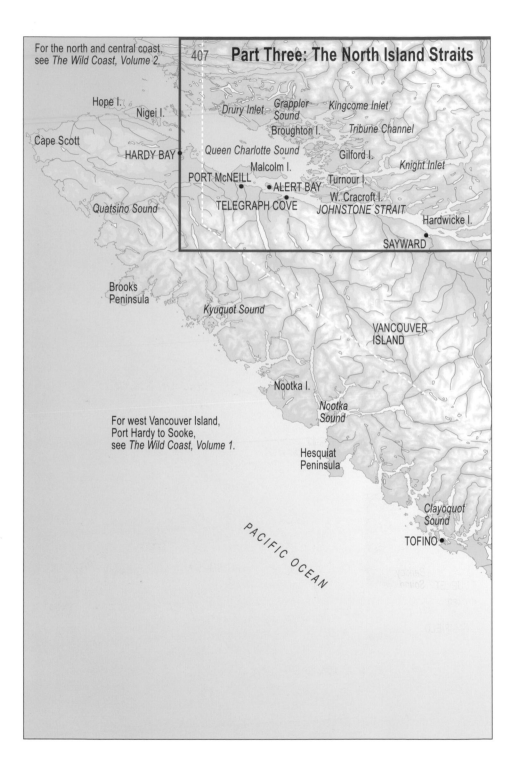

For the north and central coast, see *The Wild Coast, Volume 2.*

407 **Part Three: The North Island Straits**

Hope I.

Nigei I.

Drury Inlet   Grappler Sound   Kingcome Inlet

Broughton I.   Tribune Channel

Cape Scott

HARDY BAY   Queen Charlotte Sound   Gilford I.

Malcolm I.   Knight Inlet

PORT McNEILL   Turnour I.

ALERT BAY   W. Cracroft I.

TELEGRAPH COVE   *JOHNSTONE STRAIT*

Quatsino Sound   Hardwicke I.

SAYWARD

Brooks Peninsula

Kyuquot Sound

VANCOUVER ISLAND

Nootka I.

Nootka Sound

For west Vancouver Island, Port Hardy to Sooke, see *The Wild Coast, Volume 1.*

Hesquiat Peninsula

Clayoquot Sound

TOFINO

PACIFIC OCEAN

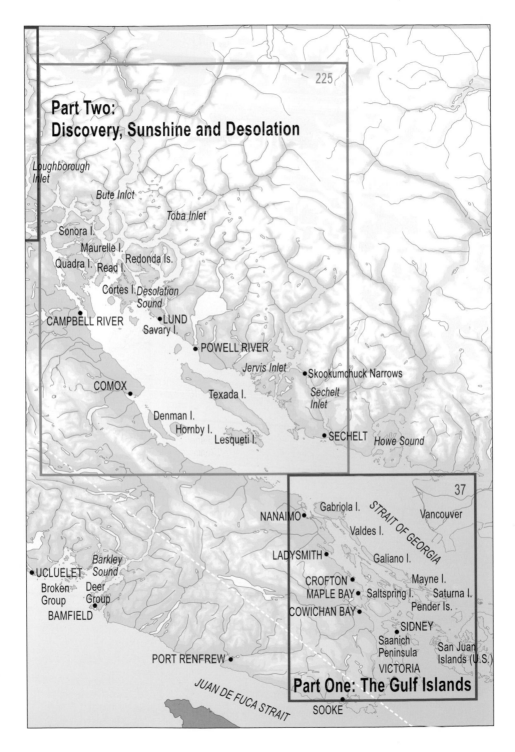

**Part Two:
Discovery, Sunshine and Desolation**

225

Loughborough Inlet

Bute Inlct

Toba Inlet

Sonora I.

Maurelle I.

Quadra I. Read I. Redonda Is.

Cortes I. Desolation Sound

CAMPBELL RIVER ●LUND
Savary I.

● POWELL RIVER

Jervis Inlet ● Skookumchuck Narrows

COMOX ●
Texada I.
Sechelt Inlet

Denman I.
Hornby I.
Lesqueti I.
● SECHELT Howe Sound

37

NANAIMO● Gabriola I. STRAIT OF GEORGIA Vancouver

Valdes I.

Barkley Sound
LADYSMITH ● Galiano I.

●UCLUELET
Broken Group Deer Group
CROFTON ● Mayne I.
MAPLE BAY ● Saltspring I. Saturna I.
COWICHAN BAY ● Pender Is.

BAMFIELD

● SIDNEY
Saanich Peninsula
San Juan Islands (U.S.)

PORT RENFREW ●

VICTORIA

Part One: The Gulf Islands

JUAN DE FUCA STRAIT
SOOKE

It might seem like camping is possible anywhere on the coast, but ideal sites are few and the competition for spots on the coast is increasing.

This volume differs because it covers large areas dominated by private shorefront, busy commercial and recreational traffic corridors and large urban centres. It follows tried-and-true routes where saturation, not isolation, is a key concern. But just like other areas of the coast, if you stray from the main routes, it won't be long before yours is the only paddle dipping into the water. This, to me, is where the real attraction of the coast begins—visiting places few other people see.

This book is a shopping list, if you like, of these types of places and a framework to travel them. It may just persuade you there's a reason to go outside the ordinary.

COMPLETING THE B.C. MARINE TRAIL

In Jennifer Hahn's book, *Spirited Waters*, there's a gripping passage where she's unable to find a campsite while kayaking the Inside Passage. Exhausted, she pulls out onto two tree trunks that have fallen at an angle side-by-side into Grenville Passage. While she naps, the tide drops a metre and a half (five feet), and she awakes to discover she and the kayak are suspended in mid-air.

This story perfectly illustrates the largest problem with kayaking the B.C. coast: the lack of campsites continues to place kayakers in peril. Create a known network of reliable sites, however, and this key safety issue disappears. And there's no reason Grenville Channel shouldn't be as safe in this day and age as, say, Sechelt Inlet, with its network of campsites.

When I paddled the north and central B.C. coast in 2005, I assumed it would be just a matter of finding campsites and creating an inventory. It was quickly apparent, though, after visiting beach after beach with the upland choked solid with vegetation, that these sites simply don't exist. This put me in the uncomfortable position of having to suggest sites that might be okay for camping on the beach at some tide levels, but which would need to be developed before they could be safe havens under all conditions. This meant, in effect, directing people to as-of-now dubious sites.

In 2006, I expected the relative urbanization of B.C.'s south coast would mean a more thorough campsite network, and in many places a network does exist. Yet stray a few miles off the established routes and the campsites disappear.

A push began in the early 1990s to create a marine trail from Washington to Alaska with a backbone of campsites every 16 km (10 miles). After a few initial victories, however, the momentum sputtered. Meanwhile, boaters have been extremely successful in a push to formalize anchorages. The Council of British Columbia Yacht Clubs prepared an inventory of anchorages, terming them "boat havens" essential to transiting the coast. The B.C. government adopted the CBCYC inventory almost as a policy document, and many of the havens became provincial parks. Others have been protected by the Land Act Notations of Interest for Use, Recreation and Enjoyment by the Public (UREP NOIs). That acronym may well be the key to establishing a marine trail.

The UREP notation has certainly come in handy for boaters. For instance, in the recently adopted Central Coast Land Resource Management Plan, there are 27 recommendations for NOIs. Sixteen are for the protection of boat havens, and 11 for marine conservation and protection. Do the math and you'll see a problem: none of these notations protect kayaking interests.

This constitutes a huge missed opportunity for kayakers. The central coast land use plan has established public policy for the use of much of B.C.'s coast without formally protecting existing wilderness campsites or holding to the ideal of establishing a marine trail. This means decisions about use of coastal lands will not be filtered through the key question: does this proposed use jeopardize the creation of a marine trail?

This is problematic, as B.C. has a dearth of kayak-friendly beaches to begin with. Meanwhile, fish farming is poised to expand. Resorts and fishing lodges are being planned and proponents are seeking Crown land to build upon or coves for floats. Commercial tour operators are hoping to eventually get exclusive tenure rights to campsites on Crown land. And First Nations land treaties are being settled, which will take huge tracts of coastland out of public hands.

Hopefully a few kayakers reading this will see the risk. I believe if there is no route of protected campsites along B.C.'s coast in the next 10 years, it will likely never exist as it could have or should have. The longer the network is delayed, the more it will become a patchwork of second-rate beaches and sites where prime locations have been lost to other interests. At worst there will be long stretches where no suitable campsites can be created, essentially killing the concept.

This edition of the *Wild Coast* series adds the final component to an on-paper marine trail system across the coast. A good first step to validating the network is creating a history of use. Every year kayaking clubs have tours that make use of existing sites along the coast. Here's a challenge: include on your itinerary a site that isn't established, and make it a working holiday by spending a day clearing a tent site.

Kayaking clubs should also become leaders in the push for a marine trail system. Clubs in British Columbia, Washington and Oregon should work together to form a marine trail committee and push the agenda forward. Such a move should help jump-start the B.C. Marine Trail Association, which has been inactive now for years, or a suitable replacement.

Individual kayakers using *The Wild Coast*'s kayaking marine trail framework can help validate the sites as well. I appreciate that clearing campsites goes against the concept of no-trace camping, but a few tent-sized clearings of salal or huckleberries have a minimal effect. Meanwhile, the survival of kayakers is at risk without them.

Anyone planning a trip can keep abreast of changes in campsite status by visiting **www.thewildcoast.ca.** Note there are already a few changes detailed in the epilogue of this book.

Rock ledges at White Cliff Islets, Broughton Archipelago.

ROCK BLUFF CAMPING

In the first two volumes I avoided including campsites that required rock ledge landings. Then came Desolation Sound, where a good number of the campsites lack beaches.

The attraction is easy to understand. Given a choice of camping on a rock bluff looking out over the ocean or in a forest setting inside a cove—well, there's no comparison. With Desolation Sound setting the precedent, it wasn't much of a leap to include other rock bluffs as potential campsites where appropriate. The only real requirement is a fairly sheltered environment to allow you to get in and out of the kayak safe from swell. Fortunately, sheltered areas are common along the south coast.

The ledges, however, come with some hazards. For instance, the rock can be slippery. Also, watch for boat wash. It's not unusual for a ship or large boat to create waves that advance 2–3 horizontal metres (8–10 feet) along a rock face.

Wind waves, swell and rough conditions can also strand you. Even a small swell can make loading or getting into a kayak difficult when there is no beach. So choosing a sheltered spot can be crucial.

The vast majority of the B.C. coast north of Campbell River is public land.

To secure a tent on rock, you'll need extra bungy cords. Fasten the cord through the tent peg loop, pull the cord taut and drop a heavy rock onto it. Voila, you have the equivalent of a tent peg. Driftwood can also work, if it's heavy enough.

Rock bluff campsites are distinguished on the maps with a brown tent icon. A small brown triangle marks spots where multiple opportunities for rock bluff camping exist but none cry out as a perfect spot. Check them out but be prepared for a backup plan, as they may not be to your liking.

Once you wean yourself from the need for a beach, a whole new world of camping will be open to you, offering some of the best camping spots on the coast.

PRIVATE VERSUS PUBLIC LAND

Canada differs from the United States in that private ownership of waterfront ends at the high tide line. This means anyone can use the beach, even if there is a mansion behind it.

This works better in theory than practice. Add a dock, boathouse, personal clutter, a barking dog and a family barbecuing on the porch of the house, and using the beach in front for a break will be an intrusion; camping on it would be next to unthinkable. This doesn't mean someone can't use the area below the highest tide level, however, and this has led to clashes between residents and campers in places like Savary Island, where backpacking visitors regularly plunk down tents in front of houses.

In rare cases there is a private foreshore right. This is usually only extended to developments such as marinas.

In the northern straits the vast majority of land is Crown land—that is, publicly owned land with no access restrictions. Farther south, however, beginning at the Discovery Islands, the balance begins to tip toward private ownership, until south of Campbell River private ownership is the rule and Crown land a rare exception.

Property borders are marked by gray outlined or shaded boxes on most island maps. Expect the higher the density of parcels, the more likely it is to have houses. Quarter-sections, on the other hand, are more likely to be Crown or forestry land. Naturally, the latter will make a far better area to explore, so these property divisions can be used to avoid planning a route alongside heavy residential areas such as north Saltspring Island.

COMMERCIAL OPERATORS AND CROWN CAMPSITES

In a few locations along the coast, most specifically Johnstone Strait and the Broughton Archipelago, commercial kayak tour companies and private kayakers are increasingly in conflict. Here's the problem: commercial kayaking groups don't want to bring clients into a camp-site only to find it overrun with casual visitors. The solution for many has been to set up a base camp—an established campsite, usually with some fairly permanent structures. They can do this through a forest use permit, but there's nothing currently on the books to stop a com-mercial operator from simply commandeering a wilderness campsite on Crown land. Many have done this. By use of tarps, tables and gear, a commercial operation can effectively block off public access, turning Crown land into a private campground as long as they keep the equipment onsite, which can be from the end of June to the be-ginning of September.

Even a forest use permit, however, doesn't give a commercial operator exclusive use to Crown land. The only exception is on First Nations–managed Crown lands (covered below). This means that even when a commercial operator has an established base camp, nothing prevents private individuals from setting up their tents among the

Kayaking the Gulf Islands.

group. The operator can restrict access to his tents, tarps and equipment, but every spot of open land is fair game for public use.

Naturally, stepping into a tour group site is undesirable for both the commercial operator and the visiting kayakers. To ward off conflict many commercial operators have created nearby tent clearings to which they can direct private kayaking parties as they arrive—a good compromise.

The only Crown land where tour operators currently have exclusivity is Hanson Island (see page 473). As part of the treaty negotiation process, the Mamalilikulla, Namgis and Tlowitsis First Nations have been given management of the island through a head lease from the provincial government. This has allowed these First Nations the right to sell leases to commercial operators. A few tour operators have established permanent base camps this way. Some, like the one near Big Bay, bar public use. Others, like the one at Weynton Point, keep an area aside for the public.

An inevitable change at some point in the future will be the formalization of the forest use permit/tenure process. Such a step was instituted a few years ago but bogged down within the government over internal jurisdiction. When the tenure system is finally formalized, there's a very real possibility it will allow tour operators exclusive use of the Crown land in their tenure. This means many beaches and camping areas, particularly in Johnstone Strait where dozens of tour companies operate, could become permanently off-limits to the public. While it would be easy to argue against granting exclusive rights to public land, a good compromise would be formalizing public sites so kayakers are ensured places to stay. At the very least, kayaking clubs should be lobbying for some form of protection now, lest many wilderness campsites are suddenly swallowed up without consideration for the marine trail concept.

ABOUT THE GULF ISLANDS NATIONAL PARK

With the creation of the Gulf Islands National Park in May 2003, the Strait of Georgia Lowlands gained federal protection. Canadians can breathe a sigh of relief that the Gulf Islands now have nationally protected status, joining 25 of the country's 39 distinct natural regions that have federal parks.

In assembling the land for the park, the focus was put on Saturna Island. In all, 1,108 ha (4.3 square miles) of Saturna is protected within the park, an area comprising almost half the national park. As for the rest, the goal was reached in large part by converting all existing southern Gulf Islands provincial parks, Crown lands and Crown islets into the national park reserve. This in effect usurped the Gulf Islands' provincial marine park system: Winter Cove on Saturna, Cabbage Island near Saturna, Beaumont on South Pender Island, Sidney Spit on Sidney Island, Isle-de-Lis on Rum Island, Princess Margaret on Portland Island and D'Arcy Island. This meant that initially the national park was created while protecting very little additional land in the Gulf Islands.

Fortunately Parks Canada has been busy filling in the holes with new land purchases, such as interior parcels on the Pender Islands and on Saturna Island to join the originally disjointed Crown parcels on Brown Ridge.

The biggest change is Parks Canada's management of the Crown islets. Many were heavily used recreationally, such as Anniversary Island and the Belle Chain Islets north of Saturna Island, Red Islets and Hawkins Island off Portland Island, Java Islets south of Saturna Island and Reay Island near Sidney. Now these all have a hands-off policy, with just two islets open to day use on the shore (Dock Island and the Belle Chain islet closest to Samuel Island).

If the resulting park appears to be a patchwork, it's not unprecedented. It follows the footsteps of the St. Lawrence Island National Park and Georgian Bay Islands National Park where various islands and portions of islands were combined into a single, although somewhat disjointed, entity.

The changes make Parks Canada a large shareholder of an extremely endangered ecosystem, the coastal Douglas-fir zone. It represents just one-quarter of one percent of B.C.'s land mass (or 2,161 square kilometres/834 square miles), of which only about one percent was protected prior to the creation of the national park.

It also makes Parks Canada a huge shareholder in the management of the only kayak-accessible campgrounds in the southern Gulf Islands. If the Broken Group is any indication, kayakers can expect strict monitoring of islands and sites to ensure campers play by the rules—that is, no use of casual undesignated sites any more, such as the fringe of D'Arcy Island. With five campsites lost

Richardson Cove, one of the newly protected properties in the the Gulf Islands National Park.

on the Crown islets, the good news is a few new areas have been earmarked for primitive camping, such as Narvaez Bay on Saturna Island. These would make important additions to a marine trail system in the area.

Parks Canada is still completing the management plan for the new park, a process that will likely take until 2012. For current information, including the status on the Narvaez Bay campsite, visit **www.pc.gc.ca**.

MANAGING WINDS

In the introduction to the other volumes of *The Wild Coast*, I tackled issues such as managing open water, weather, shipping traffic and other universal issues. All are part and parcel of a safe kayaking expedition, but nothing stops a kayaking outing quite like a strong wind. Such winds can maroon you for days, and there is seemingly little that can be done about it. However, there are a few fundamental truths about winds worth noting, plus a few tips that can help manage them.

First, the south coast has the most placid summers of any British Columbia coastal location. Usually a series of high-pressure systems will settle in between June and September, bringing warm weather (by coastal standards) and a prevailing northwest wind. A pattern should emerge of a calm early morning followed by increases over the course of the day until the winds peak in early to mid-afternoon.

In this weather pattern, your best bet is to kayak early in the day and be prepared to leave the water in early afternoon as the winds rise. Naturally, there are variations. For instance, if you wake up to a brisk wind from the southeast, you may want to think twice about your trip this day. Southeast winds usually mean unsettled weather. At the very least, consult the Coast Guard weather reports on your VHF marine radio, which is essential on any multi-day trip. (Note that wind funnels through many passages, so a northwest wind may manifest itself as an easterly or southerly in a localized area. In some areas, a southeasterly doesn't necessarily mean you'll be getting the corresponding weather condition.)

If you do find yourself facing strong winds, here are some questions to ask yourself before writing off a day's paddle.

Is the wind localized?
In many places, a wind will funnel down a valley or whip along a mountainside, affecting the water in only a small area. You may be able to paddle out of it, and the winds may be low a few miles away. Some areas are notorious for these localized winds, such as Windy Point on Johnstone Strait.

Is the wind funnelling?
In many channels, passages and inlets the wind is strongest through a central stream. In Johnstone Strait and Knight Inlet, for instance, the centre of the strait can have rough whitecaps while the area nearest to shore has comparatively small wind waves. Even if this doesn't occur, sticking to the indentations of the shore may allow you to avoid the worst of the wind. A problem with this strategy is it may work well for a few miles, then disappear around a curve in the channel or beyond an exposed point, putting you dead against the brunt of the wind.

Can I change my route?
A wind can be unpleasant to paddle against, but it might be a nice boost to have behind you. By choosing a side passage, you may be able to avoid the wind altogether. For instance, east of Quadra Island I noticed that when a northwesterly was making passage miserable in Hoskyn Channel, Sutil Channel was calm. So consider the lee

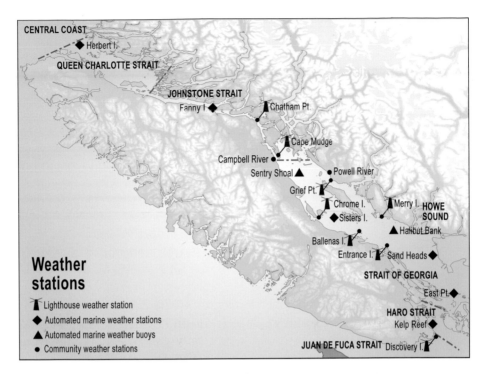

CENTRAL COAST
◆ Herbert I.
QUEEN CHARLOTTE STRAIT
JOHNSTONE STRAIT
Fanny I. ◆   ▲ Chatham Pt.
◆ Cape Mudge
Campbell River ●
Sentry Shoal ▲   ● Powell River
Grief Pt. ▲
Chrome I. ▲   ▲ Merry I. HOWE
◆ Sisters I.   SOUND
▲ Halibut Bank
Ballenas I. ▲
Entrance I. ▲ Sand Heads ◆
STRAIT OF GEORGIA
East Pt. ◆
HARO STRAIT
Kelp Reef ◆
JUAN DE FUCA STRAIT Discovery I. ▲

Weather stations

▲ Lighthouse weather station
◆ Automated marine weather stations
▲ Automated marine weather buoys
● Community weather stations

side of islands, or travel secondary channels. Taking into account prevailing wind patterns when planning a trip can also help. For instance, you may want to travel the channels north of Johnstone Strait when planning a westbound trip.

MANAGING CURRENTS

The south coast and eastern Vancouver Island are different from the other parts of the coast for the speed of many tidal currents. You may even have to plan around them, timing your trip to avoid opposing currents or ending your paddling at a predetermined location in order to run a rapid or succession of rapids the next day.

Some of these rapids can be dangerous. The Gulf Islands has Active Pass, Porlier Pass, Gabriola Passage, Sansum Narrows and Dodd Narrows, plus strong currents in many other channels. And this is nothing compared to the Discovery Islands, where you have Seymour Narrows, Surge Narrows, Hole in the Wall, Okisollo's Upper and Lower Rapids, Yuculta Rapids, Gillard Passage, Arran Rapids, Dent Rapids, Greene Point Rapids, Whirlpool Rapids, Ripple Point, Race Passage and Current Passage.

Rapids at the entrance to Hidden Basin.

The simplest and most basic safety technique is to time a transit for slack tide. Another is planning a transit for slack tide when the tide is changing in your direction of travel. This eliminates the risk of being caught having to paddle against a current growing steadily more dangerous.

A huge safety consideration is that the tide levels often have nothing to do with the tide currents. If you arrive at a rapid at high tide thinking the current is going to change to an ebb, think again. Flood currents can continue for several hours after the high tide level has been reached; conversely, ebb currents can begin long before high tide.

An indespensible tool is the *Canadian Tide and Current Tables. Volume 5* covers the Georgia Basin to Desolation Sound. *Volume 6* continues north to the top end of Vancouver Island and the start of the central coast. In the back of both volumes look for *Table 4, Reference and Secondary Current Stations.* Reference stations have times listed for the turn to flood and ebb currents earlier in the volume. Secondary stations rely on calculations based on a primary reference station.

It takes only a few moments to calculate the slack times at secondary stations. When there is a + sign, add that amount to the time of the listed slack current times for the reference station. When there is a − sign, subtract it. For instance, for Sansum Narrows in *Volume 5*, the turn to flood is 25 minutes after the turn at Active Pass. The turn to ebb is 35 minutes before. This is reflected in the symbols +0 25 and −0 35 respectively.

All times listed in the *Canadian Tide and Current Tables* are Pacific Standard Time. When you are travelling during the summer, in Daylight Saving Time, add an hour to the times listed. Therefore, to calculate the evening turn to ebb at Sansum Narrows on August 11, 2006, take the Active Pass time of 1828, convert it to a regular hour of 6:28 p.m., add the hour for Daylight Saving Time to change it to 7.28 p.m., then subtract the 35 minutes to get the final time of 6:53 p.m.

These calculations exclude idiosyncracies. On a flood tide you would generally expect a flood current. But it's not so simple.

The most common variation is a countercurrent. Since kayakers tend to stay near shore, planning your trip to coincide with the current may actually be counterproductive. Countercurrents occur along convoluted shorelines, usually in bays. Passages are generally a series of points connected by indentations, and any of these may have a countercurrent. You may be paddling along happily, thinking you're getting a boost from the current, only to discover your progress has been half what you expected.

The general rule of thumb is that shallower shorelines will have lower currents. I've actually done well paddling through many of the narrows against the current by using shoreline countercurrents to approach, then the shallows to cross. Often I've kept up with motorized yachts fighting a strong current mid-channel. Eventually these soft spots may run out. But it's surprising how often they don't.

Naturally, there are some rapids, narrows and channels where there simply is no protection, and running against the current at certain times will be impossible and travelling with the current would be foolhardy. Places such as Porlier Pass and Skookumchuck Narrows are known for dangerous eddies, whirlpools and overfalls. In any of these areas of extreme currents, it's advisable to wait for slack tide and a change to a favourable current.

Another huge consideration is the extent to which these currents change their peak speed depending on the time of the month. Some days rapids may have a top current of 3 knots, generally safe to navigate for most kayakers, while on other days the same rapids may top 12 knots—potentially deadly to all skill levels. So picking the right time of the month to cross can make all the difference.

One of the problems with the south coast is many areas have strong currents and corresponding turbulence extending over many miles, meaning that kayakers may not be clear of the area before the current grows, creating the risk of eddies and other dangers. These locations are best travelled by expert kayakers only. Seymour Narrows, Yuculta to Dent rapids and south Johnstone Strait should be attempted only by veterans. Conversely, the short narrows, including even the most dangerous, such as Skookumchuck, can be safely transited by kayakers with less experience if attention is paid to cross at a favourable slack period. Just don't dally!

About rips: These are usually created where currents clash. They often appear as waves, and can be frothing white water. They are intimidating to see and hear, as they can roar like a rapid. The best advice I can give about most rips is they look worse than they are. Kayaks are well suited for riding through them. If you run a rip to leave one current for another, or to enter a calm spot, you may find yourself turned by the clash of currents. But this should leave you in a relative calm once you're through, so no harm done. The worst risk seems to be where the two opposing currents clash to form whirlpools. The smaller ones are generally harmless, maybe twisting you a bit. And the large ones... well, I've never been sucked into one, so I can't say. But I suspect it probably isn't good. The best way to avoid large whirlpools is to stay out of currents fast enough to create them.

The single biggest safety tip I can give for rough water is to keep paddling. The paddle makes an excellent outrigger as it pushes through the water. So if you hold your paddle at the ready to brace when heading into a rapid you are probably doing yourself a disservice. From there it's simply a matter of steadying yourself and keeping your centre of balance as you are sloshed around. If you find yourself feeling tippy or uncomfortably sloshed, long, hard paddle strokes will probably help.

Assuming adequate kayaking experience and a good fundamental knowledge of coastal waters, my general rule of thumb for rapids is this: 1–2 knots—enjoy; 2–3 knots—it might shake your nerves but you'll come out okay if you follow the basic rules; 3–5 knots—experts only, or intermediate kayakers running a localized current, preferably with some type of team support; 5–7 knots—you had better be an expert and know what you are doing; above 7 knots—don't try it. Naturally, there are many variables, but the trick is to stay within your comfort level. Then push it just a little bit, to take your kayaking to the next level. You'll quickly find it usually looks much worse than it is.

The entrance to Toba Inlet.

ABOUT THE INLETS

There are eight major inlets along B.C.'s south coast: Saanich, Sechelt, Jervis, Toba, Bute, Loughborough, Knight and Kingcome. Their potential for kayaking varies greatly. For instance, Sechelt Inlet is one of the best established kayaking regions on the coast. Knight Inlet, by contrast, is rarely kayaked and highly unsuitable as a kayaking destination. Meanwhile, Loughborough Inlet is rarely visited by any form of boat but is well suited to a visit by kayak.

All inlets have their particular challenges, but the greatest will be wind. They are prone to the prevailing winds as well as their own inflow, outflow or katabatic (mountain-fed) winds. I've kayaked into all the inlets on B.C.'s coast and have found no pattern or theory to explain the conditions I've encountered. I've paddled inlets famous for outflow winds and had an inflow wind my entire trip. Others seem highly variable and shift from hour to hour, mile by mile.

The only thing I will say in general is you can expect wind, and it's likely to be far more of a factor than in the outlying channels. The higher mountains in the inlets tend to cause the winds to funnel. The variation in coastal and inland temperatures creates the wind. This makes me very wary about suggesting inlets as kayaking destinations. As bad as the wind may get in Johnstone Strait, there are always side channels to explore. Inlets give few options. For all

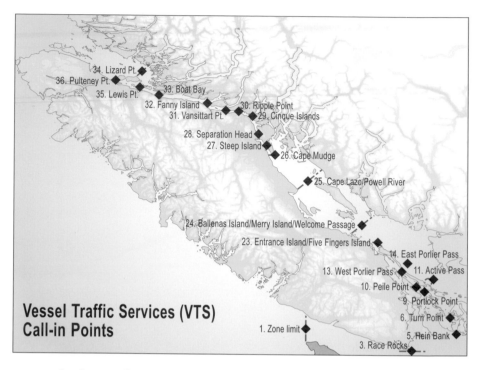

Vessel Traffic Services (VTS) Call-in Points

34. Lizard Pt.
36. Pulteney Pt.
35. Lewis Pt.
33. Boat Bay
32. Fanny Island
31. Vansittart Pt.
30. Ripple Point
29. Cinque Islands
28. Separation Head
27. Steep Island
26. Cape Mudge
25. Cape Lazo/Powell River
24. Ballenas Island/Merry Island/Welcome Passage
23. Entrance Island/Five Fingers Island
14. East Porlier Pass
13. West Porlier Pass
11. Active Pass
10. Peile Point
9. Portlock Point
6. Turn Point
1. Zone limit
5. Hein Bank
3. Race Rocks

the long miles you'll get less marine wildlife, fewer camping options and mountain views only if the clouds disperse. And deep inlets will be the last place on the B.C. coast where they disperse.

That isn't to say inlets can't be rewarding. Viewing grizzly bears is one reason to go; the simple challenge of completing an inlet is another. One great way to explore an inlet is take a water taxi to the head, then use the invariably stronger ebb current to carry you out.

Unfortunately, some inlets are simply not desirable to kayak. At the top of that list is Knight Inlet. It's long, the winds are strong and the scenery is mundane.

Other inlets are borderline. Toba and Bute are stunningly beautiful and great to visit but are probably best enjoyed near the entrance where you can take in the mountain scenery without suffering what can be miserable conditions in the inlet. Day trips from a base camp near the mouth are advisable.

Loughborough and Jervis inlets are well suited to kayaking, with some exceptional camping opportunities in Loughborough—a rarity, as inlets are known for their steep shorelines and lack of beaches. Jervis Inlet also has some beautiful camping options, plus

A ferry passes Helen Point on its way into Active Pass. Expect to see several of these during a transit of the pass.

the Holy Grail of Princess Louisa Inlet, one of the most scenic locations in B.C. It's a challenge but is highly recommended.

The most interesting, in many respects, is Kingcome Inlet. The scenery, the visible First Nations history, even the challenge of kayaking such an isolated region, made it a worthwhile place to visit. The lack of suitable camping areas is problematic, however. My suggestion for visiting this region is a water taxi to Kingcome village and a trip down the inlet back to your end point through the Broughton Archipelago—a wonderfully diverse trip.

MANAGING MARINE VESSEL TRAFFIC

I remember a crossing of Swanson Channel from North Pender Island to Portlock Point on Prevost Island when I first began kayaking. Like many paddlers, I relied on luck to make it across the main ferry route between Vancouver and Victoria. In the middle of the channel my son Damien and I heard the horn of a ferry in Active Pass. Moments later the ferry came out of the channel and proceeded down Swanson Channel, appearing for all the world like it was heading straight for us. The encounter wasn't even close in the end, though that could be because the ferry changed its course slightly to accommodate us. Either way, it didn't relieve the several minutes of panic as we paddled furiously to get out of the way.

Ferries are invariably the most challenging traffic kayakers will encounter on the south coast, particularly in the southern Gulf

Islands, simply because they are so frequent. Farther north, in areas such as Johnstone Strait, it will be cruise ships; they're often the equivalent of 16-storey buildings—small cities, almost—passing by at speeds of 20 knots through channels as narrow as Blackney Passage. Sightlines are poor along these routes, so keeping an eye open is simply not enough. This is when a marine radio comes in handy, along with a knowledge of Vessel Traffic Services call-in points.

All shipping traffic is required to check in with Vessel Traffic Services at various designated points along the B.C. coast. These points are chosen to aid transit through the most difficult portions of the coast. For instance, ships must call in to Victoria Traffic when both entering and exiting Active Pass. The station used for Victoria Traffic is Channel 11. Its jurisdiction continues as far north as the Merry Island light station near Sechelt. North of Merry Island is the jurisdiction of Comox Traffic, which uses frequency Channel 71.

While any public use of these frequencies should be limited to emergencies only, anyone can monitor them. It won't take long to get a clear picture of where vessels are, and you can plan your crossing accordingly.

A WORD ABOUT FERRY WASH

During one visit to the Red Islets off Prevost Island (in the days when camping was allowed there), I was unloading my kayak about five minutes after a ferry had passed. There was no evidence of any incoming waves, but when the wash hit the shore it was fierce. Where there had been gently lapping waves there were suddenly 60-cm (2-foot) breakers on the beach. My kayak was pounded by waves that broke over the hatches and into the cockpit. Only by hanging on for dear life was I able to keep the kayak from being washed away or trounced on the rocks.

Cruise ships can do the same. I remember talking to one fellow about an instance where he had camped on the central coast, being careful to stash the kayaks above the high tide line for the night. The group hadn't factored in the wash from a passing cruise ship, and they later found their kayaks high on shore, fortunately washed up instead of away.

Here's a simple bit of advice: don't unload your kayak in the few minutes after a ferry has passed. Don't leave your kayak unattended or sitting untied on a beach unless you're sure of the passing traffic—that is, unless you're in sight of both your kayak and the channel. Always tie up your kayak at night or during extended visits, even on higher ground. Don't tie up to drift logs. They, by nature, can drift away as well.

Always err on the side of caution. To me that means securing the kayak whenever I'm not in it. You don't want to be the one thanking the Coast Guard for retrieving a kayak making its way unpiloted down Haro Strait, nor do you want to apologize in front of the national media for setting off the ensuing international search and rescue.

LAUNCHING OPTIONS AND ISSUES

It should be easy: find a nice beach to launch your kayak and go. The problem is there are surprisingly few options, and for most of them you'll have to bring cash.

The most common launch option is to use an existing boat ramp, usually run by a municipality, where fees may apply for both launching and parking. Marinas also usually offer both launches and parking. These fees may be more expensive than municipal launches, but it's surprising how often the prices are comparable. Be sure to ask if there is a weekly or monthly rate for parking, if applicable. You may be able to negotiate a better price through a private operator, and marinas tend to have better security for your vehicle than a public or roadside pullout. Unfortunately, some marinas are less accommodating to kayakers than others, viewing them—and the extended time it takes to pack a kayak—as an inconvenience, and so discourage kayakers from using their facilities. You may want to call before arriving.

In many ways public road access to beaches is preferable to boat launches, as it is more spacious, often sand instead of concrete, less busy and generally free. Opportunities for beach launching are most common in residential areas in the Gulf Islands or southern Vancouver Island. The biggest concern is suitable parking. Residents tend to dislike transient traffic, and a few locals look for the opportunity to have someone towed. Be sure to double-check parking signs. In most cases kayakers will have to unload and then find suitable parking nearby.

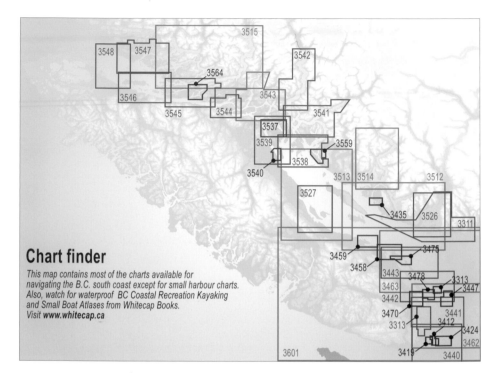

Chart finder

This map contains most of the charts available for navigating the B.C. south coast except for small harbour charts. Also, watch for waterproof BC Coastal Recreation Kayaking and Small Boat Atlases from Whitecap Books. Visit www.whitecap.ca

MAP SYMBOLS

⊼ *Rest area:* The picnic table icon denotes a beach ideal as a place for a break. While camping may be possible, the site did not meet the criteria for a desirable campsite. The most common reason is the upland is private property.

▲ *Established campsite:* The blue tent indicates a campsite with a developed camping area, usually with formal recognition, either as a forest recreation site or established within a provincial park. Expect these sites to be free.

▲ *Undeveloped campsite:* The red tent icon indicates a beach that has not yet been developed or is underdeveloped, with no official sanction or protection beyond being located on Crown land. In some cases the icon is used for wilderness sites in provincial parks when established sites are nearby.

▲ *Fee camping:* The green tent indicates formal campsites that charge fees; they may be in provincial parks, private campgrounds or reserves.

▲ *Rock ledge camping:* The brown tent icon indicates camping locations that have no or poor beaches. They are picked because the above-tide portions of rock are desirable camping locations, usually being flat, mossy bluffs. Many, like those in Desolation Sound, are established.

▲ *Possible rock ledge camping:* The smaller, solid brown tent icon indicates a cluster of islets or rocks where rock ledge camping may be possible. Individual sites were not identified because of the many possibilities. The prime locations have been given the larger rock ledge camping icon.

▩ *Car and RV campsite:* This icon indicates sites with vehicle access. These may or may not be marine-accessible, but they're generally inferior kayak camping locations. Provincial, regional or municipal sites are listed; private sites are listed only if they're strategically significant.

⚓ *Anchorage:* The anchor icon indicates some recognized all-weather anchorages. It's not comprehensive, as this guide isn't intended to replace cruising guides.

⬅ *Boat launch site:* This icon indicates locations suitable for launching trailer-carried boats, car-top boats and kayaks.

🛶 *Kayak launch:* This icon indicates places suitable for launching kayaks or other car-top boats, usually at beach accesses. They invariably have no official status.

🗼 *Lighthouse:* This symbol is used for manned lighthouses or previously manned light stations where the buildings are still in evidence. It doesn't include lighted buoys or navigation lights.

⛵ *Private marina:* This icon shows the general location of a private marina. Kayakers may find them useful in remote regions where they are often the only source of supplies and services. In urban areas many have boat ramps and long-term parking, which may be preferable for launching.

Public wharf: This icon indicates the location of government wharves. Most wharves allow several hours of free moorage. Kayaks can also tie up under stairwells or in other out-of-the-way locations so boats won't be inconvenienced.

Sea lion haulout: This icon indicates rocks or log booms that sea lions are known to frequent. They can often be seen year-round at these locations.

Trail: The purple dotted lines indicate recognized hiking routes. Most coastal routes are not maintained and may be overgrown. In some locations the maps were too congested to indicate trails; be sure to see the accompanying text.

Bird nesting area: This icon indicates a known seabird nesting location.

Bird viewing area: This icon of a bird in flight indicates a prime location for bird viewing during the summer. Winter migration staging areas are omitted.

Killer whale area of interest: This icon is used for locating key killer whale areas such as rubbing beaches and prime viewing sites. The summer orca migration route includes Queen Charlotte Strait, Blackfish Sound, Johnstone Strait and adjacent waterways.

First Nations heritage site: This stylized eagle head indicates former village sites, significant traditional-use sites and the location of key pictographs and petroglyphs. It is not comprehensive.

Parkland: Orange indicates provincial, federal and, occasionally, regional parks. Marine areas and some terrestrial areas protected as parkland are indicated by a hatched orange outline. The two can be used interchangeably. The reason is practical: in some cases shaded areas can obscure details, in others the hatched outlines can be difficult to see.

First Nations (reserve) land: Pink indicates First Nations land as allotted generally in the 1880s. It's likely the amount of reserve land will increase substantially as treaty settlements are reached.

Private property: Grey, either bordered or shaded, indicates private property. (Shaded squares are generally used only for clarity.) In some cases (such as Quadra Island), shaded areas are used where the density is too high to show individual lots. Variations are noted on the maps. Along Vancouver Island south of Campbell River, land is assumed to be private property and is therefore not always indicated on the maps.

Municipal boundary: Purple hatched lines indicate boundaries of towns, villages or cities. In southern Vancouver Island where urban development is heavy, no boundaries are indicated.

Default ground cover: On maps north of Campbell River where private property is indicated, the green is assumed to be Crown land. South of Campbell River on Vancouver Island and the off-lying islands the land is assumed to be private, even if it's the default green.

Military property: Light orange property indicates Department of National Defence lands.

Crown land: Light yellow indicates Crown land on select maps where municipalities have completed a Crown land audit or Crown land is a known quantity. Many municipalities have not completed a Crown land inventory. On areas north of Campbell River all land not marked as private is Crown land and indicated by the default green. Crown land privatized by tenures is not indicated.

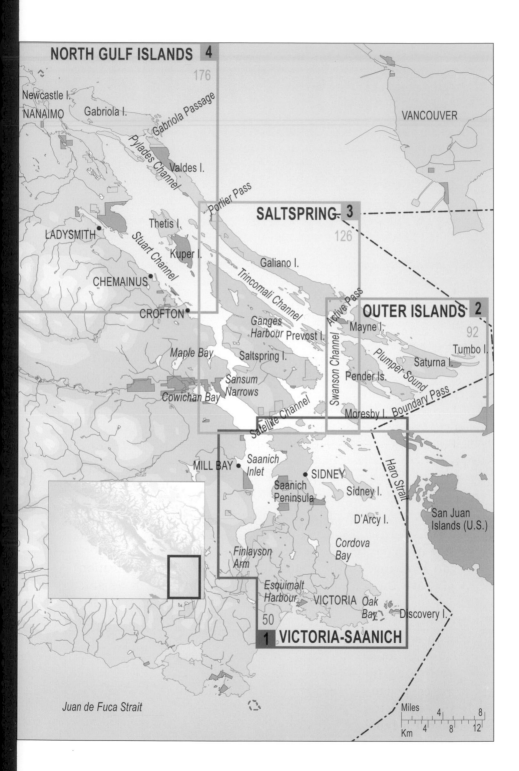

NORTH GULF ISLANDS `4`

176

Newcastle I.
NANAIMO
Gabriola I.

Gabriola Passage

Pylades Channel

Valdes I.

Porlier Pass

SALTSPRING `3`

126

VANCOUVER

Thetis I.

LADYSMITH

Stuart Channel

Kuper I.

CHEMAINUS

Galiano I.

Trincomali Channel

CROFTON

Ganges
Harbour Prevost I.

Active Pass

OUTER ISLANDS `2`

92

Mayne I.

Tumbo I.

Saturna I.

Maple Bay

Saltspring I.

Plumper Sound

Pender Is.

Swanson Channel

Sansum
Narrows

Cowichan Bay

Satellite Channel

Moresby I. Boundary Pass

MILL BAY

Saanich
Inlet

SIDNEY

Sidney I.

Haro Strait

Saanich
Peninsula

D'Arcy I.

San Juan
Islands (U.S.)

Finlayson
Arm

Cordova
Bay

Esquimalt
Harbour

VICTORIA

Oak
Bay

Discovery I.

50

`1` **VICTORIA-SAANICH**

Juan de Fuca Strait

Miles

4

8

Km

4

8

12

The Gulf Islands

THERE IS NO GULF. JUST THE GULF ISLANDS.

The Strait of Georgia was given the name "Gulphe of Georgia" by Capt. George Vancouver in 1792. The error was corrected in 1865 to rename the gulf a strait, but by that time the use of the name was entrenched, and so they remain the Gulf Islands.

Officially the Gulf Islands refers to the islands between Gabriola and D'Arcy islands only, but the boundary is increasingly being stretched. Unofficially the use is being extended to include all the Canadian islands in the Strait of Georgia, including Texada, Lasqueti and sometimes even Quadra. For the sake of historic accuracy, as well as descriptive convenience, in this book Gulf Islands refers only to islands as far north as Gabriola. But it is bucking a trend.

For decades the Gulf Islands have been a pleasant mix of occasional homesteads, cottage getaways and wilderness. A few colourful but small communities, like Ganges on Saltspring, popped up, attracting artists, hippy-style social renegades, naturalists and those few lucky enough to have discovered these places. But that all began to change in the 1960s, in particular with the creation of Magic Lake Estates on North Pender Island in 1966. It became in its day the largest development in western Canada and signalled a warning for those concerned with the future of these wonderful islands. In response, in 1970 the province introduced a minimum 4-ha (10-acre) lot size for future developments, referred to as the "10-acre freeze." In 1974 a new quasi-municipal level of government was created to oversee island development. Islands Trust began with a mandate to conserve and protect. Unfortunately, it was a vision about a hundred years too late. By 1974 many waterfronts

A reef off Valdes Island.

had been parcelled off into urban-sized lots. Initially this wasn't a problem, as most of the islands remained underdeveloped cottage country. However, a rise in demand for waterfront and the growing reputation of the Gulf Islands has led to steady infilling, and there are rows of large waterfront homes where once just the occasional quaint cottage broke the wilderness. Recreational boat traffic has multiplied, and the Gulf Islands have grown into B.C.'s most popular kayaking destination.

Sadly, urbanization is taking over this island paradise.

There has been some good news in recent years. The Gulf Islands National Park was created in 2003, and new provincial parks, such as Wakes Cove and Burgoyne Bay, are adding to the amount of protected land. So a wild coast remains. You just have to look a little harder today to find it.

GETTING HERE

By ferry

Regular and frequent ferry service is available to most of the major Gulf Islands, with the exception of Valdes. The main terminal for Victoria is at Swartz Bay at the top of Saanich Peninsula. From there ferries are available to Vancouver (Tsawwassen), Sturdies Bay on Galiano Island, Village Bay on Mayne Island, Otter Bay on Pender Island, Lyall Harbour on Saturna Island and Fulford Harbour on Saltspring

Island. Not all routes are direct—it may take as many as three stops, with the possibility of a transfer, to reach your destination. Check **www.bcferries.com** for detailed schedule information.

Saltspring and Galiano receive regular and direct ferry service from Vancouver (Tsawwassen), making both these islands convenient for starting trips from the mainland. Connections can also be made to Mayne, Pender, Saturna and Saltspring islands, although these are generally less frequent and invariably indirect.

Saltspring can also be reached from Vancouver Island between Crofton and Vesuvius Bay, to the north. Both Thetis and Kuper islands are served by a ferry in a triangle route from Chemainus. Gabriola is served from downtown Nanaimo to Descanso Bay.

During the summer a foot passenger service leaves from Sidney at the foot of Beacon Avenue to Sidney Spit Marine Park. Call **250-474-5145** for a schedule. Another foot passenger ferry leaves Maffeo Sutton Park in downtown Nanaimo to Newcastle Island Marine Park, a short hop across Nanaimo Harbour. The schedule is frequent during the summer. For times check **www.newcastleisland.ca/ferry.htm**.

From Washington: Visitors from Washington State can take the ferry from Anacortes, Washington, to Sidney. For schedule information, visit **www.wsdot.wa.gov/ferries**. An option is walking the kayak on the ferry in Anacortes and launching from the beach next to the terminal in Sidney. The cost for the kayak is the same as a motorcycle ticket. Buy your ticket, then walk the kayak onto the car deck. Wheels will help make this easier.

Another vehicle and passenger ferry operates between Victoria's Inner Harbour and Port Angeles. For schedules and more information visit **www.cohoferry.com**. Walk-on kayaks are welcome at no additional charge.

A passenger-only catamaran, the *Victoria Clipper*, operates from the Inner Harbour in Victoria to downtown Seattle. Visit **www.victoriaclipper.com**.

By road

Once on Vancouver Island, routes between various areas are generally good. The backbone of transportation on Vancouver Island is Highway 19 from Victoria with connections to all northern locations, including Mill Bay, Maple Bay, Chemainus, Ladysmith, Nanaimo and beyond. A major route between Swartz Bay and Victoria is Highway

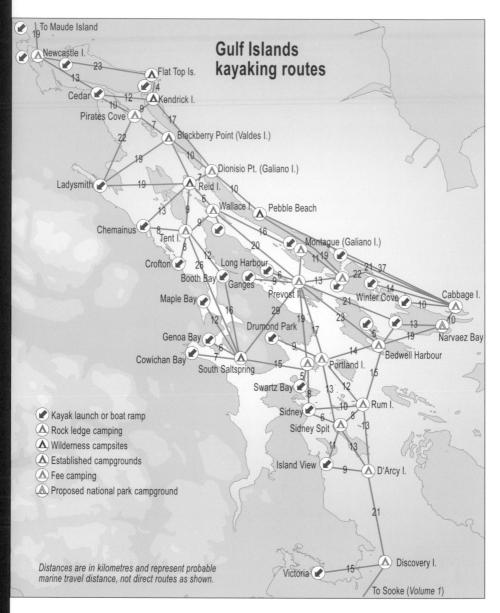

Gulf Islands kayaking routes

To Maude Island
19
Newcastle I.
23
13
Cedar 12
10
Pirates Cove 9
22
7 17
Flat Top Is.
4
Kendrick I.
Blackberry Point (Valdes I.)
19 10
Dionisio Pt. (Galiano I.)
7
Ladysmith 19
Reid I. 10
6
13 9 Wallace I.
9 Pebble Beach
Chemainus 8
Tent I. 8
16
12 20
Crofton 26 Long Harbour
Booth Bay 6
Ganges 9
Maple Bay Prevost I.
16 29 19
12 Drumond Park 17
Genoa Bay 6 9
7
Cowichan Bay 15
South Saltspring 5
Swartz Bay
8
Sidney 10
Sidney Spit 6 8
11
Island View 9

Montague (Galiano I.)
11 19
13
22 21 37
14
Winter Cove 10 Cabbage I.
21 10
23 13 Narvaez Bay
5 19
14
Bedwell Harbour
Portland I. 15
12 13
Rum I.
13
D'Arcy I.
21

Island View 9
D'Arcy I.

Discovery I.
Victoria 15
To Sooke (Volume 1)

Distances are in kilometres and represent probable
marine travel distance, not direct routes as shown.

Kayak launch or boat ramp
Rock ledge camping
Wilderness campsites
Established campgrounds
Fee camping
Proposed national park campground

17. For those driving to the Gulf Islands, roads are generally in good condition and paved, although they can be narrow, twisting and hilly. Keep an eye open for oncoming traffic, pedestrians, cyclists, pets, deer, feral goats and perhaps even a bald eagle feeding on something. Yes, despite increasing development, the Gulf Islands continue to have a charm unlike anywhere else in Canada.

By kayak

With their magnificent shorelines and better-than-average weather, the Gulf Islands are the top kayaking destination in Canada. The congestion has its drawbacks—other marine traffic, developed waterfronts and the possibility designated camping areas will be full. The first two problems can be largely avoided by picking the right locations to explore. Valdes and Saturna islands retain the most pristine shorelines, while Galiano also has long wilderness stretches. The steep slopes of south Saltspring Island have kept Sansum Narrows relatively untouched. Many of the smaller islands, such as Wallace and Kuper, also make great wilderness outings. Trip suggestions with wilderness destinations in mind are made at the beginning of each chapter.

Kayaking along De Courcy Island.

Crowding is a larger problem. Don't travel to campsites like Blackberry Point or Portland Island during the summer and expect a quiet weekend alone in the wilderness. There will be other campers, and all it takes is one tour group to push these camping areas to their limits. Worse yet, all it takes is one boat camper to unload cases of beer and a boombox and...well, you get the picture.

There are two strategies to beat the crowds. One is to travel elsewhere. There are dozens of locations on the south B.C. coast that will be vacant when campsites in the Gulf Islands are brimming over. The other solution is to kayak off-season. This is the only coastal location in Canada where you can kayak the best part of 12 months a year. Yes, it is more likely to rain in the winter, it will be colder and it will get darker earlier. But you will have privacy!

That might seem like an extreme trade-off, but there are other advantages to winter travel. Less algae in the water makes it easier to see the marine life, and the sky has less haze, allowing clear views of distant mountains, like Mount Baker in Washington. (As a footnote, the cover photo for this book was taken off Saturna Island at Murder Point in January, on a perfectly warm and sunny kayaking weekend.) On the right day it's a beautiful time to be on the water.

Wave-etched sandstone ledges with a topping of juniper, Garry oak and Douglas-fir—the signature combination of the Gulf Islands.

Transiting the region: For kayakers starting from a destination such as Washington, it's preferable to cross the border via the San Juan Islands rather than along the mainland. The scenery is better, the camping options better and the marine traffic better suited to kayaking. Kayakers entering from U.S. waters should check into Canada Customs at Sidney or Bedwell Harbour on South Pender Island.

Once in the Gulf Islands it's just a matter of choosing a route that best suits your interests—Sansum Narrows, Trincomali Channel or the Strait of Georgia. All three have their attractions and enough campsites to accommodate most agendas. See the epilogue for a suggested itinerary for running the coast.

GEOLOGY AND ECOLOGY

The Gulf Islands are primarily part of a wider geological region, known as the Nanaimo Lowlands, with a base of shale, sandstone and conglomerates. The sandstone is the most striking feature of the three, with highly eroded and sculpted cliffs along many island shorelines.

Like most areas of the coast, glaciers were instrumental in shaping the Gulf Islands. About 10,000 to 15,000 years ago the Strait of Georgia was covered by a layer of ice believed to be 1 km (0.6 miles) thick. The ice sheets from the north scoured the Gulf Islands, turning valleys into inlets and troughs into lake beds. Much of the soil cover was scoured away, leaving only a shallow layer. Hills, called drumlins, developed in the direction of the retreating ice, leaving examples like James and Sidney islands. Wave erosion ate at the hills, creating the cliffs. The result is a rugged, wave- and wind-eroded shore of cliffs, headlands, islands and reefs.

Complex erosion patterns in the sandstone are common along the Gulf Islands shore-line.

The exposed bedrock, lack of soil cover, dry summers and exposure to ocean spray have created a unique ecology in the Gulf Islands and pockets of the coast of southeastern Vancouver Island. Called the coastal bluff ecosystem, a 1990s study found just 611 ha (2.4 square miles) of this type of land. The largest example is at Fiddlers Cove on Saturna Island. Other notable examples include the Ballenas-Winchelsea archipelago, North and South Trial islands, Yellow Point near Ladysmith, Wallace Point on Pender Island, Lyall Harbour on Saturna, the bluffs through Active Pass, Komas Bluff on Denman Island and Newcastle Island near Nanaimo. Trial Islands and Newcastle Island are protected; few of the other outstanding locations are.

The lack of soil is a key component of this ecology. Hardy plants are able to thrive in crevices and depressions among the rocks. Most common are mosses and lichens, which can survive waves, wind, storms, heat and drought. The list of rare plants found in this environment includes Geyer's onion, contorted-pod evening-primrose, snake-root, Carolina meadox foxtail, dune bentgrass, Idaho fescue/ junegrass, tiny mousetail, montia, Tracy's romanzoffia, water-plantain buttercup and Macoun's meadowfoam.

More common plants include trees such as Garry oak, rocky mountain juniper and arbutus; shrubs such as baldhip rose, Nootka rose, Saskatoon, oceanspray, snowberry and salal; and an assortment of herbaceous plants.

Often adjacent to these bluffs are the coastal Douglas-fir forests. (The name is hyphenated because it is not truly a fir tree, a discovery made only after it was named.) This forest type exists in a small band down the southeastern Vancouver Island coast and in the Gulf Islands, plus a small portion on the mainland near Powell River. It covers just 2,161 square km (834 square miles), or 0.25 percent of B.C.'s land mass. The coastal location made these forests easy targets for pioneer loggers and subsequently for development, leaving very little of the original forests. Look for old-growth clusters at places like Taylor Point on Saturna Island. These monster trees can survive for hundreds of years, in part due to the fire resistence of their thick bark. Following a fire, seedlings will grow where other species have died off.

Found along with Douglas-fir are arbutus, Garry oak and lodgepole pine. In moister areas, such as along the Vancouver Island coast, their companions will be grand fir, western redcedar, bigleaf maple and western flowering dogwood. Understorey vegetation is typically salal, Oregon-grape, sword fern, salmonberry and trillium. Skunk cabbage and red alder can be found in swampy areas.

In Garry oak meadows and grassy bluffs look for blue camas. The bulbs are rich in carbohydrates and were an important First Nations food source. When cooked they are said to be soft and sweet. Don't confuse blue camas with the poisonous death camas, which can be distinguished by its cream-coloured flowers. Blue camas, not surprisingly, has blue flowers.

Large mammals were once a part of the Douglas-fir forests, but human encroachment has driven out the Roosevelt elk, black bear and cougar. Black-tailed deer and raccoons continue to flourish.

Killer whales are slowly recovering after reaching a low in the 1970s. Both the northeast Pacific transient population and the northeast Pacific southern resident population can be seen in the waters around the Gulf Islands. While more commonly found in the San Juan Islands, they can be spotted as far north as Nanaimo on occasion and are regularly seen around the islands off Sidney.

Other species of interest to look for include Steller's sea lion, barn owl, marbled murrelet, nothern goshawk (*laingi subspecies*), peregrine falcon (*anatum subspecies*), short-tailed albatross, western screech-owl (*kennicottii subspecies*), northern abalone, Olympia oyster, monarch butterfly, bog's bird's-foot trefoil, purple sanicle and twisted oak moss. All are considered species at risk.

Many species are particular to defined locations. Golden paintbrush, for instance, is limited to the Discovery Island area. Purple sanicle is found only on Saturna and Valdes islands, as well as Victoria. Water plantain buttercup is found only in the Victoria area and the Winchelseas.

FIRST NATIONS OVERVIEW

The various First Nations of southeastern Vancouver Island and the Gulf Islands are of Coast Salishan descent, with the main language Hul'qumi'num

Impressive group of petroglyphs can be found along the Gulf Islands coast.

shared by the Penelakut, Nanoose, Halalt, Lyackson, Malahat, Snuneymuxw and Cowichan. The Songhees and Esquimalt, meanwhile, speak a dialect called Lekwungen. An unfortunate aspect to European intrusion was development of the Gulf Islands and southeastern Vancouver Island that obliterated many historic areas before a full archeaological assessment could be completed. As a result much of the evidence of the historic occupation of this region is lost forever.

Esquimalt: Ashe Head on the east shore of Esquimalt Harbour was the historic home of the Esquimalt and where they make their home today. The reserve is home to about 130 people with a community hall and longhouse.

Songhees: The Songhees traditionally lived on the west shore of Victoria harbour, with village sites where the B.C. legislature and James Bay are today. In 1911 they moved to a reserve at Esquimalt Harbour, where the community is now centred.

Saanich Nation: Five bands comprise the Saanich Nation: the Tsawout, Tsartlip, Tseycum, Malahat and Pauquachin. The groups divided in 1957 but maintain a political affiliation. The Tsartlip's main community is on is South Saanich reserve at Brentwood Bay, with reserves extending as far as Helen Point on Mayne Island. The Tsawout share many of their reserves with the Tseycum, including Mandarte Island, Fiddlers Cove on Saturna and Fulford Harbour. The Tseycum's main community is at Patricia Bay on Saanich Inlet. Sixty-five of the 151 band members live on the reserve. The Tsawout's main community is the East Saanich reserve near Cordova Channel. The band has hotels, a longhouse, a cultural centre and community hall, with 474 of the band's 715 members living on the reserve.

The Pauquachin have their main community at Cole Bay on Saanich Inlet. The reserve has a recreation hall and two longhouses. It's home to 227 of the 358 band members. The Malahat band is located on the west shore of Saanich Inlet south of Mill Bay, and has 251 members.

Cowichan: The Cowichan First Nation is centred out of Cowichan Valley adjacent to the city of Duncan. The name originates from the Hul'qumi'num phrase meaning "warm country." The Cowichan have nine reserves extending between Cowichan Bay and Cowichan Lake. They are best known for their wood carvings, Cowichan sweater and the Quw'utsun' Cultural Centre, an interpretive centre in Duncan open to visitors. About 2,000 of the 4,000 band members live on the reserve.

Lyackson: The Lyackson First Nation is centred out of Chemainus today, with its traditional lands and reserves on Valdes Island. The comunity has expressed a desire to return to Valdes, but the lack of electricity and transportation links has made that difficult. The island is currently used by the band for cultural events, with possibilities for the future including a big house, youth camp and cottages. The band population is 186, with a handful living at Shingle Point.

Penelakut: The Penelakut were historically residents of Kuper and Galiano islands and on Vancouver Island near the Chemainus River. The community today is centred at Penelakut on Kuper Island where about 400 of the 800 members reside.

Halalt: The Halalt have their main community near Crofton, with two reserves, one being Willy Island. About 85 of the 205 band members live on the reserve.

Chemainus: The Chemainus First Nations territory once included villages in Ladysmith Harbour, Kulleet Bay and the Chemainus Valley. Today the main community is on the peninsula bordering Ladysmith Harbour and Stuart Channel. The band numbers over 1,100, with about 600 on the reserve.

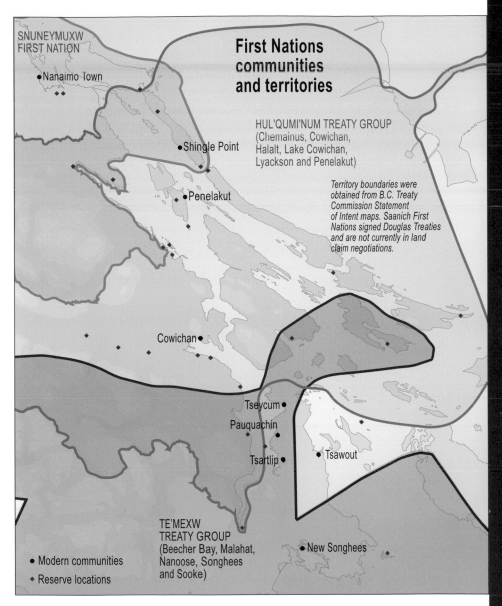

First Nations communities and territories

SNUNEYMUXW FIRST NATION

• Nanaimo Town

• Shingle Point

• Penelakut

Cowichan•

Tseycum•

Pauquachin

Tsartlip•

Tsawout

• New Songhees

HUL'QUMI'NUM TREATY GROUP
(Chemainus, Cowichan, Halalt, Lake Cowichan, Lyackson and Penelakut)

Territory boundaries were obtained from B.C. Treaty Commission Statement of Intent maps. Saanich First Nations signed Douglas Treaties and are not currently in land claim negotiations.

TE'MEXW TREATY GROUP
(Beecher Bay, Malahat, Nanoose, Songhees and Sooke)

• Modern communities
◆ Reserve locations

Snuneymuxw: This is the namesake group for the city of Nanaimo, with the main First Nations community located on the south end of the city. The traditional territory extends throughout Nanaimo to Cedar and Gabriola Island. The band numbers about 1,400.

Sunset at Sidney Spit.

Victoria-Saanich

CHAPTER ONE

WHEN I FIRST BEGAN KAYAKING, I HAD A WEEK OF HOLIDAYS TO SPARE AND a choice of either going up to Johnstone Strait to kayak with the killer whales—a long-time dream of mine—or staying closer to home and heading down to Victoria through the Gulf Islands. I chose the latter, with some regret that kayaking with the killer whales would have to wait. I needn't have worried. Just outside of Mandarte Island, a pod went by on its way toward Forrest Island. I might not have seen much more than a distant fin had they not turned back to feed near some kelp at a reef close by. The show lasted the best part of half an hour, with a big old male orca surfacing so close beside me I found myself looking up at his back. I paddled backwards a bit to give a larger buffer zone. After kayaking Johnstone Strait many times since, this was an enounter I have yet to surpass.

Victoria Harbour may not qualify as a wild coast, but don't be fooled into thinking the wilderness disappears here. One of the best trips anywhere in the Gulf Islands is a paddle through Discovery and Chatham islands, less than an hour from Oak Bay.

Kayaking Victoria Harbour or Esquimalt Harbour qualifies as urban paddling, but with a unique Victorian charm, whether it's enjoying a picnic near the historic Fisgard lighthouse or

Intricate sandstone at Rum Island.

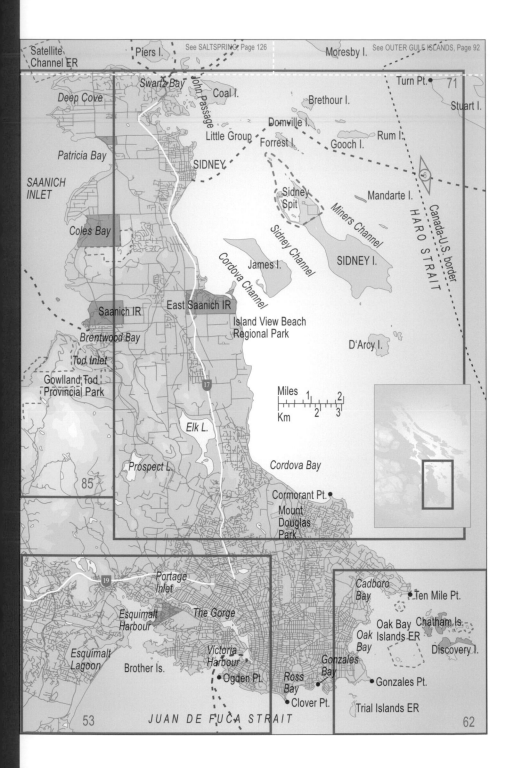

See SALTSPRING Page 126

See OUTER GULF ISLANDS, Page 92

Satellite Channel ER

Piers I.

Moresby I.

Turn Pt. 71

Swartz Bay

Coal I.

Brethour I.

Stuart I.

Deep Cove

John Passage

Domville I.

Patricia Bay

Little Group

Forrest I.

Gooch I.

Rum I.

SIDNEY

SAANICH INLET

Sidney Spit

Mandarte I.

HARO STRAIT

Canada-U.S. border

Coles Bay

Sidney Channel

Miners Channel

SIDNEY I.

Cordova Channel

James I.

Saanich IR

East Saanich IR

Island View Beach Regional Park

D'Arcy I.

Brentwood Bay

Tod Inlet

Gowlland Tod Provincial Park

17

Miles

Km

Elk L.

Prospect L.

85

Cordova Bay

Cormorant Pt.

Mount Douglas Park

Portage Inlet

19

Cadboro Bay

Ten Mile Pt.

Esquimalt Harbour

The Gorge

Oak Bay Islands ER

Chatham Is.

Esquimalt Lagoon

Brother Is.

Victoria Harbour

Ogden Pt.

Ross Bay

Gonzales Bay

Oak Bay

Discovery I.

Gonzales Pt.

Clover Pt.

Trial Islands ER

53

JUAN DE FUCA STRAIT

62

The Gorge near downtown Victoria.

exploring the tree-lined Gorge waterway that snakes its way north from Victoria Harbour. Most visitors to Victoria stroll the waterfront walkway and comment on how pretty a city it is. Little do they know how much better it gets on the water.

Exploring by kayak

Victoria and its nearby waters, such as Esquimalt Harbour and The Gorge, are best explored as day trips due to the short distances and lack of camping options. The only designated overnight marine-accessible camping area convenient to Victoria is on Discovery Island. Anyone visiting should be prepared for the possibility of wind and current issues assocated with that area of Haro Strait.

Off Sidney are three segments of the Gulf Islands National Park with campgrounds—D'Arcy Island, Rum Island and Sidney Spit. Given their close proximity, this makes an excellent region for kayakers who want to keep distances to a minimum. Novice kayakers will find this an appealing introduction to the coast. A visit to this area can also easily be expanded to include neighbouring attractions such as Portland and Pender islands.

Recommended kayaking trips

- *If you have a day*: Around Victoria, Esquimalt Harbour and The Gorge are obvious options. Esquimalt Harbour makes for an easy,

10–15 km (6–10 mile) trip with a launch from Fleming Bay or the Esquimalt Lagoon. Be sure to visit the ruins at Cole Island and take a break at the beaches near the Fisgard Lighthouse or on Brothers Islands. The Gorge requires a bit more planning due to the currents at Tillicum Narrows. Or, better yet, stay north of the narrows and simply paddle the pretty, park-lined waterway.

A more exposed option is a trip around Trial Islands. It's a good chance to see some wildlife and a rare ecology in a short, accessible trip of under 10 km (6 miles). This is best accomplished by leaving an hour or two before the current change to avoid the maximum current.

Those who want to see Discovery and Chatham islands (highly recommended) can launch from Maynard Cove and head straight across Baynes Channel. Or you can have a more thorough examination of the area by launching from Oak Bay and paddling near Great Chain Island, crossing at Plumper Passage. A good way to cheat the tides is by planning a six-hour trip. Leave at one change of current and return at the other. Explore the trails of Discovery Island during the period of peak current.

The islands around Sidney are another perfect day trip. A short option is a paddle to Sidney Spit. A longer trip, about 30 km (18 miles), continues on to D'Arcy Island (again, highly recommended). Veteran kayakers could work in a visit to Rum Island as well. For a shorter trip to D'Arcy, launch from Island View Road—it's about 16 km (10 miles) return, but through more open water.

• *If you have two days:* There are four beautiful campsites on four different islands to choose from in this region (Discovery, D'Arcy, Sidney and Rum), all within a reasonably short distance of a launch site. You won't go wrong with any choice, but I give the Discovery Islands a slight edge in beauty and suitability for kayaking—once you're past the currents of Baynes Channel, of course.

• *If you have three days:* A triangle from Sidney to Rum Island to D'Arcy Island and back is a good way to spend a leisurely three days. Be sure to explore Sidney Spit on your way back from D'Arcy Island—it's a great place for a picnic. This would be a relaxing 40-km (25-mile) trip through lots of islands, history and wildlife.

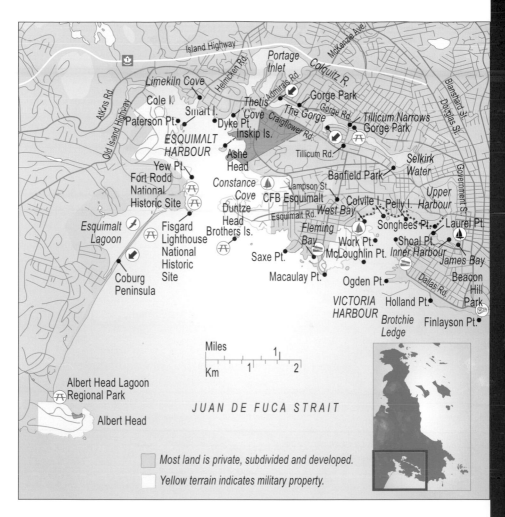

Most land is private, subdivided and developed.

Yellow terrain indicates military property.

- *The ideal trip:* The comparatively short distance between the outer Gulf Islands of the Penders and Saturna creates the opportunity for a larger exploration of the area, especially considering Sidney is an ideal launch for places such as Portland Island. A circuit including Portland Island, Bedwell Harbour on the Penders, Saturna Island, Rum Island and D'Arcy Island would be a wonderful way to spend a week.

This is the most urban of all the areas covered in the *Wild Coast* series. Industrial docks, a Canadian Forces naval base, cruise ship berths— it isn't pristine, but busy dockyards have an odd attraction nonetheless. Combined with interesting islands, a scattering of good beaches and some visible history, time won't be wasted here.

Note that access in Esquimalt Harbour is restricted to no closer than 500 m (0.3 miles) from a military ship that is stationary or 200 m (0.12 miles) from a ship that is moving. The harbour is patrolled by military craft, which along with the harbourmaster can be reached on VHF Channel 73. Don't feel you'll be unwelcome, however. The harbour is generally quite relaxed.

For information on Albert Head and the coast to the west of Esquimalt, see *The Wild Coast, Volume 1.*

Esquimalt Lagoon

This lagoon is a federally designated migratory bird sanctuary, with habitat for waterfowl including bufflehead, great blue heron and merganser. It's almost entirely landlocked thanks to a natural causeway, Coburg Peninsula, which is separated only at the north-

Fisgard Lighthouse.

east end, allowing salt water to mix with the freshwater runoff from nearby creeks. The result is a rich environment for cutthroat trout, salmon, littleneck clams, mussels and oysters. Each year thousands of surf scoters feed here.

Archaeological sites include a burial ground where the dead were placed in boxes in trees and upon a shell midden. The Royal Navy transformed it into a rifle range in the 1800s. The land adjacent to the lagoon was purchased in 1902 by coal baron James Dunsmuir for Hatley Castle, a home that later became a naval college and is now the Royal Roads University. It is prominent on the hillside behind the lagoon.

Abandoned ammunition storage buildings at Cole Island.

Launches: Lagoon Road runs the length of Coburg Peninsula. Alongside the road are diagonal parking stalls with beach access for launching.

Fisgard Lighthouse
The Fisgard Lighthouse was the first on Canada's west coast, built in 1860 before Vancouver Island was a part of Canada. Sitting on an islet accessible by a causeway, the lighthouse was automated in 1929 and is now open to the public with exhibits and videos as an adjunct to the associated Fort Rodd National Historic Site. Fort Rodd, which is set on the surrounding headland, was built in 1895 to defend Victoria and the Esquimalt naval base from attack by Russia, Britain's enemy during the Crimean War. The fort includes three gun batteries, underground magazines, command posts, guardhouses, barracks and searchlight emplacements. It remained active until 1956 and was named a national historic park in 1958. It's accessible from the water by both a beach and a visiting vessel dock.

Esquimalt Harbour
Esquimalt Harbour is a Canadian Forces base and a port for repairing large commercial vessels, including bulk carriers, tankers and passenger vessels. Most of that activity is centred in Constance Cove on the east side, where tower cranes are easily visible on the north side

Guns at the ready, Duntze Head.

of the cove. Other navy vessels are likely to be moored at large docks on the west side between Yew and Paterson points. Residences line the north end of the harbour, with little public access. Ashe Head was a long-time village site of the Esquimalt, and the band makes its home there today, as does the Songhees.

Place names: This area was known by the Coast Salish as Esquimalt, "the place of gradually shoaling water." The first European to enter Esquimalt Harbour was the Spanish explorer Don Manuel Quimper, who arrived in 1790 and named it Puerto de Cordova, a name later misappropriated for the bay near Oak Bay (see page 73).

Cole Island

The Royal Navy used this small island in the north end of Esquimalt Harbour as an ammunition storage depot as early as the 1860s. More than a dozen buildings once dotted the island, and a number still stand, including two large ammunition storage buildings. It was decommissioned after the Second World War. In 2006 the island gained protected status as part of a national historic district. Together the sites form the most intact infrastructure of the Royal Navy in British Columbia.

Northwest of Cole Island the water becomes a shallow, drying mud flat.

Duntze Head

Duntze Head forms the east entrance to Esquimalt Harbour. It is the outer extremity of the Canadian Forces Dockyard. Yes, that metal structure on the outer point, known locally as Black Rock, is indeed a gun turret. Look for a total of five guns on the point. North of Duntze Head, just inside the harbour, is an abandoned signal tower.

Just south of Duntze Head, outside the harbour, are Brothers Islands. A good beach is accessible at most tide levels on the north end. The islet to the north of the beach makes a good grassy spot for a rest. This is a possible emergency haulout, but it's shy on level areas above the high tide.

The harbour seawall in Victoria.

Juan de Fuca Strait

This vast body of water separates Vancouver Island from Washington state, beginning at Carmanah Point on west Vancouver Island. The portion from Carmanah Point to Albert Head is covered in *The Wild Coast, Volume 1*. In total the strait runs 128 km (80 miles) to end at Sea Bird Point on Discovery Island, where it joins with Haro Strait. Its narrowest point, at 19 km (12 miles), is at Race Rocks.

Place names: Juan de Fuca Strait was discovered in 1592 by the Greek mariner Apostolos Valerianos. His common name was Juan de Fuca.

Fleming Bay

This is a nicely sheltered bay used primarily as a launch site. It's also a good entry point for the local park at Macaulay Point. The park is actually Department of National Defence property leased for regional park use and features trails to bunkers and gun emplacements.

Launches: N48°25.20' W123°24.74'. This busy boat launch at Fleming Bay is augmented by a breakwater and several floats. The launch is located at the end of Lampson Street, which can be reached by turning south from Esquimalt Road, the major route through the area.

Victoria Harbour

The Inner Harbour and James Bay constitute the tourist hub of Victoria's waterfront. It wasn't always this way; a Songhees village filled the west shore in 1844 from Songhees Point to the Johnson Street Bridge. Today double-decker buses and horse-drawn carriages share the downtown roads with regular city traffic in front of historic buildings like the provincial legislature and the stately Empress Hotel. In the water, Victoria's harbour can be neatly divided into four sections, each covered in more detail below. The Outer Harbour extends from the breakwater to Shoal Point; Middle Harbour runs from Shoal Point to Laurel Point; the Inner Harbour is from Laurel Point to the Johnson Street Bridge; and the Upper Harbour is north of the Johnson Street Bridge.

The harbour is used by all types of vessels, including seaplanes, ferries and fishing boats. Non-powered boats, such as kayaks and canoes, are welcome in the harbour, but there are a few rules and suggestions to keep in mind.

- When transiting under the Johnson Street Bridge, stay between the fender piles and the shore to avoid the centre channel. This applies to both the east and west sides.

- When travelling between the Middle Harbour and Inner Harbour, stay north of the white and orange information buoy just south of Songhees Point. The buoy is used to separate powered and non-powered vessels and marks the eastern limit of seaplane traffic.

- When travelling between the Middle Harbour and Outer Harbour, stay north of Pelly Island and remain close to the north shore until west of Colvile Island.

- When entering the inner waters from the Outer Harbour, non-powered vessels can use the inbound traffic lane shared with powered vessels or stay close to the north shore. The lanes are marked by light buoys.

- Extreme caution is advised when passing docking areas such as the Huron Street Public Port Facility, located north of Ogden Point.

The message should be clear from these guidelines: stay as near to the north shore as you can, but if you choose to go near the docks, do so at your peril. Considering the amount of activity, a route north and west along the harbour near the shore is strongly advised. Many kayakers, however, may want to travel to the tourism hub at James Bay. Doing so means passing docks used by float planes, recreational traffic and frequent and fast water taxis. Be vigilant. Never expect the right of way.

Currents can run at several knots across the harbour's entrance, from Macaulay Point on the west entrance to Brotchie Ledge, a shallow bar south of Victoria Harbour. This can lead to turbulence off Ogden Point. The flood sets southeast and the ebb northwest. Currents within the harbour will be negligible until The Gorge.

North of the Johnson Street cantilever bridge is the Upper Harbour, an industrial area dominated by operations such as Lafarge, Ocean Concrete, Island Asphalt and Capital Iron.

Launches: N48°24.89' W123°23.12'. A boat ramp is located off Dallas Road between the Odgen Point Wharves and the Canadian Coast Guard property. Kayakers could also launch from either of the two government docks off Wharf Street in downtown Victoria, but be warned of considerable traffic, congestion and parking difficulties.

Weather

Victoria marine	May	June	July	Aug.	Sept.	Dec.	Av. / Ttl.
Daily average temp. (C)	10.5	12.4	14.0	14.3	13.0	4.6	9.1
Daily maximum (C)	14.1	16.1	18.1	18.5	17.2	7.0	12.6
Daily minimum (C)	6.8	8.7	9.8	10.1	8.8	2.1	5.7
Precipitation (mm)	47.0	30.6	23.2	33.2	41.8	197.4	1235.7
Days of rainfall + 0.2 mm	12.1	9.5	5.5	8.1	8.8	20.3	166.2
Days with rainfall + 5 mm	3.4	2.1	1.5	2.0	2.8	10.4	72.9
Days with rainfall + 10 mm	1.1	0.7	0.5	1.1	1.4	6.6	40.6
Wind speed (km/h)*	9.2	8.7	8.0	7.4	7.0	10.1	8.9
Prevailing direction*	W	E	E	E	E	W	W
* From Victoria International Airport							

The Gorge

A narrow channel continues northeast from Victoria's Upper Harbour, with the channel narrowing to as little as 10 m (33 feet) below the Tillicum Road Bridge at what is known locally as Tillicum

Ready to paddle The Gorge.

Narrows. This can be a tidal chute of rapids. Most of the rest of the waterway is calm with moderate currents. The distance is about 10 km (6 miles) from Ship Point to Portage Inlet. Along the way are a number of waterside parks providing beachfront access, particularly Gorge Park with waterside walking trails along a pretty, treed backdrop. On the north shore just west of the Tillicum Road Bridge is the Gorge Rowing and Paddling Centre, which offers a range of programs including kayak rentals.

The Gorge is part of Songhees folk-lore and was known as Camossung, after a girl who was turned into stone here. A midden dated at over 4,000 years is located under the south side of Tillicum Bridge at Kinsmen Gorge Park.

Portage Inlet is highly residential and many portions dry extensively in mud flats, making it a marginal destination. An option for a side trip is a short paddle up Colquitz River, which runs off the east end of the inlet.

Rapids through Tillicum Narrows.

Grass meadows and wind-twisted trees are common on the islands off Oak Bay.

Launches: N49°27.18' W123°25.18'. A good place is the west end of Gorge Park near the Admirals Road Bridge. At the waterside is a good sediment beach at all tide levels. Another option is Kinsmen Gorge Park on the south end off Tillicum Road near the bridge. Parking is ample and the beach is good, but the walk from the parking lot is longer.

Ogden Point

The waters off Ogden Point can be a problem; water from the harbour flowing into Juan de Fuca Strait can result in rips and turbulence. East of the point the waterfront is protected as part of Beacon Hill Park, a popular Victoria day-use area. The waterfront is a steep embankment with poor beaches only.

Finlayson Point, east of Holland Point, was once a defensive village site. Restored burial cairns can be seen on the hillside.

OAK BAY

Oak Bay is backed by an upscale community of the same name. A large marina is located on the south side of the bay with breakwaters extending to Mary Tod Island, a windswept and sparsely vegetated rock. On the north end of the bay is Uplands Park, with its rocky shoreland and Garry oak woodlands. Most of the rest of the shoreline is residential. A small park in the centre of the bay, Willows

Park, is a former village site known as Sitchamalth, named in reference to the drift logs and trees that lodged in the sand. It's believed it was occupied as far back as 2,700 years ago.

Launches: Overnight parking is an issue at most locations. Be sure to read the signs carefully and park elsewhere after unloading, if necessary.

N48°25.46' W123°18.25'. Just north of the entrance to Oak Bay Marina is a boat ramp with parking on Beach Drive. Alongside the launch is a gravel beach suitable for loading kayaks.

N48°25.99' W123°18.26'. At the end of Dalhousie Street is a community park, Willows Park, with ample parking. Beach access

The lighthouse at Trial Islands.

is down steps from a seawall. A nearby option is the next street south, Cavendish Avenue. It ends in a roundabout with access to a sandy beach.

N48°26.18' W128°18.10'. Turn off Beach Drive onto Estevan Avenue. Running parallel to the beach is The Esplanade. Parking is ample and convenient to the beach.

N48°26.27' W128°17.67'. A scenic road off Beach Drive leads through Uplands Park, which has two concrete boat ramps.

Trial Islands

The Trial Islands are protected as an ecological reserve, excluding a lighthouse on the southern end and radio transmission towers in the middle. The clutter and barren appearance make the islands easy to dismiss. However, they are notable for being home to more species of rare plants than any other area of comparable size in B.C. Twenty-eight rare plants can be found here, with 15 amongst the most rare.

Trial Islands Ecological Reserve

This reserve was created in 1990 to protect this remarkable example of rare and endangered plant species. The 23-ha (57-acre) reserve protects the two main rock islands and associated islets in a turbulent area of Juan de Fuca Strait. The islands are considered a living museum of the plant life in Victoria prior to its development. The islands are closed to the public.

Miracle's recovery at Oak Bay

Human-caused tragedy involving killer whales has had the odd side benefit of increasing our knowledge of this long-misunderstood creature. Such was the case with Miracle, the orphaned baby killer whale named for its odds against surviving. Miracle was shot by a fisherman somewhere in the southern Gulf Islands in 1977; the injured whale swam to Menzies Bay north of Campbell River, where a man named Bill Davis found it and began to care for it by feeding it herring. Eventually, marine biologists at Sealand in Victoria moved it by truck from Menzies Bay to an empty seawater pool at Oak Bay Beach Resort. There experts attempted to nurse it back to health before a historic helicopter trip from Oak Bay to Sealand. The move captured worldwide attention and become part of a National Geographic special. Miracle, unlike Moby Doll (see page 111), survived several years in captivity before drowning by getting caught in the mesh of the Sealand pen. Other famous killer whale names followed Miracle and Moby Doll—Shamu, Keiko and Lolita, to name a few—and all helped change the image of killer whales from pests to gentle and intelligent creatures.

Its ecology, closer to that of California and Oregon than the northern Pacific coast, was once common along Victoria's waterfront, but urban development has left only a few small pockets.

Watch for exotics such as death camas, chocolate lily, shootingstar, sea blush, Hooker's onion and blue-eyed Mary.

Birds found here include cormorant, gull, heron, hawk and eagle. Seals may be sunning on the reefs.

Getting here means crossing Enterprise Channel, which separates the Trial Islands and Vancouver Island. While a short crossing—160 m (0.1 miles) at its narrowest—tidal streams can reach 6 knots but will usually be no more than 3 knots, with rips off Staines Point, particularly on the flood tide. Race Passage is the closest reference point.

The lighthouse on the south point was built in 1906; the original lens is now a landmark in the square outside the Maritime Museum of B.C. The lighthouse is still staffed.

Place names: The Salish name was Tlikway-nung, meaning "Indian peas."

Launches: There are numerous launch options in close proximity to Trial Islands. All are easily accessible from the main road paralleling the Victoria and Oak Bay waterfront. These launch options are given west to east.

N48°24.68' W123°19.85'. Launch into Gonzales Bay (see the chapter map, page 50, for the location of the bay) at Ross Road, a short road that ends at a small waterfront public park. A paved path leads to a beach.

N48°24.79' W123°18.71'. Beach Drive runs alongside McNeill Bay, separated by a retaining wall and a seawalk. At the west end a ramp leads to a sand and gravel beach. There are also steps in the middle of the seawall. The beach may be exposed.

Typical rocks in the Chain Islets.

N48°24.68' W123°18.42'. On the east end of McNeill Bay is a more protected option. Park alongside Beach Drive on the east side of McNeill Bay. Narrow concrete steps lead to a beach protected by a small islet.

Cadboro Bay

A breakwater on the west side provides shelter for the Royal Victoria Yacht Club. Yacht races are often held in the bay. Both the yacht club and Gyro Park are former Songhees village sites. The yacht club was Sungayka, meaning "snowpatches." Gyro Park was Chee-al-thulc, also known as King Freezy for a chief with curly hair.

Place names: The brigantine *Cadboro* was the first vessel to anchor in the bay in 1842.

Launches: N48°27.52' W123°17.64'. Cadboro Bay Road skirts the bay. At the head of the bay is Cadboro Gyro Park. Turn onto Sinclair Road to enter the park. It has ample parking and a sandy beach.

Oak Bay Islands Ecological Reserve
This reserve is a dispersed collection of islands: Great Chain Island and Chain Islets, Jemmy Jones Island and Alpha Island, as well as the marine environment off Ten Mile Point. Together they protect 211 ha (521 acres) of marine bird nesting habitat, rare meadow plants and shallow-water saltwater environments. Chain Islets and Great Chain Island are considered the third-largest colony of double-crested cormorant in B.C., but the population is in rapid decline—from 686 nests in 1991 to 95 in 2000. This is also home to the largest breeding population of glaucous-winged gull in B.C. A few pigeon guillemot, pelagic cormorant and black oystercatcher also nest here and on Jemmy Jones Island and nearby Lewis Reef. The reserve was created in 1979.

Mayor Channel

This route west of Great Chain Island is divided midway by Thames Shoal. The north entrance is between Lewis and Fiddle reefs, known as the Goal Posts. Both are marked by buoys. Tidal currents flood north and ebb south at 2–3 knots. A number of other obstructions, such as Lee Rock and Tod Rock, are in the area.

Chain Islets and Great Chain Island

Dominated by Great Chain Island, this island cluster represents one of the three largest seabird rookeries in the Georgia Basin. Residents are hundreds of pairs of double-crested cormorant, pelagic cormorant and several thousand pairs of glaucous-winged gull. Pigeon guillemot and black oystercatcher also nest here. Expect to see seals hauled out on the smaller reefs.

Place names: The effect of a great flood is remembered in Songhees legend. Chain Islets was Thleethlayakw, meaning "broken in pieces." During the great flood of legend, there was a single rock high enough for people to tie their canoes. When the flood was over the island is said to have broken into pieces.

Cadboro and Ten Mile points

These two points mark a residential headland. Between them is tranquil Maynard Cove. Numerous reefs line the shore.

Place names: There is a long history of Cadboro Point and Ten Mile Point changing positions on charts. Ten Mile Point is now frequently used to refer to the entire peninsula. It is 10 nautical miles on a course by water from Esquimalt Harbour (18.5 km).

Launches: N48°27.09' W123°16.01'. Maynard Cove is beautifully sheltered and secluded. Turn off Cadboro Bay Road onto Tudor Avenue, then turn right onto McAnally Road. The cove is visible on the right side with level access to a pretty gravel beach. Parking is limited to near the cove along the narrow residential road.

Baynes Channel

Baynes Channel leads between the Chatham Islands and the peninsula of Ten Mile Point. Currents will run 4–6 knots at the north entrance by Strongtide Islet, and 2–3 knots on the southern end. The

Typical scenery at the Chatham Islands.

flood sets northeast and the ebb southwest. Expect rips on the outside of Strongtide Islet as well as various other points along the channel.

Place names: Rear Admiral Sir Robert Lambert Baynes was commander-in-chief of the Royal Navy's Pacific station 1857–60.

Plumper Passage

This passage runs northwest between the Chain Islets to the west and Chatham and Discovery islands to the east. Currents run 3–5 knots. The tide change is more complex than in neighbouring Baynes Channel. The flood turns almost immediately after low water, then runs for about 3 hours, 45 minutes until a slack, then runs on the ebb for about 7 hours until low water. Expect the possibility of rips and turbulence. To calculate the low water, use Victoria as a reference station, then add 22 minutes.

Place names: The *Plumper* was a steam sloop built in Portsmouth in 1848. It was used to survey the B.C. coast 1857–61.

Chatham Islands

This twin set of islands is a First Nations reserve. Both are charmingly undeveloped, with wonderful arbutus and Garry oak stands. Numerous shallow passages with moderate to strong currents snake

A view toward Alpha Island.

between these and the various outlying islands, islets and reefs. The currents are variable and can run like a river. Even so, this is prime kayaking territory. The lagoon off Puget Cove can be a nicely sheltered place to visit. Two nearby islands, Strongtide and Vantreight, are both private and have conspicuous radio and communications towers.

Place names: *Chatham* was the small consort ship of the *Discovery* under command of Lieutenant Broughton. It was an armed tender with four three-pound guns and a crew of 55. It was named after the Earl of Chatham.

Griffin and Alpha Island

Alpha Island is less than 1 ha in size (2.5 acres), but home to 63 plant species. Mid-April is a great time to visit, as 18 of those plants will be in bloom: camas, golden paintbrush, sea blush and chocolate lily among them. Rare plants include California buttercup and snake-root.

Griffin Island is distinct for the large, open, grassy meadow in the island's centre. Foot access is restricted to both these islands as part of the Oak Bay Islands Ecological Reserve.

Unusual trees at Discovery Island.

Discovery Island

Numerous bays and beaches protected by offshore rocks and kelp beds make this island challenging for boat traffic but ideal for kayaks. Rudlin Bay is the recreational centre of the park with picnic tables, a designated camping area on a sloping grassy bank, an outhouse and trails. Numerous reefs and lack of a suitable anchorage keep boaters away from the bay, though water taxis provide a drop-off service. The mooring buoy is for B.C. Parks staff only.

Grassy banks line good portions of the shore, with trails leading along most of the park side of the waterfront and to the lighthouse. Between Commodore Point and the lighthouse the trail is well groomed, while much of the rest is rough and overgrown. A side trail near Commodore Point leads to the rubble and foundations of the Beaumont pioneer home.

Discovery Island Marine Park

Capt. E.G. Beaumont donated the southern half of this island, about 61 ha (150 acres), for a marine park in 1972. It was one of three he donated, including Beaumont Marine Park on South Pender Island (now part of the Gulf Islands National Park).

Sea Bird Point on the east end of Discovery Island is the junction for Haro and Juan de Fuca straits. The lighthouse on the point was built in 1885 and automated in 1996 after being manned for 111 years.

The north end of the island is a First Nation reserve, a Skingeenis village that predates Victoria.

If you circumnavigate the island, watch for rips near Sea Bird Point and off the reefs at Commodore Point.

Place names: The *Discovery*, with a crew of 134 and 20 guns, was the ship Captain Vancouver used to explore the B.C. coast 1792–94. Built on the Thames, it was christened New Year's Day in 1790. The American paddle steamer *Commodore*, built in New York in 1852, came to the B.C. coast in 1858 as part of the Fraser River gold rush, along with the *Sea Bird*. The *Sea Bird*, the first steamer to travel up the Fraser as far as Murderer's Bar, caught fire on a trip to the Fraser River shortly after leaving Victoria and was run aground near Sea Bird Point.

Camping: B.C. Parks urges campers to stick to the designated area at Rudlin Bay to protect the sensitive meadows. This directive doesn't seem to be working, though, as dispersed camping remains popular.

N48°25.43' W123°13.99'. Camping is designated in the open field at Rudlin Bay. Picnic tables and an outhouse are provided.

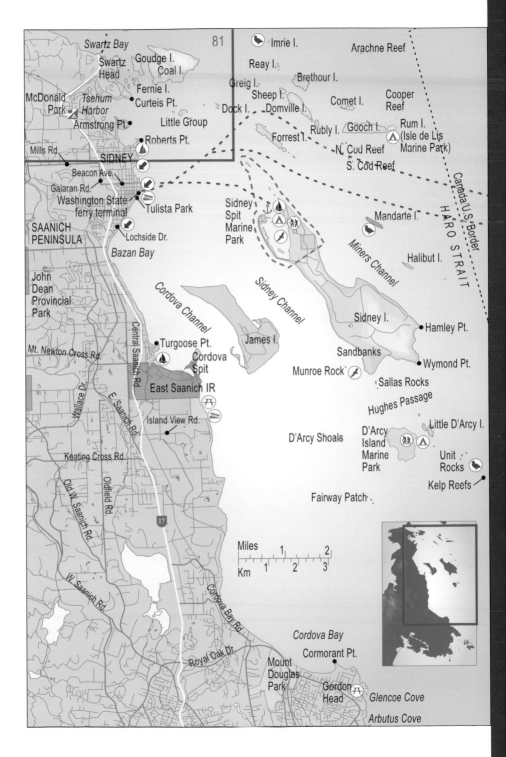

81

Swartz Bay

Imrie I.

Arachne Reef

Swartz Head

Goudge I.
Coal I.

Reay I.

Brethour I.

McDonald Park

Tsehum Harbor

Fernie I.
Curteis Pt.

Greig I.

Sheep I.
Dock I. Domville I.

Comet I.

Cooper Reef

Armstrong Pt.

Little Group

Rubly I. Gooch I.

Rum I.
(Isle de Lis Marine Park)

Mills Rd.

Roberts Pt.

Forrest I.

N. Cod Reef

S. Cod Reef

SIDNEY

Beacon Ave.

Galaran Rd.

Washington State ferry terminal

Tulista Park

Sidney Spit Marine Park

Mandarte I.

SAANICH PENINSULA

Lochside Dr.

Bazan Bay

Miners Channel

Halibut I.

John Dean Provincial Park

Cordova Channel

Sidney Channel

Sidney I.

Hamley Pt.

Mt. Newton Cross Rd.

Turgoose Pt.

James I.

Sandbanks

Wymond Pt.

Cordova Spit

Munroe Rock

Sallas Rocks

East Saanich IR

Hughes Passage

Island View Rd.

D'Arcy Shoals

D'Arcy Island Marine Park

Little D'Arcy I.

Unit Rocks

Keating Cross Rd.

Kelp Reefs

Fairway Patch

Miles

1   2

Km   1   2   3

Cordova Bay Rd.

Cordova Bay

Cormorant Pt.

Royal Oak Dr.

Mount Douglas Park

Gordon Head

Glencoe Cove

Arbutus Cove

Central Saanich Rd.

E. Saanich Rd.

Wallace Dr.

Oldfield Rd.

Old W. Saanich Rd.

W. Saanich Rd.

17

Canada/U.S. Border

HARO STRAIT

N48°25.48' W123°14.94'. The cove at the western border of the park is dotted with rocks and kelp. A small beach here provides access to a level, grassy area.

N48°25.26' W123°14.52'. West of Commodore Point is a small cove with a good beach backed by a grassy area. This site has trail access to Rudlin Bay. Another option is just east of Commodore Point, on the beach or the grass atop the embankment. An outhouse is located nearby.

HARO STRAIT

Haro Strait lies between Juan de Fuca Strait to the south and Boundary Pass to the north. Sea Bird Point on Discovery Island is the southern limit, while the strait extends north through Piers Island, Kanaka Bluff on Portland Island, Reynard Point on Moresby Island to Turn Point on Stuart Island in the San Juans. Part of the main shipping route to Vancouver, it's travelled frequently by large container ships.

Enjoying the evening at Sidney Spit.

The strait is prone to a huge countercurrent east of Discovery Island on the flood tide. The northward tide hits San Juan Island then shifts northwest, creating a countercurrent that results in a southerly flood flow off Discovery Island. This delays the turn of the tide to an ebb off Sidney Island 1–2.5 hours after the turn predicted for Race Passage. Kayakers can avoid this by staying within the island clusters.

Cordova Bay

This bay is part of a stretch of fairly exposed coast. It's a moderate trip of 19 km (12 miles) between the campsites at Discovery Island

and D'Arcy Island. Regional parks can be found at Gordon Head and Mount Douglas. Given the limited beach access and lack of islands, this stretch is not a common kayaking destination. A torpedo firing area is located from the north end of Cordova Bay north to Cordova Spit.

Place names: The name Cordova Bay is actually a Hudson's Bay Company error. Manuel Quimper of the Spanish navy anchored in Esquimalt Harbour in 1790, naming it Puerto de Cordova after Don Antonio Maria Bucareli y Ursua Henestrosa Lasso de la Vega Villacis y Cordova, the 46th viceroy of Mexico. It was mistaken for this bay by HBC officials.

A view through the remains of the caretaker's residence at the D'Arcy Island leper colony.

D'Arcy Island

D'Arcy Island is a pleasant little park with a black mark in its history. Between 1890 and 1924 it was home to a leper colony, a reflection of how misunderstanding can breed fear. Today we know leprosy is one of the least communicable of all communicable diseases, but in 1890 the appearance of cases among Chinese coal mine workers brought a sense of panic to Victoria. The city responded by banishing the lepers to this island colony. In 1924 the colony was moved to Bentinck Island (see *Volume 1*, page 354). While numerous relics of the colony can still be seen, the most visible reminder is the crumbling foundation and walls of the caretaker's residence. Except for the historic remnants, the island is wonderfully pristine and has an assortment of trails. It became a provincial park in 1967, and has since been transferred to the Gulf Islands National Park.

The best access to the island and its trails is on the east side in a cove near Little D'Arcy Island. You'll find a beach, a day-use area with picnic tables, an information kiosk, washrooms and tent pads. Little D'Arcy Island is privately owned. Both Unit Rocks and Kelp Rocks (east of the regional map) are nesting sites for glaucous-winged gull.

The outer bar of Sidney Spit as high tide approaches.

Place names: Lieut. John D'Arcy was mate aboard the *Herald* on a surveying expedition of the Pacific Ocean 1852–1854.

Camping: N48°34.04' W123°16.40'. Tent pads and a group site can be found along a trail leading from the day-use area on D'Arcy Island's east side. Undesignated spots dot the island, but campers should be aware that Parks Canada patrols the national park islands and dispersed camping is not allowed.

Island View Beach

This is a popular Saanich day-use park, with a beach, sand dunes and trails that can be reached from Highway 17 by Island View Road.

Launches: A boat ramp is available at Island View Beach Regional Park. Kayakers may prefer to use the gravel beach, though this may mean crossing drift logs.

Cordova Channel

This channel separates James Island from Saanich Peninsula. Currents reach 2–3 knots flooding north and 1–2 knots on the southerly ebb. On the west side Cordova Spit creates a bay for the Saanichton Bay government wharf. The rest of the bay and most of the spit is part of the community at East Saanich Indian Reserve.

James Island

Back in 1913 James Island became a TNT manufacturing plant for Canadian Explosives. Rather than a bombed-out hole, however, it was a thriving community with homes, a school and its own railway. The plant was closed in 1978 and the village removed. In 1989 a consortium bought the island, but their plans to develop it into a luxury subdivision were destined for failure. In 1994 Seattle cell phone billionaire Craig McCaw purchased it, and it now boasts a Jack Nicklaus-designed golf course, six cottages, a seaplane ramp, runway and dock. The white earth cliff along the south shore is conspicuous, while the east side is low and sandy.

Place names: James Douglas was governor of Vancouver Island at the time it was named in 1853.

Sidney Channel

Sidney Channel runs between James Island and Sidney Island with a width of little more than a mile (1.8 km). The flood current runs northwest. The turn to flood is 1 hour after the turn at Race Passage, and the turn to ebb is 1 hour and 30 minutes later.

Sidney Island

Sand is the main characteristic of this island. There are tall earth cliffs on the southwest and south ends, and the whole island is fringed with a sandy mud flat that will dry about 320 m (0.2 miles) offshore. Then there's the sandy spit that extends about 1.6 km (a mile) north from the main island. A light marks the northern extent of the spit. The spit forms part of a lagoon with luxurious sand beaches now part of the Gulf Islands National Park reserve.

Originally a provincial park, it's serviced by foot passenger ferry from Sidney at the end of Beacon Avenue during the summer season. This makes it popular with backpackers and families. The protected anchorage makes it an ideal waypoint for boaters, and during the summer season several dozen boats will be at anchor here or moored at the dock.

Smelt, also called sandlance, reproduce in the lagoon's sand, attracting sandpiper, murrelet, auklet, cormorant, gull and other shorebirds each summer. This is one of the top bird habitats in the Georgia Basin. Brandt cormorant stop here on the fall migration and mew gull and brant during the spring migration. Black oystercatcher

Killer whales feed near Mandarte Island.

nest in the area. The beaches are also a great place to see great blue heron. About 50 regularly feed here. As late as 1988, 100 pairs were reported nesting here, but the colony has since disappeared.

Boaters are asked to stay outside the lagoon to protect the wildlife. A wharf and landing floats are provided for visiting boaters at the east entrance to the lagoon. A trail leads to lookouts over the northern side of the island toward Gooch and Domville islands.

On the north side of the lagoon are remnants of Sidney Island Brick and Tile, founded in 1906. The bricks were used in projects such as the Empress Hotel and Hotel Vancouver. The factory went bankrupt in 1925. Bricks, building foundations and equipment are still scattered along the shorefront. Hidden deeper within the park is a memory from the Second World War: a bomb shelter. It lies off the main path east of the camping area in an open field. It was built because James Island, as an explosives manufacturing site, was considered a target.

Outside park boundaries Sidney Island is mostly residential. The property was sold in 1981 for a sustained-yield tree farm. The central property is a common area managed for forestry. The exterior of the island is 24 large residential lots. The intent is to make it a model for sustainable development.

Camping: N48°38.17' W123°19.77'. Camping is in an open, grassy clearing on the east side of the lagoon. A good sand beach surrounds

The Sidney waterfront from Sidney Spit.

the site. Group camping for 15 or more is available in a field set back from the water. On-site staff collect fees. For group reservations call **1-877-559-2115.**

Mandarte Island

This elongated rocky island is the perfect combination of environment and seclusion to attract thousands of nesting birds. Residents include double-crested cormorant, pelagic cormorant, glaucous-winged gull and pigeon guillemot. It's also one of just a few places on the B.C. coast where tufted puffin is known to breed. The island is a Tsawout and Tseycum reserve; with their cooperation it's maintained as a seabird reserve and research area.

Like many nesting sites on the Vancouver Island coast, the number of double-crested cormorant nests on Mandarte Island is in rapid decline. In 1983 1,100 nests were recorded. In 2000 there were 215.

Place names: Father Mandarte was the first Roman Catholic priest in Saanich in about 1870. He built Saanich's first church.

Sidney

This is a full-service residential community of about 10,000. The commercial centre tends to cluster around Beacon Avenue, which ends at a wharf used as a terminal for foot passenger ferry service

The beach facing north at Rum Island.

to Sidney Island. A customs office is located at Port Sidney Marina north of the wharf behind breakwaters. Just south of the wharf off Beacon Avenue is a beach suitable for a kayak haulout. About 650 m (0.4 miles) south of the wharf is the Washington state ferry terminal. It's bracketed by a small waterfront park to the north and Tulista Park, a day-use area with a busy boat ramp, to the south.

Currents along the Sidney waterfront can be variable and strong, especially along the ferry wharf. In other locations the flood sets north and the ebb south.

Launches: Kayaks can launch from a number of residential streets that end in beach access within Sidney. Here are a few key options, from south to north.

N48°38.14' W123°24.33'. Lochside Drive runs parallel to the ocean. Parking is along the shoulder. A slope leads to a seawall running parallel with the ocean. Stairs provide beach access at regular intervals.

N48°38.57' W123°23.91'. Tulista Park is located immediately south of the Washington State ferry terminal. Within the park is a busy boat launch; a gravel beach to the north is suitable for kayak launches.

N48°38.93' W123°23.61'. The main road in Sidney is Beacon Avenue, which ends in the dock for the Sidney Island foot passenger ferry. To the south of the terminal is an open beach. Steps lead from the seawall. Unload at the seawall, then find parking nearby. A better option might be the end of Rothesay Road. To get here turn north off Beacon Road to Third Street, then east on Rothesay. The dead-end road has beach access through a short, paved path over rocks. Parking is available on Third Street. Another nearby option to the north is Amherst Avenue. There concrete steps lead to a sheltered gravel beach.

Camping: The Gulf Islands National Park includes McDonald Park, located on the western outskirts of Sidney off Highway 17, just minutes from the Swartz Bay ferry terminal. This is a convenient staging ground for kayak trips. There are 50 vehicle-accessible and 6 walk-in campsites.

Gooch and Rum islands

Gooch and Rum islands are connected by a neck of land with beaches on both sides. These give access to a trail skirting Rum Island.

Gooch Island is privately owned. Rum Island was formerly Isle-de-Lis Marine Park and is now part of the Gulf Islands National Park. It was made a park in 1978 thanks to a donation by Mrs. Rennie McCaud Nelson, who asked that the park be named for the lilies on the island.

HMCS *Mackenzie* lies in about 30 m (100 feet) of water just north of Gooch Island. The anti-submarine destroyer was sunk in 1995 as an artificial reef for divers. Four buoys mark its location.

Place names: Rum Island was used as a liquor cache during Prohibition.

Camping: N48°39.76' W123°16.84'. Designated camping is on the south side of Rum Island on a grassy headland. Land at the isthmus and take a short trail to reach the campsite.

Domville Island and area

Domville and the other nearby islands are all privately owned. Despite cottages and homes dotting the islands, many reefs and complex shorelines make for an interesting area to explore. Reay and Grieg islands are former Crown islets transferred into the Gulf Islands National Park; both are undeveloped. Public access is prohibited to protect the sensitive habitat.

Low, treed islands are typical for this region.

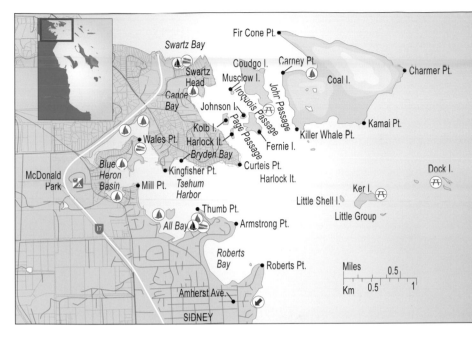

Imrie Island

This low rock makes a good landmark on a crossing from Coal Island to Moresby Island. A nesting site for black oystercatcher, glaucous-winged gull and pigeon guillemot, it's now part of the Gulf Islands National Park and access is prohibited.

COAL ISLAND

Most of the islands in this cluster are privately owned and the passages busy with marine traffic. Coal Island is the largest in this area. Pocket pebble beaches dot the shoreline, along with many private property signs. The Saanich Peninsula shore in this region is heavily developed, with marinas in most coves. For most kayakers it will simply be a transit area.

Ecological oddities: The second-largest rocky mountain juniper in B.C. is located on the southwest end of Coal Island.

Little Group

The Little Group is a cluster of islands and rocks surrounded by a number of drying ledges and shoals. Two islands, Ker and Little Shell, remain private. The other smaller islets and rocks have been

Rocks at the south entrance to John Pass.

incorporated into the Gulf Islands National Park reserve. Dock Island, on the east end of the Little Group, is a rocky mound with an east-facing cove. It's also part of the national park now. Day-use access is allowed at the beach shoreline, but not in the upland area. Camping is prohibited.

Ecological oddities: Most of the Canada geese found across B.C. are not native. They came from central North America and were introduced across North America as game stock after being hunted to near-extinction in the 1960s. (The native subspecies of Canada geese on the west coast are smaller and migratory.) The birds appeared in the Gulf Islands in the mid-1980s, nesting there from March to July, and they appear to be helping non-native grasses invade the islets and replace native wildflowers. Geese eat the grass, carry the seeds in their digestive systems to new islands and deposit them there. For both invaders the relationship works well—the geese spread the grasses, and the grasses feed the geese. The losers are the native wildflowers, which are being forced out by the introduced grasses. UBC researchers are investigating this relationship on six islets in the Gulf Islands National Park Reserve and on Ker Island. The intent is to aid park staff in protecting the Gulf Islands' fragile coastal bluff ecology from these invaders.

Tsehum Harbour

This harbour, also known as Shoal Harbour, has numerous marinas within the various coves. A public wharf and customs float are located in All Bay. The north shore of the harbour, between Curteis and Kingfisher points, is fringed by drying and submerged rocks. A plan is in place to dredge the tidal flats of the lagoon to enlarge a marina, which, like others in this area, has reached capacity.

Iroquois, Page and John passages

Three passes can be used to head north-south between Coal Island and the Saanich Peninsula. The islands that create the passes—Fernie and Goudge—are privately owned. Look for a good beach on the south of Goudge Island for a low-tide break. Tucked into Saanich Peninsula is Canoe Bay, where a marina and customs office are located.

A speed limit of 4 knots is in place in all three passages, as the traffic tends to be busy and the sightlines poor. Numerous reefs dot the waters here, making it a difficult area for boats to transit. Currents will reach several knots, with the flood north and ebb south.

Swartz Bay

This bay is the main ferry terminal and point of departure for BC Ferries vessels headed for Tsawwassen (Vancouver) and the Gulf Islands. There are five ferry berths, with another used for freight ferries operating between here and the Fraser River. The ferry terminal tends to be a busy place, with several arrivals and departures in any given hour. It is highly recommended that kayakers do not transit in front of Swartz Bay. Instead, cross to the outlying islands where sightlines are better. Ferries will sound horns and call in to Vessel Traffic Services only when leaving the terminal, and this does not give kayakers enough notice to safely clear the area. For more advice on travelling this area by kayak, see page 139.

Launches: N48°41.21' W123°24.43'. The Swartz Bay public wharf is located immediately to the east of the ferry terminal, but getting to it by car can be tricky. If you're coming from the Tsawwassen ferry and heading south, get off the highway and turn back onto Highway 17 northbound. Take the last exit before the toll booth (Dolphin Road). Follow the edge of the ferry terminal fence to Barnacle Road. There you'll find a busy wharf with limited parking.

Typical bluffs in Squally Reach.

If you're walking a kayak onto the ferry, you can walk it off to the wharf. Wheels for the kayak would make this easier. You can launch a kayak from the wharf or squeeze through the rough beach access and launch from the gravel. Good alternative launch sites can be found in Saanich.

SAANICH INLET

Saanich Inlet extends 24 km (15 miles) south from Satellite Channel. The northern end is wide with a gently rolling topography until Tod Inlet; south of Tod Inlet it becomes narrower, twisting and hemmed in by mountainous slopes. It was created by a single retreating glacier, and the direction differs from the pattern elsewhere in the Gulf Islands, indicating it was created in an earlier ice age. It's the only example of a coastal fiord on east Vancouver Island. Its mountains may lack the height of the mainland inlets, but the exposed bluffs and arbutus forests have a charm quite unlike the heavy pine forests of the more northerly fiords.

Ferry service: A regular BC Ferries passenger and automobile ferry service crosses Saanich Inlet from McPhail Point to Brentwood Bay. This is a convenient and scenic option for those crossing between points north of the Malahat and the Saanich Peninsula.

Patricia Bay

This portion of Saanich Inlet is the widest, at 8 km (5 miles) from Mill Bay to Patricia Bay. Residential development is heavy. Deep Cove has a decaying public wharf (unusable) and a marina. On the southeast side of Patricia Bay is the Institute of Ocean Sciences and its wharf for Fisheries and Oceans research vessels and the Victoria Airport seaplane base. Northwest of Yarrow Point is a 1.6-km (1-mile) square in the middle of Saanich Inlet designated as a military torpedo and air-to-sea firing range.

Launches: The Tseycum reserve in Patricia Bay has a boat launch, a convenient entry point for those arriving from the Tsawwassen terminal. It's near the totem pole on the north end of the bay.

N48°41.26'W123°28.48'. Deep Cove has a beach access of so-so quality that kayakers might like to use, especially for trips from Victoria heading toward

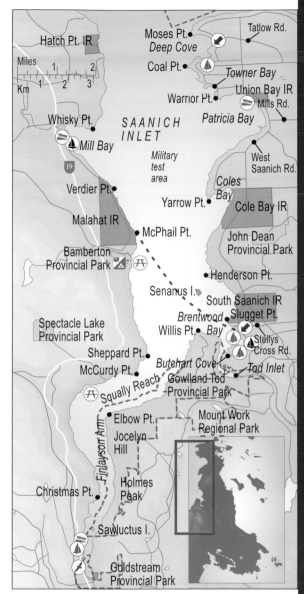

Saltspring. From Highway 17 take Wain Road (17A) west to West Saanich Road. Take West Saanich Road north to Tatlow Road, then Tatlow Road west. Follow it to the beach access at the end. Cape Keppel is just 4 km (2.5 miles) away.

The old Portland Cement factory at Bamberton.

Mill Bay to Sheppard Point

Mill Bay is a small waterfront community on the west shore of Saanich Inlet with a marina protected by a breakwater and a public wharf. The Mill Bay ferry terminal is at McPhail Point on the Malahat reserve. Almost immediately south of the reserve is Bamberton Provincial Park. From the park to Sheppard Point the waterfront is steep, almost tall enough to be called mountainous and almost completely undeveloped—with one huge exception. A cement plant and its silos sit in ruins on pilings north of Sheppard Point. Portland Cement operated here in the early 1900s; Butchart Gardens, across the inlet, was originally the quarry for the operation. In the 1990s a plan by the owner to develop the 592-ha (1,460-acre) property into a 12,000-resident development raised local opposition. In 2005 the property was sold to a new owner with no immediate plans to develop it, but be sure a new subdivision will be on the agenda in the next few years.

Bamberton Provincial Park

This park's sandy beaches are known for invitingly warm water. The land for the park was donated by the British Columbia Cement Company in 1959. Kayakers may want to use the beach for a break but camping isn't an option. The sites are considerably uphill from the waterfront.

Launches: From the Island Highway follow Mill Bay Road to downtown Mill Bay. Across from the shopping centre is Handy Road, which ends in the gently sloping boat ramp.

The waterfront at Bamberton Provincial Park.

Brentwood Bay

Brentwood Bay is a busy village centre with several marinas, a public wharf and a small ferry terminal. The ferry wharf is just south of Sluggett Point; the public float is in the southeast end of Brentwood Bay. The area is a major tourist draw due mainly to Butchart Gardens, 22 ha (55 acres) of manicured gardens, including the Sunken Garden set in an old limestone quarry. A highlight is the summer-long weekend fireworks. Boats often anchor in the adjacent waters to watch the spectacle.

Place names: Brentwood was the estate and home in England of Mr. Horne-Payne, chairman of the B.C. Electric Railway.

Launches: N48°34.65' W123°27.89'. South of the ferry terminal at Mill Bay is a small community park with a stretch of limited parking. A trail leads through the park to a beach. This is about the best southernmost launch for day trips into Finlayson Arm on the Victoria side. To get here from Highway 17, turn east onto East Saanich Road, then left onto Stellys Cross Road.

Jocelyn Hills alongside Saanich Inlet.

Tod Inlet

This inlet is a boat haven and popular anchorage. Much of the east shore is protected by Gowlland Tod Provincial Park. Two village sites on the inlet have been dated at 1,500 years old or more. Physical reminders of pioneer days include the Vancouver Portland Cement Company. An industry town thrived here between 1904 and 1920. Hiking trails use the original roads and railway right-of-way.

Ecological oddities: Species considered rare that can be found on the inlet include the phantom orchid and peregrine falcon.

Gowlland Tod Provincial Park

This park protects over 1,200 ha (2,965 acres) of coastal Douglas-fir forest and 8 km (5 miles) of shoreline. A pioneer copper mine is located within the park and many of the hiking and horse trails use previous logging and mining roads. Twelve middens line the park's shoreline. Most sites were used for seasonal hunting, fishing and gathering. The park was established as part of the Commonwealth Nature Legacy to commemorate the 1994 Commonwealth Games in Victoria.

Squally Reach

This portion of the inlet extends from Willis Point to Elbow Point. Some residential development is clustered around Willis Point but otherwise Squally Reach is undeveloped. The topography rises as you head south. Beaches are generally rough.

Finlayson Arm

This is the southern extent of Saanich Inlet, running 6.8 km (4 miles) from Elbow Point to the intertidal muck at the mouth of Goldstream River. Development is limited, though an abalone farm is located just north of Christmas Point. A marina, the Goldstream Boathouse, is on the lower western shore north of Goldstream Provincial Park. Sawluctus Island is privately owned. The Goldstream River estuary is considered a "quiet zone" with no boat access. Occasionally canoeists try to launch from the park into Goldstream River, but this should be discouraged due to the estuary's shallow depth and sensitivity as a salmon spawning ground and waterfowl habitat.

Rugged shoreline along Finlayson Arm.

Launches: Goldstream Boathouse has a boat ramp allowing marine access to Finlayson Arm. Access is from the Island Highway's northbound lane. Note the turnoff can be difficult to see.

Ecological oddities: The arm's steep and deep shoreline supports a rare community of giant cloud sponges as well as sea plumes and lampshells.

Goldstream Provincial Park

Goldstream Provincial Park is popular for its trails, interpretive programs, campground, huge old-growth trees and the chance to see salmon travelling upriver to spawn. The park was donated by the Greater Victoria Water Board in 1958, with additions made in 1994 and 1996. Every year from late October to December chum, coho and chinook salmon enter the Goldstream River to spawn. There is no marine access, as the Goldstream River estuary is closed to the public. A viewing platform allows observation of the birds in the estuary, including many bald eagles, particularly during spawning. The campsite is located a considerable distance from the estuary across the Island Highway, making it inappropriate for kayak camping. A favourite day-hike is up Mount Finlayson.

A fine January day at Murder Point.

The Outer Gulf Islands

CHAPTER TWO

PARKS CANADA COULDN'T HAVE PICKED MORE WISELY WHEN TAYLOR POINT, Narzaez Bay and Monarch Head on Saturna Island were included in the new Gulf Islands National Park. These are all exceptional places to kayak. I have many memories of this area: sunsets at Cabbage Island; being stared down by large, moody, long-horned cattle in the old-growth forest at Taylor Point; encountering herds of feral goats and their babies at Murder Point; sunny, warm January weekends paddling Bedwell Harbour and Bruce Bight; and, more recently, casually thinking I could run Boat Passage only to find myself trounced by the rapids—to name just a few.

Parks Canada has been busy adding parcels to the national park reserve since its inception in 2003, with most within this area. Now most of the upper portion of Brown Ridge and as far as Mount David are protected. Other new parcels protect Greenburn Lake on South Pender and Loretta's Wood on North Pender.

Given a choice of venues to visit anywhere on the B.C. coast, it's hard to top Saturna and the magnificence of Monarch Head, the serenity of Taylor Point, the cliffs of Fiddlers Cove and the beauty of Cabbage Island.

Exploring by kayak

The main constraint to kayaking this area is the lack of campsites. Marine-accessible camping is desperately needed on south Saturna and Mayne islands to complete a marine trail through the area. As it stands, the distance from the campsite at Bedwell Harbour to Cabbage Island is about 25 km (16 miles)—not an impossible distance, but a long haul through a scenic area where kayakers will

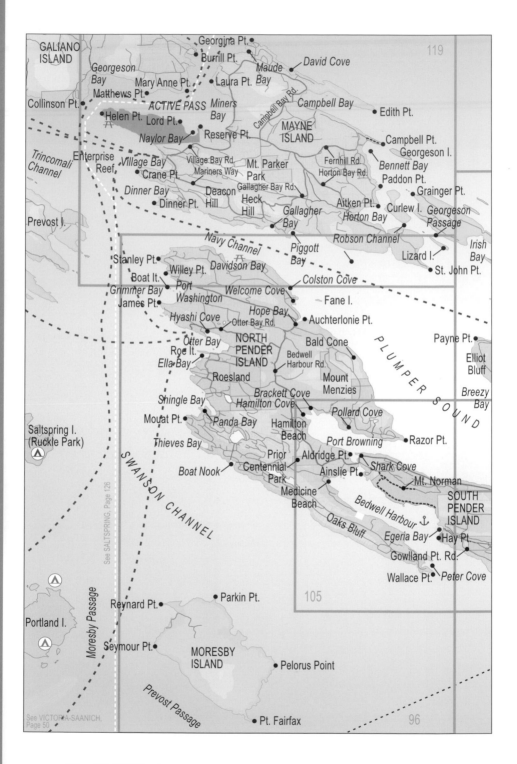

GALIANO
ISLAND

Georgina Pt.

Burrill Pt.

David Cove

Georgeson
Bay

Maude
Bay

Mary Anne Pt.

Laura Pt.

Matthews Pt.

Collinson Pt.

ACTIVE PASS

Miners
Bay

Campbell Bay Rd.

Campbell Bay

Edith Pt.

Helen Pt.

Lord Pt.

MAYNE
ISLAND

Campbell Pt.

Naylor Bay

Reserve Pt.

Georgeson I.

Trincomali
Channel

Enterprise
Reef

Village Bay

Fernhill Rd.

Bennett Bay

Village Bay Rd.

Crane Pt.

Mariners Way

Mt. Parker
Park

Horton Bay Rd.

Paddon Pt.

Grainger Pt.

Prevost I.

Dinner Bay

Deacon
Hill

Gallagher Bay Rd.

Dinner Pt.

Heck
Hill

Aitken Pt.

Curlew I.

Georgeson
Passage

Gallagher
Bay

Horton Bay

Navy Channel

Piggott
Bay

Robson Channel

Irish
Bay

Stanley Pt.

Davidson Bay

Lizard I.

St. John Pt.

Boat It.

Willey Pt.

Colston Cove

Grimmer Bay

Port
Washington

Welcome Cove

Fane I.

James Pt.

Hyashi Cove

Hope Bay

Auchterlonie Pt.

P
L
U
M
P
E
R

Otter Bay Rd.

Otter Bay

NORTH
PENDER
ISLAND

Bald Cone

Payne Pt.

Roe It.

Bedwell
Harbour Rd.

Elliot
Bluff

Ella Bay

Roesland

Mount
Menzies

Breezy
Bay

Saltspring I.
(Ruckle Park)

Shingle Bay

Brackett Cove

Pollard Cove

S
O
U
N
D

Hamilton Cove

Mouat Pt.

Panda Bay

Hamilton
Beach

Port Browning

Razor Pt.

Thieves Bay

Prior

Aldridge Pt.

Boat Nook

Centennial
Park

Ainslie Pt.

Shark Cove

Mt. Norman

SOUTH
PENDER
ISLAND

Medicine
Beach

Bedwell Harbour

Egeria Bay

Hay Pt.

Oaks Bluff

Gowland Pt. Rd.

Wallace Pt.

Peter Cove

See SALTSPRING, Page 126

S
W
A
N
S
O
N

C
H
A
N
N
E
L

Portland I.

Moresby Passage

Reynard Pt.

Parkin Pt.

Seymour Pt.

MORESBY
ISLAND

Pelorus Point

Prevost Passage

See VICTORIA-SAANICH,
Page 50

Pt. Fairfax

119

105

96

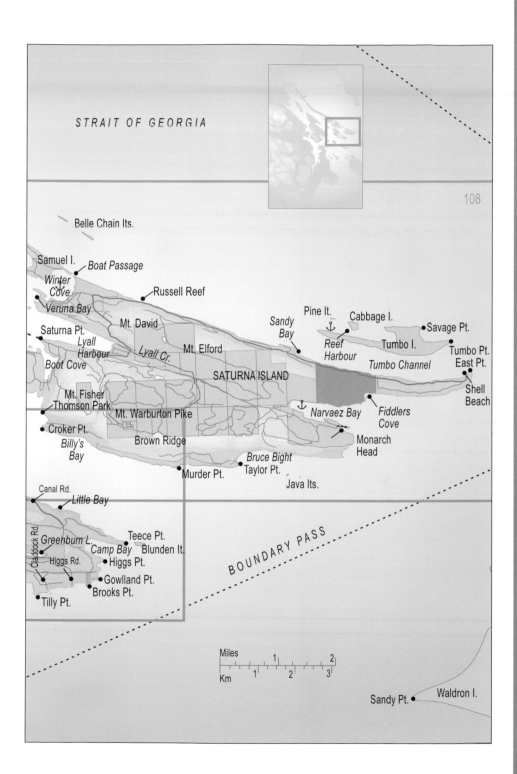

STRAIT OF GEORGIA

108

Belle Chain Its.

Samuel I. *Boat Passage*

Winter Cove

Russell Reef

Veruna Bay

Saturna Pt.
Lyall Harbour
Mt. David
Lyall Cr.
Mt. Elford
Boot Cove

Mt. Fisher
Thomson Park

Croker Pt.
Billy's Bay

Mt. Warburton Pike
Brown Ridge

Murder Pt.
Taylor Pt.

Bruce Bight

SATURNA ISLAND

Sandy Bay

Pine It.
Cabbage I.
Savage Pt.
Reef Harbour
Tumbo I.
Tumbo Pt.
Tumbo Channel
East Pt.

Shell Beach

Narvaez Bay
Fiddlers Cove
Monarch Head

Java Its.

Canal Rd.
Little Bay

Claddock Rd

Greenburn L.
Teece Pt.
Camp Bay
Blunden It.
Higgs Rd.
Higgs Pt.
Gowlland Pt.
Brooks Pt.

Tilly Pt.

BOUNDARY PASS

Miles
1
2
Km
1
2
3

Sandy Pt.
Waldron I.

want to linger. In addition, there is no public campsite between Montague Harbour on Galiano and Cabbage Island, a distance of almost 30 km (18 miles).

Recommended kayaking trips

- *If you have a day:* The best day trip in the Gulf Islands in my mind is from Breezy Bay to Monarch Head or as far as Fiddlers Cove, then back, a trip of 20–25 km (12–16 miles). Of course, this means a possibly time-consuming ferry to Saturna. Another good day trip is from Hamilton Beach on North Pender through Bedwell Harbour—from 8–25 km (5–16 miles), depending on how thoroughly you wish to explore the harbour. I've done both these trips in the middle of winter and found the weather wonderful. A day trip from Swartz Bay or Sidney to circumnavigate Moresby Island would also be pleasant, but would be best when combined with a visit to Portland Island (covered in Chapter 3). Naturally, stronger kayakers could pick longer routes, such as a trip to South Pender from Sidney.

- *If you have two days:* A popular trip is from Winter Cove to Cabbage Island and back, though circumnavigating Saturna Island is recommended (32 km/20 miles in total). Another good weekend trip from Sidney is to Bedwell Harbour, possibly returning via a circumnavigation of South Pender (40–54 km/24–33 miles).

- *If you have three days:* With a launch from Winter Cove, consider a trip around Saturna Island by staying at Cabbage Island and Bedwell Harbour on South Pender.

- *If you have five days:* An adventurous route would be to launch from Bennett Bay on Mayne Island, overnight at Cabbage Island, Bedwell Harbour, Portland Island, Prevost Island then return to Bennett Bay. This is an easily achievable 88 km (55 miles). For details on Portland and Prevost islands, see Chapter 3.

- *If you have a week:* I would suggest a launch from Sidney, a trip up Iroquois Pass to Portland Island, an exploration of Prevost Island, a trip through Active Pass, a run to Cabbage Island, a trip to Bedwell Harbour, then south to Rum Island, D'Arcy Island or Sidney Spit before returning home. This combines destinations from chapters 1 to 3.

Near Hope Bay.

- *The ideal trip:* Any trip of this area must involve several days exploring Saturna Island. The ideal circuit of this area would have to include Active Pass, the area around Georgeson Island and Belle Chain Islets, Tumbo Island, Monarch Head, Bedwell Harbour and Moresby Island. With this agenda you can simply connect the dots. An itinerary might be launching from Sidney, then travelling Portland Island, Prevost Island, Active Pass, Cabbage Island; spending a day exploring Tumbo Island; continuing to Narvaez Bay; heading to Bedwell Harbour, then south to the islands off Sidney before returning to your launch site. Substitute Montague Harbour on Galiano as a good staging area for trips from Vancouver.

NORTH PENDER ISLAND

The two Pender islands are home to about 3,500 people, with most living on the larger North Pender Island. While more developed than many of the Gulf Islands, North Pender still retains much of its natural charm along the shorelines. The best places to explore by boat are Oaks Bluff, Bedwell Harbour and the north shore from Stanley

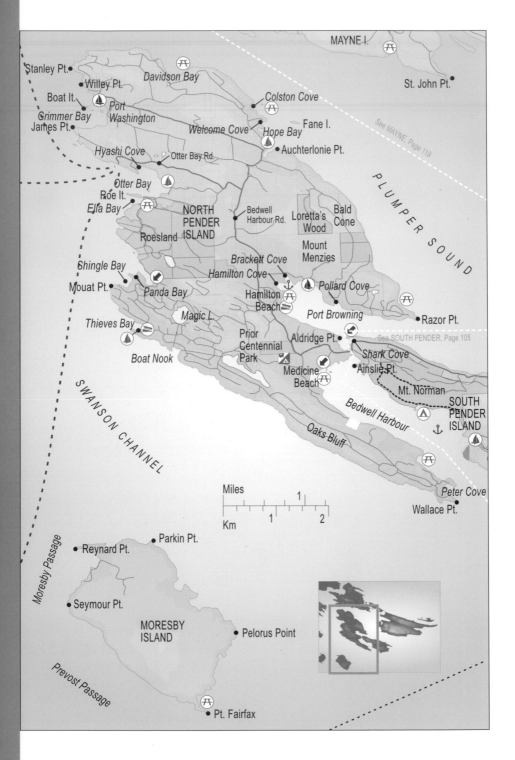

MAYNE I.

Stanley Pt.

Willey Pt.

Davidson Bay

St. John Pt.

Boat It.

Colston Cove

Port
Washington

Grimmer Bay
James Pt.

Welcome Cove

Fane I.

Hope Bay

See MAYNE, Page 119

Hyashi Cove

Auchterlonie Pt.

Otter Bay Rd.

PLUMPER SOUND

Otter Bay

Roe It.

Ella Bay

NORTH
PENDER
ISLAND

Bedwell
Harbour Rd.

Loretta's
Wood

Bald
Cone

Roesland

Mount
Menzies

Shingle Bay

Brackett Cove

Hamilton Cove

Mouat Pt.

Panda Bay

Hamilton
Beach

Pollard Cove

Magic L.

Port Browning

Razor Pt.

Thieves Bay

Aldridge Pt.

See SOUTH PENDER, Page 105

Boat Nook

Prior
Centennial
Park

Shark Cove

Ainslie Pt.

Medicine
Beach

Mt. Norman

SOUTH
PENDER
ISLAND

Bedwell Harbour

Oaks Bluff

Peter Cove

Wallace Pt.

SWANSON CHANNEL

Miles

1

Km

1

2

Parkin Pt.

Moresby Passage

Reynard Pt.

Seymour Pt.

MORESBY
ISLAND

Pelorus Point

Prevost Passage

Pt. Fairfax

Point to Razor Point. Expect to see wildlife, as the islands are rich in deer, mink, shrew and about 140 species of birds.

Place names: In 1791 Spanish explorers named the island San Eusbio. Daniel Pender was master aboard the surveying vessel *Plumper* in 1857, the *Hecate* in 1861 and the *Beaver* in 1863.

Camping: North Pender lacks a marine-accessible campground, but Prior Centennial campground could serve as a staging area for those arriving by ferry. Now part of the Gulf Islands National Park, the campground has 17 drive-in sites set in thick forest cover, plus a short 1-km (0.6-mile) walking trail within the campground. Reservations can be made through the province's Discover Camping service at **1-800-689-9025.**

Moresby Island

Development on Moresby Island is limited to a farm on the western shore in a bay between Reynard and Seymour points. Its history includes ownership in 1887 by Capt. Horatio Robertson, the man credited with being the first European to pilot the Yangtse River in China. He built the island's unusual home with its two octagonal towers. The island was later purchased by T.W. Paterson, British Columbia's lieutenant-governor, in 1909. It is a mixture of rock bluffs and numerous pocket sand and gravel beaches. A wonderful area to explore is Point Fairfax, a long, thin strip of land with good beaches and a cairn on the point. Expect to see seals, otters and mink on a circumnavigation.

Place names: Rear Admiral Fairfax Moresby was commander of the Pacific Station of the Royal Navy from 1850 to 1853. His flagship was HMS *Portland*.

Prevost and Moresby passages

Prevost and Moresby passages are shipping routes connecting traffic in Haro Strait to Swanson Channel and Active Pass. The passages are bordered by Portland Island to the west and Reay, Brethour, Comet, Gooch and Rum islands to the south. At the narrower north end of Moresby Passage currents can run at 2–3 knots. The flood sets north and the ebb south.

The name is apt at Oaks Bluff.

Swanson Channel

This busy channel leads from Boundary Pass between Moresby, Saltspring and Prevost islands to connect with Active Pass. It's the main route for ferry traffic between Victoria and Vancouver, as well as a considerable amount of recreational and commercial traffic heading to and from the mainland via Active Pass. The Pender Island ferry crosses into Otter Bay via Swanson Channel, and ferries also head to Village Bay on Mayne Island or Lyall Harbour on Saturna through Swanson Channel.

Currents flood northwest and ebb southeast. The highest flood current will be near Enterprise Reef off Mayne Island's Village Bay. It can reach 5–7 knots in the entrance to Active Pass at spring tides and 3–5 knots during lesser tides.

Kayaks may have to cross Swanson Channel, and a lull when no ferries will be crossing your route may be difficult to find. Monitoring VHF Channel 11 is advised. See Active Pass, page 131, for information on navigating this area.

Place names: Capt. John Swanson was in charge of several Hudson's Bay vessels including the *Beaver*, *Labouchere*, *Otter* and *Enterprise* between 1858 and 1870.

An old cabin at Roesland.

Oaks Bluff

Aptly named, the high bluffs along the south end of North Pender Island are topped with Garry oak. Houses line the top of the bluff, but the rugged shoreline is generally undisturbed. The two bays along this stretch, Thieves Bay and Boat Nook, are developed with homes and docks, development that continues around Mouat Point in Shingle Bay.

Place names: Thieves Bay is named for an incident dating back to pioneer days, when poaching was a problem. On one lucky occasion poachers in a fishing sloop were caught and made to row to Mayne Island's jail under police guidance. As the policeman stepped from the boat, the thieves took the opportunity and paddled off into Active Pass, never to be seen again. Or so the story goes.

Launches: N48°46.19' W123°18.67'. A beach behind the marina at Thieves Bay is a pleasant launch site. Use the turnabout for unloading, then park elsewhere.

Otter Bay

This bay is dominated by the BC Ferries terminal. It was home to a saltery from 1929 to the early 1940s; rusting machinery, pilings

Looking toward Mayne Island from Colston Cove.

and a concrete foundation mark the operation. It produced tonnes of salted herring before it was expropriated in 1942 from the Japanese owners as part of Canada's wartime internment policy. The saltery burned down in 1956.

The south side of Otter Bay is protected as part of the Gulf Islands National Park. The park property, purchased in 1996, encompasses the Roesland Resort, a destination popular in the 1920s. The previous owner still retains a small portion of the land within the park boundaries. Roe Islet, included in the parkland, is accessible by a footbridge. The islet contains some old-growth Douglas-fir.

Numerous buildings dot the Roesland property. Most are deserted cabins from the old resort; the most dilapidated were torn down after its inclusion in the national park. Visiting kayakers can use the beach south of Roe Islet at Ella Bay.

Historic buildings in the parkland include the 1908 Roes homestead, rebuilt and now the home of the Pender Island Museum.

Grimmer Bay and Port Washington
Grimmer Bay is a developed bay with a harbour called Port Washington. The public wharf favours commercial use, with a well-

An attractive islet for a break off Colston Cove.

used seaplane float at the end of the dock. Watch for a chain of rocks that extends northwest from the central head of the bay. Boat Islet sits at the extremity of the rocks.

Place names: Washington Grimmer was an early postmaster here.

Navy Channel

This channel joins Plumper Sound and Swanson and Trincomali channels between Mayne and North Pender islands. The flood current runs southeast at 2–3 knots, with the ebb a maximum of 1–2 knots northwest. Note these directions are in the opposite direction of Plumper Sound and other prevailing tide directions in the area. This is because the current from Swanson Channel splits as it reaches Active Pass. Turbulence from the clash occurs in Plumper Sound.

Davidson Bay

Sandy beaches line Davidson Bay. This makes a good place for a break below the tide line. Farther south, Fane Island, Welcome Cove and Hope Bay are developed. A good place to stop is the clamshell beach on the little islet just outside Colston Cove. It's uninhabited but privately owned.

Bald Cone

Shoreline near Bald Cone.

The stretch of coast from near Auchterlonie Point to Razor Point is the steepest and wildest on North Pender Island. Tall, exposed cliffs drop to the waterline; Bald Cone, at 140 m (460 feet), and the nearby cliffs are a visual highlight. In 2005 Loretta's Wood, the inland area north of Mount Menzies, was added to the Gulf Islands National Park reserve. Access is currently only possible through private property. Loretta was the original donor of the land to the Islands Trust Fund in 2003.

Port Browning

Port Browning Marina and Resort occupies the head in Hamilton Cove. The marina has a store, beer and wine sales, showers and laundry. A public wharf is located northeast of Brackett Cove. Hamilton Beach, to the south, is a long, sandy stretch of shoreline. Just up the road is the Driftwood Centre with a bank, bakery, liquor store and post office (V0N 2M0).

Launches: N48°46.50' W123°16.44'. A strip of road leads to a pebble beach at the Pender Islands Lions Club boat ramp at Port Browning. To get here, take Hamilton Road from Bedwell Harbour Road.

Pender Canal

This pretty channel is crossed by a 23-m (75-foot) trestle bridge. Currents can run as high as 4 knots. The flood sets north and the ebb south. Kayakers can avoid the boat traffic and much of the current by staying in the shallows. Boats are restricted to 10 km per hour (5 knots).

The canal is an ancient Coast Salish burial site. Studies have shown that between 1,500 and 1,000 years ago the graves were often elaborate, with intricate goods, such as carved horn spoons, buried with the deceased. Around 1,000 years ago the practice of below-ground burials disappeared and was replaced by boxes, canoes or houses above ground behind the village.

The only bridge linking Gulf Islands crosses Pender Canal.

A bar joined North and South Pender islands until 1903, when it was dredged for boat traffic. The bridge—the only one between any of the Gulf Islands—was added in 1956.

Travel notes: New legislation allows the RCMP to use radar and hand out speeding tickets for boats similar to speeding tickets for cars. Pender Canal has been targeted due to a chronic problem with speeders. So if you're thinking of seeing how fast you can paddle through the canal when being pushed by a favourable current, you can make history by being the first kayaker to get a speeding ticket.

Medicine Beach

While much of the North Pender Island side of Bedwell Harbour is dotted with homes, cabins, resorts and camps, Medicine Beach is a nature sanctuary. The gravel beach is a popular day-use area. Coast Salish used the plants that grow here for medicinal purposes. The 8-ha (20-acre) nature sanctuary includes the beach, a wetland, an upland forest and a few bluffs. It is accessible by road.

At the south entrance of Bedwell Harbour, Peter Cove is developed but strewn with rocks where seals haul out—a destination for day-tripping kayakers.

Bedwell Harbour from Medicine Beach.

Launches: N48°45.67' W123°16.05'. At Medicine Beach a parking lot is provided for public beach access. This is a good starting point for kayakers or canoeists who want to explore Bedwell Harbour while avoiding open water or the currents of Pender Canal.

SOUTH PENDER ISLAND

Mount Maxwell from outside the campground.

This island is a fraction of the size of North Pender and has a permanent population of about 200. Kayakers will appreciate the various beaches along the south end, the bluffs near Mount Norman, the rocks at Skull Islet and the campsite at Bedwell Harbour. South Pender has been the beneficiary of several additions to

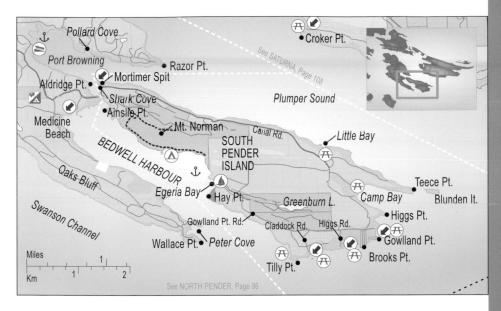

the Gulf Islands National Park reserve, notably a 69-ha (170-acre) property around Greenburn Lake, added in 2004, and a 50-ha (123-acre) addition south of the lake the following year. It is notable, as freshwater lakes in the Gulf Islands are rare.

Bedwell Harbour

Bedwell Harbour is formed by an overlap of North and South Pender islands. It's a recreational highlight for the region, popular as an anchorage for boaters and for kayakers exploring or camping at the former Beaumont Marine Park (see the separate entry below). Add mooring buoys, commercial crabbing, float planes and the possibility of water skiers, and you have a potentially congested area.

South Pender's main settlement is centred on Egeria Bay. A breakwater extends from Richardson Bluff to protect an upscale marina and resort on the north end of the bay. A public wharf and customs office are on the south end of the bay. Public mooring buoys are located east of Skull Islet.

Mortimer Spit

This is a popular road-accessible day-use area. Mortimer Spit is a long sandy bank that protects Shark Cove to the south, an intertidal wetland that dries in a mud flat at low tides.

Launches: N48°46.03' W123°15.46'. Driving and parking is possible along the spit. Kayakers can launch just about anywhere, as the water here is well sheltered.

The wetland at Shark Cove.

Beaumont/Mount Norman

Formerly two separate parks, one provincial and one regional, these two properties have been amalgamated into the Gulf Islands National Park. Trails lead from an access off Ainslie Point Road to a viewpoint, a wooden platform and benches atop Mount Norman at 244 m (800 feet). From there a trail leads down to the Bedwell Harbour waterfront and the campsite.

Capt. E.G. Beaumont donated the land for the park in 1963, along with the park at Discovery Island and Beaumont Provincial Park in the Nechako Plateau west of Prince George.

Camping: N48°45.25' W123°14.42'. While mainly a marine-based camping opportunity, hardy hikers can get to the Beaumont campsite in Bedwell Harbour via Mount Norman. There are 11 walk-in campsites. Tent clearings are set behind the beach north of Skull Islets.

Skull Islet.

Blunden Islet

This former ecological reserve is now included in the Gulf Islands National Park. The islet marks the convergence of Boundary Pass and Plumper Sound, and there are often confused seas with rips in the vicinity.

Nearby Teece Point is capped by a large residence. The north side of South Pender Island is generally steep with rough beaches.

Kayaking toward Blunden Islet.

Place names: Edward Raynor Blunden was the master's assistant aboard the surveying vessel *Hecate* in 1861.

Camp Bay and the south shore

Camp Bay is a popular beachcombing spot, and kayakers will appreciate the interesting rock formations and numerous reefs. The Land Conservancy of BC owns Gowlland Point, to the south. The beach, accessible by a wooden stairwell, could conceivably be used as a kayak launch. The 4-ha (10-acre) Brooks Point Park protects a portion of the shoreline at Brooks Point. The rest of the south shore of South Pender is lightly residential.

Launches: N48°43.96' W123°12.13'. At the end of Craddock Road is Craddock Beach. Beach access is down some steps that may be awkward. The beach is fine for launching but may be more exposed than some other options.

N48°44.05' W123°11.58'. Drummond Bay, at the end of Higgs Road, is accessible by a dirt trail that leads through some bushes and ends at a rocky beach. Climb over some rocks to the left and there is a perfectly sheltered sandy beach. Access with gear may be difficult over the rough trail.

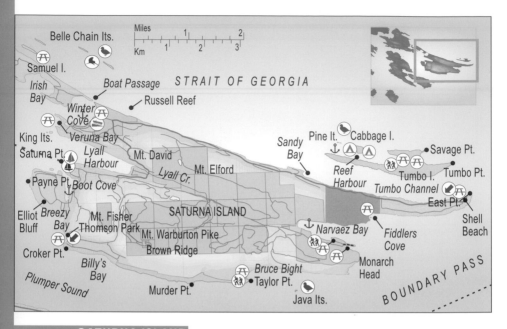

SATURNA ISLAND

Saturna Island lies at the eastern extremity of the string of outer Gulf Islands—so far east, in fact, that if you go any farther north, south or east you'll end up in the United States.

Picture Saturna as two ridges of land, both tilting upward from the north to create impressive south-facing cliffs, particularly those at Monarch Head. Between these ridges lies a deep valley with inlets at either end—Narvaez Bay to the east and Lyall Harbour to the west. Particularly distinctive are the open grassy slopes of Brown Ridge.

Saturna is home to about 350 people—a tiny number for an otherwise large island. Development tends to favour the area around Lyall Harbour, though housing does stretch along the north coast and along both sides of the peninsula that ends at East Point.

Visitors looking for land-accessible portions of the Gulf Islands National Park will find access limited to trails at Winter Cove, Lyall Creek and foot access to Narvaez Bay. Access to Taylor Point is possible but not sanctioned by Parks Canada, as the route can be dangerous.

Nearby Tumbo and Cabbage islands are also part of the national park reserve, with camping at Cabbage Island. More camping is being considered at Narvaez Bay.

The westernmost point on Tumbo Island.

Place names: The *Saturnina* was the naval schooner used by Spanish explorer Capt. Jose Maria Narvaez during his exploration of the Pacific Northwest in 1791.

Russell Reef
This popular swimming area on the north shore near Winter Cove is known for its shallow pools that build up behind rocky ridges. Most of the rest of Saturna's north shore is gently sloping upland that's either private property or bordered by road. Beaches are non-existent until Sandy Bay, which is backed by residential and resort properties.

Tumbo Channel
Due to the complex currents in the area, the current in Tumbo Channel, between Tumbo and Saturna islands, flows east regardless of the tide.

Cabbage and Tumbo Islands
Cabbage and Tumbo islands are popular boating destinations, due largely to the protected anchorage. The main recreational beach is

Expect wonderful sunsets at Cabbage Island.

located on the south end of Cabbage Island. Look for oyster beaches on the island's east and west shores.

Both Tumbo and Cabbage islands have been folded into the Gulf Islands National Park. Tumbo was first settled in 1877, and relics remain, including an early log cabin and a bunkhouse built for Japanese miners in 1888. A life-tenancy agreement with the previous owner means there is still one private cabin on the north end of the island. A three-hour trail around the island leads through Douglas-fir forest and Garry oak meadows. Good beach access to the trail is immediately east of Cabbage Island. Another pebble beach on the island's east side has picnic tables and an outhouse.

Place names: Lieut. Charles Wilkes labelled this Tumbow Island on a chart by in 1841, supposedly after the village of Tumbou in Fiji, which Wilkes had surveyed in 1840.

Camping: N48°47.84' W123°05.24'. A few campsites spread out along the waterfront of Cabbage Island face west, south or east.

East Point
East Point is aptly named for its location on the eastern edge of the Gulf Islands. The point is a regional park with a grassy headland

and wooden buildings associated with the old lighthouse, which was built in 1888.

A good landing spot for a break is at Shell Beach, tucked into the cove on the west side of East Point and backed by a shell midden. Kayakers can stop here and walk the headland to check for conditions outside East Point before rounding the point. Off East Point is Boiling Reef—a hint of the turbulent waters in the area, with rips, overfalls and eddies. Even in calm conditions currents can be moderate, and submerged rocks among the kelp pose a hazard. (As a side note, I've travelled the point numerous times and never had a problem beyond moderate currents by staying immediately adjacent to the shore.)

East Point is a Vessel Traffic Services call-in point for ships navigating Boundary Pass.

Launches: N48°47.05' W123°02.79'. This isn't a recommended launch, as the trail from the road is quite long, but Shell Beach is an option for those who want a short day trip out to Tumbo Island. A trail leads about 100 m (300 feet) downhill from the road to Shell Beach.

Boundary Pass
This is the main channel between the Canadian Gulf Islands and the

Moby Doll's claim to fame
In 1964 a sculptor named Samuel Burich was hired to create a life-size model of a killer whale for the Vancouver Aquarium. To do this, he was given permission to kill an orca for use as a model. A harpoon gun was set up at East Point and two months later it was fired at a young male.

The whale didn't initially die, and in an odd about-face the aquarium rallied to save the whale. It was towed to Vancouver with the harpoon still in its back. It was christened Moby Doll and put in a pen near Burrard Dry Dock, the first killer whale in captivity. But Moby's health never fully recovered and after 87 days the whale died. The *London Times* published a two-column obituary.

Moby Doll's legacy was two-edged. It furthered our understanding of killer whales and raised their profile, but it also created a demand for whales in aquariums. Over the next decade about 65 resident killer whales were taken from the waters off Vancouver Island, including 38 of the now-endangered southern resident population. A lot of those were young females, removed from their pods during the peak of their reproductive years. That practice was halted in 1976 when the population dipped to a low of about 68. It has since increased to about 90.

Sandstone rock formations at Fiddlers Cove.

U.S. San Juan Islands. The international boundary runs down the middle of the pass. This is a key shipping route for huge ocean-going freighters. Kayakers are most likely to use Boundary Pass on a trip between South Pender Island and Rum Island. You could travel it straight, but that would bring you into the shipping lane plus put you in U.S. waters just off Stuart Island, so a dogleg route to Point Fairfax on Moresby Island is recommended. Tidal currents can run at several knots, with the highest at 5 knots off East Point.

Fiddlers Cove

South of East Point, Saturna's coastline changes from the gentle slope of the north shore to high, intricately fretted sandstone cliffs rising sharply from the ocean. The small inlet called Fiddler's Cove, an uninhabited Tsawout/Tseycum reserve, is remarkable as the largest single example of the coastal bluff ecosystem in the Gulf Islands, at 19 ha (47 acres). It is an established recreation area. Permission to use it must be obtained from the Tsawout at **250-652-9101** or **1-888-652-9101** in Canada.

Narvaez Bay

The land surrounding Narvaez Bay is steep and forested, with a small patch of private land and a few homes at the head of the bay; much of the rest is protected within the national park reserve. The forest cover is maturing second-growth forest.

A small point on the bay's south shore was the site of the first settlement on Saturna. Here a sand and gravel beach facing northwest gives access to a picturesque headland that could become a camping area; it is currently an option being considered for the Gulf Islands National Park. The headland is a wide, clear area with an outhouse. A trail leads to a narrow and beautiful little cove north of Monarch Head. The tall cliffs and tropical hue of the water make it a scenic highlight of the area, by land or water. If you paddle in, there is a good beach at the head of the cove. Be sure to walk out to the point.

Bluffs near Monarch Head.

The old homestead shack at Taylor Point.

Hiking: Narvaez Bay is accessible by road, but a gate at the park entrance means foot access only.

Place names: Jose Maria Narvaez was the sailing master in command of the *Saturnina* in 1791. This bay was named during an extensive survey Narvaez and Eliza made between Nootka Sound and Cape Lazo.

Monarch Head

The cliffs at Monarch Head tower hundreds of feet up from the water, creating a scenic highlight of the Gulf Islands.

Place names: HMS *Monarch* was the 84-gun flagship of Rear Admiral Henry William Bruce (Bruce Bight). The ship was built in 1832 and arrived at Esquimalt in 1855, serving here until 1857.

Java Islets

These islets lie just southwest of Monarch Head. They are a seal haulout and nesting site for black oystercatcher, pigeon guillemot and glaucous-winged gull. The islets are now part of the national park reserve. Access is prohibited.

Currents in the area can be troublesome. They tend to be strong and irregular.

Bruce Bight

This bight is backed by a superb stretch of sand beach in a cove sheltered by Taylor Point. The point has wonderful old-growth Douglas-fir forest, arbutus and Garry oak. A stone farmhouse on the point is part of a pioneer sandstone quarry. The farmhouse is now fenced off, but a quick look inside the shed behind it revealed newspapers used as insulation with dates of 1908 and 1911 still visible—at least for now.

A thin wedge of national park property extends west from Taylor Point for 4 km (2.5 miles)—the longest uninterrupted stretch of protected shoreline in the southern Gulf Islands. Its upland neighbour is farm property used by cattle (many with large horns) that often cross into the park.

Paddling past Java Islets with Brown Ridge in the distance.

Hiking: There is no formal trail to Taylor Point, although routes do exist along Brown Ridge down to the bight. As these are not designated trails and occasionally follow cliff edges, attempt them at your own risk. Other unofficial trails follow the shore west of Taylor Point. Many of these are simply feral goat tracks, so don't be fooled into navigating them along cliff edges.

Murder Point

When near Murder Point, keep an eye open for feral goats. This whole stretch of coast is a beautiful area to explore by kayak. The backdrop is Brown Ridge and Mount Warburton Pike, topping the island at 401 m (1,315 feet), the second-highest point in the Gulf Islands. The Coast Salish used the mountaintop for spiritual purposes, collecting feathers for ceremonies they performed here. A narrow, twisting road goes to the summit, but all vehicles, including bicycles, are restricted.

Place names: Warburton Pike was an early settler on Saturna. He's best remembered for his 6,430-km (4,000-mile) canoe journey in 1897 up the Stikine River, into the heart of the Northwest Territories and out into the rough, cold waters of the Bering Sea. His account of the trip, *Through the Arctic Forest*, became something of a bestseller in its day. Murder Point, meanwhile, is named for an unfortunate incident in March 1863. Frederick Marks and his 15-year-old daughter, Caroline Harvey, were killed during their move to Miners Bay on Mayne Island. During a storm they sought shelter on Saturna and were accosted by a First Nations group. The British Navy's retribution for their murders led to the incident at Lamalchi Bay (see page 184).

Breezy Bay

A community park, Thomson Park, is set on the shoreline of Breezy Bay just north of Croker Point. The point and the immediate shoreline to the east have been fairly recently developed. Tucked in behind the development is Saturna Island Vineyards.

Launches: N48°46.58' W123°12.03'. Thomson Park offers parking and a beach suitable for kayaks and car-top boats. To get here from the ferry, take East Point Road south and turn onto Harris Road. The latter is a twisting, private dirt road that becomes very steep and narrow at some points.

Plumper Sound

This sound, bounded by Saturna, Samuel, Mayne and the Pender Islands, joins Navy Channel with Boundary Pass. Currents flood northwest as high as 2–3 knots and meet with the eastbound current from Navy Channel off Hope Bay, forming rips. The current reverses on the ebb, with the strongest stream around Croker Point.

Winds can be problematic here, funnelling along Elliot Bluff and off Samuel Island to create choppy water when conditions are moderate to low elsewhere. Anecdotally, conditions tend to be worst outside Irish Bay in the area north of St. John Point on Mayne Island. The trouble is usually localized, extending sometimes as far as Bald Cone on North Pender Island.

Lyall Harbour

This is the village centre for Saturna, where you can find a general store, a liquor store and a pub adjacent to the ferry terminal at Saturna Point. There is a public wharf just west of the ferry terminal and a marina just east. Within the harbour are several small private islets. Boot Cove, easily missed due to its narrow entrance, is tucked into the south side of Lyall Harbour. Cliffs dominate the cove's western shore, making it prone to funnelling wind. Homes surround Boot Cove and top the high cliffs of Elliott Bluff. Veruna Bay, north of Lyall Harbour, is a popular local beach; a reef ridge off the bay poses a hazard when entering Winter Cove.

Hiking: A trail leads from Narvaez Bay Road to the mouth of Lyall Creek—one of the few salmon-bearing streams remaining in the Gulf Islands. It also passes a scenic waterfall.

Winter Cove
Winter Cove is a recreational centre for Saturna, with a sheltered anchorage and a beach. The park was created in 1979 and transferred into the Gulf Islands National Park in 2003. Its salt marsh is one of the few protected examples in the Gulf Islands. Trails lead around the marsh and along the shoreline to a lookout over Boat Passage. This is a day-use park only.

Tucked into the south end of Winter Cove is tiny Church Cove, backed by St. Christopher's Church. Not currently used, it was a Japanese boathouse that was converted to the church in the 1930s.

Launches: N48°48.56' W123°11.38'. A public boat launch and gravel beach lie at the end of a small public parking lot within Winter Cove park.

Boat Passage
This tiny opening between Ralph Grey Point on Samuel Island and Winter Point on Saturna Island is prone to currents as strong as 7 knots; the flood sets northeast into the Strait of Georgia and the ebb southwest into Winter Cove. The flood turns 15 minutes before the turn at Active Pass and the ebb 45 minutes prior. At times other than slack expect rips and turbulence well outside the passage. The turbulence can be dangerous and a crossing at or near slack tide is advised.

Belle Chain Islets
The Belle Chain Islets and Anniversary Island are long, thin, forested wedges of rock. A lengthy line of reefs extends to the west of the islets. In winter sea lions congregate here; in April 2002 an estimated 460 Steller's sea lions and 141 California sea lions were recorded. Other residents are nesting black oystercatcher, glaucous-winged gull and pigeon guillemot. All these islets, islands and rocks are now

part of the national park reserve. Some of the headlands have traditionally been used as wilderness campsites, with the most popular at Anniverary Island. That is now prohibited by Parks Canada, although access to the island closest to Samuel Island, locally called Little Samuel Island, is permitted as a place for kayakers to take a break—shoreline access only.

Samuel Island

This private island is residential on the side facing Winter Cove. Irish Bay in the centre of the island is largely uninhabited, as is the west end to Grainger Point. Much of the shoreline is steep and cliffy. There is a good beach for a picnic near Grainger Point.

MAYNE ISLAND

This island of about 900 residents has a town-like atmosphere, with the village centre at Miners Bay. Residences line the various bays and most of the outer shores, leaving few pristine areas. The only protected portion of shore is at Bennett Bay and local parks at Dinner Bay and Georgina Point. The tallest peak on the island, Mount Parke at 263 m (863 feet), has a lighted radar tower at the summit. The peak is the focal point of a 47-ha (116-acre) regional park. Highlights for kayakers are the pretty reefs around Georgina Point, the uninhabited reserve lands at Helen Point, the steep bluffs near St. John Point and the national park properties at Bennett Bay and Georgeson Island.

Georgeson Passage

Georgeson Passage runs between Samuel Island and Lizard and Curlew islands. Boaters will have problems with the rocks in the north entrance. The currents have not been rated for speed, but run at several knots and can be strong enough to thwart a crossing against the current by paddle. When this is the case, neighbouring Robson Channel is usually still navigable as an alternative. The strongest current is fairly localized at the narrowest point between Curlew and Samuel islands.

The turn to flood is 15 minutes before the turn at Active Pass and the turn to ebb 45 minutes prior.

Place names: One of the most prominent settlers on Galiano Island was Henry (Scotty) Georgeson, who owned land at Georgeson Bay

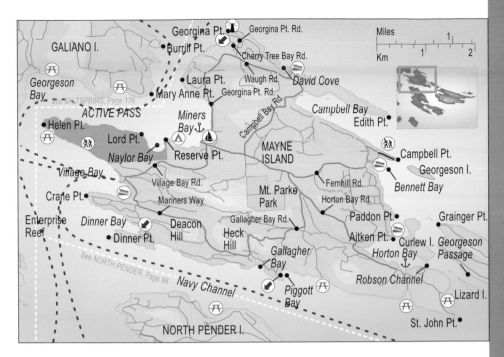

along Active Pass. In 1885 he became the first lightkeeper at Georgina Point on Mayne Island, not retiring until 1923 at the age of 89.

Robson Channel

This passage leads between Curlew Island and the southeast peninsula of Mayne Island. It's shallow with moderate currents. Anecdotally, when currents make Boat Passage dangerous and Georgeson Passage impassable for kayakers, Robson Channel will simply be a good workout. Hug Mayne Island to avoid the currents near Lizard Island.

Horton Bay

Horton Bay, just north of Aitken Point, is a developed cove with a sandy beach. All the outlying islands are privately owned.

Launches: N48°49.88' W123°14.78'. A steep road leads to the beach at Aitken Point. The grade may be uncomfortable for some motorists. To get here, follow Horton Bay Road to a Y-junction and then turn left, following Steward Road to its end.

Looking toward the bluffs near Heck Hill.

Campbell Bay

The south arm of this bay ends at Campbell Point, a peninsula in near-pristine condition. Remnants of old-growth forest can be found along a walking trail to the point. This property, the land fronting Bennett Bay and neighbouring Georgeson Island are all part of the national park reserve. Georgeson Island is notable for its old-growth forest, which has escaped both logging and invasive species. Access to the island is prohibited.

Below Campbell Point is Bennett Bay, home to a pleasant sand beach with the Mayne Inn to the southwest. There are no other services in the area.

Currents can be strong through this area, with turbulence from Georgeson Passage extending to Georgeson Island on the flood.

Launches: N48°50.78' W123°15.05'. The beach at Bennett Bay park is ideal for launching; it's relatively level with an expansive sandy beach.

David Cove

This residential cove on the north shore of Mayne Island is used as a moorage and anchorage for local craft.

Georgeson Island (in the days before access was banned).

Launches: N48°51.92' W123°16.43'. The level boat ramp at David Cove is nicely sheltered for access to the outer coast.

Piggott Bay

The south shore of Mayne Island facing Navy Channel is lightly residential; houses cluster around both Gallagher and Piggott bays. The undeveloped stretch east of Piggott Bay is a highlight; it's backed by an unnamed hill toward the peninsula of St. John Point. Nice beaches for a break are set in the bays on both sides of the hill.

Launches: N48°49.47' W123°16.78'. From Village Bay follow Mariners Way to Marine Drive, then turn onto Piggott Road. At the end of a dirt road Piggott Bay has a level spot with a very small beach area for launching. Logs may clutter the beach at high tide.

Village Bay

This is a residential area dominated by the ferry terminal. Dinner Bay, south of Village Bay, is also mainly residential with a community park at the head.

Launches: N48°50.48' W123°19.29'. From the ferry terminal, turn right at Mariners Way and right onto Callaghan. A winding road leads

Waterfront near Helen Point.

down to a pleasant boat ramp on the south side of Village Bay. An alternative for kayakers is Dinner Bay at the community park.

Helen Point

The peninsula capped by Helen Point is a Tsartlip reserve. A midden on the peninsula reveals three different periods of habitation: 1300 to 800 BC; 100 BC to 300 AD and 1200 to 1400 AD. Look for a good, but small, beach for a break on the peninsula's south side. An established trail skirts the shoreline above some pretty ridges.

Miners Bay

Miners Bay was first settled in 1859, making it one of the first places on the West Coast to be inhabited by Europeans. Today it has a public wharf, a pub, coffee shops, a post office (V0N 2J0) and numerous bed and breakfasts. The former jail, Plumper Pass Lockup, is now a museum. Float planes use the bay and tie up at the public wharf. Note the strong countercurrents in the bay from Active Pass. (See page 131.)

Place names: This bay was a way station for miners drawn to the Cariboo gold rush of 1858.

Weather

Mayne Island	May	June	July	Aug.	Sept.	Dec.	Av./Ttl.
Daily average temp. (C)	12.3	14.7	16.8	16.9	14.4	4.3	10.2
Daily maximum (C)	17.3	20.0	22.5	22.6	19.8	6.8	14.4
Daily minimum (C)	7.2	9.4	11.0	11.1	9.0	1.8	6.0
Precipitation (mm)	40.7	35.2	22.1	28.1	32.6	130.4	828.8
Days of rainfall + 0.2mm	12.2	10.2	6.1	6.0	8.1	19.3	157.2
Days with rainfall +5mm	2.8	2.3	1.6	1.8	2.3	8.3	55.0
Days with rainfall +10mm	0.9	0.8	0.5	0.6	1.0	4.4	24.5

Camping: N48°51.10' W123°18.51'. There are no marine-accessible public campgrounds on Mayne Island. Mayne Island Eco-Camp in Miners Bay is an option. Kayakers can land at the beach east of Reserve Point and camp at the oceanfront sites.

Georgina Point

On June 12, 1792, Capt. George Vancouver camped on Georgina Point, making Mayne Island the only Gulf Island he visited. His crew left a 1784 coin and a knife that were found almost a century later. A lighthouse built in 1885 was replaced with the current tower in 1969. The lighthouse is no longer staffed but is open to the public as the main attraction of Georgina Point Lighthouse Heritage Park, which protects the headland.

The north end of Mayne Island east of Georgina Point is residential, but Georgina Shoals and the various reefs and rocky islets that line the shoreline help hide that fact. Maude Bay, to the south of Georgina Point, can make a rough kayak launch.

Georgina Point is the north Vessel Traffic Services call-in point for ships entering and leaving Active Pass. For more on the Active Pass call-in system, as well as details about transiting Active Pass, see page 129.

The superb shoreline on Prevost Island.

Saltspring Island

CHAPTER THREE

SALTSPRING ISLAND IS THE LARGEST AND MOST HEAVILY POPULATED OF THE Gulf Islands with about 10,000 residents. A community of artists and artisans drawn to the relaxed island lifestyle includes renowned painter Robert Bateman. This deep artistic imprint is reflected in Saltspring's many galleries and craft stores. The Saturday market in Ganges Harbour is always a popular draw. The mountainous terrain and the complex shoreline that extends to the smaller surrounding islands provide a natural attraction. Many of those nearby islands—Wallace, Prevost and Portland, in particular—are among the best kayaking locations in the Gulf Islands.

Saltspring was historically used by First Nations, but there is no evidence it was a permanent village site. The first known permanent settlers chose Vesuvius Bay in 1857, when nine black families, ex-slaves from Kentucky and Mississippi, bought their freedom and moved to Canada. Descendants of those pioneers still live on the island.

Geographically, Saltspring has several clear divisions. The northeast half of the island is dominated by low-rolling bedrock hills. The southeast half of the island is mountainous, composed of massive sedimentary rocks. Satellite Channel has formed along the line of the San Juan Fault. Glacial erosion created the Fulford Harbour–Burgoyne Bay valley. South of that valley are some of the highest summits in the Gulf Islands. The shoreline is a pleasant mixture of rock cliff, rock platform and cobble and gravel beaches. A few choice sand beaches dot the island.

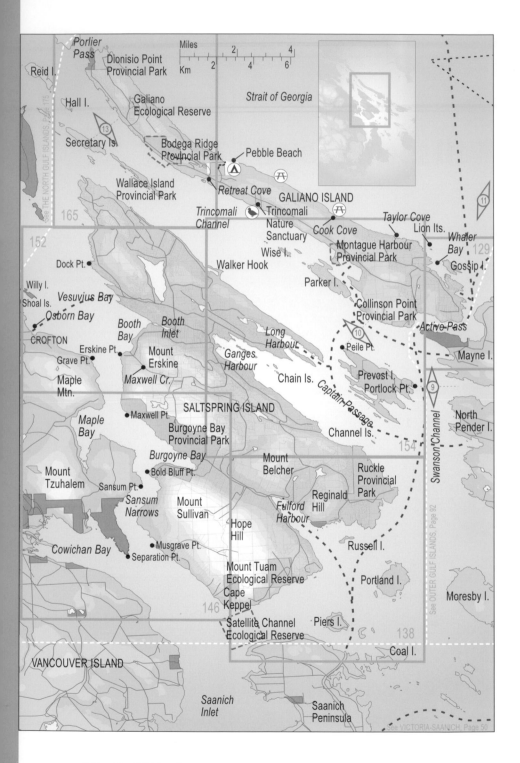

Porlier
Pass

Reid I.

Hall I.

Dionisio Point
Provincial Park

Miles

Km

Strait of Georgia

Galiano
Ecological Reserve

13

Secretary Is.

Bodega Ridge
Provincial Park

Pebble Beach

Wallace Island
Provincial Park

Retreat Cove

GALIANO ISLAND

165

Trincomali
Channel

Trincomali
Nature
Sanctuary

Cook Cove

Taylor Cove

Lion Its.

Whaler
Bay

11

152

Wise I.

Montague Harbour
Provincial Park

129

Dock Pt.

Walker Hook

Gossip I.

Willy I.

Shoal Is.

Vesuvius Bay

Parker I.

Osborn Bay

Booth
Bay

Booth
Inlet

Long
Harbour

Collinson Point
Provincial Park

Active Pass

CROFTON

Erskine Pt.

Peile Pt.

Mayne I.

Grave Pt.

Mount
Erskine

Ganges
Harbour

Maple
Mtn.

Maxwell Cr.

Chain Is.

Prevost I.

Portlock Pt.

9

Maxwell Pt.

SALTSPRING ISLAND

Captain Passage

North
Pender I.

Maple
Bay

Burgoyne Bay
Provincial Park

Channel Is.

154

Burgoyne Bay

Mount
Belcher

Swanson Channel

Mount
Tzuhalem

Bold Bluff Pt.

Sansum Pt.

Sansum
Narrows

Mount
Sullivan

Reginald
Hill

Ruckle
Provincial
Park

Fulford
Harbour

Cowichan Bay

Musgrave Pt.

Separation Pt.

Hope
Hill

Russell I.

Portland I.

Moresby I.

Mount Tuam
Ecological Reserve

Cape
Keppel

146

Piers I.

138

Satellite Channel
Ecological Reserve

Coal I.

VANCOUVER ISLAND

See VICTORIA-SAANICH, Page 50

Saanich
Inlet

Saanich
Peninsula

See THE NORTH GULF ISLANDS, Page 175

See OUTER GULF ISLANDS, Page 92

10

Place names: Saltspring is one of the most misspelled locations in Canada, including the use of "Salt Spring" by locals, road signs, BC Ferries, publications and governments including Islands Trust. There is only one official spelling, though: Saltspring, the name given it by officers of the Hudson's Bay Company due to the 14 briny springs on the island. For a time it was called Admiral Island in honour of Rear Admiral Baynes. Other references relating to him include the island's highest mountain. Ganges Harbour is named after his flagship; Fulford Harbour after its captain; Burgoyne Bay after the commander; Southey Point after the admiral's secretary; Mount Bruce after the previous commander-in-chief; and Cape Keppel after a friend of the admiral's.

Exploring by kayak

Portland and Wallace islands are the most-visited destinations in this region. Adventures in Sansum Narrows can be as simple as a day trip from Maple Bay to the nearby Saltspring shores or a full transit through the mountainous narrows.

Adventurous kayakers will enjoy the challenge of transiting Porlier Pass and reaching Dionisio Point on Galiano. The outer side of Galiano is a wonderful area to explore, one not often visited.

Recommended kayaking trips

- *If you have a day:* From Maple Bay, paddle to Maxwell Point on Saltspring and have lunch or a break on one of the pleasant beaches nearby. From Galiano, paddle the islands off Montague Harbour to Ballingall Islets then back along the cliffs. From Ganges, a trip out to Third Sister Island will be appealing. Extend the trip to Prevost if you can.

- *If you have two days:* An overnight trip to Prevost Island is highly recommended. Launch from Long Harbour and overnight at James Bay. If you can make the distance, be sure to circumnavigate Prevost Island. An alternative is to head from Fernwood Point to a campsite on Wallace Island. From Sidney or Swartz Bay, an overnight trip to Portland Island is recommended. These trips will appeal to novice kayakers.

- *If you have three days:* Beginner kayakers should extend a visit to James Bay with a circumnavigation of Prevost Island on the middle day. The east side is about the best kayaking in the Gulf

Islands, so don't pass up the chance. A circumnavigation of Saltspring Island is possible for hardy kayakers, though four days is recommended. An itinerary could be launching at Genoa Bay and visiting Portland Island, Prevost Island, Wallace Island and back (a trip of about 80 km/50 miles). Experienced kayakers can circumnavigate Galiano in three days. Launch at Montague then head to Dionisio, Pebble Beach and back (about 60 km/38 miles in total).

• *If you have five days:* A leisurely trip around Saltspring is suggested. Campsites could be Montague Harbour, Wallace Island, Tent Island, South Saltspring, Portland Island or Prevost Island. You can launch from Swartz Bay, Montague Harbour, Genoa Bay, Crofton or any of the Saltspring Island launches.

• *If you have a week:* Kayakers could expand on a circumnavigation of Saltspring by adding side trips to Thetis-Kuper, Active Pass, Dionisio or Bedwell Harbour. However, my week-long trip of this region would be designed like this: a launch from Montague to Wallace Island, then Dionisio or as far as Pebble Beach, a continuation along the outer coast to Cabbage Island, a return around East Point to Bedwell Harbour on South Pender, then Portland Island and Prevost Island before returning to the launch.

• *The ideal trip:* This is a variation on the last trip I took in 2006. I would launch from Evening Cove near Ladysmith and make my way to the De Courcy Group, staying at Pirates Cove. I'd leisurely explore those islands and south Valdes Island before going into Gabriola Passage to stay at Kendrick Island. I'd run the outside of Valdes to Dionisio, then the outside of Galiano and Saturna to Cabbage Island. The return route would be along the inside via either Trincomali or Sansum Narrows. My route was Sansum Narrows via Bedwell, Sidney Spit, Portland Island then Sansum Narrows. Tent Island would make a good venue on the final night. This route could easily be accomplished in a week, and would be a fantastic run of the wildest sections of the Gulf Islands. A simpler agenda would be to stay off the Strait of Georgia side, instead heading down via Trincomali and back via Sansum Narrows.

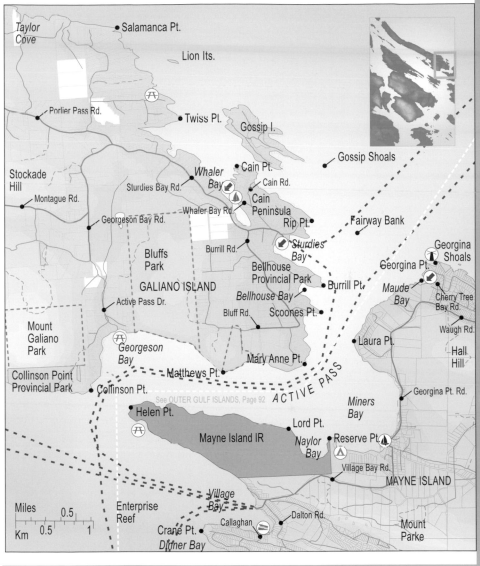

Taylor Cove
Salamanca Pt.
Lion Its.
Porlier Pass Rd.
Twiss Pt.
Gossip I.
Gossip Shoals
Stockade Hill
Whaler Bay
Cain Pt.
Sturdies Bay Rd.
Cain Rd.
Montague Rd.
Whaler Bay Rd.
Cain Peninsula
Rip Pt.
Fairway Bank
Georgeson Bay Rd.
Bluffs Park
Burrill Rd.
Sturdies Bay
Georgina Shoals
GALIANO ISLAND
Bellhouse Provincial Park
Georgina Pt.
Maude Bay
Cherry Tree Bay Rd.
Active Pass Dr.
Bellhouse Bay
Burrill Pt.
Waugh Rd.
Mount Galiano Park
Bluff Rd.
Scoones Pt.
Collinson Point Provincial Park
Georgeson Bay
Laura Pt.
Hall Hill
Matthews Pt.
Mary Anne Pt.
Collinson Pt.
ACTIVE PASS
Georgina Pt. Rd.
See OUTER GULF ISLANDS, Page 92
Miners Bay
Helen Pt.
Lord Pt.
Mayne Island IR
Naylor Bay
Reserve Pt.
Village Bay Rd.
MAYNE ISLAND
Enterprise Reef
Village Bay
Dalton Rd.
Miles 0.5
Crane Pt.
Callaghan
Mount Parke
Km 0.5 1
Ditner Bay

ACTIVE PASS

This deep and twisting route between Mayne and Galiano islands is known for its scenery, strong currents and considerable boat traffic. The latter is particularly problematic, as the large Spirit-class ferries navigate this channel, and it's not unusual—actually, it's almost certain—to have two ferries in the pass at the same time, even though the channel is just 500 m (0.3 miles) at its narrowest. Other

Active Pass.

commercial boats, fishing boats, yachts and recreational boats also dot the waters, creating the potential for a disastrous collision. (I have heard the analogy that navigating a ferry through Active Pass is like driving a truck through a playground.)

The currents are complex in the pass, and can be dangerous for kayaks and small craft. For current information, consult the *Canadian Tide and Current Tables, Volume 5.*

Call-in points: Kayakers and mariners transiting Active Pass should monitor VHF Channel 11. There are three Vessel Traffic Services call-in points for ships transiting Active Pass, and vessels have to call in at two of them. The southern call-in points are either Peile Point or Portlock Point (see the main chapter map on page 126 to locate the points).

- *9, Portlock Point:* Before the west entrance to Active Pass, ships entering or leaving the pass via Swanson Channel must call in at a line running east-west through the Portlock Point light.

- *10, Peile Point:* Ships entering or leaving the area via Trincomali Channel call in at Peile Point on northwest Prevost Island in a line running 45°–225° through the Peile Point light.

- *11, Active Pass:* Ships entering or leaving Active Pass will call in at the east entrance, 3 miles (5 km) northeast of the Georgina Point light.

Note the standard navigation reference for the entrance from the Strait of Georgia is the east entrance, not the north entrance, while the Helen-Collinson points entrance is considered the west entrance to Active Pass.

Ferries are required by law to signal with a prolonged blast when visibility is limited around corners. This can help warn kayakers of ship traffic, but it's problematic as the signal is no indication of direction of travel.

Place names: USS *Active* was a U.S. surveying and revenue steamer, the first steamer to navigate the pass in 1855.

Transiting Active Pass by kayak: The safest way to transit the pass is to travel with the direction of the current and avoid travelling at peak current. Generally, this means avoiding the middle two hours of any ebb or flood current. Novice kayakers may want to travel at slack, but during most non-peak times the current is safe. Ferry and boat traffic will probably be more of a headache.

On the flood, the current generally conforms to the turns of the channel, with the main stream running close to Matthews Point (so you might want to paddle against the current on the Mayne Island side).

Problems occur in several areas of the flood. One is at Miners Bay, where a portion of the current is deflected south of Laura Point to create a clockwise countercurrent. It can be felt at the Mayne Island wharf, where it can be up to 2.5 knots. The problem for kayakers is that avoiding the countercurrent by staying out of Miners Bay will put you in open water. If a ferry passes, it's difficult to tell its course through the turns and you might think yourself at risk of being hit. You can generally avoid the ferry lane by travelling a straight line between Laura Point and Reserve Point. If you do see a ferry coming in mid-transit between these points, you will probably want to head into Miners Bay a bit to keep your distance (a good strategy), but you should be safe nonetheless.

A side effect from the eddy in Miners Bay is turbulence where it rejoins the main flow. This will take place just south of Mary Anne Point.

Another problem will be encountered leaving the pass. A weak current flows along the north shore of Mayne Island, meeting the Active Pass current between Georgina Point and Fairway Bank. The

A common site in Active Pass—two ferries passing.

result can be rips as far south as near Mary Anne and Laura points. More rips can be encountered at Fairway Bank to Gossip Island.

The ebb sets south-southeast in the Strait of Georgia entrance to Active Pass. It then turns west around Laura Point. Unlike the flood tide, the main current passes Matthews Point south of the middle of the channel on the Mayne Island side. It then hits the shoals at Helen Point and Collinson Point before mixing into the current in Trincomali Channel.

There are two possible areas of concern. A countercurrent in Miners Bay runs anti-clockwise on the ebb along the south shore, reaching as high as 2 knots at the Miners Bay wharf. Another anti-clockwise eddy forms west of Helen Point as the tidal stream rushes past Collinson Point, causing a back-pull toward Helen Point. Fortunately the current in this counter-flow is relatively low—just 1–1.5 knots at the highest. Throughout the pass there are no rips or turbulence on an ebb flow, making this a potentially safer route to transit on the ebb than the flood.

Kayakers should pick a side during a transit of Active Pass and stick to it. Crossing mid-pass is hazardous considering the volume of traffic.

Managing shipping traffic: Ferries will be the most frequent and most troubling commercial traffic in Active Pass. There are likely to be two Spirit-class ferries (the large ones) travelling between Tsawwassen and Swartz Bay at any time. They leave the terminals at roughly the same time and meet at the midway point, which happens to be Active Pass, so there's a good possibility of two ferries being in the pass at any one time. Gulf Islands ferries to Sturdies Bay and/or Village Bay can add to the congestion.

Travelling Active Pass will be much safer and simpler if you have a VHF marine radio and monitor Channel 11. Ferries will call in when leaving Swartz Bay, Tsawwassen or the Gulf Island terminals. They will also call in at Portlock Point and when nearing Georgina Point on their way in or out of the pass. This should eliminate any surprise encounters. You will know, for instance, that ferries have recently departed Tsawwassen and Swartz Bay and are headed into Active Pass. You will then be informed when they reach the approaches. Commercial ships and even large motor yachts also call in.

If you don't have a marine radio, the best strategy is to anticipate that ferries will be travelling through the pass during your transit, with two likely to cross in very quick succession. When these two Spirit-class ferries have passed and are clear, you may have a window of ferry-free travelling. Of course, this does not help predict any other Gulf Island ferries that may be en route. And even a detailed calculation of ferry times does not help with delays or unscheduled extra sailings. So there is no magic answer except for a VHF marine radio.

Crossing Active Pass: For many reasons it's likely kayakers will want to cross Active Pass rather than transit it. A crossing is potentially risky as sightlines are poor and you'll clash with the prevailing direction of ship traffic. Given the narrowness of the pass, larger vessels will have very little room to accommodate slower kayakers.

For those crossing the Strait of Georgia side of the pass, I recommend a crossing at the narrow portion between Burrill Point and north of Laura Point. The crossing is about 700 m (2,300 feet). It should take no more than 10 minutes, and will probably be much less as you'll be motivated. The sightline is good into the Strait of Georgia but poor into the pass.

On the west entrance you can cross between Collinson and Helen points, the shortest route. You can also cross between Portlock and Stanley points at Prevost and North Pender islands to avoid any currents or turbulence associated with Helen Point. The Collinson Point crossing is about 600 m (2,000 feet); the Portlock Point crossing is about 1.9 km (1.2 miles).

Steep bluffs at Collinson Point.

Georgeson Bay

This bay indents the northwestern end of Active Pass on Galiano Island. Bluffs Park, a large regional park that lives up to its name with a steep shoreline, occupies a half-mile of shore in the bay. The park was bought in 1947 for $1,000. It has been logged, but that appears to be more than a century ago now, making it a good example of a coastal Douglas-fir forest. Near the shore are some Garry oak meadows and wildflowers. The west side of Georgeson Bay is residential. There is a good beach in the bay. Look for the petroglyph of a face on two sides of a square boulder.

Behind Collinson Point is Mount Galiano. The peak and surrounding land is owned by the Galiano Conservancy. A trail from Active Pass Drive leads to the top through Douglas-fir forest. A new provincial park is set on the shoreline and lower elevations of the mountain. In all, this is a pleasantly wild stretch of scenery along the southern shore of Galiano Island.

Travel notes: **A** large fire on the southeast end of Galiano in 2006 caused the evacuation of several hundred residents and has made all Gulf Islands residents, and particularly those on Galiano, cautious about open fires. Campfires are not allowed in Gulf Island parks and are a poor idea during summers anywhere on these islands.

Bellhouse Bay

This bay is capped on the north headland by a small and pretty provincial park. The bay is shallow and prone to breaking waves from ferry wash, so don't hug too close to shore when a ferry passes.

Sturdies Bay

This bay has a combined public wharf and ferry terminal and forms a village centre for Galiano Island; services are available near the terminal.

Launches: N48°52.68' W123°19.01'. A path alongside the ferry terminal vehicle waiting area leads to a good beach for launching kayaks. This would make a possible entry point for anyone walking a kayak off the Galiano ferry.

Whaler Bay

Whaler Bay is dotted with homes and reefs. Crown land adjacent to Whaler Bay, together with Bluffs Park, provide the only wilderness corridor and trail from Trincomali Channel to the Strait of Georgia. A public wharf is located in Whaler Bay south of Cain Point. Gossip Island, privately owned and heavily subdivided, shelters Whaler Bay. Lion Islets are also private. Watch for rips around Salamanca Point, Lion Islets and Gossip Island on the flood tide.

Launches: N48°53.10' W123°19.29'. From the ferry terminal at Sturdies Bay, take the second right, Cain Road. This narrow dirt road leads to level beach access in a small and mildly sheltered cove. Parking is available for a few cars. Another option is to turn left off Cain Road to Whaler Bay Road and launch from the Whaler Bay public dock. Parking near the dock is ample.

Bellhouse Provincial Park

This small, 2-ha (5-acre) park on Galiano Island is a popular day-use area with a circular trail leading through Garry oak to Burrill Point and views over Active Pass. The land was donated by the Bellhouse family in 1964 and was part of the farmland used for grazing. Visitors are asked to stick to the trail, as the headlands are considered sensitive.

Crowds on Pebble Beach.

Taylor Cove

West of Taylor Cove the heavy residential concentration ends, and housing is intermittent throughout the entire remaining outer coast of Galiano. Taylor Cove is backed by a power station—a good landmark for those approaching from the northwest. The beach in the cove is too rocky for landings.

Pebble Beach

Travelling the outside of Galiano Island from Dionisio to Whaler Bay is a unique trip in the Gulf Islands, especially by paddle. (For references, see the main chapter map on page 126.) The distance is about 24 km (15 miles) in open water with few areas for breaks, as the shore is largely unbroken rock platform. One place to stop is Pebble Beach.

The beach is on the opposite side of the island from Retreat Cove, where a block of Crown land encompasses almost a kilometre of shoreline (0.6 miles), with mature Douglas-fir, some over 350 years old. A trail leads from the end of McCoskrie Road through an ecological reserve to Pebble Beach.

Public access to Pebble Beach makes it a favourite day-use and backpack camping area. There are two beaches accessible by trail. The main Pebble Beach is to the east. A smaller, second beach is located in a cove to the west. It's generally quieter, so should you wish to avoid crowds, this would be the place to stop.

Camping: N48°56.93' W123°28.82'. Pebble Beach is the only parcel of Crown land on outer Galiano, and it also has one of the best sandy beaches on the island. A wide, level grassy clearing is adjacent to the beach. Kayakers may appreciate the level expanse of gravel at the south end of the beach. Note there may be a surf landing to contend with. Should conditions be particularly rough, the second beach to the east is in a more sheltered cove. Watch for rocks near the entrance point.

FULFORD HARBOUR

The southeast Saltspring Island shoreline is steep, mountainous and only sparsely developed, with most of the peaks protected either as regional parks or Crown land. The height of the peaks has even surprised a few pilots over the years: the remnants of plane crashes litter the mountainsides, including a couple of Second World War planes that were left to rot and the more recent addition of a Cessna.

Fulford Harbour is 5 km (3 miles) deep and well sheltered, with a BC Ferries terminal at its head for service to Swartz Bay, 10 km (6 miles) away. A public wharf is south of the terminal, and a marina to the north.

Colburne, Goss and Stranger passages

Colburne Passage runs between Pym, Knapp and Piers islands on the north and Saanich Peninsula to the south. Between the three islands on the north side of the passage are Gosse and Stranger passages. Gosse Passage, between Piers and Knapp islands, is the most common route for ferries, though ferries also use Satellite Passage via Arbutus Island or travel east around Portland Island via Moresby Passage. Sightlines are not good when navigating near these islands. The multitude of routes means ferries can appear from just about anywhere, including both sides of Portland Island. Currents can run 1–2 knots with the flood setting west and the ebb east.

The shoreline of Saanich Peninsula facing Colburne Passage is steep, but it's residential and in some places heavily developed with housing.

Navigating by kayak: The most common kayaking route is likely to be from east of Swartz Bay (Swartz Head) to Portland Island. The hazardous portion is from Swartz Head to Knapp or Pym islands. Ferries may leave Swartz Bay for Moresby Passage, and as they

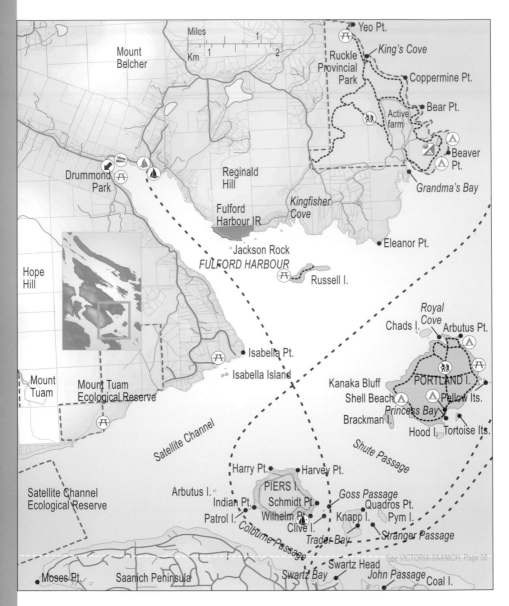

don't call into Vessel Traffic Services on Channel 11 until leaving the terminal, your warning period is minimal. It's a short crossing, however, just 800 m (half a mile), so all you need is about 10 minutes or less of clearance. You can increase your sightline marginally by transiting from Fir Cone Point on Coal Island to Pym Island. Once in the safety of Pym or Knapp islands your crossing is clear.

Ferries do not navigate Shute Passage.

A worst-case scenario would be a ferry leaving Swartz Bay through Moresby Passage when you're in mid-channel across Colburne Passage. In that event, if you feel you are really in danger, consider using the marine radio on Channel 11 to state you are caught in mid-channel, and ask: "Do you have me in sight?" The ferry captain will likely appreciate it, though Vessel Traffic Services likely won't, as Channel 11 is a restricted channel and traffic-to-traffic chatter is not allowed. You may get a rebuke from Vessel Traffic Services. You can also contact the ferry on Channel 11 and ask to switch to another frequency to discuss the situation, but given time constraints a direct conversation is probably appropriate. Channel 16, the emergency channel, is another option.

Fulford Harbour from Russell Island.

If you are crossing the region from Swartz Head to Saltspring Island, head to Knapp Island or even Portland Island (recommended) before crossing Satellite Channel. A route directly in front of the ferry terminal through Colburne Passage would be foolhardy. A crossing of Gosse Passage need not be hazardous, as the shipping route is narrow and marked by navigation lights. Your only at-risk portion will be between the navigation lights, little more than 100 m (330 feet). The sightlines should be sufficient for that distance.

Piers Island

This is a privately owned and heavily subdivided residential island with a multitude of private docks. A public wharf is located just northwest of Wilhelm Point. Nearby Knapp and Pym islands are also privately owned. Pym has been developed with a massive retaining wall, dyking, a dock and a variety of buildings. A breakwater and

Chiselled cliffs of Brackman Island.

docks have been built on Knapp Island in Trader Bay.

Piers Island has one of the most unusual histories among the Gulf Islands: it was the prison for 540 Doukhobors in the 1930s. The Doukhobors were a communal Russian religious group, also known as the Sons of Freedom, that had the habit of demonstrating consternation by disrobing. By

Shell Beach, Portland Island.

unfortunate coincidence, the Canadian criminal code was amended to give parading in the nude a mandatory three-year sentence. So when a Doukhobor leader was arrested for perjury in 1931, the community disrobed, causing the RCMP to arrest about 600 people and place them in tents and temporary shelters.

Without enough jails to imprison them all, the federal government expropriated Piers Island to house the Doukhobors. But the Depression set in, the government lost interest and none of the Doukhobors served the full sentence. The incident did, however, ruin a great many lives; families were left destitute and many split apart in a huge foster parenting program. The prison closed in 1935 and the island's ownership reverted back to private hands.

Brackman Island

This island on the southwest of Portland Island is a former ecological reserve now part of the Gulf Islands National Park reserve. A surrounding 200-m (656-foot) marine habitat is also protected. Sculpted cliffs grace the northeast side. There is no public access. When paddling nearby, take care to avoid nesting seabirds. Bird residents include bald eagle, oystercatcher, great blue heron, cormorant, gull and various songbirds. The island was first made a reserve in 1989.

Portland Island

Portland Island was aquired by the province in 1958 and made a gift to Princess Margaret. In 1967 she returned it to B.C. as a park for

Canada's centennial year, named Princess Margaret Marine Park. It has since been transferred into the Gulf Islands National Park. At 220 ha (544 acres) it's a mixture of protected coves, sandy beaches and a rich intertidal ecology. I consider the northwest shore of Portland Island near Kanaka Bluff one of the best places in the Gulf Islands to visit at low tide. Keep your eyes open for all manner of intertidal and subtidal marine life.

Trails criss-cross the island. Boaters can anchor in Princess Bay (sometimes called Tortoise Bay) or Royal Cove and use the park's two dinghy docks. Allow a good three hours to complete the trail around the island.

Most of the outlying islands—Chads Island, Tortoise Islets and Hood Island—are privately owned. The MV *G.B. Church* was sunk to the south of Pellow Islets as an artificial reef for divers (N48°43.33' W123°21.34'). Two buoys mark the spot.

Place names: **HMS** *Portland* was built in 1852 at Plymouth and was the flagship of Rear Admiral Fairfax Moresby. Chads Island was named after *Portland*'s captain 1850–1853.

Camping: N48°43.29' W123°23.03'. On the south side of the island, tucked into the cover of Brackman Island, is Shell Beach. Behind it you'll find an open, grassy area suitable for numerous tents, some picnic tables and an outhouse. Kayakers often camp on the open beach. Other more private spots can be found along the western extension of the beach.

Satellite Channel Ecological Reserve

Most people are likely to pass this ecological reserve without noticing, as it is B.C.'s only completely underwater reserve. It's located in the middle of the channel off the north end of Saanich Peninsula and south of Saltspring. The boundary comes within 200 m (655 feet) of Cape Keppel on the north and within the same distance of Moses Point to the south. Most of the reserve is relatively shallow, with depths from 80 m (262 feet) to a low of 18 m (60 feet) on the southwest corner.

The sea floor is sand, silt and clay—ideal for a rich benthic (sea bottom) ecology. This and a strong tidal current result in a highly productive area that is home to 67 species of marine life—from polychaetes (segmented worms) to pelecypods (bivalve molluscs related to the giant South Sea Tridacna clam, though the ones here are much smaller). The wiry and regenerative brittle star, a close relative of the sea star, is also found here. Another is the sea cucumber, an often warty-looking creature with no head or brain.

The 343-ha (848-acre) ecological reserve was created in 1975.

N48°44.10' W123°22.00'. On the north end of the island is Arbutus Point, above which six tent pads have been built in the forest cover. Beaches on both sides of the point are suitable for landing a kayak; at certain tide levels and conditions the point itself can be used.

N48°43.24' W123°22.23'. Princess Bay is an option but lacks views and involves packing gear up stairs. Stair access from a beach is located north of the dinghy dock. Above is an open, grassy area with picnic tables, some set in an old, overgrown orchard.

Satellite Channel

Satellite Channel runs between Swanson Channel in the north through to Cowichan Bay and the south end of Sansum Narrows. Ferries frequently use the channel, either as the route to Fulford Harbour or north through to Swanson Channel. Currents flood northwest and ebb southeast, reaching 1–2 knots.

Isabella Island

This small island and a small associated islet to its west are connected to Saltspring via a drying ledge. The island and surrounding rocks are part of the national park reserve. Access is prohibited.

Drummond Park

This park at the head of Fulford Harbour is a popular local children's playground with beach access.

Launches: N48°46.19' W123°27.65'. From Fulford-Ganges Road turn onto Isabella Point Road. A rough launch is located at the north end of Drummond Park. The access is level, but the beach can be muddy at low tide.

Shoreline at Mount Tuam.

Mount Tuam Ecological Reserve

This 362-ha (895-acre) reserve was created in 1971 to protect an example of dry coastal Douglas-fir forest. Two sections of steep, rugged slope overlook Satellite Channel. The pure stands of arbutus on the upper elevations are considered about the best representation left in British Columbia.

The beach at Russell Island.

Russell Island

Russell Island plays a rich but fairly obscure role in the history of the Gulf Islands—the arrival and settlement in the late 1800s by Hawaiians. Called Kanakas, they settled on islands including Portland, Russell and Saltspring. Russell Island was first settled in 1886; the house and orchard on the island date back to about 1906. This is one of the few Kanaka homesteads still standing in the Gulf Islands. Now part of the national park reserve, Russell Island has a day-use area and trails; a good clamshell beach on the western tip provides access. The caretaker's home on the north end is considered private property.

Beaver Point

This is the site of a former community, with remnants of the government wharf and store still visible at the northern tip of the point. The wharf was used between roughly 1890 and 1960 as a steamer landing, while the general store operated from 1914 to 1951. The area is now protected as part of Ruckle Provincial Park. A trail follows the shoreline of the park from the south end to Yeo Point, with several branches criss-crossing the interior of the park.

Place names: The Hudson's Bay Company steamer *Beaver* was the first steam-driven ship on the B.C. coast.

Camping: Ruckle Park has eight vehicle-accessible campsites available on a first-come, first-served basis. Walk-in campsites are located on the grassy meadow overlooking Swanson Channel. The meadow is separated from the parking area by a thin strip of forest. Officially there are 78 sites, but anywhere on the grassy slopes appears to be fair game, as the sites are not plotted. The campsite could be used by kayakers, but the shoreline is mainly rocky and beaches generally poor. Expect a potentially difficult rock-ledge landing. Portland Island and Prevost Island are nearby alternatives.

Yeo Point

Sand beaches line both sides of the headland that forms Yeo Point. Kayakers can enter the shoreline trail by landing at the beach.

Ruckle Provincial Park

This park protects 7 km (4.3 miles) of shoreline with a mix of rocky headlands and pocket beaches backed by inviting grass meadows. The grasslands and the nearby headlands near Beaver Point are the recreational focus of the park. The first homesteader was Henry Ruckle in 1872; his descendants still raise sheep on private land at the campground entrance. The family donated the parkland but maintains life tenancy over the farm portion. The buildings include an early 1870s home built by Henry Ruckle, recently stabilized but unoccupied and closed to the public. Archaeological sites in the park include 11 shell middens, boulder cairns (one believed to be associated with a native burial site, near Beaver Point) and one known traditional inland camping area where several artifacts were uncovered.

SANSUM NARROWS

Sansum Narrows separates Vancouver Island and Saltspring Island between Satellite and Stuart channels, becoming as narrow as 300 m (0.2 miles).

Bruce Peak, Baynes Peak and Mount Erskine on Saltspring are each identifiable by distinct cliffs near the summits. Bruce Peak is the highest, at 709 m (2,326 feet), with red obstruction lights on the ridge between it and Mount Tuam. Look for cliffs near the summits of Baynes Peak and Mount Erskine. The steep slopes have kept development on Sansum Narrows to a minimum. It can be a challenging place to navigate, though, with funnelling winds, strong currents and some turbulence. The current floods north and ebbs south, but is rarely above 3 knots, with less than half that in wider portions. Even so, whirlpools and rips can appear near Burial Islet and in the area between Sansum and Bold Bluff points.

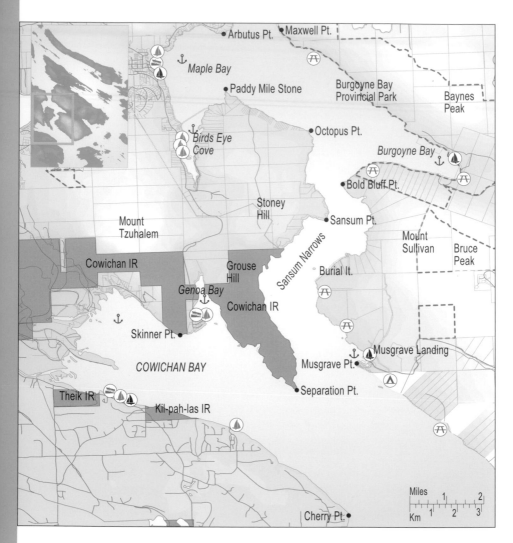

Place names: Arthur Sansum was first lieutenant aboard HMS *Thetis* 1851–53.

Cape Keppel

The cape, the southernmost point on Saltspring Island, gently curves to conform to the outer edge of Mount Tuam. The area remains largely undeveloped but for a few scattered homes. Watch for the pure arbutus stands.

Place names: Rear Admiral Sir Henry Keppel was the fifth son of the fourth Earl of Albermarle, and a friend of Admiral Baynes.

Sansum Narrows looking toward Bold Bluff Point.

Cowichan Bay

The community spreads out along the south shore of the bay, with a public wharf, marinas, restaurants, pubs, a hotel, a post office (V0R 1N0), galleries and cafés. This is a working harbour; a lumber wharf and barge slip at the outer end of a causeway across the mud flats at the head of the bay bring in large freighters. Two rivers, the Cowichan and Koksilah, flow into the bay across the mud flats.

The bay is named for the primary First Nation of the region, a group that prospered and eventually divided into present-day bands such as the Saanich, Chemainus, Lamalchi and Penelakut.

Place names: Cowichan comes from the Coast Salish word *khowutzun*, meaning "the warm land."

Launches: N48°44.50' W123°37.49'. From the Island Highway take the Cowichan Bay Road turnoff and continue along the waterfront to the commercial centre. Northwest of the marinas is a public boat ramp.

Genoa Bay

This pretty cove set inside the north entrance of Cowichan Bay is accessible by road from Maple Bay. The east side of the bay is a log

Separation Point.

booming ground with private mooring buoys. A marina is on the west side. Mount Tzuhalem is the backdrop.

Launches: N48°45.55' W123°35.91'. The launch at Genoa Bay is public but the marina is private. Parking is designated for marina customers, so expect to park elsewhere after unloading. To get here, find your way from the Island Highway to Maple Bay Road in Duncan, then take Genoa Bay Road.

Separation Point
The north entrance to Cowichan Bay is a steep, undeveloped peninsula that is part of an uninhabited portion of the Cowichan Indian Reserve. It's a visual highlight, with a dome-shaped bluff at the point.

Musgrave Landing
Musgrave Landing is a small community in the cove on the north side of Musgrave Point. It's accessible by land via a rough road through the mountains from Fulford Harbour. The final leg into Musgrave Landing is private road. The community is serviced by a government dock.

Musgrave Landing was once a farm, the barns of which are still visible. Watch for the petroglyph just off shore on a rock at the beach. The landing is home to a patch of rare and delicate phantom orchids growing at two vacant Crown properties near the waterfront.

They're remarkable for blooming for only a single day in June.

Camping: N48°44.63' W123°32.60'. Just south of Musgrave Landing is a small Crown islet. On Saltspring, behind the islet, is a gravel and rock beach. An embankment above it is suitable for perhaps a single small tent. Camping is also possible on the beach, north of the headland. Or follow the old road up from the grass embankment to a large clearing that appears to be an old road junction. Hidden in the nearby bushes is an outhouse. The Saltspring Paddling Group created the camping area, which appears to be rarely used.

Rough beach at the campsite near Musgrave Landing.

Burial Islet
This low islet with a scrub top is positioned in the midst of Sansum Narrows. A navigation light is on the northwest side. The nearby water is prone to rips and is in the vicinity of the strongest current in the narrows.

Burgoyne Bay
Burgoyne Bay is a deep, sheltered inlet with silt and cobble beaches. The steep slope of Baynes Peak has deterred development; the largest protected stand of Garry oak in British Columbia grows on the sloping southwest corner of the mountain. Southeast of the bay is Bruce Peak, which is covered with trails. Part of the peak is used for communication towers. The north end of the mountain was logged and has never truly grown back.

Burgoyne Bay ends in a drying mud flat. Behind a public wharf on the north side of the bay near the head is the wharfinger's home. The only other homes in the area are on the lowlands near Bold Bluff Point. Across from the bay is Octopus Point. Throughout its history it has alternatively been known as Burial Point, and is marked as that on many maps, charts and documents.

From the dock at Burgoyne Bay.

Place names: Commander Hugh Talbot Burgoyne was an officer aboard HMS *Ganges* under Captain Fulford. He was awarded the Victoria Cross for gallant action during the Crimean War. In 1870 Burgoyne perished, along with most of the 500 crew, when the turret ship *Captain* capsized and sank off Cape Finisterre, the westernmost point of Spain.

Maxwell Point
The steep slopes of Saltspring are undeveloped in this region except for overhead power cables suspended from towers north of the point. There are numerous pocket beaches, and this is a favourite area of mine to introduce kayaking to beginners. A launch at Maple Bay, a paddle to Saltspring and a break at a beach at Maxwell Point is a perfect way to spend a few hours on a sunny day.

Maple Bay

The picturesque little community of Maple Bay hugs the shoreline. Here you'll find a public wharf, a rowing club and a pub. The backdrop is Maple Mountain. Marinas and a public float cluster in Birds Eye Cove to the south.

Launches: N48°18.93' W123°36.57'. You can launch at the beach at the Maple Bay Rowing Club. To get here, follow the signs to Maple Bay from the Island Highway in Duncan. Turn onto Herd Road north of Duncan or Maple Bay Road in Duncan's city centre; either route will take you to the Maple Bay waterfront. Once there turn left and follow the waterfront road to the rowing club. The launch is from a clean, level sand beach.

SOUTH STUART CHANNEL

This is generally an uninspiring area to visit, so I won't dwell on it. The Saltspring Island side is low and heavily residential, while the pulp mill at Crofton dominates the Vancouver Island side. The proximity to smokestacks and busy industrial wharves detracts from the nearby islands. It is useful, however, as the northern ferry link to Saltspring, with regular ferry service from Crofton to Vesuvius Bay.

Crofton

This community has grown around the pulp mill and the industrial buildings and emissions are visible for miles. It's a major shipping area serving cargo ships, tankers, tugs and barges. The town centre is at Osborn Bay, where there's a public wharf, a ferry landing at the head of the wharf and a small craft basin to the south. The north end of Osborn Bay is a drying bank with a log sorting facility and a causeway to Shoal Islands. The largest, Willy Island, is the Halalt reserve.

South of Crofton is Grave Point. It and Erskine Point are the north entrances to Sansum Narrows. Grave Point is recognizable by a conspicuous red cliff. A booming ground and breakwater are located just south of the point.

Launches: N48°51.94' W123°38.40'. To the north of the ferry terminal there's a boat ramp and north of that a rocky beach suitable for launching kayaks. From the launch it's about a 5-km (3-mile) crossing to Saltspring.

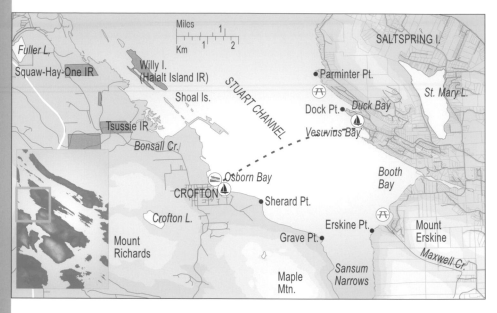

Booth Bay

Booth Bay is backed by a narrow inlet near a biologically rich tidal flat. Residences surround the bay, with a background of Mount Erskine and Mount Belcher. South of Erskine Point the houses disappear, and there are a few rough beaches that make ideal picnic locations. At Maxwell Creek there's a recreational beach with potential as a kayak launch at the end of Collins Road.

The pulp mill dominates the skyline at Crofton.

Vesuvius Bay.

Place names: Eric Booth was one of the original settlers on Saltspring Island and served as reeve of the township.

Vesuvius Bay

Vesuvius Bay is a small village centre; services are limited to a restaurant, a pub and a biffy on the ferry dock. The public wharf immediately north of the ferry terminal is usually busy and requires rafting. Restaurant customers from boats can use the dock behind the restaurant, then the wooden stairs. Numerous submerged rocks and reefs line this stretch of the shore. On the south end of the bay there's a good beach popular as a local day-use area, backed by houses.

Place names: The paddle sloop *Vesuvius* was built at Sheerness in 1840 and served in the Russian War 1854–56. The commander was Sherard Osborn (Osborn Bay).

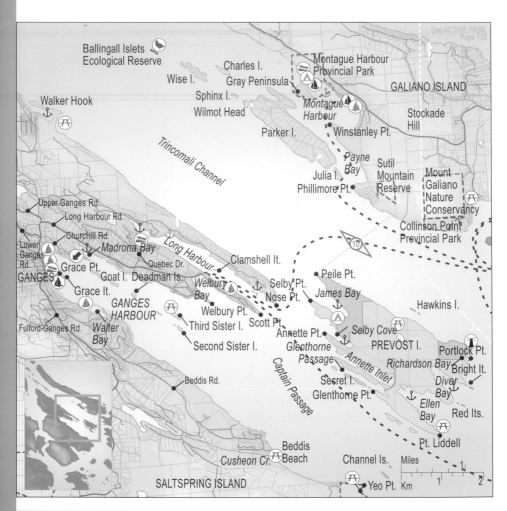

See ACTIVE PASS, Page 128

Map labels:

Ballingall Islets Ecological Reserve
Walker Hook
Wise I.
Charles I.
Gray Peninsula
Sphinx I.
Wilmot Head
Parker I.
Montague Harbour Provincial Park
Montague Harbour
GALIANO ISLAND
Stockade Hill
Winstanley Pt.
Trincomali Channel
Payne Bay
Julia I.
Phillimore Pt.
Sutil Mountain Reserve
Mount Galiano Nature Conservancy
Collinson Point Provincial Park
Upper Ganges Rd.
Long Harbour Rd.
Churchill Rd.
Lower Ganges Rd.
Madrona Bay
Quebec Dr.
Long Harbour
Clamshell It.
Peile Pt.
GANGES
Grace Pt.
Goat I. Deadman Is.
Welbury Bay
Selby Pt.
Nose Pt.
James Bay
Hawkins I.
Grace It.
GANGES HARBOUR
Welbury Pt.
Scott Pt.
Fulford-Ganges Rd.
Walter Bay
Third Sister I.
Second Sister I.
Annette Pt.
Glenthorne Passage
Selby Cove
PREVOST I.
Richardson Bay
Portlock Pt.
Bright It.
Diver Bay
Beddis Rd.
Captain Passage
Annette Inlet
Secret I.
Glenthorne Pt.
Ellen Bay
Red Its.
Beddis Beach
Cusheon Cr.
Channel Is.
Pt. Liddell
Miles
SALTSPRING ISLAND
Yeo Pt. Km

GANGES

The community of Ganges is the cultural and economic centre of Saltspring Island. A multitude of services cater to tourists, including the popular Saturday market. There are also a grocery store, cafés, tourist information, restaurants, kayak rentals, banking and a post office (V0S 1E0). Ganges is a common staging area for kayak trips in the region, of which Prevost Island is a highlight.

Place names: HMS *Ganges* was the 84-gun flagship on the Royal Navy's Pacific station 1857–60. Built in 1821, it was the last British sailing battleship commissioned for service outside British waters.

Launches: N48°51.16' W123°29.88'. The public boat launch is located at the head of the harbour in the midst of the busy commercial centre. It's behind the market, off Fulford-Ganges Road, in a small public boat basin for commercial and transient vessels in the harbour's south side. Parking is an issue. The ramp itself is narrow and busy, so leisurely loading of a kayak will likely cause a jam.

Point Liddell, Prevost Island.

N48°51.36' W123°29.34'. From Ganges take Long Harbour Road north, then the first right onto Churchill Road. At the end of Churchill Road a set of curving, awkward concrete stairs give beach access. Note the street is narrow and residential and parked vehicles can quickly clutter the area.

Weather

Saltspring (Cusheon L.)	May	June	July	Aug.	Sept.	Dec.	Av./Ttl.
Daily average temp. (C)	11.4	14.0	16.2	16.3	13.2	2.6	9.0
Daily maximum (C)	16.9	19.5	22.1	22.3	18.6	5.3	13.5
Daily minimum (C)	5.9	8.5	10.3	10.3	7.6	-0.2	4.4
Precipitation (mm)	48.9	37.5	22.9	27.6	35.0	148.0	1028.1
Days of rainfall + 0.2mm	13.7	11.2	6.7	7.0	9.5	19.0	
Days with rainfall +5mm	3.1	2.4	1.7	1.8	2.3	9.3	
Days with rainfall +10mm	1.0	0.8	0.4	0.7	0.9	5.6	

Channel Islands

These three low, grassy rock ridges are now part of the Gulf Islands National Park. Access is prohibited. Seals use the nearby reefs as a haulout.

Islets near Nose Point, Long Harbour.

Beddis Beach

Beddis, a popular day-use area for Saltspring, is in the most developed part of a relatively pristine stretch of shore. Wooded cliffs extend northwest from Yeo Point to Beddis Beach.

Ganges Harbour

The harbour is a busy recreational corridor surrounded by residences. Its main charm for kayakers is the Chain Islands. Numerous hazards and shallows keep most of the boat traffic to the south of these islands, while most kayakers travel along the islands. Walter Bay, on the south end of the harbour, is a waterbird sanctuary.

Chain Islands

This line of islands, islets and reefs includes Goat Island, Deadman Island and First, Second and Third Sister islands. All are private. Third Sister Island is the only uninhabited one, with a superb beach known as Chocolate Beach on the west end. On most summer days, groups of novice kayakers from Ganges congregate here.

Watch for a wreck underwater southwest of Goat Island.

Long Harbour

Long Harbour is deep, narrow, sheltered and home to a BC Ferries terminal that serves large ferries arriving from Tsawwassen (Vancouver) on the mainland and other Gulf Islands destinations. Several Crown islets, private islands and reefs dot the harbour. The largest of the cluster of islands at Nose Point is private; the rest are Crown reefs. Watch for foul ground around them. The harbour ends in a muddy tidal flat. The Royal Vancouver Yacht Club has docks northwest of Scott Point. Homes and other private wharves line the harbour.

Launches: N48°51.56' W123°27.81'. From Long Harbour Road, turn onto Quebec Drive. The roads may be confusing, as the signs aren't easily seen, but the road eventually leads down a hill to a spacious boat ramp with a nice beach area for loading kayaks alongside the ramp. Parking is limited, but it's a good starting point for destinations such as Prevost.

Walker Hook

This crooked headland and the lagoon it creates are landmarks along this mostly flat stretch of north Saltspring Island. The base of the hook is a natural causeway connecting what would otherwise be an island. The west side of the causeway is a sandy beach—the remnants of glacial deposits; north Saltspring is one of the few locations in the Gulf Islands where glaciers didn't strip the bedrock of sediment, allowing the erosion from stream runoff to create a few choice sand beaches like this one.

Place names: Edward Walker (1826–1902) was one of the first residents of Nanaimo. He owned trading schooners that, among other endeavors, carried material for the construction of the Fisgard Lighthouse. He built the schooner *Alpha* for trade on the coast.

Captain Passage

This passage runs between Prevost and Saltspring islands, linking Swanson and Trincomali channels. Currents can run as high as 3 knots on the flood toward Trincomali and 4 knots on the ebb that runs south. There may be enough turbulence between Nose Point and Prevost Island to intimidate novice paddlers. Large ferries cross Captain Passage on the way to or from Long Harbour. Monitor Channel 11 for the Active Pass call-in points to avoid surprises.

Place names: Captain John Fulford was commander of Admiral Baynes' flagship *Ganges*.

The historic lighthouse at Portlock Point.

Prevost Island

Few islands exemplify the beauty and serenity of the Gulf Islands as well as Prevost. For a relatively tiny entity it has a remarkably diverse range of features—essentially all the best of the Gulf Islands rolled into one tidy package. The majority of the island has not been sub-divided. Most development is clustered on Secret Island and around Annette Inlet. The remainder is sandstone cliffs and undisturbed bays with off-lying island clusters. Several portions are now part of the Gulf Islands National Park. Feral goats outnumber human residents. Look for them on the island's steeper shorelines.

The island was bought from the Crown in the 1920s by Hubert DeBurgh. He was offered Secret Island as well for an extra $50, but declined.

Place names: James Charles Prevost was captain of the *Satellite* 1857–60.

Secret Island

Both Acland and Secret islands are inhabited. Secret Island shelters Glenthorne Passage, a popular mooring location. In 1967, Wallace Island resort owner David Conover purchased Secret Island for $25,000, logged it and put it back on the market for $125,000. The next buyer put a road down the centre and split the island into 40 lots. The development is reflected in the number of private docks along Glenthorne Passage. It's a marked contrast to the pristine southern shoreline of Prevost Island. Steep, arbutus-lined bluffs stretch from Glenthorne Point to Point Liddell.

Place names: Secret Island was originally Iskit Island, but it was seized from the unlucky German owner in 1941. Later owner David Conover asked it be renamed Secret Island in recognition of his relationship with his friend Marilyn Monroe. It wasn't much of a secret, though. Conover wrote four books, one of which is titled *Find Marilyn, a Resource.*

James Bay

James Bay, on the northwest end of Prevost Island, is sheltered between two headlands, with a sand and gravel beach at the head of the bay. A second beach behind a ridge on the southwest end of the bay is backed by an old orchard. A rough trail leads from here to the head of the bay, then along the peninsula to Peile Point, the junction of Captain Passage and Trincomali Channel. Peile Point is a Vessel Traffic Services call-in point.

Public mooring buoys are available in James Bay. Note that the prevailing northwest winds can funnel down Trincomali Channel and blow straight into the bay, making for choppy conditions and possibly a windy camping spot.

Camping: N48°50.43' W123°23.98'. Camping is open in the orchard behind the beach on the south-central portion of the bay. A few clear, private areas can be found on the ridge overlooking the bay. The choice location is on the point.

Looking toward the campsite at James Bay from Peile Point.

A feral goat on the shore near Hawkins Island.

Hawkins Island

Formerly a recreational island with wilderness campsites on the flat headlands, these islands are now off-limits as part of the Gulf Islands National Park. An aquaculture operation is located between Hawkins and Prevost islands.

Portlock Point

Portlock Point is the eastern extremity of Prevost Island and the junction of Trincomali and Swanson channels. Ships transiting Active Pass are required to call in to Vessel Traffic Services in Victoria on Channel 11 when passing the line due east of the light. A lighthouse built on the point in 1895 is now closed, but the grounds can be visited by a trail from the beach at the head of Richardson Bay, immediately to the south of the point. Other ruins from pioneering days dot the shoreline here, particularly northwest of the point. The point, head of the bay and north shore of the headland have been recently added to the national park reserve. Also in the park is Bright Island, a rounded and treed rock at the north entrance to Diver Bay. Access is prohibited. Numerous rocks and reefs surround the island.

Richardson Bay, Prevost Island.

Red Islets

These islets are off the south end of Diver Bay on east Prevost Island. They have long been recreational islets, but are now part of the national park reserve. Access is prohibited.

South of Red Islets is Ellen Bay, another deep channel with an old shack at the head of the bay. A nice beach is tucked into Point Liddel.

GALIANO ISLAND

Galiano Island is 26 km (16 miles) long and as narrow as 2 km (1.2 miles). The island's ridges rise as high as 341 m (1,118 feet) at Mount Galiano, but most of the island is a sloping ridge that rises gradually from the Strait of Georgia and leaves rocky bluffs or cliffs on the Trincomali Channel side. Most of the residences are concentrated near Sturdies Bay and in a few other pockets, such as Phillimore Point, Retreat Cove, Cain Peninsula and North Galiano.

The Coast Salish visited Galiano Island for thousands of years, leaving remnants of that habitation, including middens in both Montague Harbour and Dionisio Point parks. European settlement began in the 1870s, but with mixed success as agriculture proved

On the bluff overlooking Trincomali Channel.

difficult. It was surveyed in 1889, and all land not pre-empted prior to the survey—about half the island—was bought by Samuel Robbins of the Vancouver Coal Mining and Lands Co. Most of these properties were on the northwest of Galiano. They went through a variety of owners over the years, including forestry company MacMillan Bloedel in the 1950s, which was the largest landholder on Galiano for many years. This led to arguably the largest land feud in Gulf Islands history. The slow growth of trees prompted MacBlo to get out of the forestry industry on Galiano and focus on development instead. Much to the dismay of the local government, Islands Trust, the land had been zoned in such a way that it could be subdivided. Islanders, naturally, rankled at the idea of a huge subdivision and the zoning was changed to prevent subdivision. A court battle ensued. The company argued against the new zoning and won, so the subdividing continued. Islands Trust appealed and also won. Since many of the properties had been sold in the interim, the purchasers ultimately became owners of small parcels usable only as forestry land.

As a result, much of the island remains in a natural state. Long, winding roads lead through scenic areas such as Lovers' Leap viewpoint over the high cliffs of Bodega Ridge. These are popular with hikers and cyclists. Dionisio Point Provincial Park remains a key attraction on the island's northwest.

Because of the size of the island, descriptions of Galiano are split between three sections. The shoreline adjacent to Active Pass is covered beginning page 129, while the northwest end is described starting page 168.

Ballingall Islets.

Place names: Dionisio Alcala Galiano aboard *Sutil*, accompanied by Valdes in the *Mexicana*, travelled the Gulf Islands in 1792 while under orders from the viceroy of Mexico to explore Juan de Fuca Strait. While exploring the inner channels they met Vancouver and accompanied him until they came out into the Pacific. Galiano waskilled in the Battle of Trafalgar in 1805.

Payne Bay

Most of southern Galiano plunges steeply into Trincomali Channel, but at Phillimore Point, the southern entry into Payne Bay, it flattens considerably. This has allowed residential development southeast of the point. Behind the point is Mount Sutil, with an elevation of 280 m (919 feet). The peak was purchased for a transmission tower that was never built. It's now a protected area with no safe legal access, which helps maintain its natural state. Payne Bay serves as the entry to Montague Harbour. A conspicuous hydro line runs to Galiano from Parker Island, which is private and almost completely developed. Julia, Sphinx and Charles islands are also privately owned. Wise Island is heavily subdivided.

Ballingall Islets Ecological Reserve

These low, rocky islets are distinctive for their gnarled juniper snags. The ecological reserve was established in 1963 to protect colonies of nesting glaucous-winged gull, double-crested cormorant and pigeon guillemot. It's a tiny parcel—just 0.2 ha (half an acre)—and when first created protected 28 double-crested cormorant nests and 11 pelagic cormorant nests in the snags. Unfortunately, the last nest was recorded in 1987. The islets remain a reserve in the hope that the birds will return. Access is prohibited.

Montague Harbour Marine Park

Created in 1959, this is the province's oldest marine park. The 97-ha (240-acre) park includes a saltwater marsh, a tombolo, foreshore habitat for heron, eagle, cormorant and other seabirds and a rich intertidal ecology that includes plumose anemones, cockles, mussels, clams and oysters. This led to several unusual rules for the park, such as replacing overturned rocks, plus a hands-off policy for shells and other marine organisms.

Shell middens indicate a village site with occupation spread through three periods over the last 3,000 years. A dock accommodates vessels up to 11 m (36 feet). A day-use fee is charged for vehicles and a nightly fee for dock and mooring buoy use.

Montague Harbour

Montague Harbour is a well-used anchorage with public floats and a marina with a store. Gray Peninsula, protected as Montague Harbour Marine Park, has a dock, public mooring buoys and a campground.

Launches: N48°54.00' W123°24.46'. A launch ramp is located in the provincial park at the end of Montague Park Road. A long, sandy beach is perfect for launching kayaks.

Camping: N48°53.81' W123°24.31'. Montague Harbour has 25 drive-in campsites, with 13 reservation-only (call **1-800-689-9025**) and 12 available on a first-come, first-served basis. Due to the park's popularity during the summer, it's a good bet that unless you have a reservation you'll be relegated to the overflow camping area in the clearing behind the wharf—essentially a field. Even if campsites are available, they're akin to regular provincial park campgrounds as opposed to wilderness camping. Wilderness alternatives nearby are James Bay on Prevost Island and Wallace Island.

TRINCOMALI CHANNEL

Trincomali Channel extends from Portlock Point on Prevost Island to Pylades Island and links Swanson and Pylades channels. The part of the channel covered in this section is the portion to Porlier Pass at the north end of Galiano only.

On the north shore of Trincomali are the impressive cliffs of Galiano northwest of Gray Peninsula—a marked contrast to the relatively featureless shore of north Saltspring. Coromorants nest on some of these cliffs; the key area is protected as Trincomali Nature Sanctuary.

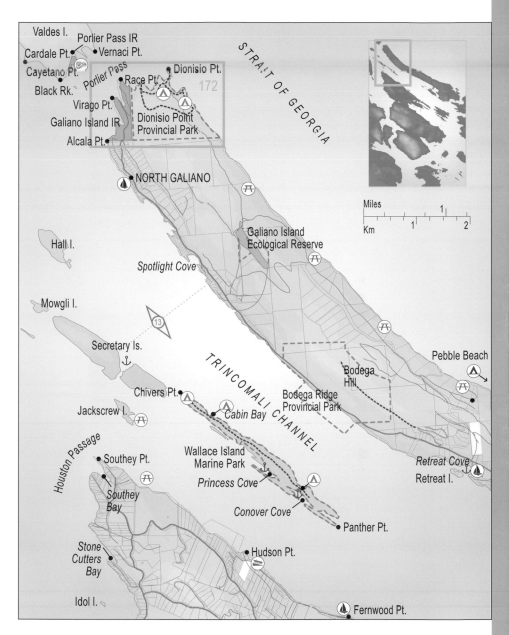

Currents in Trincomali flood northwest and ebb southeast. They rarely go above 1.5 knots in the wider sections and will be fastest north of Wallace Island, where currents run up to 3 knots.

Typical outer shoreline of Galiano Island facing the Strait of Georgia.

Place names: HMS *Trincomalee* was a sailing frigate equipped with 24 guns that served on the Pacific 1853–1856. It was built in Bombay in 1819.

Southey Point

Southey Point, rather ironically, sits on the northernmost tip of Saltspring Island. It is residential and development is essentially unbroken between Vesuvius Bay and the area toward Hudson Point. This stretch has little appeal for paddlers, especially if travelling south with views of the mill at Crofton.

Southeast of Southey Point is a long and sandy beach. A public pier extends over the extensive tidal flats at Fernwood Point.

Launches: A boat ramp is located northwest of Fernwood Point at Hudson Point (a local name, not an official one) off North Beach Road. It offers the most direct access to Wallace Island Marine Park. The boat ramp is northwest of a public pier.

Houston Passage

Houston Passage curves around Saltspring Island, from the east side of Kuper Island to the south end of Wallace Island as far as Panther and Fernwood points. Current is low, with the flood northwest and the ebb southeast.

An evening storm breaks up at Chivers Point.

Wallace Island

Wallace Island is one of a number of small islands that separate Trincomali Channel and Houston Passage. The group is well sheltered and remarkable for long, thin ridges that appear at some tide levels like skeletal rock ribs. They are particularly prevalent along the southwest shore of Wallace Island. All the islands are private except for the park at Wallace Island; the southwest central portion of the island remains in private hands. The island was once a resort, a past that's still visible in many of the cottages. The resort dates back to just after the Second World War when David and Jeanne Conover said goodbye to California and bought Wallace Island for $20,000. Their adventures are captured in David Conover's book *Once Upon an Island*.

The channel between the neighbouring Secretary Islands runs dry at lower tides. At the north side of the drying channel is a boat haven. Nearby Jackscrew Island has a pleasant cove and beach on the southeast side, along with a breakwater and private floats.

Place names: Originally Narrow Island, Wallace was renamed in 1905 for Capt. Wallace Houston (Houston Passage) of HMS *Trincomalee*. The coal ship *Panther* sank when it struck Panther Point. The island's original owner, Chivers (Chivers Point), was a gold prospector famous for paying for items in gold pieces. When he died, no gold was found—giving rise to the legend that a supply of gold is hidden somewhere on the island.

This is a popular destination for both boaters and kayakers. Development is limited to campsites in three locations, pit toilets, picnic tables, the dock at Conover Cove and the dinghy dock at Princess Cove. Anchorages and stern tie rings can be found at both locations. Once the Royal Cedar Cottages resort, many of the cottages remain as part of the parkland, including one modified as a picnic shelter. In the late 1960s the resort was bought by a group of teachers from Seattle, and a subsequent disagreement and eventual court-ordered sale resulted in a chance for the province to purchase the island for use as a marine park in 1990. Trails run the length of the island.

Camping: N48°57.35' W123°34.40'. A rock and crushed shell beach lies between bedrock ridges at Chivers Point. A path from the beach leads to six campsites with gravel tent pads.

N48°57.14' W123°34.02'. A half a kilometre (0.3 miles) from Chivers Point is Cabin Bay. Off the bay is a rock ridge connected by a natural causeway. The best kayak landing spot is on the west side of the causeway. A flat area on Wallace Island is the designated camping area, a small location for two to three tents in close proximity. Two picnic tables are provided, but no outhouse. The rock ridge makes a good day-use area.

N48°56.25' W123°32.64'. Conover Cove is near the southeast end of Wallace Island. Camping is on a grassy, flat and open area. The main access is from Conover Cove, but a tiny bay on the northeast side of the island opposite Conover Cove is suitable as a kayak pullout (N48°56.33' W123°32.60').

A water pump is located about 300 m (1,000 feet) north along a trail.

Retreat Cove

This is a small residential area on Galiano Island. A portion of Retreat Island, including an intact Garry oak stand, is protected as conservancy land. The island is connected to shore by a drying shoal. A public wharf is located on the south end of the cove. The east side of Retreat Island is considered a safe anchorage.

Bodega Ridge

Bodega Ridge rises to 328 m (1,076 feet). It's recognizable for its single tree above prominent cliffs. The day-use-only park has no facilities beyond trails and the natural attractions, which include sandstone formations, wildflowers and cliffs that are home to bald eagle and peregrine falcon.

Place names: Capt. Juan Francisco de la Bodega y Quadra was the Spanish naval commander at Nootka when Captain Vancouver arrived in 1792.

Ecological oddities: Unusual plants include the arbutus-like shrub hairy manzanita and Gray's desert-parsley. Underwater, look for the weathervane scallop. The park shoreline is one of just two areas in the province with noteworthy populations of this variety of scallop.

Bodega Ridge Provincial Park
The park includes both the ridge and a marine area designated to protect the rockfish habitat that includes quillback, lingcod, sea perch, sea urchin, shrimp and sponge. The ridge was originally purchased as an ecological reserve by the Pacific Marine Heritage Legacy in 1995; it was the first acquisition for the Gulf Islands National Park, though it was never included in the park reserve. It was made a provincial park in 2001.

Spotlight Cove

Between Bodega Hill and Alcala Point the shoreline is mostly residential with a cluster of homes at Spotlight Cove. A village centre, North Galiano, is located northwest of Spotlight Cove. There you can find a general store and public wharf, known as the Spanish Hills dock, alongside Porlier Pass Road.

Porlier Pass

This pass is deceiving for it appears too wide—about 0.8 km (0.5 miles)—to be a rapid. But the amount of water that passes through it during each tide change is substantial enough to create considerable currents, as much as 9 knots on the flood and 8 knots on the ebb. The current pours into the Strait of Georgia on the flood and into Trincomali Channel on the ebb. It's famous for its overfall, often several feet (up to a metre) in height.

Divers will have a special interest in this pass. Wrecks include the *Del Norte*, a steam schooner that struck a reef northeast of Porlier Pass in 1868, and the *Point Grey*, a 30-m (100-foot) tug that hit and sank at Virago Rock.

The Lyackson had a village on the Valdes Island shore called Th'xwe'ksen, or "Shining Point."

Call-in points: Vessel Traffic Service call-in points are required for ships entering and leaving Porlier Pass. As with Active Pass, the orientation of the pass is considered east-west; the west entrance refers to the Trincomali side and the east entrance, the Strait of Georgia side. The call-in points are within 4.8 km (3 miles) of entering or leaving the pass.

- *13, West Porlier Pass:* The call-in point is considered N48°57.92' W123°34.20' in the middle of Trincomali Channel north of Chivers Point.

- *14, East Porlier Pass*: This is 4.8 km (3 miles) northeast of the pass at N49°03.01' W123°32.20'.

Place names: Jose Maria Narvaez named it Boca de Porlier in 1791 after Antonio Porlier, a Spanish official.

Navigating Porlier Pass by kayak: The rule is simple. Don't travel through Porlier Pass at peak current. Wait for slack or near slack. Current change times are listed in *Canadian Tide and Current Tables, Volume 5*.

On an ebb tide the current will split outside of Porlier Pass to run west under Valdes Island and east past Galiano. For those simply paddling past Porlier Pass via Trincomali Channel, approaching the pass will put you potentially against the current in either direction. Hug the Valdes or Galiano shore to take advantage of countercurrents on your approach, or drop down to Reid and Hall islands.

On a flood tide, Porlier Pass will look deceivingly calm from Trincomali Channel. The turbulence will be past Race and Vernaci points, so kayakers will see only silk-smooth water from Trincomali Channel when winds are calm. This could lull you into complacency.

If you are travelling between Cardale Point on Valdes Island and Alcala Point on Galiano, be sure you're not being pulled unawares into Porlier Pass by the current. With a GPS you can set a course and watch your bearing to ensure you're not drifting. Without a GPS you can use dead reckoning. Find a reference point in the direction you're headed, and a second reference point in the distance as directly behind it as possible (for instance, a distinctive tree on the point and the peak of a hill behind it). If the nearer reference point moves to the right of the point behind it, this means you are drifting left—an alarm bell if you're travelling across the pass to Alcala Point.

Trincomali Channel from above the bluffs of the Trincomali Nature Sanctuary.

To pass the Strait of Georgia side on an ebb tide, keep your distance by heading to the navigation bell near Canoe Islet.

On a flood tide, be aware that the current runs north through the pass near Canoe Islet. If you are crossing from Dionisio you'll have the current in your favour. Enjoy it and stay out of the worst of the turbulence. If you're crossing from Valdes, you'll have to fight the main stream of the current and potentially much of the turbulence to reach Dionisio. This method works well, but avoid peak currents. Stay along the Valdes Island shore between Shah Point and Vernaci Point. You'll get a good countercurrent until Vernaci Point. Once near Vernaci Point, break off before the worst of the turbulence and head to Dionisio. Paddle like mad. This will take you sideways to the current until out of the main stream east of Race Point. You'll make good time, but you may run into rips and turbulence. If the rips are troublesome, aim into them, then return to paddling in the direction of Dionisio once you're through. Once out of the main current, getting to Dionisio Point should be simple.

Naturally, the level of turbulence and strength of the current will be directly proportional to how close you time your trip to peak current. Travelling at slack tide will be simple; travelling at peak current will be potentially dangerous. It pays to wait.

Dionisio Point

This area, known locally for decades as Coon Bay, gained a reputation in the 1960s as a place for free accommodation. A number of shacks were built here, but the vandalism and uncontrolled fires led landowners MacMillan Bloedel to bulldoze the shacks in 1975. Many of the residents returned, however, and didn't leave until the park was designated in 1991. In 1995 road access was removed.

Earlier residents were the Cowichan, with archaeological evidence showing 5,500 years or more of habitation. The area is believed to have been a camp for collecting eggs, roots and berries as well as for fishing and hunting marine mammals. Evidence remains in the middens, burial sites and in five rectangular depressions that indicate a village site.

For those arriving by paddle or small boat, there are two places to land at Dionisio: Coon Bay and Perry Lagoon. Both can be problematic. If there is a current and/or if the wind is blowing from the northwest, the wind waves will blow straight into Coon Bay, forcing a surf landing on a fairly steep beach. Continuing to the east of Dionisio Point you might be able to thread your way through the rocks protecting Perry Lagoon, but if it's a low tide the way in could be blocked or hidden, especially if there are wind waves or swell to

Coon Bay, Dionisio Provincial Park, on a beautiful February day.

contend with. The clearest path will be to the extreme east of the lagoon entrance. Beware of the possibility of partially submerged or submerged rocks along the lagoon entrance. Note that swell and wind waves may be greatly exaggerated around Dionisio Point in some tide conditions as rips mix with wind waves. Potential difficulties will be greatly reduced if you wait till slack or near-slack tide to enter Dionisio.

Once here, a trail leads out to the headland of Dionisio Point for views into Porlier Pass. In all, the park contains about 7 km (4.3 miles) of trails. The beaches at Coon Bay and within the lagoon are popular day-use areas.

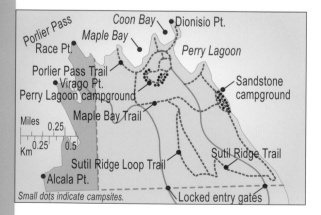

Camping: N49°00.73' W123°34.40', Perry Lagoon. Campsites can be accessed from Coon Bay or Perry Lagoon. They're located uphill from the beaches. They're not particularly convenient for those arriving by boat, though a park warden may have a dolly available to help move camping gear. Campsites that formerly faced the lagoon have been closed to protect the nearshore environment.

N49°00.46' W123°34.00', Sandstone. Under the right conditions, Sandstone campground can be an option along the outer shore of Galiano. It's located about 430 m (a quarter-mile) southeast of the end of Perry Lagoon and can be identified by the wooden ladder leading to the forested upland. There is no beach and no shelter, which means a rock ledge landing on an exposed portion of the Strait of Georgia. Consequently it's a fair-weather stop only, with a risk you may land in calm conditions but have to leave in wind waves—a potentially dangerous situation, as even a 15-cm (6-inch) swell can make a rock landing or launch difficult. If you do land, you'll find 12 sites with picnic tables, 8 of which face the water.

Dionisio Point Provincial Park
Dionisio Point was made a provincial park in 1991 through the purchase of two upland lots and forestry company MacMillan Bloedel's donation of two waterfront lots. The park is accessible only by water, the road access having been closed in 1995. There are trails leading through old-growth forest, alongside picturesque creeks and to lookouts at the park's various points. A midden facing Maple Bay is fenced off to help preserve it.

Travel notes: Dionisio Provincial Park advertises itself as a marine-accessible park only. A gate blocks the access road, but the road is paved and in good condition, making it ideal for cyclists as there is no car traffic. Hiking trails also lead into the park, but they cross private property, so officially they don't exist. Regardless of the rules, cyclists will almost certainly outnumber the few (if any) kayakers at the Sandstone campsite. This is an odd outcome for a campsite created for paddlers in a park where land access supposedly isn't possible.

Sculpted sandstone is a common feature in the northern Gulf Islands.

The North Gulf Islands

CHAPTER FOUR

LIKE MANY NEW KAYAKERS ON VANCOUVER ISLAND, MY FIRST OVERNIGHT
kayaking adventure was to Pirates Cove on De Courcy Island. The
beautiful eroded sandstone of De Courcy, the sheltered channels
and the great camping make this a great introduction to the area,
all without having to stray far from shore. To be more adventurous
I began to go farther afield, to Blackberry Point and trips around
Thetis Island. And finally I was ready for the big, open water on the
outside of Gabriola Island, with a trip to the Flat Tops.

Everyone has to start somewhere, and this makes a perfect place,
as two large islands, Gabriola and Valdes, shield the inner waters and
the multitude of inner islands scattered around Trincomali, Pylades
and Stuart channels.

Gabriola is 14.5 km (9 miles) long and about 4.2 km (2.6 miles)
wide and home to around 5,000 people who travel via a ferry from
downtown Nanaimo. The island contains a stunning collection of
petroglyphs, evidence of thousands of years of First Nations occupation. Since European settlement Gabriola has never gone far beyond
cottage country, with little industry but cheap land; as late as 1969
lots were advertised for as little as $25 down and $25 a month. A
smattering of waterfront parkland has been increased in recent years
with the addition of a bankrupt campground north of Descanso Bay
purchased as a regional park.

If there's one last frontier in the Gulf Islands, it's Gabriola's
neighbour, Valdes Island. Two imposing waterways isolate this long,
thin island: Gabriola Passage to the north and Porlier Pass to the
south. The two sides of Valdes are distinct. The more easterly side
facing the Strait of Georgia has a low rock-shelf shoreline with a

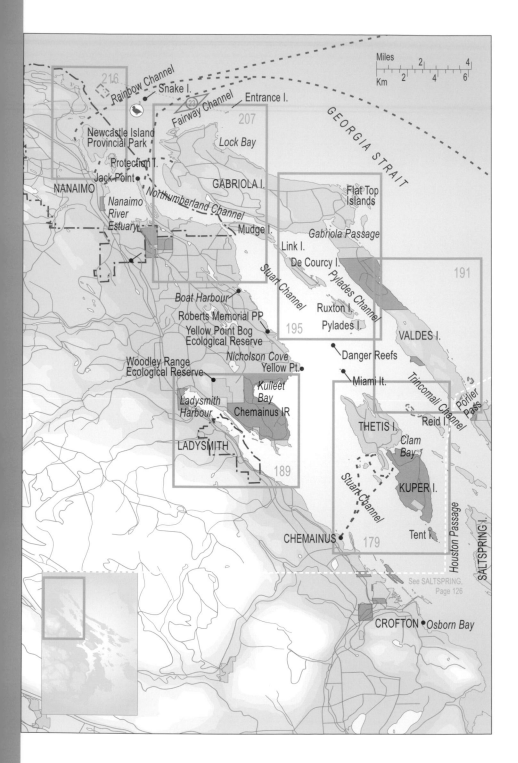

Miles 2 4
Km 2 4 6

Rainbow Channel

Snake I.

216

Entrance I.

Fairway Channel

23

Lock Bay

Newcastle Island
Provincial Park

GEORGIA STRAIT

Protection I.

Jack Point

NANAIMO

GABRIOLA I.

207

Flat Top
Islands

Nanaimo
River
Estuary

Northumberland Channel

Gabriola Passage

Mudge I.

Link I.

De Courcy I.

Boat Harbour

Roberts Memorial PP

Yellow Point Bog
Ecological Reserve

Stuart Channel

Pylades Channel

Ruxton I.

Pylades I.

195

191

VALDES I.

Woodley Range
Ecological Reserve

Nicholson Cove

Yellow Pt.

Danger Reefs

Miami It.

Trincomali Channel

Porlier Pass

Ladysmith
Harbour

Kulleet
Bay

Chemainus IR

THETIS I.

Reid I.

Clam
Bay

LADYSMITH

189

KUPER I.

Stuart Channel

Houston Passage

SALTSPRING I.

CHEMAINUS

179

Tent I.

See SALTSPRING,
Page 126

CROFTON • Osborn Bay

Paddling De Courcy Island.

gently sloping upland and a scattering of cottages along its length. The southwest shore, facing Pylades and Trincomali channels, is a mix of beach, forested hills and impressive cliffs. It's the last of the larger Gulf Islands without ferry service, ensuring a good measure of isolation.

Place names: Jose Maria Narvaez named Gabriola "Punta de Gaviola" in 1791. There are three theories for the name: one suggests it's a misspelling of *gaviota*, that being a nautical term for a schooner's topsail; another is that *gaviota* could be translated as "Seagull Island"; a third is that Gaviola was a family name whose significance is lost. Cayetano Valdes was in command of the exploring vessel *Mexicana* during the Spanish exploration of the Gulf Islands in 1792. In 1791 he was first lieutenant with Malaspina in the corvette *Descubierta*.

Recommended kayaking trips

- *If you have a day:* From Nanaimo a day trip around Newcastle Island is highly recommended. It can be expanded with side trips to the caves at Jesse Island and possibly the pub at Protection Island. A day trip around Thetis and/or Kuper is also highly recommended, but does entail an hour of open water from the launch to the island. Recommended is a launch from Elliott's Beach Park at Evening Cove. The virtual land bridge of the De Courcy Group—from Mudge Island to De Courcy Island—is also a great day trip. Launch from Cedar and picnic at Pirates Cove. From Gabriola, a trip to the Flat Top Islands and outer Valdes Island is a good way to spend a calm day.

- *If you have two days:* Pirates Cove, Blackberry Point on Valdes and Tent Island all make great overnight destinations.

- *If you have three days:* A good trip is to Blackberry Point, spending the middle day hiking and exploring Valdes.

- *If you have five days:* Launch at Cedar for a trip to Blackberry Point, a run down Valdes Island to the islet off Reid Island and an exploration of Kuper Island, ending the day at Tent Island. Explore Thetis, Cross to Pylades Island and stay at Whalebone Island or Pirates Cove, then return to Cedar. This is a thorough but relaxed exploration of the inner waters, covering as little as 70 km (43 miles).

- *The ideal trip:* I don't think an exploration of this area is complete without seeing the outside of Valdes Island. My itinerary would be to launch from Cedar and spend a first night at Pirates Cove; travel through Gabriola Passage to stay at either the Flat Tops or Kendrick Island; paddle along the outside of Valdes to Dionisio Provincial Park; return through Porlier Pass to Blackberry Point; then head back to Cedar. This trip could be extended by heading to Tent Island and exploring Thetis and Kuper islands.

THETIS-KUPER

Smaller than the other major islands of the Gulf Islands, both Thetis and Kuper can be navigated in day trips from the Chemainus or Ladysmith area. The two islands were originally joined by mud flats, but in 1905 a channel was dredged to allow boat traffic through what is now officially known as The Cut. Thetis is about 3 km wide and 5 km long (2 by 3 miles), with tall ridges for such a small island— Burchell Hill is 180 m (591 feet) and Moore Hill 178 m (584 feet).

These are the smallest of the Gulf Islands to be served by BC Ferries. Thetis has about 350 residents and a community hall, a library, tennis courts, an elementary school for grades K–7 and a

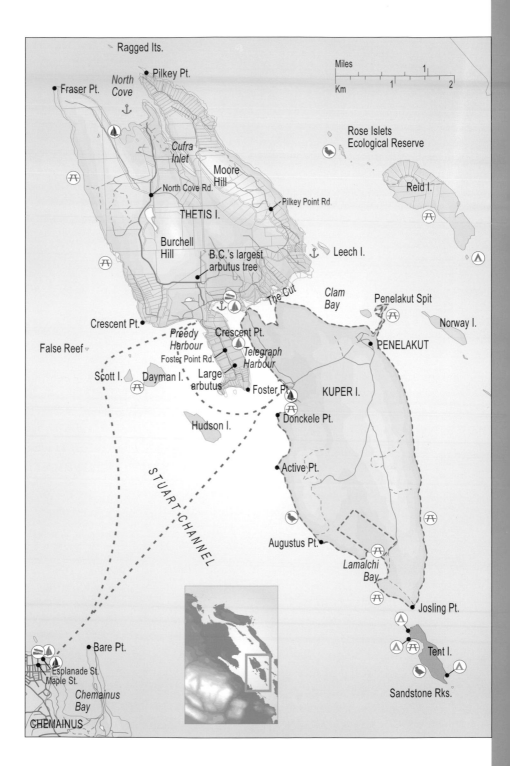

Ragged Its.

Pilkey Pt.

Fraser Pt.

North Cove

Cufra Inlet

Moore Hill

North Cove Rd.

Rose Islets
Ecological Reserve

Reid I.

THETIS I.

Pilkey Point Rd.

Burchell Hill

B.C.'s largest arbutus tree

Leech I.

The Cut

Clam Bay

Penelakut Spit

Norway I.

Crescent Pt.

Preedy Harbour

Crescent Pt.

Foster Point Rd.

Telegraph Harbour

PENELAKUT

False Reef

Scott I.   Dayman I.

Large arbutus

Foster Pt.

KUPER I.

Hudson I.

Donckele Pt.

Active Pt.

S T U A R T   C H A N N E L

Augustus Pt.

Lamalchi Bay

Josling Pt.

Bare Pt.

Tent I.

Esplanade St.
Maple St.

Chemainus Bay

Sandstone Rks.

CHEMAINUS

Miles
Km

Tent Island.

church. It is bible camp country, with Capernwray Bible College, the Anglican Church's Camp Columbia and Pioneer Pacific, a 30-ha (74-acre) Christian camp at North Cove. These and other large holdings tend to keep the west shore of Thetis between Fraser Point and Crescent Point in a near-natural state, which is ideal as it's one of the few locations with gently sloping shore that isn't developed. Many grassy banks are in a near-natural state. Students from these camps can often be found venturing out in kayaking groups to the nearby islands.

Kuper Island is a First Nations reserve. First Nations traditionally occupied both islands, but the largest reminder—a huge midden—was destroyed by a commercial venture on Thetis Island at the turn of the last century.

Today Kuper Island is home to about 185 people, with the community divided between homes near the ferry terminal at Telegraph Harbour and at Penelakut south of Penelakut Spit. Most of the island is in a natural state.

Place names: HMS *Thetis*, commanded by Captain Kuper, was stationed in Esquimalt 1851–53.

Ecological oddities: Thetis is home to B.C.'s largest arbutus tree. It has a 6.64-m (21.8-foot) circumference and a height of 35.5 m

(116.4 feet). It's located 115 m (375 feet) north of the northeast corner of the community centre.

Chemainus

Chemainus is a picturesque Vancouver Island mill community that diversified its economy by adding murals to its quaint downtown commercial sector. The result was a worldwide success, spawning imitators across North America. Chemainus Bay, however, clings to its industrial history with booming grounds, wharves, floats and a sawmill on the southwest. The public wharf is just north of the sawmill. North of that is the Thetis Island ferry terminal and a marina. On the east side of the peninsula forming the bay is a B.C. Hydro generating station and an oil wharf.

Travel notes: Chemainus is home to the Seaward Kayaks factory. Seaward helped equip expeditions for *The Wild Coast* series. Visit **www.seawardkayaks.com**.

Launches: N48°55.72' W123°43.06'. A sand and gravel beach to the north of the Chemainus boat ramp is suitable for launching kayaks. It's located in the heart of Chemainus near a popular waterfront park. To get here, take Chemainus Road to Oak Street, which ends at the ferry terminal. From Oak Street, turn north onto Maple Street. The boat launch is located at the end of the street.

Stuart Channel

This channel runs from Dodd Narrows to Sansum Narrows, bordered by the islands of Saltspring, Kuper, Thetis and the De Courcy Group to the north. The water in the channel is fairly benign, with flood tides generally weak and variable and ebb tides usually running south at 1 knot or less. Currents tend to be strongest in the area near Dodd Narrows, where they can reach 3 knots.

Tent Island

Off the southern tip of Kuper is Tent Island, a reserve of the Penelakut First Nation. The cove on the west side is a popular day-use area. The island is a former marine park that reverted back to the Penelakut when the lease expired. It's an exceptionally pretty island—one of the prettiest in the Gulf Islands. The pockmarked cliffs on the southwest side are a cormorant nesting area. Be sure to give the nests a wide berth.

The northern beach at Tent Island.

Camping: Camping is possible anywhere on Tent Island. The Penelakut First Nation asks that you make a donation—$10 to $20, depending on the party size, is suggested—to Penelakut First Nation, Box 360, Chemainus, V0R 1K0. There's no limit to the length of a stay. Sites don't need to be reserved and you can make the donation after your visit. The band was clearing trees in 2006 to make the north headland more camper-friendly but ran into bones, which halted the work. Plans include building an outhouse and barbecue pit. For information call **250-246-2321**.

N48°55.77' W123°37.98'. The northwest corner of Tent Island has a reef connected by a sandy bar. Beaches continue on both sides of the point. The point is an established camping area, while another is on the headland overlooking the larger cove to the south. A trail joins the two areas. Also, look for a level area upland from the centre of the larger cove.

N48°55.34' W123°37.49'. On the southeast end of the island an attractive headland overlooks Houston Passage. Access is either by the beach to the immediate south or, if conditions are right, on the sandstone ledge directly below the headland.

Lamalchi Bay

This shallow, sheltered bay has a good beach with derelict buildings on reserve property. The west side of the head of the bay is private land, with the beach portion a pioneer cemetery. A few old head-

Historic Lamalchi Bay.

stones and some newer ones dot the field. The outer shore toward Josling Point has a few good beaches to stop and stretch the legs. Given the broad, rocky shoreline, it's possible to take an extended walk. North of Augustus Point, Kuper Island's western shoreline becomes steep cliff with intricate sandstone. The cliffs make ideal cormorant nesting sites. Give the nests a wide berth when passing.

Penelakut Spit

This is a noteworthy clamshell beach that forms a natural break-water. South of the spit the First Nation community of Penelakut nestles on the hillside. A small wooden church is a landmark.

Penelakut was the site of one of the bloodiest recorded First Nations battles in 1859. A group of Bella Bellas visiting Fort Victoria on a trading mission killed most of the island's inhabitants on their return journey.

The rest of the east side of Kuper Island has long stretches of stone beach backed by steep, impenetrable forest and tangled undergrowth. The shore itself is shallow and sandy. On a calm day at low tide look for flatfish hiding along the sandy bottom. They'll be no more than a faint outline until you approach, at which point they'll swim away to find a new spot in the sand.

Nearby Norway Island is private land, with a home, pool, tennis court and dock. It has never been logged. Reefs and islets dot the area around the island.

A pioneer headstone at Lamalchi Bay.

The Lamalchi Bay battle
Lamalchi Bay was the site of a bloody encounter on April 20, 1863, when the British gunboat *Forward* attacked the village for allegedly harbouring fugitives wanted for attacks on European settlers (see page 116). The first assault was repelled, at the cost of a sailor's life, and was followed by one of the largest military operations in the province's history. (The sailor who was killed, 16-year-old Charles F. Gliddon, was the first and last British soldier killed in action in British Columbia.)

The *Forward* headed to Willy Island to anchor for the night after the attack, leaving the villagers' canoes and boats intact—a tactical error. The Lamalchi used the opportunity to scatter to other villages or hiding spots. Later the *Forward* returned with the *Grappler*, only to find the community empty. Their response was to burn the village. After a manhunt that turned into an embarrassment for the British navy (it was reported that canoes outpaddled the British gunboats), enough prisoners were rounded up to satisfy the enraged Europeans. Three men were eventually hung in Victoria. The entire incident was a black eye for the British, who flogged band members for information and took a newspaper editor prisoner over bad press. The trial was also called unfair. The final fugitive, Acheewun, was taken prisoner after a chase along the mountains at Montague Harbour. It goes down in history as the largest military operation on the B.C. coast and the only war against a First Nations tribe. The Lamalchi band, numbering just 15 in 1905, joined with the larger Penelakut band.

Place names: **Pelelakut means "two logs in sand."**

Scott, Hudson and Dayman islands

Three privately owned islands are located just outside Preedy Harbour. Numerous rocks and reefs surround them. Hudson Island is the largest, with 10 properties around a grass airstrip in the island's centre. Note that while official route maps show the BC ferry travelling on either side of this group, the ferry may also travel between Dayman and Hudson islands on its way to Thetis.

Telegraph Harbour

Telegraph Harbour is a long, narrow waterway sheltered by the overlap of both Thetis and Kuper islands. On the Kuper Island side north of Donckele Point a beautiful stretch of beach is backed by undeveloped forest. To the north is a public wharf and the Kuper Island ferry terminal, behind which is a cluster of homes. On the Thetis

Nesting cormorants, Kuper Island.

Island side of Telegraph Harbour are two marinas. Thetis Island Marina has a pub, restaurant, store and post office (V0R 2Y0) on the harbour's west shore. Telegraph Harbour Marina has a general store, café/soda fountain, fuel dock, laundromat, washrooms and showers. It's located at the east end of the harbour's head.

Thetis Island's community centre is a short walk up North Cove Road, where you'll find a number of businesses, including craft stores. Expect the possibility of a roadside store selling fresh goods on the honour system. Walk in, pick what you want, leave the money in the tray. A similar system is used for a donut bakery at a house up Pilkey Point Road.

Launches: N48°59.06' W123°40.28'. A concrete boat ramp is located just north of Telegraph Harbour Marina.

The Cut

First dredged in 1905, this channel is a narrow, man-made strip through muddy intertidal clam beaches between Thetis and Kuper islands. The Thetis Island side is developed; you may even hear lawn-mowers. The Kuper Island shoreline is undeveloped; there's a vast drying mud flat where clams are harvested.

The Cut is a navigational hazard for boaters but kayakers will have few problems at higher tides. At lower tides even kayaks will run aground. The current floods east and ebbs west.

A provincial boat haven in Clam Bay is protected in the cover of Leech Island. Boaters often use it to await high tide for navigating The Cut. Leech Island is privately owned.

Preedy Harbour

Preedy Harbour is home to the BC Ferries terminal and a public wharf. The carefully groomed, resort-like grounds and buildings to the north are part of the Capernwray Harbour Bible College. To its west, set back in the trees, is Overbury Farm Resort. The resort was a poultry farm during the 1930s. It went bankrupt when Canadian Pacific stopped making weekly steamer trips to Thetis. The owners dismantled the chicken coops and used the lumber to make four cottages. The original cabins are still being used, along with newer cabins and an updated farmhouse.

Between Fraser Point and Crescent Point, there are numerous pocket beaches and grassy meadows are common. Development is minimal.

North Cove

North Cove has a public float and breakwater in the southwest corner. Cufra Inlet, a clam harvesting area, makes an interesting place to paddle at higher tides, but it dries extensively at lower tides. Several islets form a route for those paddling between Thetis and the De Courcy Group. The closest is Ragged Islets, about 0.6 km (0.4 miles) northwest of Pilkey Point. Farther afield, 2.3 km (1.4 miles) northwest of Pilkey Point is Miami Islet (see the main chapter map on page 176 to locate it). The islet is surrounded by numerous rocks and boaters should keep their distance; a reminder is the wreck 370 m (1,214 feet) northwest of the island at N49°02.42' W123°42.75'. It's visible at low water. Miami Islet is 3 km (1.8 miles) from Pylades Island.

Moore Hill

Unlike the gently sloping west shore of Thetis Island, the east shore is steep and bluffy, dominated by Moore Hill. Part of the hill broke away, apparently during a severe earthquake, creating sheer rock

A view from the Crown islet off Reid Island toward Galiano.

faces and horizontal fissures known locally as the Caves. The Caves are deep and hazardous and should not be visited casually, if at all.

Ecological oddities: The Caves at Moore Hill are the winter home of the lumpnose bat. This is the northern limit of the bat's range and one of the few places in Canada where it's known to winter (other known locations are Williams Lake and the Okanagan). The Thetis colony is home to between 20 and 40 bats each winter. If the roost is disturbed they'll likely abandon it. They emerge about an hour after dark, so if you see a flash past your campsite at night, look for distinctly long ears. It might be a lumpnose.

Reid Island

Reid Island is the large neighbour of Hall Island. At just over 2 km (1.2 miles) end to end, it's developed into 36 properties, making for a patchwork of homes along the waterfront and about 10 km (6 miles) of trails criss-crossing the island. The island is cliffy to the southwest, with a pretty cove surrounded by beach.

Rose Islets.

Rose Islets Ecological Reserve

The Rose Islets are a series of exposed rock ridges west of Reid Island. The area was protected in 1971 as a nesting site for double-crested cormorant, but since then the numbers have dramatically declined. By 1987 there were no active nests at all, but in 1998 they began to return, and 15 nests were recorded in 2000. The decline is a reflection of a larger trend; overall in the Strait of Georgia the double-crested cormorant population has fallen by 70 percent between 1987 and 2003. While human interference could be to blame, it could also be simply nature at work: there has been a rise in the population of bald eagles, which snack on cormorants.

Public access to the islets is prohibited. The reserve protects 0.8 ha (2 acres).

Off the south tip of Reid Island is a small Crown island. Landing is difficult, as the shoreline is a jumble of rocks and ledges. On the island you'll find a mix of arbutus, gnarled old Garry oak and coastal bluff meadows. Expect a colourful show here each spring. A rough trail crosses the island to viewpoints of Reid Island and Penelakut.

Place names: Capt. James Murray Reid served in the Hudson's Bay Company for 28 years, leaving when his ship, the brigantine *Vancouver*, ran aground in 1854.

Camping: N48°59.41' W123°36.93'. There is an established camping area on the Crown islet. Be sure to treat the surrounding meadow lightly. Expect this islet to gain protected status in the future, as

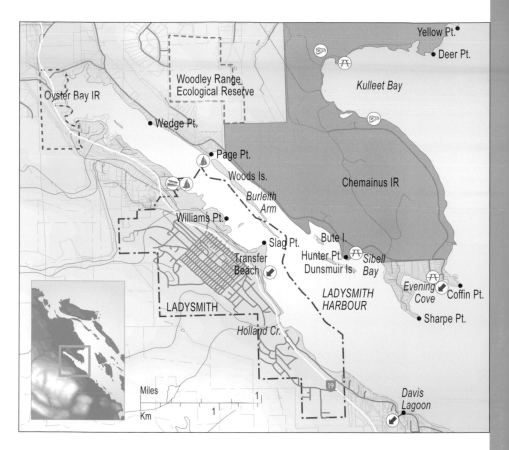

it's one of the few Crown islets in the north Gulf Islands not yet protected and a great example of the coastal bluff ecology.

LADYSMITH

Ladysmith Harbour is a popular launch point and a favourite place for novice kayakers to explore. It's sheltered but developed, with the residential community of Ladysmith on the south side and an active logging operation and log boom on the north shore. Most recreation is focused around Transfer Beach, south of Slag Point. Northwest of Williams Point is a pair of industrial wharves. Farther northwest is a marina, with another at Page Point. Beyond the marinas the harbour is mostly shallow bog.

Watch for float planes landing and taking off southwest of Woods Islands. The Dunsmuir Islands are an outstation used as moorage by the Seattle Yacht Club.

Southeast of Ladysmith is Davis Lagoon. It's crossed by a bridge and dries extensively at low tides. It's a possible launch point for kayaks.

Place names: Coal baron James Dunsmuir named the town after Ladysmith in South Africa in 1900, when he heard the town had been relieved from a long Boer War seige the previous day. The South African town was named after the wife of Major General Sir Harry Smith, governor and commander-in-chief at the Cape. She was a descendant of Ponce de Leon, making Ladysmith probably the only town on Vancouver Island to have a connection with the famous 15th-century Spanish explorer.

Transfer Beach

This is the main waterfront community park for Ladysmith, with a concession, washrooms and a playground behind the expansive beach. Much of the beach is cordoned off as a swimming area during the summer.

Launches: N48°59.42' W123°48.42'. Launching from Transfer Beach is a matter of carrying the kayaks from the parking area across a short grassy stretch to the beach. The turnoff from the Island Highway is a set of lights at the south end of Ladysmith.

Evening Cove

A small community park, Elliott's Beach, backs onto the cove, with a pleasant, day-use beach area protected by the headland at Coffin Point.

Launches: N48°59.23' W123°45.71'. At Elliott's Beach Park a trail leads from the parking lot to the beach, which is sheltered under most conditions but can be mucky at lower tides. To get here from the Island Highway north of Ladysmith, turn east onto Brenton-Page Road and follow it as it changes names to Shell Beach and then Evening Cove roads. Near the end of Evening Cove Road is a short road to your right that ends in the parking lot for the park. Launching from here rather than Transfer Beach will cut about 3 km (2 miles) off a crossing to Thetis.

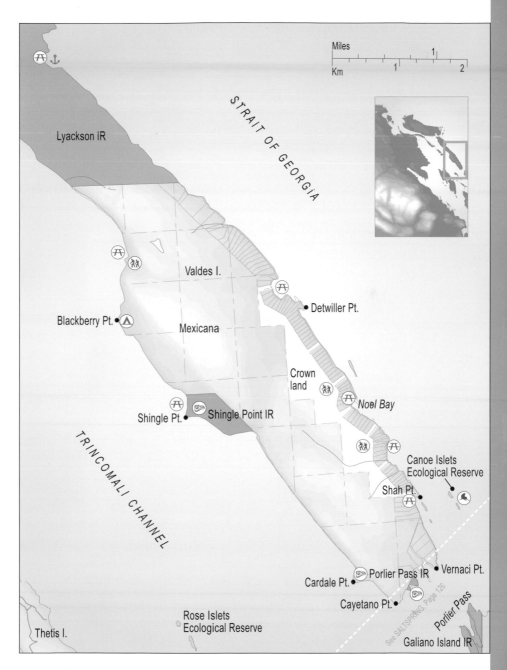

Miles

Km

STRAIT OF GEORGIA

Lyackson IR

Valdes I.

Detwiller Pt.

Blackberry Pt.

Mexicana

Crown land

Noel Bay

Shingle Pt.

Shingle Point IR

TRINCOMALI CHANNEL

Canoe Islets Ecological Reserve

Shah Pt.

Cardale Pt.

Porlier Pass IR

Vernaci Pt.

Cayetano Pt.

Rose Islets Ecological Reserve

Thetis I.

See SALTSPRING, Page 120

Porlier Pass

Galiano Island IR

Kulleet Bay

This bay is surrounded by reserve land, with still-visible reminders
of a long history of Chemainus First Nation occupation. Carving can

be seen on a large boulder on the south shore of the bay that was moved from its original location. If you look carefully you can see how the natural marks and etching create a mythical beast referred to as the Rain God. On the north inner side of the bay, along a small creek in a sandstone basin known as the Shaman's Pool, is a variety of petroglyph figures. The basin has a ritual significance for initiation into secret dance societies. The pool and petroglyphs may be overgrown.

North of Kulleet Bay is Yellow Point, where up to 10,000 surf scoters feed in the intertidal area between Yellow and Deer points. A lodge is located on the point.

SOUTH VALDES ISLAND

Both sides of Valdes are wonderful areas to explore. The outer shore is unique in that the rock ledge shoreline continues unbroken for miles, raising the possibility of long waterfront rambles. The down-

Sandstone cliffs on the Trincomali shore of Valdes Island.

side is it has been heavily subdivided and is being increasingly filled in with cottages. Fortunately, many portions are still in pioneer stages, with shacks or even just campsites. The lack of ferry service to Valdes, along with few anchorages and no marinas, ensures the island doesn't progress beyond cottage country. A highlight of this area is the large Crown parcel inland (marked in yellow on the map), which has wonderful old-growth forest traversed by trails. A good way to reach the area is by logging road from the log dump near Blackberry Point. Bring a GPS, though, as the various ridges can be difficult to tell apart and it's easy to get lost. Spelunkers will also appreciate Valdes, as the island is dotted with caves.

Shingle Point

This is a low, sandy spit with a few homes on the reserve property behind the point. In Hul'qumi'num this is T'a'at'ka, meaning "place of many salal berries." It was formerly a traditional Lyackson village

Sunset at Blackberry Point.

site. Another village located at Cardale Point was called Th'a'xel, or "gravelly place."

Blackberry Point

This point is the recreational highlight for the Trincomali side of Valdes Island, and it makes a great base for exploring the island's many attractions. One of those is the long section of cliff, conspicuous from the De Courcy Group, that extends northwest of Blackberry Point. Visit at low tide to get a close look at the starfish, anemones and many strange marine creatures that cling to life on the intertidal cliff face.

Canoe Islets Ecological Reserve

Sitting at the northwest entrance to Porlier Pass, about 400 m (a quarter-mile) off Valdes Island, Canoe Islet Ecological Reserve is composed of two small, low, rounded bedrock islets. It was made a reserve in 1971 to protect the double-crested cormorant nesting sites here. They were numerous in the 1960s, but the last nests were recorded in 1974. The islets aren't desolate, however. Sea lions have moved in. As many as 100 Steller's and 800 California sea lions have been counted here.

South-southeast of Canoe Islet is the final resting place of the sidewheel steamer *Del Norte*. Look for an information/mooring buoy at N49°01.58' W123°35.30'. The vessel hit rocks here in 1868.

Fretted sandstone at Lyacksun facing the Strait of Georgia.

Camping: N49°03.34' W123°39.40'. Blackberry Point's upland has been made available for public use through an agreement with the logging company owners. Beaches are on either side of the point, behind which is a flat, grassy clearing suitable for group camping. More private tent areas are just south of the point on the edge of the forest cover. A composting toilet has been constructed.

Shah and Detwiller points
The stretch of outer shore between Shah and Detwiller points is heavily subdivided, but so far only sparsely developed. South of Shah Point is a string of south-oriented reefs that act as a good breakwater. Outside the reefs the tidal effects of Porlier Pass may be felt; caution is advised in this area. See page 169 for details on travelling Porlier Pass.

Place names: HM *Shah* was the flagship of Rear Admiral Algernon Frederick Rous DeHorsey on the Pacific coast 1876–78. Lloyd Detwiller was an RCAF pilot, a long-time administrator of the UBC Health Sciences Centre and an early property owner on Valdes Island.

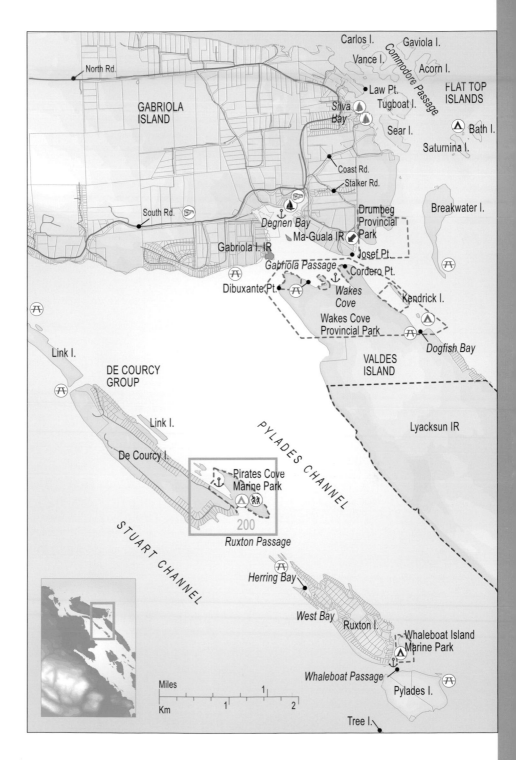

Carlos I.
Gaviola I.
Vance I.
Acorn I.
Commodore Passage
Law Pt.
Tugboat I.
FLAT TOP
ISLANDS
Silva
Bay
Sear I.
Bath I.
Saturnina I.

GABRIOLA
ISLAND

North Rd.

Coast Rd.
Stalker Rd.

Breakwater I.

South Rd.

Drumbeg
Provincial
Park
Degnen Bay
Ma-Guala IR
Josef Pt.

Gabriola I. IR
Gabriola Passage
Cordero Pt.
Dibuxante Pt.
Wakes
Cove
Kendrick I.

Wakes Cove
Provincial Park
Dogfish Bay

Link I.
VALDES
ISLAND

DE COURCY
GROUP

Link I.
Lyacksun IR

De Courcy I.
PYLADES CHANNEL

Pirates Cove
Marine Park

200

Ruxton Passage

STUART CHANNEL

Herring Bay

West Bay
Ruxton I.
Whaleboat Island
Marine Park

Whaleboat Passage
Pylades I.

Miles
1
Km
1
2

Tree I.

Gabriola Passage from Wakes Cove Provincial Park.

Lyacksun

This uninhabited reserve extends from one side of Valdes Island to the other. It is Lyackson First Nation land, used historically for hunting and fishing, with known traditional bathing and burial sites. While private property, there is beautiful shoreline on both sides. A highlight is a picturesque unnamed cove on the Strait of Georgia side. Wonderful arbutus and Garry oak stands dot the upland meadows and fretted sandstone lines the shore. The cove is an established recreation area that's occasionally used as an offbeat but nicely sheltered anchorage. Kayakers may be tempted to camp here. Permission should be sought in advance by contacting the band manager at **250-246-5069.**

PYLADES CHANNEL–GABRIOLA PASSAGE

Pylades Channel connects False Narrows and Gabriola Passage to Trincomali Channel. The De Courcy Group, a line of idyllic islands with numerous passages, coves and sandstone cliffs to explore, borders the southwest side. Tidal currents run as high as 2 knots. The flood sets northwest and the ebb southeast.

Place names: HMS *Pylades* saw service here in 1859–60. She was a 21-gun corvette built in 1854.

Crossing Whaleboat Passage.

Whaleboat Island Marine Park

This diminutive provincial park is sheltered between Ruxton and Pylades islands. The harbour on the west side is popular for over-flow from Pirates Cove as well as residents of Ruxton Island. Most of the shore of the island is steep and rocky. The passage between Whaleboat and Ruxton is a picturesque stretch where eagles invariably watch from the trees.

Whaleboat was made a park in 1981 and protects the entire 10-ha (25-acre) island.

Camping: N49°04.42' W123°41.64'. Whaleboat Island offers the prospect of wilderness backcountry camping. The best landing opportunity is on the southwest corner, where some crushed shell appears at some tide levels; haul out on the rocks at other levels. There are no designated sites but there are places for those looking for rugged wilderness camping. Expect this site to become more popular and developed in the coming years due to congestion at Pirates Cove.

Ruxton and Pylades islands

Ruxton Island was heavily subdivided between 1967 and 1971 and is steadily being built up with cottages. Herring Bay is used mainly for moorage, as is West Bay. North of Herring Bay are numerous islets that become joined by crushed shell at low tides. They are ideal kayak haulouts for a lower-tide picnic or stroll. In the small bay on the northeast side of the peninsula from Herring Bay is a level boat landing where a trail/road leads around the interior of

Sandstone cliffs line the southwest shore of De Courcy.

Ruxton Island. Cars are banned from the island, with the exception of one truck for communal use, so don't expect much in the way of traffic. Neighbouring Pylades Island is divided into just a few properties, with a handful of residences facing south. Some appear derelict. Watch for the abandoned pioneer cabin on the east shore. Cliffs run along the west side of both Ruxton and Pylades. Off Pylades is tiny Tree Island, heavily modified for private use. Tree Island and Danger Reefs, located 1.4 km (0.85 miles) southwest of Tree Island, are part of a series of landmarks that can be followed between the De Courcy Group and Thetis Island, an otherwise open crossing of 4.5 km (2.8 miles). See page 186 for more information.

De Courcy Island

The southwest shore of De Courcy has long been one of my favourite stretches to paddle. The fretted sandstone cliffs are wonderfully intricate. While the shores are mostly residential, the homes on this side of the island are usually above and behind the bluffs and unobtrusive. "The Farm," a large property that has defied subdivision, breaks a road that would otherwise circle the island. On the northeast side of De Courcy, the passages among various off-lying islands are shallow and may run dry at low tides, but they're rich in marine life, particularly shellfish.

Place names: Capt. Michael De Courcy served aboard HMS *Pylades*. While in the Spanish West Indies he is credited with destroying a Spanish force at Carthegena said to be three times the size of his own.

Pirates Cove

This is an excellent place to explore, though it's suffering from overuse. It's most popular as an anchorage, and a volunteer host staffs the float in the cove during the summer. As the cove doesn't flush well, this is a no-discharge zone. Unfortunately, not all boats

Brother XII

Edward Arthur Wilson was a short, slim man who had a history of ship and railway work before turning to the occult. He founded the Aquarian Foundation with the premise that 12 Brothers would become the new leaders of a post-Apocalyptic race known as the Aquarius. Wilson named himself Brother XII. The chosen birthplace for the new race was Cedar-by-the-Sea. The colony spread over time to Valdes Island, on a ridge above locally named Dogfish Bay on the island's east side, and to De Courcy and Ruxton islands. The foundation gained fame and followers; when the dirty laundry was aired in a series of court cases and counter-charges, it made front-page news the world over with stories of free love, black magic and a whip-wielding dominatrix called Madame Zee. Before paying the court-ordered reparations, Brother XII blew up his yacht and destroyed most of the buildings. An enduring story is that boxes of gold coins remain buried on the island.

Pirates Cove toward Ruxton Island.

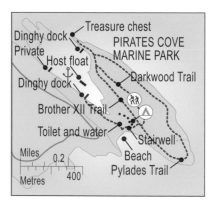

comply and coliform counts in the cove are traditionally high. Two dinghy docks are associated with the provincial park on the east and west shores of the cove; a private wharf and floats are in the northwest corner on private property.

The head of the cove is a rich intertidal area that backs onto a marsh. Because the only beach within Pirates Cove is mucky, visiting kayakers will want to land in the cove on the south side of the island. There you'll find a pleasant beach backed by driftwood and a clamshell and grit causeway and midden. The causeway connects the main De Courcy Island with an off-lying ridge. A wooden stairwell leads up the ridge to a plateau where the camping area is located. A second stairwell leads to the top of the ridge and the various trails that criss-cross the peninsula. On the north headland of the peninsula is a treasure chest filled with tidbits that can often be entertaining—not quite treasure, but not always garbage either. Along the west side of the park is a hand-operated water pump, a composting toilet and a trail that continues north past the dinghy dock to De Courcy's main road.

Camping: N49°05.66' W123°43.54'. Campsites used to be located on both the east and west sides of the causeway, but now the only sites are clustered on the east side on the ridge up the stairwell. A half-dozen wooden tent pads and picnic tables are scattered across the ridge. The old sites have been closed and are covered with slash to deter use. The beach is capped by driftwood that can make carrying gear and kayaks difficult, after which the gear must be carried up the stairs to the camping area—not an easy prospect for some. This can also be a busy campsite—well beyond the capacity of the number of tent pads. Expect the possibility of clustering on summer weekends.

In 1965 the province began negotiating with the owners of De Courcy Island to purchase the peninsula at Pirates Cove. An additional 4 ha (10 acres), including the isthmus, was exchanged for a water lot lease in the cove, and the present-day shape of the park was born. The size is 31 ha (77 acres) with about 2.7 km (1.7 miles) of shore. It tends to be busy, with an average of about 50 boats in the cove on summer weekends and possibly dozens of kayakers.

The role of Brother XII is played up in park literature, while middens, including a large, intact midden between the two coves, reflect a much longer history. Four other middens can be found around the park.

A large sunstar is plucked out of the low tide at Pirates Cove for a short kayak excursion.

Travel notes: The raccoons on De Courcy are veteran camp robbers that have learned to associate campers with food. They are fearless and will dismantle anything improperly secured. Be sure to secure food and garbage at the end of the day, otherwise you'll find your belongings pillaged, dispersed and fought over in loud raccoon disputes in the middle of the night. Don't imagine that closed coolers are secure or that a food bag on a tree branch is out of the way. Tent vestibules are also fair game.

Link Island

This tiny island has never been subdivided, and the only housing is on the south side. It's aptly named for the permanent bar that connects it to Mudge Island. The channel to the south between Link and De Courcy, locally known as Hole in the Wall, is one of those special places—a narrow passage between sculpted sandstone with a crushed shell bed. It will run dry at lower to moderate tides. Current through the gap tends to be low. On the northeast side is a pleasant cove lightly ringed with houses. An appealing island off the north end of Link Island is private property, but a smaller, level rock islet to the north is not. I have seen it used as a campsite; you may want to pass by on your way to Pirates Cove to see if it's appropriate for you (N49°07.39' W123°45.93').

Gabriola Passage

This passage separates Valdes and Gabriola islands. At its narrowest, between Josef and Cordero points, currents can run as high as 8 knots. The flood sets east into the Strait of Georgia. Watch for rips, turbulence and strong currents well beyond the narrows, as far as Breakwater and Kendrick islands. The ebb sets west into Pylades Channel at a maximum of 9 knots.

Southeast of Dibuxante Point is a booming ground. Expect to have to paddle around the extensive log boom.

Navigating by kayak: Running Gabriola Passage is a simple matter of not passing during peak currents. At lesser currents it will be either fun or nerve-wracking. The fastest current is in the vicinity of Josef and Cordero points—the line of no return. You can use the shore to edge quite close to these points to eyeball the danger, and either turn back or run the current, if you feel it is safe.

Degnen Bay

This bay is popular as an anchorage. There is residental development, particularly in the area of the government dock on the northeast shore. Most of the shore is rock bluff or a steep earth embankment. Islands dot the entrance; the largest, Ma-Guala, is a Snuneymuxw reserve.

Opinion is split on the type of creature carved into the rock at Degnen Bay.

The bay has a rich native history. The west entry point of the bay is a burial site. A large petroglyph (of a dolphin, porpoise or killer whale—take your pick of interpretations) is etched into the sandstone just northeast of the government wharf above the high tide line. Look for it between the second and third private docks east of the government dock. More petroglyphs are just a short walk away. If you dock at the government wharf and walk about 1 km (0.6 miles) along south road to the Gabriola United Church property, a trail leads into a park dotted with about 50 petroglyphs. The Weldwood site was discovered in 1977 and includes a serpent 2.5 m (8 feet) long.

Gabriola Island	May	June	July	Aug.	Sept.	Dec.	Av./Ttl.
Daily average temp. (C)	11.7	14.4	16.9	16.8	13.8	3.3	9.5
Daily maximum (C)	16.6	19.3	22.2	22.3	19.2	6.0	13.8
Daily minimum (C)	6.6	9.6	11.4	11.2	8.4	0.6	5.3
Precipitation (mm)	44.9	40.9	26.0	28.2	38.5	137.8	924.0
Days of rainfall + 0.2mm	10.7	9.2	5.9	5.7	7.3	15.2	137.9
Days with rainfall +5mm	3.1	3.0	1.9	1.8	2.3	8.1	58.7
Days with rainfall +10mm	1.0	0.9	0.6	0.9	1.3	4.9	29.1

Wakes Cove

Since Wakes Cove was made a provincial park in 2003, a dinghy dock and mooring buoys have been constructed, giving access to trails that run through the park. Wakes Cove is divided by a headland in the middle. The dinghy dock is located on the east portion along with a private dock along the north headland. All three headlands are private holdings within the park.

Wakes Cove.

Wakes Cove was made a provincial park in 2002. It protects 132 ha (326 acres) of land on Valdes Island and 73 ha (180 acres) of foreshore on the edge of Gabriola Passage across from Degnen Provincial Park. The park includes a stand of old-growth Douglas-fir forest, First Nations middens, rare plants and remnants of an early settlement, including an orchard, the original homestead and farm buildings.

As a new park, interim plans do mention the possibility of overnight camping, but it is currently not allowed. For a break there is a good, gently sloping rock ledge that gives access to a large grassy, forested meadow on the west headland. This would make a good future camp area.

Kendrick Island

Kendrick Island, just outside Gabriola Passage, is ideally located as a base for exploring the Strait of Georgia side of the Gulf Islands. It's owned by the West Vancouver Yacht Club as an outstation. A pair of Crown islets are located just to the southeast. The bay behind the islets, on Valdes, is known locally as Dogfish Bay; it was once a Brother XII settlement (see page 199). It has a passable beach.

Camping: N49°07.22' W123°41.27'. On the more northerly of the two Crown islets is a large, level camping area suitable for a group.

The rock platform dries extensively at low tide at the islet near Kendrick Island.

The Crown Flat Top islet.

The difficulty is the lack of a beach for landing. You can exit onto the sandstone platform shore on the inside (west) side of the island to avoid swell, but the current can be strong.

Flat Top Islands

This group of islands off the east end of Gabriola Island is almost entirely privately owned—even the exposed and wave-battered outer Carlos Island, the reef just north of Tugboat Island, the exposed Brant Reef out in the Strait of Georgia and the small rock to the southwest of Saturnina Island. Only two islets between Saturnina and Bath islands are Crown land. They become joined at low tides. Breakwater Island is remarkable for its sandy dunes along the southern spit. Tucked in behind the Flat Tops is Silva Bay, home to a popular marina with an associated boat-building school. To the south is Page's Resort Marina.

Launches: N48°07.91' W123°41.99'. The best option for reaching the outer waters of Gabriola near the Flat Tops is from the road adjacent to Drumbeg Park. Follow the well-marked road to the park (turn off North Road to Coast, then Stalker), but instead of turning into the park take Stalker to the end. There you'll find a turnabout with two short paths leading to a beach. This will set you at the edge of the

The outer headland of the park at Drumbeg Provincial Park.

Drumbeg Provincial Park

This park protects 20 ha (50 acres) of rolling upland behind a kilometre (0.6 mile) of shoreline on Gabriola's southeast edge. Here you'll find Douglas-fir forest and a midden extending along the majority of the park's shoreline, along with a trail. The park was created in 1971; the name is a tip of the hat to the Scottish roots of former owner, Neil Stalker. It's a day-use park only with picnic tables, benches, an information shelter and a parking lot.

tidal stream from Gabriola Passage, though you may want to stay to the shallows until well away from the influence of the current. An alternative is to enter Drumbeg Park and take the 30-m (100-foot) trail from the parking lot to the beach.

Camping: N49°08.78' W123°40.60'. The two Crown islets between Saturnina and Bath islands are beautifully flat-topped (which should be no surprise), creating level camping areas. The beaches are rough and access points shift with the tide. You may have to make a rock-ledge landing.

NORTH GABRIOLA

On a calm day a trip along the cliffs, bays and wave-etched sandstone rocks of outer Gabriola Island can be worthwhile. But it can also be an exposed place, and winds are often strong near Entrance Island when Pylades Channel is calm. In addition, currents can be strong in Dodd Narrows and False Narrows, and industrialization along Northumberland Channel means dodging log booms, tugs and even large ferries. It's not an area to visit casually unless you stick to short day trips around Taylor, Pilot and Descanso bays.

Cedar-by-the-Sea

Cedar-by-the-Sea is the local name for the oceanfront portion of the large rural area south of Nanaimo known more simply as Cedar. Most recreational use centres on the boat launch south of Dodd Narrows or the moorage at Boat Harbour. Close to the launch is Round Island, a private island with reefs on the south side often used by seals.

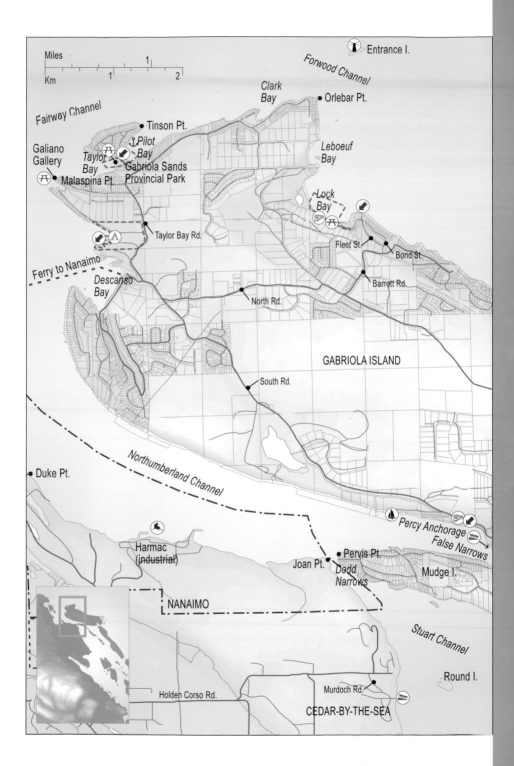

Miles

Km

Entrance I.

Forwood Channel

Clark
Bay

Orlebar Pt.

Fairway Channel

Tinson Pt.

Pilot
Bay

Leboeuf
Bay

Galiano
Gallery

Taylor
Bay

Gabriola Sands
Provincial Park

Malaspina Pt.

Lock
Bay

Fleet St.

Bond St.

Taylor Bay Rd.

Barrett Rd.

Ferry to Nanaimo

Descanso
Bay

North Rd.

GABRIOLA ISLAND

South Rd.

Duke Pt.

Northumberland Channel

Percy Anchorage

False Narrows

Harmac
(industrial)

Joan Pt.

Pervis Pt.

Dodd
Narrows

Mudge I.

NANAIMO

Stuart Channel

Round I.

Holden Corso Rd.

Murdoch Rd.

CEDAR-BY-THE-SEA

Launches: N48°06.89' W123°48.29'. This is a busy site conveniently located for trips to the De Courcy Group. A sand and gravel beach is adjacent to the concrete boat ramp, though carrying gear across the rock from the ramp to the beach can be a problem. To get here, turn east off the Island Highway under the flyway for the Nanaimo Parkway onto Cedar Road. Follow that road straight until the stop sign. Turn right onto McMillan Road. Holden Corso is the next left after the convenience store and gas station. Follow it until Murdoch Road. Parking is congested at the launch; pay close attention to the signs to avoid being towed.

Mudge Island

This is the most developed of the string of islands in the De Courcy Group. It is the only small Gulf Island blessed with electricity, telephone and cable service thanks to power lines crossing the island to Gabriola. What makes it popular for development—accessible, low-banked shoreline—makes it a poor draw for sightseeing. The south shore is close to Dodd Narrows, so use caution. By landing at the beach shared with Link Island you can walk to a park with a bench overlooking Dodd Narrows.

Place names: William Tertius Fitzwilliam Mudge was a lieutenant aboard HMS *Pylades*.

Dodd Narrows

This narrow passage between Vancouver Island and Mudge is prone to currents as high as 9 knots. This can create rips and overfalls on spring tides. Because slower traffic tends to wait for slack before crossing, slack can be a busy period, with tugs, barges, log booms and recreational boaters all using the narrow passage in a short period. The flood sets northwest and the ebb southeast. Watch for the worst rips off Joan Point on the flood and near the overhead cable on the ebb. False Narrows, an alternative route, has currents generally half those in Dodd Narrows.

Place names: Capt. Charles Dodd (1808–60) served the Hudson's Bay Company for 25 years, arriving in British Columbia aboard the paddle steamer *Beaver* in 1835.

Kayaking Dodd Narrows: I sat at Joan Point one afternoon during peak current on a spring tide and had a chance to see the rapids in action. The main stream rushed through the narrows smoothly enough, then collided with the water in Northumberland Channel, creating a nasty series of rips. Where the main stream ran into the eddy alongside Joan Point, the water would crash and spin together and form large whirlpools that would twist along the line where the currents merge, then finally disperse some distance away.

Like all narrows, difficulties diminish at periods of lower current and disappear at slack tide. If you want to run the narrows, heed this advice in *Sailing Directions*: "no attempt should be made to alter course out of the main stream until clear of the turbulence." Given the whirlpools I saw, the advice makes sense for kayakers who may see calm water to the side and wish to escape into it. You may find yourself upon a forming whirlpool if you do.

Duke Point

This point on the shore of Vancouver Island facing Northumberland Channel is home to a large industrial complex, including the Harmac pulp mill with its conspicuous chimneys and emissions, plus Canadian Occidental Petroleum, a deep-sea port and a BC Ferries terminal for service to Tsawwassen. North of Duke Point is a peninsula that ends at Jack Point. The point and a portion of the west headland are part of Nanaimo's Bigg Point Park. A parking lot and access are located off the Duke Point Highway just outside the ferry terminal. A trail leads to the headland. Look for a good picnic beach southwest of the point. Camping isn't allowed. Currents can be strong around Jack Point.

Ecological oddities: **Some businesses have rats as pests. Others have birds. At Harmac, the pests can weight as much as 1,000 kg (2,200 pounds). Every year in late fall hundreds of Steller's and California sea lions converge on the Harmac log boom, lounging on the logs stored in the boom south of the mill. Since this is a working harbour, it often means attempting to move or lift logs with sea lions still resting on them. The bulk of the crowd usually disperses in early December for other points, while a few remain for most of the winter.**

Place names: **The point is named in association with the adjacent channel, which is named after the Duke of Northumberland.**

False Narrows

False Narrows connects Pylades Channel and Northumberland Channel. It moves at half the current of Dodds Narrows, making this a relatively stress-free route between Nanaimo Harbour and the inner Gulf Islands. The flood sets northwest and the ebb southeast. The difficulty is an extensive, shallow shoal at the narrowest portion. It's easy to run aground.

A Coast Salish seasonal village, Senewelets, was located on the Gabriola shore. A midden extended 1.3 km (0.8 miles), with habitation estimated at 2,000 years.

Launches: N48°08.09' W123°46.85'. This popular local boat launch is often used by residents of Mudge Island. To get here, follow South Road to El Verado Drive. Halfway along El Verado is a road leading to the beach. Parking is ample and there's a long shell beach for kayakers to use.

N49°08.39' W123°47.35'. A tiny local park on the waterfront just west of the False Narrows boat launch has parking, picnic tables and a jumble of rocks leading to a beach with some sand areas. This might be preferable for kayakers who want to avoid the boat traffic at the boat launch or want to launch west of the narrows.

Northumberland Channel

This channel extends from False Narrows to Nanaimo Harbour between Vancouver Island and the southwest shore of Gabriola. Due to a more rapid tidal change in the Strait of Georgia than the channels within the shelter of the Gulf Islands, Northumberland Channel runs to the east in both flood and ebb tides. The maximum current is 1–2 knots, even at spring tides. The Gabriola shoreline along the channel is notable for its sheer cliffs. Unfortunately, this is a busy log boom area. Expect several booms and tugs at work, even on weekends. Most kayakers will probably want to navigate the shore near booms nonetheless, as the south shore is heavily industrial and the centre of the channel busy with motorized traffic.

Large BC Ferries vessels regularly transit the entrance to Northumberland Channel to and from the Duke Point terminal. Also, expect the possibility of barges. Sightlines are good, but for extra insurance monitor VHF Channel 11 for the Entrance Island call-in point.

The beach at Descanso Bay Regional Park.

Descanso Bay

The terminal for the ferry to Nanaimo is located in the northeast of Descanso Bay. The former Gabriola Campground, located along the small bays just to the north, is now Descanso Bay Regional Park, with both camping and day-use areas. Not far from the ferry terminal, the Gabriola village centre offers public washrooms, phones, a museum, a post office (V0R 1X0), stores and groceries. The campground's day-use beach is suitable for launching kayaks or canoes.

Place names: Spanish naval officers Galiano and Valdes circumnavigated Vancouver Island in 1792 and used a small anchorage on Gabriola Island. They named it Cala del Descanso—"small bay of rest." The shelter was welcome after a difficult time that day with the currents in Porlier Pass. The explorers spent several days gathering food and resting.

Camping: This is not a marine campground, but conceivably kayakers could land at the beach and walk up the hill to a campsite. It's probably better suited as a staging area for day trips from Gabriola. There are 32 campsites scattered throughout the 24 ha (40 acres) of the regional oceanfront park. Fees apply.

Galiano Gallery.

Malaspina Point

Tucked into a cove here is Galiano Gallery, an overhang of sandstone shaped somewhat like a breaking wave. It's about 90 m (300 feet) in length and 3.5 m (12 feet) high. Spanish explorers Galiano and Valdes found it when they anchored in Descanso Bay in 1792. Galiano's report and an accompanying sketch ultimately made the gallery famous, but not for a hundred years, with much of the credit going to Captain Malaspina (one of the reasons it's often called Malaspina Gallery). A picture of the gallery was included in the book *Voyages by Malaspina*, which went unpublished and sat in Madrid's archives until 1885.

Gabriola Sands Provincial Park
The park was established in 1960 by a donation from the Gabriola Sands Resort Company. Additional land was added in 1983 for a total protected area of 6.7 ha (16.5 acres). Shell middens are at the heads of both Taylor and Pilot bays. This is a day-use park only.

Gabriola Sands

This provincial park extends on both sides of a sandy neck that joins a sizable peninsula to Gabriola. Beaches are to either side of a road that bisects the park. The portion facing Taylor Bay is an open, grassy field. The portion facing Pilot Bay is narrower but treed and in a more natural state. A shopping centre is located a short distant from the beaches.

Launches: N49°11.68' W123°51.48'. Follow Taylor Bay Road north from the ferry terminal; it turns into Berry Point Road. Turn left on Ricardo Road and park facing Pilot Bay. The beach at Pilot Bay is sandy, level and sheltered.

Snake Island

Snake Island, northwest of Gabriola, is about 2.8 km (1.7 miles) from Taylor Bay, 2.4 km (1.5 miles) from Five Finger Island and 3.1 km (1.9 miles) from McKay Point on Newcastle Island. Low, grassy and surrounded by drying rocks, it's the perfect setup for a seabird nesting colony and seal haulout. Access is restricted to protect nesting birds. A shell beach on the south side provides access when allowed. A sign explains access restrictions. If you do get a chance to explore here, a highlight is the sandstone overhangs. For divers, both HMCS *Saskatchewan* and HMCS *Cape Breton* have been sunk nearby as artificial reefs.

Most ferry traffic between Departure Bay and Vancouver uses Rainbow Channel, passing west of Snake Island between it and Four Finger islands. However, ferries from Duke Point to Tsawwassen travel east through Fairway Channel. In addition, the southern extent of Fairway Channel is used by the Gabriola ferry to Descanso Bay.

Sandwell Provincial Park
A long sandy beach, forested upland and saltwater marsh are protected in this park on the north side of Gabriola Island. Picnicking and strolling the beach are favourite activities. The park was founded in 1988 and preserves 12 ha (30 acres), with shell middens and petroglyphs.

Entrance Island

Entrance Island is a bare wedge of rock with a manned lighthouse off the north shore of Gabriola Island. The original light was built in 1875 at a cost of $4,450 plus the loss of three workers who drowned. The first lightkeeper lasted just six months. His successor, Robert Gray, stayed 30 years. Cormorants, ducks and sunning seals use the island's rocks. Most ship traffic will pass north of the island. The line from Entrance Island to Five Finger Island is a Vessel Traffic Services call-in point.

Lock Bay

This bay is a provincial park and popular day-use beach. Be sure to look for two carvings on a large sandstone boulder at the high tide line. Another is carved on a sloping sandstone rock near the high tide line. The depth of the lines indicates they were made with a metal instrument, so they are not considered ancient.

Fretted sandstone at Snake Island.

East of Lock Bay the shoreline becomes sharp, angular cliffs. The uplands above the cliffs were purchased as part of a land settlement, still being negotiated, with the Snuneymuxw First Nation.

NANAIMO AND NEWCASTLE ISLAND

A city harbour normally wouldn't rank a mention in a volume dedicated to wild coasts, but Nanaimo is deceiving that way. At the heart of Nanaimo Harbour is Newcastle, an island protected in its entirety as a provincial park. The park contains wonderful wilderness shoreline just a few minutes of paddling away from a launch site. Other small islands dot the area and include an ecological reserve and the Gulf Islands' only paddle-through cave.

Nanaimo is formerly a coal-mining city; it was first occupied in the 1850s after a rich coal vein was found. Over the following years mines dotted the area. Newcastle Island's heyday, meanwhile, was in the 1930s when the Canadian Pacific Railway expanded its summer steamboat excursion business. In 1930 CPR purchased the island from the Western Fuel Corporation for $30,000. A resort opened in 1931, and CPR vessels were soon bringing as many as 2,500 passengers a day from Vancouver to enjoy the beaches, the pavilion (still on site today), a restaurant and sports grounds. Service was shut down in 1941 due to the war, and a re-launch in 1945 was doomed when automobiles replaced steamers for family getaways. The resort closed in 1950 and was purchased as a city park in 1955. In 1960 it was handed over to the province as B.C.'s second marine park.

Nanaimo Harbour

This is a busy commercial area where ferries, marina traffic and float planes all share the water. Much of the activity centres on the small area of water bounded by the walking/fishing pier and the Visiting Vessel Pier, which is reserved for cruise ships and larger vessels. Moorage for smaller boats is available in the commercial Boat Basin. The harbour monitors VHF Channel 67. Harbour amenities include showers, a laundromat, washrooms, gas, water, ice and a waste pump.

The distinctive, bastion-shaped building north of the Boat Basin is a restaurant and pub with a float plane jetty. Nearby is the historic Bastion, the last remaining defensive fort built by the Hudson's Bay Company. It dates back to 1853 and is now a museum during the summer. Five First Nation villages were located in the area

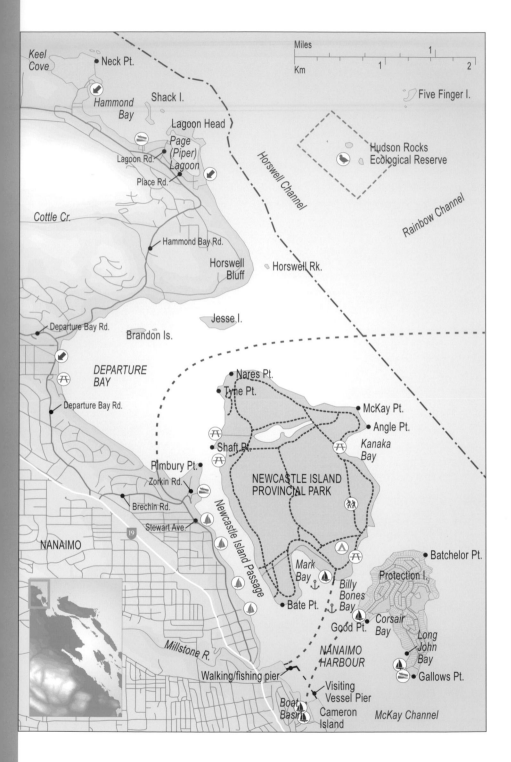

Keel Cove

Neck Pt.

Hammond Bay

Shack I.

Lagoon Head

Page (Piper) Lagoon

Lagoon Rd.

Place Rd.

Cottle Cr.

Hammond Bay Rd.

Horswell Bluff

Horswell Channel

Five Finger I.

Hudson Rocks Ecological Reserve

Rainbow Channel

Horswell Rk.

Jesse I.

Departure Bay Rd.

Brandon Is.

DEPARTURE BAY

Departure Bay Rd.

Nares Pt.

Tyne Pt.

McKay Pt.

Angle Pt.

Shaft Pt.

Kanaka Bay

Pimbury Pt.

Zorkin Rd.

NEWCASTLE ISLAND PROVINCIAL PARK

Brechin Rd.

Stewart Ave.

19

NANAIMO

Newcastle Island Passage

Mark Bay

Bate Pt.

Batchelor Pt.

Protection I.

Billy Bones Bay

Good Pt.

Corsair Bay

Long John Bay

Millstone R.

NANAIMO HARBOUR

Walking/fishing pier

Visiting Vessel Pier

Boat Basin

Cameron Island

Gallows Pt.

McKay Channel

Miles

Km

1

1

2

Paddling past Old Man and Old Woman rocks.

now occupied by the city: Solachwan, Tewahlchin, Anuweenis, Kwalsiarwahl and Ishihan.

Cameron Island, so named despite now being connected to Nanaimo with landfill, is topped with a tower and residential complex. Walkways connect the waterfront from Cameron Island to beyond the Departure Bay ferry terminal. Plans are in place to eventually complete the waterfront walk to the beach at Departure Bay.

Just south of Cameron Island is the ferry terminal for service to Gabriola Island. To get there, take the old Island Highway (19A) through Nanaimo and turn east onto Esplanade at Port Place Mall. The entry is south of the Cameron Island residential tower. South of the ferry terminal is a bulk freight and barge facility.

South of Nanaimo is a huge, drying mud flat that ends in the Nanaimo River estuary, with industrial use and substantial log booming.

Place names: Nanaimo is the anglicization of the Hul'qumi'num word for the area. Various translations are "meeting place," "group of many people" or "people of many names."

Protection Island

This island is within city limits, which gives residents the unusual luxury of services such as municipal water and sewer. There's an eclectic assortment of homes and shacks along with a good percentage of parkland. Its only commercial amenity is the Dinghy Dock Pub, on floats by the island's ferry dock. The island is served by regular foot passenger service from Nanaimo's Boat Basin.

Place names: The name is a description of the island's role in protecting Nanaimo Harbour. Two First Nations men were hanged at Gallows Point in 1853 for the murder of a Hudson's Bay Company employee in Fort Victoria. They were the first people in British Columbia to be condemned to death by jury.

Billy Bones Bay

This bay is protected by the small passage that runs between Newcastle and Protection Islands. It and Mark Bay are popular anchorages. The passage between the islands runs dry at low tide. The upland on Newcastle Island adjacent to Billy Bones Bay has a public dock, a playground, washrooms, the historic pavilion and the camping area.

Camping: N49°10.96' W123°55.59'. The 18 designated walk-in sites on Newcastle Island are located in a forest setting northeast of the dock, relatively convenient to the beach for kayakers. Amenities include flush toilets, showers, water and a food concession in season. Group camping is available in a large grassy clearing.

Newcastle Island Passage

This busy navigational channel between Vancouver and Newcastle islands is lined on the west side with marinas, wharves and jetties. The Newcastle Island side is undeveloped parkland. Float planes land in Departure Bay and taxi through the northern limit of the passage to a dock near Pimbury Point. There is a 5-knot speed limit in the channel. Wind in the channel is usually a fraction of that in the outer waters. Currents are not quite minimal; they won't stop you, but may slow you.

Place names: Hudson's Bay Company officers named the island and channel in 1853 after the coal city of Newcastle upon Tyne in Northumberland.

Launches: N49°11.42' W123°56.94'. There are two boat ramps and two associated docks at the Brechin boat ramp. Kayakers normally use the south ramp. You can launch from the dock or the rough beach south of the boat ramp. A kayak rental centre is located adjacent to the boat ramp. The launch is opposite the ferry terminal off Zorkin Road.

Shaft Point

South of Shaft Point is a remnant of Newcastle Island's limestone mining history. The limestone was used for buildings such as the US Mint in San Francisco. The *Zephyr* was carrying 800 tonnes of limestone for the mint in 1872, including two 8-m (27-foot) pillars, when she ran aground and sank at Mayne Island. In 1987 one of the pillars was raised from the water and transported back to where it was mined 105 years earlier. It's visible from the water almost directly across from the Brechin boat ramp. On both sides of Shaft Point are pleasant sandy beaches with grassy uplands. North of Shaft Point the sea floor is shallow and sandy well offshore. Watch for swell created by recreational boat traffic and the ferries, as it's amplified in the shallows. A strobe light just off the point is activated when float planes are landing or taking off.

Nares to McKay points

This stretch on the north side of Newcastle Island contains impressive cliff scenery, with exposed bedrock looming 25 m (80 feet) up from the water. These bluffs are among the best examples of coastal bluff ecology on the coast. Near Nares Point look for Old Man Rock and Old Woman Rock, thought to be powerful spirits.

Toward McKay Point as you leave the protection of Departure Bay the mood of the water can change. Novice kayakers should be especially wary of the shallow water around McKay Point. Swell will be steep and amplifed by the shallows. Also, watch for submerged rocks.

Newcastle Island Marine Park

This 306-ha (756-acre) park in Nanaimo Harbour is just five minutes by ferry from the bustle of downtown Nanaimo. As well as being a wildlife preserve, it's rich in history. A midden marks a Salish village abandoned before the arrival of the first Europeans. Coal was mined here from 1853 to 1883, and there are remnants of two separate operations, one at Kanaka Bay. Remains of a Japanese settlement north of Shaft Point are still visible: machinery, bricks and timbers are what's left of a saltery and shipyard dismantled by the Canadian Navy in 1945. Harkening back to the 1930s heyday of the island is the CPR pavilion, which is still open for special events during the summer. Other resort-era reminders are the old wading pool, shuffleboard and checkers structures. Connecting the various points of interest on the island are 21 km (13 miles) of trails.

Kanaka Bay

This sheltered cove on the outside of Newcastle Island is a popular recreation beach. It dries extensively; a rocky islet in the centre of the bay becomes landlocked at lower tides.

Place names: Peter Kakua was an early settler from Hawaii, one of the people known collectively as Kanakans, who were recruited by the Hudson's Bay Company. Peter was common-law partner to a First Nations woman, Que-en, whom he murdered with an axe, along with his father-in-law, mother-in-law and infant baby, in a drunken rage. He then got in a rowboat and set off for the mainland, but only made it as far as Kanaka Bay, where he built a fire, drank more and was soon arrested. He was hanged in 1869 and buried near where he was captured.

Departure Bay

This bay is a focal point for Nanaimo; housing is clustered on the nearby hills to take advantage of the ocean views. The recreational hub of the bay is the expansive sandy beach at its head, backed by a breakwater and seawall, a grassy picnic area and parking. From the ferry terminal, in the south part of the bay near Pimbury Point, a regular stream of large, fast ferries transit the bay in a route south of Jesse Island. Sightlines are generally good but the ferries move quickly and create a large wash that might intimidate novice kayakers.

Within Departure Bay are several islands. The Brandon Islands are used by the Pacific Biological Station and are home to B.C.'s first fish farm, which started in 1974. It still has fish pens but they're now used for research, which lately has been focusing on generating new species for farming. The Pacific Biological Station, run by Fisheries and Oceans Canada, is located on the north shore of the bay. Other research by the station includes working in the Philippines to save the endangered sea horse.

Jesse Island is privately owned. Watch for guard dogs. The north shore is sandstone cliff and includes a short paddle-through cave— the only one in the Gulf Islands. Horswell Rock, just outside the north entrance to Departure Bay, is a seal haulout.

Place names: This was originally known as Wintuhuysen Inlet but was renamed by Hudson's Bay Company officers in 1852 for its role as an appropriate place for ships to depart Nanaimo Harbour. Entrance

The cave at Jesse Island.

Island, by contrast, was considered the ideal entry route. The Salish name is Tslalup, meaning "country around Nanaimo."

Launches: N49°12.27' W123°58.10'. The beach at Departure Bay is accessible via steps from the seawall. Day parking is adjacent to the seawall. This is a well-used local launch for day trips. A drawback is the extent to which the beach dries at low tide.

Weather

Departure Bay (Nanaimo)	May	June	July	Aug.	Sept.	Dec.	Av./Ttl.
Daily average temp. (C)	12.3	15.2	17.7	18.1	14.9	4.1	10.2
Daily maximum (C)	16.3	19.1	21.8	22.1	18.8	6.4	13.6
Daily minimum (C)	8.3	11.4	13.6	14.0	10.9	1.7	6.8
Precipitation (mm)	45.8	41.8	25.1	32.0	41.3	151.7	937.8
Days of rainfall + 0.2mm	12.6	10.4	6.9	6.8	9.0	18.4	
Days with rainfall +5mm	3.2	2.8	1.7	2.3	2.7	8.9	
Days with rainfall +10mm	1.0	1.1	0.6	0.8	1.1	5.1	
Wind speed (km/h)	9.4	9.3	10.0	9.2	8.1	9.0	
Prevailing direction	E	E	NW	NW	NW	SE	

This 50-ha (124-acre) reserve was established to protect seabird habitat for glaucous-winged gull, pelagic cormorant, black oystercatcher and pigeon guillemot. It was also a double-crested cormorant nesting site, but the last recorded nests were in 1995. Pelagic cormorant numbers have also fallen dramatically, from a population once considered nationally significant—142 nests—to just 3 nests in 2000. The rocks were made a reserve in 1996.

The reserve protects five low, rocky islets, the nearby reefs and the surrounding marine area.

Five Finger Island

This is the largest of a group of rugged, windswept rocks located off the north end of Departure Bay. They are home to numerous marine birds and the occasional sunning seal. It's a favourite trolling area for recreational fishermen.

Five Finger Island is bare and rugged. It gets its name from its five hillocks, which can look like the knuckles of a clenched fist. The island is the northern limit of the Vessel Traffic Services call-in point for Entrance Island.

Piper Lagoon

Once upon a time whales were common in the Strait of Georgia, and until the early 1900s whales were hunted, floated into Hammond Bay and beached on Shack Island. In 1907 Pacific Whaling purchased the upland at the lagoon and built a whaling station complete with docks, ramps and bunkhouses for 125 workers. In 1907, 97 whales were beached, each averaging 50 tons. But the whales disappeared from the Strait of Georgia and the last was beached in 1908. In 1912 the whaling station's machinery was moved to Rose Harbour in the Queen Charlotte Islands.

The neck of land, Lagoon Head, was slated for development but instead was purchased as a local park. Trails lead along the causeway to the cliffs at Lagoon Head. It's an exceptionally pretty area.

Place names: The real name for this lagoon is Page Lagoon, a name registered in 1911. The local name is exclusively Piper Lagoon, with no known significance for either Piper or Page.

Launches: N49°13.40' W123°56.81'. Kayaks can be launched from the outer beach adjacent to the parking lot. Slightly north of the park is a local boat ramp with a steep shore area and not much beach space for loading kayaks. Parking is available at the top of the hill.

Five Finger Island.

Shack Island

This is one of the most-painted locations on Vancouver Island. Picturesque old shacks are crammed onto the island's rocky shore, many built under jagged cliffs. The first shacks popped up in the 1890s as driftwood shelters. Because it was Crown land they were rent free. By the 1930s, during the Depression, about 20 cabins filled the island. Not all were escaping poverty, either. One Finnish family, the Luomas, built highly valued rowboats using cedar driftwood. The shacks remain today thanks to squatter's rights. At low tide the island can be reached by foot from the peninsula at Piper Lagoon.

Neck Point

This is another city park with trails leading around the headlands. The rocks just off the point are popular with divers.

Launches: N49°13.98' W123°57.85'. Across from the main parking lot in Neck Point Park is a steep cobble beach that is nicely sheltered in most conditions. To get here, find your way onto Hammond Bay Road and turn at Morningside Drive.

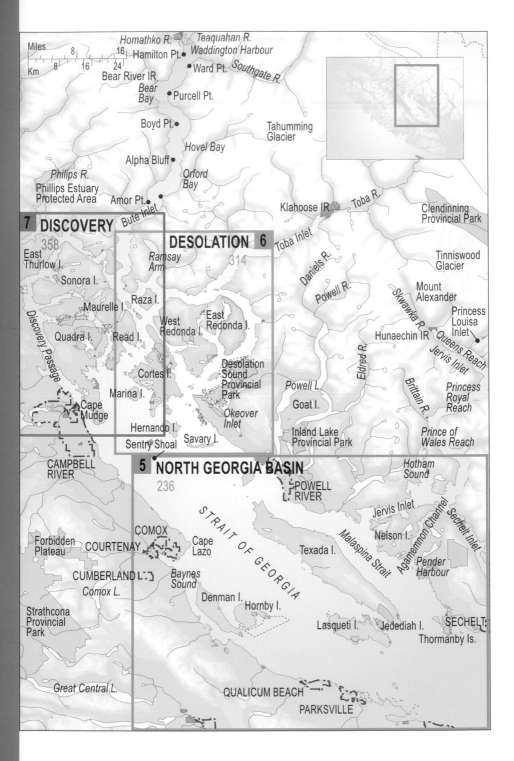

Miles
Km

Homathko R.
Hamilton Pt.
Teaquahan R.
Waddington Harbour
Ward Pt.
Southgate R.
Bear River IR
Bear Bay
Purcell Pt.
Boyd Pt.
Tahumming Glacier
Hovel Bay
Alpha Bluff
Orford Bay
Philips R.
Phillips Estuary Protected Area
Amor Pt.
Bute Inlet
Klahoose IR
Toba R.
Clendinning Provincial Park

7 DISCOVERY
358
East Thurlow I.
Sonora I.
Ramsay Arm
DESOLATION 6
314
Toba Inlet
Daniels R.
Tinniswood Glacier
Maurelle I.
Raza I.
Powell R.
Mount Alexander
Skwawka R.
Princess Louisa Inlet
West Redonda I.
East Redonda I.
Hunaechin IR
Queens Reach
Jervis Inlet
Quadra I.
Read I.
Eldred R.
Discovery Passage
Cortes I.
Desolation Sound Provincial Park
Powell L.
Brittain R.
Princess Royal Reach
Marina I.
Goat I.
Cape Mudge
Okeover Inlet
Inland Lake Provincial Park
Prince of Wales Reach
Hernando I.
Savary I.
Sentry Shoal

5 NORTH GEORGIA BASIN
236
Hotham Sound
POWELL RIVER
CAMPBELL RIVER
Jervis Inlet
Nelson I.
Agamemnon Channel
Sechelt Inlet
COMOX
Cape Lazo
Forbidden Plateau
COURTENAY
STRAIT OF GEORGIA
Texada I.
Malaspina Strait
Pender Harbour
CUMBERLAND
Baynes Sound
Comox L.
Denman I.
Hornby I.
Strathcona Provincial Park
Lasqueti I.
Jedediah I.
SECHELT
Thormanby Is.
Great Central L.
QUALICUM BEACH
PARKSVILLE

PART TWO

Discovery, Sunshine and Desolation

WHAT WONDERFUL NAMES TO INSPIRE THE IMAGINATION: DISCOVERY islands, Sunshine Coast and Desolation Sound. These three key regions include the north end of the Strait of Georgia and several of the largest inlets in British Columbia. They arguably encompass the greatest range of sightseeing options anywhere on the B.C. coast, from charming island clusters north of Lasqueti Island to the precipitous mountains of Toba and Jervis inlets. Key communities for this region are Powell River, Sechelt and Lund on the mainland and Campbell River and Comox on Vancouver Island. These make good jumping-off points to wilderness that is never far away.

GETTING HERE

By road

There are two potential road routes into this region. On the mainland Highway 101 extends as far north as Lund. Getting to Lund from Vancouver, however, requires two ferries—one across Howe Sound and another across Jervis Inlet. The alternative is to approach from the Vancouver Island side along Highway 19, which follows most of the east coast of Vancouver Island. North of Campbell River the highway veers inland, and logging roads are the only access to north Discovery Passage and south Johnstone Strait. This transportation hurdle makes the Discovery Islands much more difficult to reach, keeping Desolation Sound and Sechelt Inlet, both of which have good road access from Vancouver, as the main kayaking routes.

Chatterbox Falls, Princess Louisa Inlet.

By ferry

Extensive travel in this region is almost certain to require multiple ferry links. The mainland highway link, Highway 101, requires two ferries: across Howe Sound from Horseshoe Bay to Langdale and across Jervis Inlet from Earls Cove to Saltery Bay. There are also ferries from Comox on Vancouver Island to Powell River and to Texada Island from Powell River.

For those wishing to reach the Discovery Islands, ferry service is available from Campbell River to Quadra Island, with a second ferry between Quadra and Cortes islands. This makes Cortes a difficult place to reach from the mainland. Paddling from Lund could well be quicker!

BC Ferries offers vehicle service to Denman Island with a link between Denman and Hornby Island. Lasqueti is serviced only by an independently run foot passenger ferry that has limited room for kayaks. BC Ferries promotes a coastal circle tour for trips from Vancouver to Sechelt to Powell River to Courtenay to Nanaimo (or Victoria) and back to Vancouver—a great way to combine an exploration of Vancouver Island, the Gulf Islands and the Sunshine Coast without backtracking. Side trips by ferry are possible to Texada,

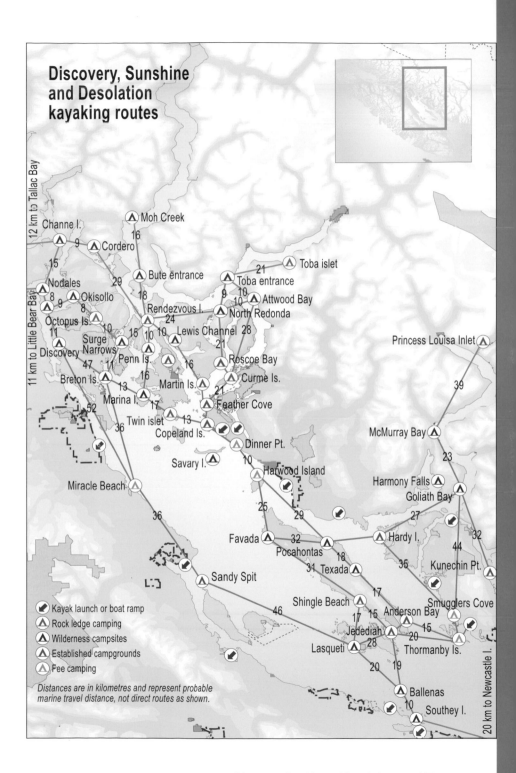

Discovery, Sunshine and Desolation kayaking routes

12 km to Tallac Bay

11 km to Little Bear Bay

Channe I.

Moh Creek

16

9

Cordero

15

Nodales

29

Bute entrance

8

9

Okisollo

18

8

Octopus Is.

10

Surge

11

Narrows

15

10

10

Lewis Channel

Discovery

47

Penn Is.

11

Breton Is.

13

16

16

Martin Is.

Marina I.

17

Twin islet

13

36

Copeland Is.

Savary I.

Miracle Beach

36

Favada

32

Pocahontas

18

31

Texada

Sandy Spit

Shingle Beach

46

Jedediah

Lasqueti

28

20

19

Toba islet

21

Toba entrance

9

10

10

Attwood Bay

North Redonda

28

21

Roscoe Bay

Curme Is.

21

Feather Cove

Dinner Pt.

10

Harwood Island

25

29

Princess Louisa Inlet

39

McMurray Bay

23

Harmony Falls

Goliath Bay

27

Hardy I.

32

44

35

Kunechin Pt.

17

15

Anderson Bay

Smugglers Cove

17

15

20

Thormanby Is.

24

Rendezvous I.

Ballenas

10

Southey I.

20 km to Newcastle I.

11 km to Little Bear Bay

Kayak launch or boat ramp

Rock ledge camping

Wilderness campsites

Established campgrounds

Fee camping

Distances are in kilometres and represent probable marine travel distance, not direct routes as shown.

Codfish Bay, Jedediah Island.

Lasqueti, Denman or Hornby islands. This offers a superb opportunity for kayakers who prefer day trips to overnight kayaking. It would be possible to car-camp or stay at bed and breakfasts while cherry-picking the best day trips. This would allow you to see a wide range of geography without having to mount a kayaking expedition—a leisurely way to see lots of coast.

By kayak

The established kayaking areas for this region are Desolation Sound and Sechelt Inlet. Jedediah Island is a growing alternative, while a few kayakers stray as far as Cortes Island, Toba Inlet and Surge Narrows on Quadra Island. From there the routes tend to peter out, with no real established campsites through Okisollo or Cordero channels. This creates a striking contrast: Desolation Sound and Sechelt Inlet can be filled to capacity during the summer, while the northern regions are rarely visited. Day trips are most popular around places such as Thormanby Islands, Pender Harbour and Hornby Island.

Transiting the region: The B.C. coast is made for adventures, and every year a handful of kayakers attempt to run the coast from Vancouver or Washington State to Alaska, while others choose to travel portions of the coast—such as Bella Coola to Vancouver (a highly recommended trip). Whatever the agenda, it makes sense to travel north to south to get the assistance of the prevailing northwest winds of the B.C. coast. If you don't, you will essentially be travelling against the weather when those good high-pressure systems set up offshore.

Anyone passing through the south coast has a choice of routes through this region: the mainland, along Vancouver Island or along either side of Texada Island. As someone who has travelled these routes, I strongly suggest avoiding the Vancouver Island coast unless you are a strong kayaker whose only goal is to make good time. There are few attractions and just as few campsites. I've included Miracle Beach on the kayaking route map as a key campsite option as it is the only designated spot along

Basaltic volcanic bedrock is the foundation for much of Lasqueti, Texada and Jedediah islands.

that stretch of Vancouver Island, though I suspect kayakers will have little trouble finding a good beach somewhere other than the park to throw up a tent. The portion from Denman Island (Sandy Spit) to Nanaimo is particularly problematic. The best beaches tend to be public property—such as along the Qualicum Beach waterfront, through downtown Parksville and at Rathtrevor Beach Provincial Park—and beachfront camping is restricted. For that and a plethora of other reasons, including the famous Qualicum winds, I suggest leaving the Vancouver Island side to travel along Lasqueti—a transiting itinerary being maybe Ballenas-Jedediah-Favada-Copeland Islands. Or from the mainland switch Thormanby for Ballenas. The countryside on this route is prettier and casual campsites more plentiful.

More about travelling the coast is offered in the epilogue.

GEOLOGY AND ECOLOGY

Two things will strike kayakers along this part of the coast. One is the lack of sandy beaches across most of the region. The other is how sand is concentrated in certain places, such as Savary and Marina islands.

As with most of the geography on the coast, you can blame the ice age. When the Cordilleran Ice Sheet covered the coast as little as 14,000 years ago, it scoured most of the region down to the granite bedrock, leaving what it scoured in occasional pockets of sand and gravel. So while Cortes Island mostly has granite shoreline, nearby Twin Islands is sedimentary bedrock and Marina Island has a sandy beach, thanks to erosion of the glacial debris by waves.

Another feature of this region is differences in water temperatures. Some areas, like Desolation Sound, are known for warm water, while other nearby channels may be frigid in comparison. One reason for this is that many of the inlets and channels are deep and don't flush well. This leads to stratified water levels, where the deepest water doesn't mix with the surface. This and fresh water on the surface can create a warm water temperature, causing another common feature for this area—frequent algae blooms, which can include dangerous red tide.

Another influence on the water temperature is the flow from Howe Sound and the Fraser River. This causes a distinct difference in the water salinity and temperature between Cortes and Texada islands, for instance.

This region is shy on seabird nesting sites, but it does support spring and fall migrations of marine and shore birds, especially in the north end of the Strait of Georgia and Desolation Sound. Loons, cormorants, diving ducks and gulls winter in this area, while Desolation Sound is remarkable for its healthy population of about 5,000 marbled murrelet. The number was established following a five-year banding study.

Whale and orca sightings in this area are rare, though killer whales were once common around Campbell River. Rare species you stand a better chance of seeing in this region are Steller's sea lion, barn owl, marbled murrelet, northern goshawk (*laingi* subspecies), peregrine falcon (*anatum* subspecies), short-tailed albatross, western screech-owl, coast tailed frog, northern abalone, Olympia oyster and monarch butterfly. The coastal wood fern is found only on Denman,

Hornby and the Winchelsea-Ballenas islands. The Winchelseas are also one of the few places to find water-plantain buttercup.

FIRST NATIONS OVERVIEW

This region is inhabited by First Nations of both Kwakwaka'wakw and Coast Salish descent. The Kwakwaka'wakw is a relatively new term to refer to the collective of First Nations that speak the Kwak'wala language, one that falls under the larger Wakashan umbrella. The Kwakwaka'wakw group was previously referred to as Kwakiult, which now names a single First Nation based out of Port Hardy. If you visit this region, you are likely to enter the traditional lands of some of the following First Nations.

Sechelt: The traditional territory of the Sechelt First Nation includes Jervis Inlet, Sechelt Inlet, Nelson Island and the south end of Texada Island. There were originally four groups, or septs—the Kunechin, Tsonai, Tuwanek and Skaiakos. They have since combined to live in one area, Chatelech, which centres on the old Roman Catholic mission location in Sechelt. Today the band numbers just over 1,000 members.

The Sechelt also go by the historic name Shishalh. The Sechelt First Nation was the first in Canada to be granted self-government.

Sliammon (Tla'amin): The Sliammon had three main historic villages: Tohk natch at Okeover Inlet, Toh kwon non in Theodesia Inlet and Kah Kee Ky in Grace Harbour. Through the treaty process the band is gaining new territory in the Desolation Sound area, including the eastern side of Okeover Inlet and the lands northwest of Theodesia Inlet. Plans for the band include reopening its Mermaid Oyster Producers processing plant on the south end of Okeover Inlet and processing wild clams from Savary Island.

The Sliammon today are centred just outside Powell River. About 650 of the band's 1,000 members live in the main village. Harwood Island falls within their land holdings.

Klahoose: The main Klahoose village is located at Squirrel Cove on Cortes Island. About 60 families live on the Tork reserve on the cove's east shore, with a community centre, church, band office and playground. There is no road access. The band numbers about 290.

Xwémalhkwu (Homalco): The main Xwémalhkwu village was located in Calm Channel at Church House, but is now largely abandoned. Today the band is centred out of Campbell River, where it maintains a cultural centre and band administration offices. Its membership is about 448.

In years past the Xwémalhkwu territory was extensive, with villages on Thurlow, Sonora and Stuart islands as well as Philips Arm and Bute Inlet up to Southgate and Homathco rivers. The band's nine reserves protect many traditional village sites.

Kwiakah: This is a small group numbering just over 20 members, with reserves in Philips Arm and just north of Stuart Island. Most band members live at the reserve in Campbell River.

Wei Wai Kum (Campbell River First Nation): The Wei Wai Kum First Nation has 598 band members, about 332 of whom are centred at the reserve in Campbell River. The band has unoccupied reserves in Loughborough Inlet and Cordero Channel.

We Wai Kai (Cape Mudge First Nation): The band membership of the We Wai Kai First is 845. The community is centred at its name-sake Cape Mudge reserve with other lands on Quadra Island and at Quinsam River.

K'omoks (Comox): The K'omoks originally had territory along Vancouver Island from the Salmon River area to Cape Lazo, including portions of Quadra Island and other nearby islands. A main settlement was a village at Comox River. That was abandoned in 1917 and is now the Salmon River Indian Reserve. The K'omoks are considered the Northern Coast Salish, but they spoke a different dialect, with the last speaker of the language having died in 1995. The band numbers 273. There are currently about 160 members living on the main reserve in Comox, with the band numbering 273. The reserve has a recreation building and gallery/gift shop.

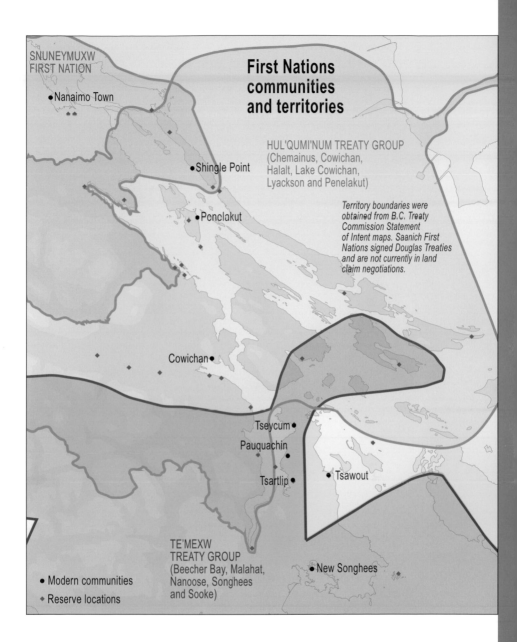

First Nations communities and territories

SNUNEYMUXW
FIRST NATION

•Nanaimo Town

•Shingle Point

•Penelakut

HUL'QUMI'NUM TREATY GROUP
(Chemainus, Cowichan,
Halalt, Lake Cowichan,
Lyackson and Penelakut)

*Territory boundaries were
obtained from B.C. Treaty
Commission Statement
of Intent maps. Saanich First
Nations signed Douglas Treaties
and are not currently in land
claim negotiations.*

Cowichan•

Tseycum•

Pauquachin
•

Tsartlip•   •Tsawout

TE'MEXW
TREATY GROUP
(Beecher Bay, Malahat,
Nanoose, Songhees
and Sooke)

•New Songhees

• Modern communities

◆ Reserve locations

Jervis Inlet.

The North Georgia Basin

CHAPTER FIVE

SECHELT INLET IS THE ONLY PLACE IN BRITISH COLUMBIA WITH A designated system of campsites created specifically for marine-based camping—a half-dozen camping locations each protected as part of Sechelt Inlets Marine Park. It has become one of the busiest kayaking spots in the province, thanks to the convenient campsite network and its proximity to Vancouver.

Of course, busy does not mean better, especially when it comes to kayaking campsites, so it should be no surprise that when the park in Sechelt Inlet is battling capacity issues, nearby Jervis Inlet is rarely visited by paddle, despite having some of the best scenery in the province, including legendary Princess Louisa Inlet. This could be because so many people say it can't be paddled. Don't believe it. It makes a perfect kayaking destination, as you'll see.

Gaining popularity as a destination is Jedediah Island, a relatively new provincial park that sits amid an archipelago perfect for kayaking. The archipelago lies in the centre of the north end of the Georgia Basin, a huge inland sea that extends to the United States and includes Juan de Fuca Strait, the Strait of Georgia and Puget Sound, as well as the adjacent drainage systems of valleys, lowlands and mountain slopes.

This portion of the basin offers probably the most diverse range of options for exploration on the coast—from imposing Texada Island to the sprinkling of small islands and islets that form the Winchelsea-Ballenas archipelago. And, naturally, kayakers rarely visit many of the best features.

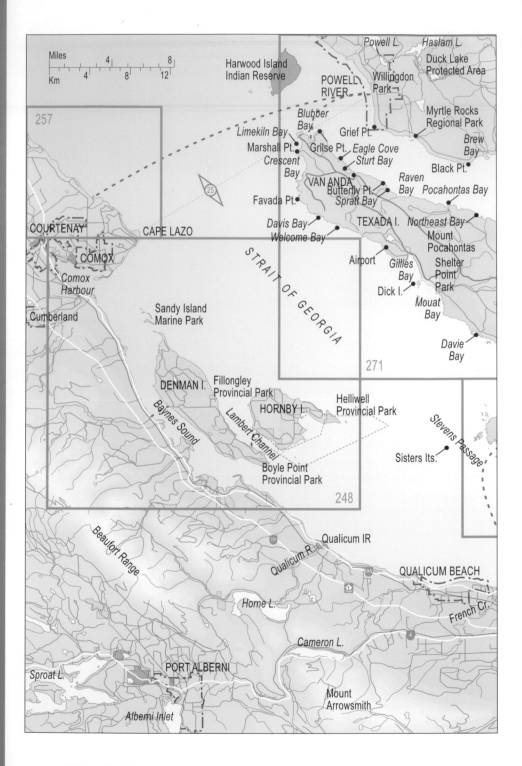

Miles
4   8
Km
4   8   12

257

Powell L.   Haslam L.
Duck Lake
Protected Area

Harwood Island
Indian Reserve

POWELL
RIVER

Willingdon
Park

Blubber
Bay

Myrtle Rocks
Regional Park

Limekiln Bay   Grief Pt.

Marshall Pt.   Grilse Pt.   Eagle Cove

Brew
Bay

Crescent
Bay   Sturt Bay

Black Pt.

VAN ANDA

Favada Pt.   Butterfly Pt.

Spratt Bay

Raven
Bay   Pocahontas Bay

Davis Bay   Northeast Bay

Welcome Bay   TEXADA I.   Mount
Pocahontas

Airport   Gillies
Bay   Shelter
Point
Park

Dick I.

Mouat
Bay

Davie
Bay

COURTENAY   CAPE LAZO

COMOX

Comox
Harbour

S T R A I T   O F   G E O R G I A

271

Cumberland

Sandy Island
Marine Park

DENMAN I.   Fillongley
Provincial Park

Helliwell
Provincial Park

Baynes Sound

Lambert Channel   HORNBY I.

Stevens Passage

Sisters Its.

Boyle Point
Provincial Park

248

Beaufort Range

Qualicum IR

Qualicum R.

QUALICUM BEACH

Horne L.

French Cr.

Cameron L.

Sproat L.

PORT ALBERNI

Mount
Arrowsmith

Alberni Inlet

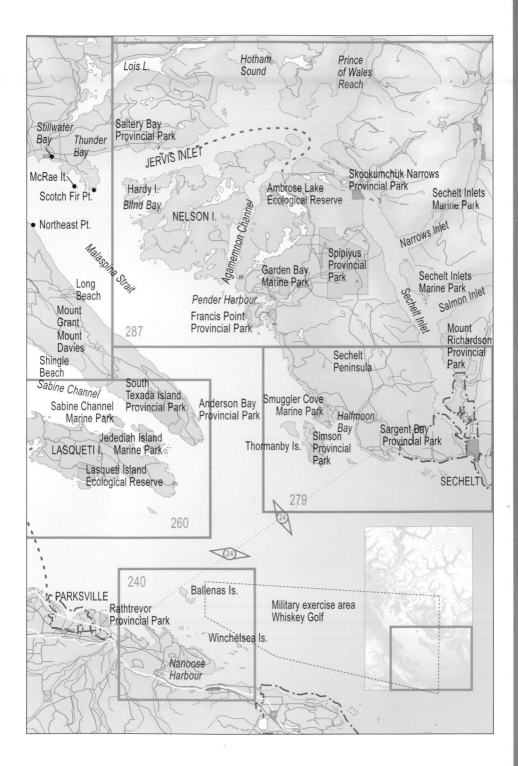

Lois L.

Hotham
Sound

Prince
of Wales
Reach

Stillwater
Bay

Thunder
Bay

Saltery Bay
Provincial Park

JERVIS INLET

McRae It.

Scotch Fir Pt.

Hardy I.

Blind Bay

Ambrose Lake
Ecological Reserve

Skookumchuk Narrows
Provincial Park

Sechelt Inlets
Marine Park

Northeast Pt.

NELSON I.

Agamemnon Channel

Narrows Inlet

Malaspina Strait

Long
Beach

Garden Bay
Marine Park

Spipiyus
Provincial
Park

Sechelt Inlets
Marine Park

Sechelt Inlet

Salmon Inlet

Mount
Grant

Pender Harbour

Mount
Davies

Francis Point
Provincial Park

Mount
Richardson
Provincial
Park

Shingle
Beach

Sechelt
Peninsula

Sabine Channel

South
Texada Island
Provincial Park

Anderson Bay
Provincial Park

Smuggler Cove
Marine Park

287

Sabine Channel
Marine Park

Halfmoon
Bay

Sargent Bay
Provincial Park

Jedediah Island
Marine Park

Thormanby Is.

Simson
Provincial
Park

LASQUETI I.

SECHELT

Lasqueti Island
Ecological Reserve

279

260

24

240

24

PARKSVILLE

Ballenas Is.

Military exercise area
Whiskey Golf

Rathtrevor
Provincial Park

Winchelsea Is.

Nanoose
Harbour

19

Exploring by kayak

This area differs in that most destinations are more easily reached from the mainland than Vancouver Island. Beginner locations would be areas like Baynes Sound, Thormanby Island or Sechelt Inlet. Advanced kayakers will relish the challenge of Jervis Inlet or the extra distance to Jedediah Island.

Recommended kayaking trips

- *If you have a day:* Good day trips would be to the Thormanby Islands from Halfmoon Bay, Harmony Falls from Egmont, Harwood Island from Powell River, Sandy Spit from Comox, Hornby Island from your choice of Denman, Hornby or Vancouver islands, or the Winchelsea Islands from Lantzville. You may also want to play around Skookumchuck during a tide turn.

- *If you have two days:* A trip up Sechelt Inlet and back would be fun, preferably getting as far as Tzoonie Narrows for the best scenery. A circumnavigation of Denman Island, launching from Deep Bay, would be interesting. For shorter trips you could overnight at Thormanby Islands, Hotham Sound from Egmont, or possibly Smuggler Cove from Pender Harbour or Halfmoon Bay.

- *If you have three days:* From Halfmoon Bay a good fairweather trip would be to Jedediah Island, spending the middle day exploring the islands.

- *If you have five days:* Texada Island is an interesting circumnavigation for people who don't mind chalking up the miles. An itinerary could be Halfmoon Bay, Anderson Bay, Pocahontas, Favada, Jedediah and back. You could easily extend this by spending more time at Jedediah and Lasqueti. For others, exploring Sechelt Inlet is a great way to spend five days, though be warned about the crowds during summer. Princess Louisa Inlet is a more adventurous destination but achievable in that time frame—and in my mind far more rewarding.

- *The ideal trip:* An itinerary would be a launch from Halfmoon Bay, a stay at Thormanby Islands or Smuggler Cove, a run up Agamemnon Channel to Goliath Bay, a run up to Princess Louisa Inlet, a return via lower Jervis Inlet, a run around the top end of Texada Island to Favada Point, a run down the west side of

Texada to Jedediah Island, and a thorough exploration of the islands around Jedediah before a return to Halfmoon Bay. This would be best as a two-week trip, but it's well worth the investment in time, combining incredible mountain scenery with remote island paddling.

About the Strait of Georgia: The north end of the Strait of Georgia is the meeting place—or dividing line, if you prefer—of the two tides that separate into either Queen Charlotte Strait or Juan de Fuca Strait and into the Pacific Ocean. The point of division is usually near Cape Mudge (see chapter 7), but that can vary:

Typical shoreline near Jedediah Island.

it can be near Cape Lazo (Comox) depending on the wind and the phase of the moon. It would be intuitive to think this area of joining waters would be a calm location, but instead it can be prone to considerable currents, such as those off Savary Island. Through most of this part of the Strait of Georgia the current will set northwest on the flood and southeast on the ebb. Tides tend not to relate to the highs and lows normal along the outer coast during full and new moons (spring tides); instead, the high tides remain fairly static over the course of a month, while the greatest range in daily height differences lies in the low tide levels.

Call-in points: Though sightlines are generally good, kayakers may wish to monitor Channel 11 on the west side of Texada Island (in Sabine Channel, in particular) for cruise ships. Also, freighters may be travelling to or from Powell River or along Malaspina Strait. Ferries regularly travel the north end of the island to and from Powell River to either Vancouver Island or Blubber Bay on Texada.

- *24, Ballenas Island/Merry Island/Welcome Passage:* This is a line from the Reception Point lights to Merry Island lights and Ballenas Island lights.

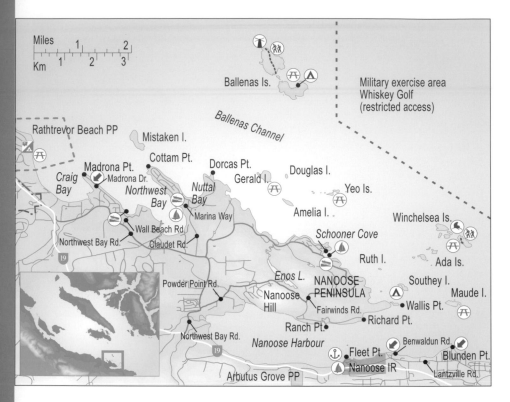

- *25, Cape Lazo/Powell River:* This is a line joining Cape Lazo and the south entrance light of the Powell River floating breakwater. Vessels heading south state whether they'll be travelling via Malaspina Strait, Sabine Channel, Stevens Passage or west of Sisters Islets.

BALLENAS-WINCHELSEAS

This group of islands, like the Trial Islands near Victoria, may appear barren, but they have earned the Conservation Data Centre's highest biodiversity ranking, one shared by just nine other sites in the Gulf Islands. Many of the islands are standout locations for Douglas-fir, Garry oak and arbutus forests in an undisturbed state—a rarity, considering only about one percent of the original area remains. This makes sightings of plants such as prickly pear cactus and camas a distinct possibility. Unusual species include short-tailed albatross, northern abalone, coastal wood fern and water-plantain buttercup.

The lighthouse at North Ballenas Island.

Fifteen of the islands are Crown land. The private islands are Gerald, Mistaken, Maude, North Winchelsea and North Ballenas. South Winchelsea is a nature reserve, while North Winchelsea is a Department of National Defence naval monitoring station—part of the Canadian Forces Maritime Experimental Test Ranges (CFMETR) based out of the south tip of Nanoose Peninsula.

Lantzville

This village of about 3,500 residents is strung along the waterfront north of Nanaimo. It's blessed with a gently sloping shoreline with numerous beaches. A multitude of roads dead-end at public access points to the beach, making Lantzville an ideal location to launch a kayak trip to the Winchelseas.

Launches: N49°15.25' W123°05.88'. This is the most westerly place to launch from Lantzville, providing the quickest route to the outer Winchelseas. The launch is from the end of Benwaldun Road, just before the Nanoose reserve off Lantzville Road. The short street dead-ends at a beach access. At low tide the beach dries extensively, with the possibility of gravel bars.

Southey Island.

Maude Island

This is the easternmost island in the group, located east of Nanoose Peninsula. As Crown land it's a popular recreation destination with casual camping or picnicking on its south-facing treeless bluffs.

Nanoose Harbour

This harbour is protected by Nanoose Peninsula, which is steep and thickly wooded on its south shore and topped by Nanoose Hill at 261 m (856 feet). Part of it is a Canadian Forces naval base with a pier and mooring buoys at Ranch Point. Public landing is restricted at the shore along the base property. The head of the harbour is a swampy mud flat. The harbour ends at Wallis Point, off which is an islet that's connected to the point at low tides. The south end of the islet is a pretty cove with a beach for landing. The point is the end of a popular local hiking trail.

Southey Island

This Crown island located just north of Wallis Point is a pleasant recreational island with a few beaches on the south end. Rough trails lead around the island through Garry oak and arbutus forest. Drying reefs extend to nearby Ruth Island, a long, thin mound of rock with some scrub used as a haulout by seals.

Wildflowers in bloom on South Winchelsea.

Camping: N49°16.59' W124°06.25'. The best beach on Southey faces Nanoose Peninsula. A few camping areas are set upon a level headland near a beach.

Ada Islands

This group is made up of two principal islands plus a host of reefs. The main island is a large mound of rounded, exposed bedrock. Three rocks southeast of Ada Islands are a winter haulout for Steller's sea lions; as many as 351 were observed here in 1978. The yellow buoy is for the Department of National Defence.

South Winchelsea Island

This island, owned by The Land Conservancy of BC, has been an ecological reserve since 1998. Access to most of the island is restricted, including a ban on camping, pets and fires. A short trail leads through the portion open to visitors.

A cabin on the island's west end is intended for research but can also be rented, with funds going toward the island's mortgage and maintenance. For information, contact the office of TLC at **250-479-8053**. An outhouse is located north of the cabin and a small dock is to the west. This is a solid metal structure built to replace a wooden one that was destroyed by sea lions, which haul out in the hundreds on rocks west of the dock.

Holding their fins above water helps keep sea lions warm.

Pinnipeds—it's a male's world

Two types of sea lions converge on the Gulf Islands during winter. The Steller's, or northern, sea lions are much larger and lighter in colour, growing to 3.3 m (11 feet) in length and weighing in at as much as 1,100 kg (2,500 pounds). They have a boxy, bear-like head. California sea lions are generally brown and many reach 450 kg (1,000 pounds) and 2 m (7 feet) in length. They have a more dog-like face than the Steller's and by the age of five develop a bony bump on the top of the skull called a sagittal crest.

The sea lions found in the Gulf Islands will almost certainly be male. Steller's sea lions mate in the Gulf of Alaska and Aleutian Islands; the pups are born May to July. In winter, as early as November, the males head south. The California sea lions generally breed in southern California's Channel Islands and as far south as Mexico, and the pups are born in June and July. Come winter, the males separate and head north as far as Vancouver Island. By coincidence, the two geographically distinct species of males congregate together here.

After about a century of being shot because they compete for fish, sea lions are now protected. At one time driven from this region, by the 1970s California sea lions began to return to the Strait of Georgia to feed on herring. Today they number about 200,000, with about 40,000 Steller's sea lions.

Sea lions are pinnipeds—aquatic mammals with limbs ending in fins. If you see them lying in the water snoozing or relaxing with their fins in the air, it's because their fins are not as protected by blubber as their torsos. Holding their fins in the air helps keep sea lions warm.

A trail leads from the cabin to a small beach about mid-island on the south side. The rock beach is a poor entry point to the island, but can be used by kayakers. At lower tides, a crushed shell beach emerges in the intertidal rocks on the island's west end. Approach from the south. Another (possibly awkward) option for landing is the dock.

Ecological oddities: South Winchelsea Island is a superb example of the coastal bluff ecology. Watch for Geyer's onion, western pearlwort and dune bentgrass in a pool near the south end of the trail. Visit in May to see the many showy wildflowers.

North Winchelsea Island

Conspicuous buildings topping the island include a white radar dome and communication towers—part of the CFMETR torpedo tracking facility. In conjunction with the Whiskey Golf seabed, the facility tests torpedoes and their instruments, including sonar. It's one of a kind for Canada and the west coast of North America.

Schooner Cove

This cove is dominated by the 350-berth full-service Schooner Cove Marina, which is nestled in the protection of a large rock breakwater. Services include water, a pump-out station, gas, a boat ramp, tackle shop, café and store. Accommodation is available at the Schooner Cove Hotel. Kayak rentals are also available.

Gerald Island

This private island is a mix of steep cliff, jumbled rock and pocket beaches. Look for prickly-pear cactus on the easternmost headland. Nearby Yeo Islands are thin strips of bedrock that resemble many of the more remote islets of the outer coast. Island residents include cormorants, gulls, turkey vultures and snakes. Nearby Amelia Island is capped with arbutus trees. It's privately owned but uninhabited.

Place names: Gerald Yeo was a surgeon aboard HMS *Ganges* 1857–60. Amelia Connolly was the wife of Sir James Douglas.

Ballenas Channel

This channel runs 2.5 km (1.5 miles) between Ballenas Islands and Gerald Island. Prevailing summer north-westerlies can make this a troublesome crossing for novice kayakers, as the channel is quite exposed.

Ballenas Islands

These two islands are separated by a narrow, rocky channel. The rocks form part of a fairly sheltered cove on the north end of South Ballenas Island. Within the cove is an expansive beach backed by scrubby forest. Much of the rest of the south island is bare; it's accessible by a trail leading up the bluffs from the east end of the beach. A trail from a beach on

Prickly-pear cactus on Gerald Island.

A view from the campsite on South Ballenas Island.

the south side of the north island crosses private property to the old lighthouse station, now an unmanned weather station. The light was first built in 1900, and buildings associated with the station remain.

Place names: Capt. Narvaez named the islands Islas de las Ballenas, Island of the Whales, during his 1791 visit in the Spanish armed vessels *San Carlos* and *Saturnina*.

Ecological oddities: The south island is home to the very rare water-plantain buttercup, which was recently added to the national COSEWIC list of endangered species. Look for it in a pond inland from the southernmost bay.

Camping: N49°20.30' W124°08.86'. A trail up the bluff from the north-facing cove on South Ballenas Island leads to a clear, level area. The path is steep and may be difficult with gear, but it's a pretty location. At lower high tides it may be possible to use the beach.

Northwest Bay

This is the largest of three bays on the northwest side of Nanoose. The south shore and head of the bay is fringed with pleasant beaches. The inner south shore is a busy booming ground, with sea lions using the logs as a haulout. The inner north shore is home to the Beachcomber Marina, which has a good boat ramp. Homes line most of the rest of the shore, including both Nuttal and Craig bays.

Launches: N49°18.64' W123°14.29'. Partway along Madrona Drive is a pleasant public beach access by way of a 30-m (100-foot) trail leading through a treed area. A parking lot is provided. The beach becomes rock shelving at lower tides. To get here, find your way to Northwest Bay Road, turn onto Beaver Creek Wharf Road and turn left onto Madrona Drive.

Continuing northwest: Three communities lie in close succession northwest of Nanoose before Baynes Sound: Parksville, French Creek and Qualicum Beach. These are residential communities, with extensive park areas along the beachfronts in both Parksville and Qualicum. Rathtrevor Beach Provincial Park is popular for its extensive sandy beach, which dries considerably at lower tides. Reservation camping is possible here, but access is poor for kayaks. A seawalk extends much of the length of the waterfront at Qualicum Beach. Launching from here would be possible, though nearby attractions are few. French Creek is a boat harbour with public floats and the ferry terminal for passenger service to False Bay in Lasqueti. A Coast Guard rescue unit is also based here. In all, this is a poor area for kayaking.

Beware of torpedoes

Venturing into the open water past Ballenas Islands could put you in the middle of a war zone. CFMETR (Canadian Forces Maritime Experimental and Test Ranges) at Nanoose has been testing torpedoes in the waters of Whiskey Golf since the 1960s. It's considered the top torpedo testing range in the world, having tested about 30,000 U.S. and Canadian torpedoes. At the heart of the range are hydrophones on the seabed floor at 400 m (1,300 feet) in depth. It's a desirable testing area due to the deep, flat seabed.

The testing is done by ships, submarines and aircraft. Explosives aren't used, but that probably wouldn't matter much if a kayak or small boat sat in the path of one during a test. A transit area 914 m (3,000 feet) north of Winchelsea Island and east of South Ballenas Island allows mariners to pass the active area.

Entering Whiskey Golf is likely only a concern to kayakers on a crossing from Lasqueti Island to Ballenas Islands on a day when a strong westerly is blowing. This could push you off course into the range. This isn't just hypothetical—it happened to me. Fortunately I didn't have to worry, as Whiskey Golf was inactive that day. The VHF marine weather stations give warnings for the days when Whiskey Golf is active.

Place names: Qualicum is the Salishan name for a strong west wind that blows in from the Pacific and funnels through the Qualicum Beach area.

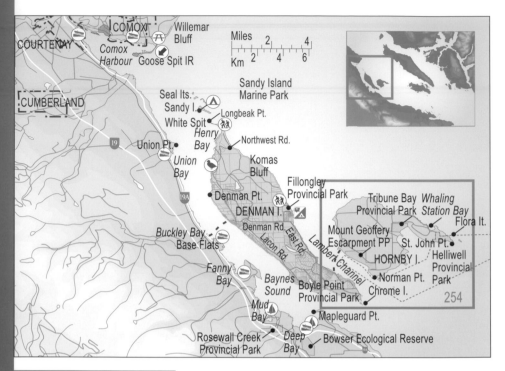

BAYNES SOUND

Baynes Sound separates Vancouver and Denman islands. It's as wide as 2.3 km (1.5 miles) to the north and 1.6 km (1 mile) to the south. It is a treasure chest of bivalves: Pacific oysters, Olympia oysters, foolish mussels, varnish clams, Manila clams, littleneck clams, butter clams, geoducks, horse clams, basket cockles, soft-shell clams, Baltic macomas, bent-nose macomas and pointed macomas; the sound produces about half the province's cultured shellfish from 119 shellfish beaches. Together 50 commercial tenures produce about 3,360 tonnes per year.

Not surprisingly, it's also key staging, breeding and wintering habitat for migratory birds—the second most important in the province after the Fraser River estuary. It sees about 176 bird species. Herring spawn in the sound and neighbouring streams serve as spawning and rearing areas for coho, chum, chinook, pink, sockeye, coastal cutthroat and steelhead.

Currents can reach 2–3 knots at the south entrance by Chrome Island but decrease substantially as the sound widens to the north.

A sandstone ledge off Downes Point.

Place names: Admiral Sir Robert Lambert Bayne was commander-in-chief at Esquimalt 1857–60. He is credited with averting war when the Americans placed troops on San Juan Island to hold it for the United States. As a younger officer in 1827, Baynes commanded the Asia station and helped secure the independence of Greece.

Deep Bay
Deep Bay is an anchorage for large vessels; a marina protected by the headland at Mapleguard Point has a boat ramp that makes a good launch location for trips to Hornby Island. Another marina is located at Mud Bay.

Fanny Bay
Fanny Bay has a public wharf, with extensive mud flats around it. The ferry to Denman Island leaves from Buckley Bay to the north. A barge-loading berth is also located there. Union Bay to the north is a coal and lumber port.

Comox Harbour
This harbour is one of the largest deltas on the east coast of Vancouver Island, making it well-used winter habitat for a large number of birds, including American widgeon, mallard, northern pintail, and black, surf and white-winged scoters. Up to 425 bald eagles have

Sandy Island.

been counted feeding in the valley and estuary. It's also key trumpeter swan habitat; as many as 2,009 birds have been counted here—about 10 percent of the world's population.

This is also a busy boat harbour, with four marinas and a commercial fishing fleet. Goose Spit, a lengthy natural causeway of sand, provides protection for the harbour. Additional breakwaters protect the marinas. On the north shore is a government pier used for Department of National Defense vessels only. Upland from the harbour north of Cape Lazo is a Canadian Forces base and airfield.

Don't plan on paddling far up the Courtenay River: a seal barrier stops navigation. Watch for the signs.

Place names: The Euclataw name for Vancouver Island was Komuckway or Comuckthway, which means "plenty," "abundance" or "riches." The name was gradually shortened. It was once known as Port Augusta.

Launches: The Comox Marina is run by the municipality and offers a boat launch next to Marina Park. Parking is ample and there are washrooms. There are several other launch ramps within the harbour, but kayakers may want to avoid the marinas, marine farms, float planes, oil wharf and DND wharf by using Goose Spit. Parking is plentiful along much of the spit.

Weather

Comox	May	June	July	Aug.	Sept.	Dec.	Av./Ttl.
Daily average temp. (C)	12.1	15.0	17.6	17.6	14.2	3.4	9.7
Daily maximum (C)	16.5	19.4	22.4	22.5	18.8	5.9	13.5
Daily minimum (C)	7.6	10.6	12.7	12.7	9.5	0.8	5.8
Precipitation (mm)	46.6	44.2	29.7	34.8	45.0	181.1	1179.0
Days of rainfall + 0.2mm	12.6	11.6	8.4	7.7	9.3	18.6	166.0
Days with rainfall +5mm	3.2	2.8	1.8	2.1	3.0	9.4	66.1
Days with rainfall +10mm	1.2	1.0	0.7	1.1	1.3	5.3	35.6
Days with rainfall +25mm	0.07	0.13	0.03	0.1	0.13	1.4	7.6
Wind speed (km/h)	12.4	12.3	11.8	10.9	9.9	14.3	12.5
Prevailing direction	SE	SE	NW	NW	W	SE	SE

Cape Lazo

Cape Lazo is a prominent headland with cliff faces of yellow clay. A couple of km north (about a mile) is a large radar dome that's part of Comox Airport.

Place names: Narvaez named it Punta de Lazo de la Vega in 1791. Lazo is Spanish for "snare."

Denman Island

Denman Island is an agricultural and residential island. Much of its outer coast is composed of sandy cliffs, especially at Komas Bluff, and extensive rock flats at lower tides. The spit at Fillongley is remarkable, as is Sandy Spit, a series of islands, islets and boulders that dry in a line extending over 4 km (2.5 miles) off the north end of the island. Known as White Spit, the beach is the result of erosion, mainly from Komas Bluff and the area around Fillongley Provincial Park.

Henry Bay, south of the spit, was the site of a large summer village in the late 1880s. Middens are a reminder. It's now an anchorage with commercial oyster beds in the bay.

The inner shoreline facing Baynes Sound has sand beaches and a pastoral upland setting. Cormorants nest on the northwest corner

Denman Island's provincial parks

Boyle Point Provincial Park is a small day-use park with a forested 1.5-km (about a mile-long) trail leading to a view at the point. The park is 125 ha (309 acres) and was established in 1989. Watch for the sea lions on Chrome Island.

Sandy Island Marine Park includes Sandy Island and the nearby Seal Islets. At low tide the island and islets become connected to Denman Island. It's former Department of National Defence land once used for military exercises involving explosives, mainly during the Second World War. Volunteer staff help visitors protect the fragile island ecology. The land was made a park in 1966.

The land for Fillongley Park was donated in 1954. It features trails, a beach with an extensive spit and a small vehicle-accessible campsite on the park's southeast corner. It's one of the few locations on Denman Island that has never been logged and a great example of old-growth Douglas-fir forest. In the park is the grave of George Beadnell, who donated the land. The park is named after Beadnell's home village in England. A fountain in a clearing is the only remnant from the homestead. Middens along the east boundary of the park indicate a long history of First Nation occupation.

of the island. The ferry lands at Denman Landing where there is a store and post office (V0R 1T0).

This is a deceivingly large island, about the equivalent of Gabriola Island in size; circumnavigation is 48 km (30 miles), or longer if the tide is low. Boyle Point at the south end of the island has steep, yellow sandstone pillars. Just south of the point is Chrome Island, conspicuous for its lighthouse. The station was established in 1891 and is still staffed. Unfortunately the modern tower was built on the site of petroglyphs. Carved figures can still be seen on the island's granite bedrock.

Place names: Rear Admiral Joseph Denman was commander-in-chief of the Pacific station 1864–66. Capt. David Boyle served on HMS *Tribune* on the B.C. coast 1859–60. He became governor and commander-in-chief in New Zealand 1892–97.

Camping: Vehicle-accessible camping is located in Fillongley Provincial Park, but the 10 sites usually fill quickly during the summer. Kayakers will probably find Sandy Island preferable.

N49°37.17' W124°51.36'. Wildnerness camping is allowed within Sandy Island Marine Park. The most popular location is Sandy Island. On the western point facing Comox Harbour is a good sand beach— probably the best on the island. There is no tree cover, however. On the south side facing the anchorage is a beach area backed by trees—probably a better location on a windy day. Here you'll find various clearings, including a tent pad set on a bit of a hill on the east side. There are two pit toilets. The waypoint is for the sandy western beach.

N49°37.64' W124°51.58'. Kayakers may be tempted to pull out at one of the Seal Islets. The largest is to the north of Sandy Island. A good beach is on the west end. The upland is level and lightly vegetated sand, but beach camping is probably preferable to protect the ecology.

HORNBY ISLAND

Mount Geoffrey is the high point on Hornby, with steep slopes to the water on the west side and a gentler slope on the east. The island is about half the size of Denman, but is more geographically varied. Tribune Bay is a popular day-use area with an extensive sand beach and warm water. Upland from the bay is the Hornby co-op store and the post office (V0R 1Z0). East of the bay at Helliwell Provincial Park the shore features a wonderfully etched cliff rock face. This is a beautiful area to explore on the trails or from the water. Off St. John Point is Flora Islet, which has a good west-facing beach. It has recently been added to Helliwell Provincial Park and camping is prohibited. Watch for seals hauled out on the rocks. St. John Point is a nesting site for about 100 pairs of pelagic cormorant. Glaucous-winged gull and pigeon guillemot also nest at the point.

At Dunlop Point and Downes Point the shore is rugged, with a large sandstone ledge at low tides. It features intriguing etched and rounded sandstone mounds. A midden is located at Downes Point.

More recreational beach is located at Whaling Station Bay, but unfortunately housing is heavy along much of the bay. Development continues west along most of the outer shore of Hornby past Grassy Point, where a gravel beach is accessible by land.

Watch for petroglyphs at various locations and a fish trap at Boulder Point. An interesting etching is a dancing figure on the east side of Whaling Station Bay at the high tide line. Others are along Ford Creek near a waterfall, on Galleon Beach at the park, Downes Point and scattered around Tralee Point.

Scuba divers will be drawn to the abundant marine life at Norris and Heron rocks off Norman Point. At the point is an unusual private camping location, with scattered cabins and semi-permanent tent sites along the shorefront.

If you visit Collishaw Point, keep an eye open for the fossils and rock formations.

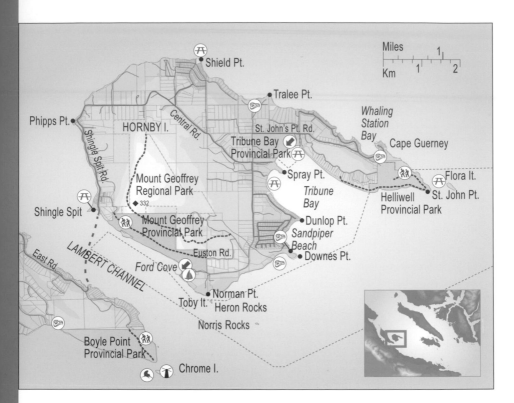

Hornby Island's provincial parks

The newest addition is Mount Geoffrey Escarpment Provincial Park. Created in 2004, it protects about 2 km (1.2 miles) of shoreline and 187 ha (462 acres) of the escarpment. Hiking trails lead through the area; look for maps at the island's Co-op store.

Tribune Bay Provincial Park was created in 1978 and includes a former lodge along with its tennis courts and picnic shelter. But the main feature is the extensive white sand beach. In the park are an open grassy area, picnic tables, fire rings, a water pump, change rooms and pit toilets. It's a day-use park only with no camping; a private campground is adjacent. A midden is located at the east end of the beach.

Mount Geoffrey escarpment.

The land for Helliwell Provincial Park was donated in 1966. It features mature Douglas-fir forest and arbutus in the eastern portion with grassy clearings atop the sea cliffs. Be sure to give the nesting birds a wide berth while paddling past the cliffs.

The grasslands have historically been maintained by sheep. Without them, salal and shore pine are beginning to encroach. Look for the fences and cart left over from the sheep farm, which operated from 1914 to 1942.

The ferry crosses from Denman Island to Shingle Spit. Adjacent to the terminal on the spit is a beautiful beach. Southeast of Shingle Spit the sheer slopes of Mount Geoffrey, newly protected as a provincial park, form the shoreline.

Ecological oddities: Helliwell Provincial Park is habitat for one of the last known populations of the endangered Taylor's checkerspot butterfly. Flora Islet is a popular diving location due to the occasional appearance of six-gill sharks. Normally a deep-sea shark, the six-gill is known to frequent the shallows around the island.

Place names: Rear Admiral Geoffrey T. Phipps Hornby was commander-in-chief of the Pacific station of the Royal Navy 1847–51. He was captain of HMS *Tribune*, a 31-gun screw frigate that was sent to B.C. for the San Juan Islands boundary dispute 1859–60.

Lambert Channel

Lambert Channel runs between Denman and Hornby islands. Herring spawn here, usually in early March. This draws huge numbers of birds, specifically pelagic cormorant, surf and white-winged scoter, gull, oldsquaw, bufflehead, goldeneye and merganser. In 1990, 692 bald eagles were recorded here.

The view from Flora Islet.

Sandy bluffs near Cape Lazo.

Camping: N49°53.16' W125°07.11'. While it might be possible to camp at the provincial parks at Kitty Coleman or Miracle Beach, they are not well suited to kayaks, especially since a reservation is recommended during the summer. There are numerous beaches of varying quality along this stretch, but my vote is for Kuhushan Point. Pick a low-tide spot out of sight of both marinas on the beach of Oyster River Nature Park. A consideration may be that banks are susceptible to erosion during high water. There is also foot access to the area. This is recommended only for a transit, not as a destination.

Mitlenatch Island

This tiny island sits 6.3 km (4 miles) off the south tip of Cortes Island. Despite its size it's the second-largest seabird colony in the Strait of Georgia, with large populations of pelagic cormorant, glaucous-winged gull and pigeon guillemot. As many as 300 marbled murrelet have also been seen here during the summer. It's possible to land in the cove in the southeast corner of the island (Camp Bay), where

Mitlenatch Island Nature Park
Mitlenatch Island and its surrounding 300 m (1,000 feet) of foreshore is a nature sanctuary, providing protection for the nesting seabird colonies as well as a rich marine ecology of abalone, scallop and sea cucumber. The unusual vegetation of the island is aided by the fact it's in a rain shadow, receiving about half the annual precipitation of nearby Campbell River. No pets are allowed. Good times to visit are May when spring wildflowers bloom and July when coastal cactuses flower. The park protects 155 ha (383 acres) and was created in 1961.

you'll see a naturalist hut used by Simon Fraser University and the Canadian Wildlife Service during the summer. A volunteer host will help keep visitors within the designated boundaries, as much of the island is off-limits. A bird blind faces north. Steller's and California sea lions haul out here from the late fall to May; as many as 100 might be found. The island is also home to some of the largest garter snakes in the province. Look for an old fish weir in Camp Bay.

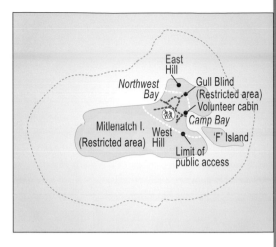

Place names: Mitlenatch is a Coast Salish word meaning "calm waters all around." But it might also derive from Sliammon: *metl* meaning "calm" and *nach* meaning "posterior"—a description, perhaps, of the calm waters found behind the island during a storm. In Kwagiulth, *mah-kwee-lay-lah* means "it looks close, but seems to move away as you approach it." Most kayakers will probably agree with that interpretation.

LASQUETI AND SOUTH TEXADA

Tucked away in the middle of the north Georgia Basin between Texada and Lasqueti islands is Jedediah Island. Despite its remoteness it has become a key boating and kayaking destination. A choice of camping options provides a base for exploring the nearby archipelagos and three other provincial parks in the area. Two of those are on Texada Island, part of a precipitously mountainous shoreline. Lasqueti Island, on the other hand, is low terrain dominated by private property. Pronounced bluffs and the most scenic shoreline tend to be on the south and west shores. Capping the island is Trematon Mountain, recognizable for the summit's so-called turret shape.

Lasqueti is not on an electrical grid, so expect minimal services.

Ferry service: Foot passenger ferry service to Lasqueti is from French Creek near Parksville on Vancouver Island aboard the *Centurion VII*. The service, independent from BC Ferries, runs several times a day,

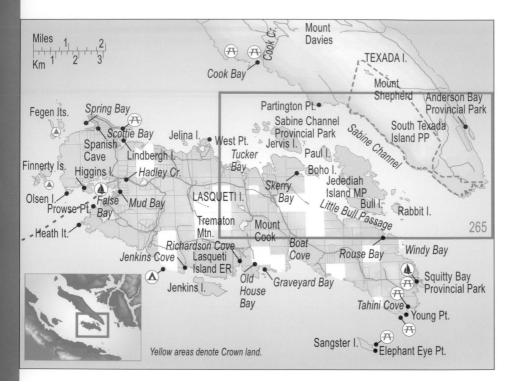

Yellow areas denote Crown land.

but does not take reservations. The number of kayaks it will take is limited, varying with the number of passengers and the weather. Once on Lasqueti you can launch from the beach at the ferry wharf.

Kayaking to Jedediah: From the mainland, an obvious route is from Thormanby Islands to Texada Island. The open water portion of a trip from this direction would be a touch under 8 km (5 miles) to Upwood Point on Texada. Any of the Sechelt launches would be appropriate. From Vancouver Island, the shortest route is Ballenas Islands to Sangster Island. From beach to beach is about 10 km (6 miles), with the open water portion about 8.2 km (5.1 miles). This route is for experienced kayakers only, as conditions can deteriorate in mid-channel if the wind picks up. The normal safety rule applies: open water crossings should be planned for the morning before the day's winds rise.

Place names: Jose Maria Narvaez of the *Saturnina* named the island in 1791 for Juan Maria Lasqueti, a Spanish naval officer.

Home Bay, Jedediah Island.

Sangster Island

This island off the southeast side of Lasqueti Island is well positioned for a break before or after crossing from Ballenas Islands. The main attraction is a bay backed by a wide beach on the island's east end, north of the navigation light at Elephant Eye Point (N49°25.55' W124°11.68'). This beach has been used recreationally for years as an option for a low-tide campsite. The island is uninhabited but privately owned.

Place names: Capt. James Sangster served the Hudson's Bay Company in command of the brig *Llama* in 1837 and *Cadboro* 1848–54. He ended his career as the postmaster in Victoria.

Squitty Bay and East Lasqueti

From Boat Cove to Rouse Bay, the shoreline of Lasqueti Island is mainly steep, with pronounced bluffs of volcanic rock. Numerous coves and islets make the area a wonderful place to explore by kayak. Squitty Bay is protected as a day-use provincial park. The main feature of the park is a government dock used as moorage by island residents. Upland from the dock is road access, a pit toilet and picnic tables. Camping and fires are not permitted.

South Lasqueti Island

The south shore from Young Point to False Bay is pocketed with small bays, most of which are backed by private property. The most outstanding shoreline is along Lasqueti Island Ecological Reserve, which includes tall cliffs and bald bluffs extending toward Trematon Mountain. Jenkins Island is privately owned.

Camping: N49°27.70' W124°19.24'. Just west of Jenkins Cove is a parcel of Crown land with a small cove near the centre. The cove is bracketed on both sides by tall cliffs and ends in a stone and cobble beach. The beach is high-backed and suitable for camping at, I would suspect, most tide levels. There is no established campsite here, but a rough trail leads up the shore to the west cliff face, where there are level mossy areas for those who aren't afraid of heights, as the tent areas are atop the cliff. This is a beautiful property that would make a great addition to the area as a marine park.

Squitty Bay.

False Bay

False Bay is the village centre of Lasqueti with a post office (V0R 2J0), restaurant, store and public wharf that doubles as the ferry terminal. The bay is used by float planes and as an anchorage. A sheltered lagoon connects with False Bay just east of Prowse Point. The current can run 3–4 knots at the lagoon entrance. Inside is a shellfish farm.

Finnerty Islands

Three island clusters sit off the west end of Lasqueti. The southernmost is Finnerty Islands,

Lasqueti Island Ecological Reserve.

Lasqueti Island's provincial parks

Two rock headlands on the east side of Lasqueti Island protect Squitty Bay Provincial Park, creating an anchorage and setting for a picnic area and public dock. The 13-ha (32-acre) park was created in 1988.

On the south shore, Lasqueti Island Ecological Reserve protects some of the largest rocky mountain junipers in the province. Another 15 species of plants found here are considered rare. Watch for turkey vulture, osprey, great horned owl, pygmy owl and the Pacific tree frog. The park was created in 1971 and protects 201 ha (497 acres). Access is prohibited.

a group with some tight passages and reefs that make for good exploration by kayak. Watch for the aboriginal fish weir at low tides. North from the Finnerty Islands is Fegen Islets, while another cluster sits west of Spring Bay. All are uninhabited Crown land. By contrast, all of western Lasqueti Island is private, with houses lining the shore.

Camping is possible on almost any of these islets, but with mostly large rock or boulder beaches, they are difficult to access. Probably the best option is the westernmost of the cluster, to the west of Spring Bay. Camping is possible on the level upland that runs most of the length of the island. Other level headlands can be found on other islets, but a lack of beaches makes them dubious campsites.

A view from Finnerty Islands.

Place names: Capt. Edward Stephen Fegen was captain of the armed merchant cruiser *Jervis Bay*, sunk by a German warship in the North Atlantic in 1940 while protecting a convoy. It was incorrectly named Fegan Islets in 1945 and was not corrected until 1984. As a result many charts and maps still name them the Fegan Islets.

North Lasqueti

Tucker Bay was the site of the first community on Lasqueti in 1912. A salmon cannery moved into False Bay in 1916. Today it's largely undeveloped, with a few rough beaches and a few homes. Scottie Bay is more built up, with a dock in the southern limit of the bay.

JEDEDIAH ISLAND

This island gem in the waters between Texada and Lasqueti islands has a multitude of coves, beaches and trails. The main point of entry is at Home Bay on the island's east side, where an old homestead is located. It was built around 1905 by the Foote family. They purchased the island in 1890 and used it for 30 years. A second house at Long Bay was built in the 1980s. Four archaeological sites on the island include a fish weir.

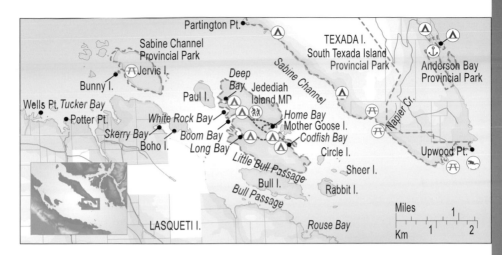

Behind the homestead is a field where feral sheep still graze. At the far end of the field the trail to Deep Bay continues through the forest. The sheep can be found in the grassy clearings that dot the island; feral goats tend to stay on the rock bluffs. The plan is eventually to remove the feral animals to stop them grazing on native vegetation, but their departure will be a mixed blessing as the pleasant open fields will eventually become overgrown. The island was home to a wild horse named Will that has since passed away; the grave is lovingly maintained along the trail to Long Bay. Rare species of animals to look for here are the short-tailed albatross, marbled murrelet, western screech-owl (*kennicottii* subspecies), northern abalone and monarch butterfly.

Jedediah is a great base for exploring the nearby area, which includes about 30 islands, islets and reefs. Many of the neighbouring islands, such as Rabbit, are private.

Hiking: Trails criss-cross the island between Home Bay and bays on the west side. The main trail leads to Long Bay and also skirts Boom Bay, while another leg leads to White Rock Bay. To get to this trail to Deep Bay, cross the open meadow at Home Bay. It may be obscured by grass at some points.

Camping: There are a half-dozen main spots to camp on Jedediah. Each area is connected by trail, so none of the choices will leave you isolated.

Boom Bay, Jedediah Island.

N49°29.82' W124°11.67', Home Bay. On the south side of the bay opposite the homestead is Sandy Beach (or Club Jed, if you must). This is the best kayak beach due to the sand, with many flat upland areas behind the beach plus an outhouse, information kiosk and even an old fire pit at the high tide line. Another option in Home Bay is the cove just to the north of the homestead. A small mud beach leads to the meadow behind the homestead.

N49°29.70' W124°11.57', Codfish Bay. Located just south of Home Bay, this is a pleasant bay backed by a gravel beach. Its short-coming is a lack of level clearings. It's best suited for a single tent on the upland at the trailhead. Camping on the beach may be possible during some tide levels.

N49°30.29' W124°12.74', Deep Bay. This bay on the northwest corner of the island features a rough beach that tends to disappear at higher tides. After a rock scramble there are many level and clear areas in the uplands to choose from. An outhouse is located on the trail midway to Boom Bay.

N49°30.14' W124°12.51', Boom Bay. This is a pretty area with a beach leading to a small, level area. More level areas can be found on a second tier up the hillside behind the beach.

N49°29.86' W124°12.48', Long Bay. There are two possible landing points. One is immediately north of the abandoned cottage. Look for the rusting fire pit at the high tide line. Note the rough beach tends to disappear at higher tides. A trail leads from the water to a level area with a makeshift picnic table and a cooking ledge. An outhouse is also located here. The cottage is locked and signs declare it unsafe. Just south of the cottage is a landing via a rough stone beach. An old road, now covered with grass, leads from the beach to a large meadow with a variety of places to camp.

N49°29.82' W124°12.67'. South of Long Bay are two small coves. The southern of the two has a beach where the upland looks over both Bull Passage and the cottage site in Long Bay.

Jervis Island

This is the largest of a cluster of islands northwest of Jedediah Island. It and Bunny Island to the west are protected as Sabine Channel Provincial Park. Jervis is steep and inaccessible except for a few small beaches on the west side, with the best due east of Bunny Island. From here you can gain access via steep rocks to flat headlands suitable for camping. The difficult access makes this appealling to a few rugged wilderness campers only; the majority of visitors will be much more comfortable on Jedediah. If you do stop here and can make the scramble, the bald bluffs provide wonderful viewpoints.

Bunny Island and the unnamed islands to its north tend to have rock shoreline only.

Bull Passage

This passage separates Lasqueti and Bull islands. Here the Lasqueti Island shore is low

A feral goat, Jedediah Island.

Jedediah Island and Sabine Channel marine parks

In 1995 Jedediah Island was purchased from owners Al and Mary Palmer. They lived on the island beginning in 1972 after Mary had purchased it with her previous husband in 1949 for use as a summer retreat. The acquisition of the park was aided by the estate of the late Daniel Culver, which committed $1.1 million. Culver, the only Canadian to climb both Everest and K2, died in 1993 while descending K2. Other major contributors were the Friends of Jedediah, the Marine Parks Forever Society and the Nature Trust of British Columbia. The park protects the entire 243 ha (600 acres) of the island.

Sabine Channel Provincial Park protects both Jervis and Bunny islands in their entirety. The two islands are composed of rocky cliffs and outcrops and are recognized for their rich marine environment. The park was created in 2001 and protects 95 ha (235 acres).

Jervis Island.

and rolling except for tall cliffs south of Boho Island. Any of the few beaches along this stretch are generally poor and backed by private property. Most kayakers and some boaters will prefer Little Bull Passage. Watch for rocks in the middle of the channel. The cliffs on the southeast side of Jedediah in Little Bull Passage are stunning. Bull Island is privately owned.

Sabine Channel

This channel separates Jedediah, Lasqueti and the various other smaller islands from Texada Island. Currents can run as high as 2 knots but are usually much less. It's a possible cruise ship route.

Place names: Sir General Edward Sabine (1788–1883) was a scientist in magnetic research and president of the Royal Society.

South Texada Island

Southeast of Cook Bay the topography of Texada soars higher, topping out at Mount Shepherd, 887 m (2,910 feet). The impressive backdrop is enhanced by steep, precipitous bluffs along the shoreline. For kayakers there are numerous beaches. At Cook Bay the fine beaches are backed by a number of homes and a log dump. The cottages end at the South Texada Provincial Park boundary, where the shoreline is steep and rugged. A cottage is located at the southernmost of the coves, a private holding within the park.

Camping: N49°31.43' W124°11.93'. Two km (1.2 miles) southeast of Partington Point a rocky headland has a good-quality grit and stone beach. A flat, grassy area on the headland provides views along both sides of Sabine Channel. Within the forest is more level ground suitable for camping. This pretty site would accommodate a large group.

N49°30.52' W124°10.45'. A clean beach that's easily visible from Jedediah, this makes a good camping location similar to the one above.

South Texada Island Provincial Park

This former forest reserve was made a provincial park in 1997; it protects 900 ha (2,224 acres) of the tallest portion of the island and arguably the most dramatic shoreline. It's not easily reached—abandoned logging roads are the only land access. Boat access is also difficult, as there are few reliable anchorages, though kayakers will be drawn to the many rock and gravel beaches that line the park. There are no facilities.

Anderson Bay

This bay is bounded by mainly inaccessible shore that includes a steep-sided islet. The surrounding upland is protected as a provincial park while the bay is used as a boat haven and a log dump.

South Texada Island.

Camping: N49°31.03' W124°08.08'. The park's peninsula has very rough beach access from both the Anderson Bay and Malaspina Strait sides. On the peninsula you'll find a rudimentary camping area with a fire pit, benches and clearings for a tent or two among the encroaching salal. Unfortunately, though, both beaches are rocky and increasingly so at lower tides. The advantage is views both down the Strait of Georgia and up Malaspina Strait.

N49°31.22' W124°08.39'. The head of the bay provides a better beach than the peninsula and is capped by a clear, level, grass upland. You'll find benches, a table and an old road access that connects with nearby logging roads for a stroll, if you like. This site can accommodate a large group.

Anderson Bay Provincial Park

This small provincial park was created in 2000 and protects part of the bay, including the outer portion of the peninsula, the adjoining island and the steep shoreline on the bay's west side. It does not protect the head of the bay, though that is well used recreationally. The park is undeveloped and protects 35 ha (86 acres).

Favada Point.

TEXADA ISLAND

Texada Island runs 50 km (30 miles) northwest to southeast with an average width of about 8 km (5 miles). A ridge of mountains runs along its length, growing taller to the southeast. Hundreds of miles of logging roads criss-cross the island, including the mountainous spine, making it a good place to hike for views from places like Mount Pocahontas. Also notable are the island's limestone deposits, which have created numerous caves, some over 300 m (1,000 feet) in length. Areas like the cliffs at Blubber Bay are popular among rock climbers. Swimming lakes include Heashell Lake, an abandoned quarry filled with water, and Bob's Lake, a forest recreation camping site in an area known for its wildflowers.

The west coast of the island tends to be the most rugged, with numerous shell, cobble and pebble beaches, such as Cook Bay, Rocky Point, Shingle Beach and Shelter Point. Interesting pockets to explore include Grilse Point, Favada Point, the area around

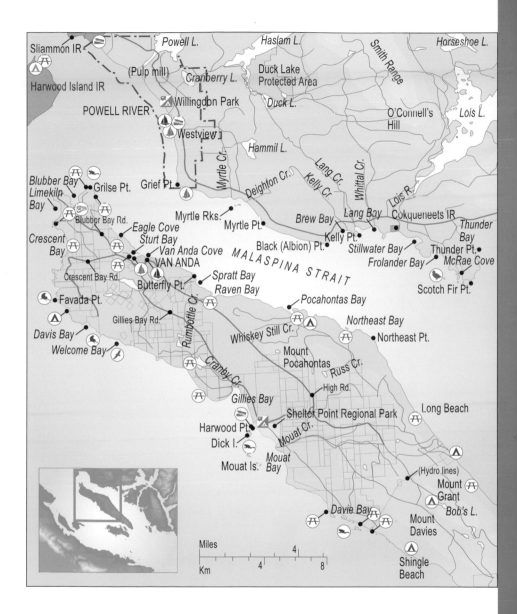

Map labels:

Sliammon IR
Harwood Island IR
(Pulp mill)
POWELL RIVER
Willingdon Park
Westview
Powell L.
Cranberry L.
Haslam L.
Duck Lake Protected Area
Duck L.
Smith Range
Horseshoe L.
O'Connell's Hill
Lois L.
Hammil L.
Myrtle Cr.
Deighton Cr.
Lang Cr.
Kelly Cr.
Whittal Cr.
Lois R.
Blubber Bay
Limekiln Bay
Grilse Pt.
Grief Pt.
Myrtle Rks.
Myrtle Pt.
Brew Bay
Lang Bay
Cokqueneets IR
Thunder Bay
Crescent Bay
Eagle Cove
Sturt Bay
Van Anda Cove
VAN ANDA
Black (Albion) Pt.
Kelly Pt.
Stillwater Bay
Frolander Bay
Thunder Pt.
McRae Cove
Blubber Bay Rd.
MALASPINA STRAIT
Crescent Bay Rd.
Butterfly Pt.
Spratt Bay
Raven Bay
Scotch Fir Pt.
Favada Pt.
Pocahontas Bay
Northeast Bay
Gillies Bay Rd.
Davis Bay
Welcome Bay
Rumbottle Cr.
Whiskey Still Cr.
Mount Pocahontas
Russ Cr.
Northeast Pt.
Cranby Cr.
High Rd.
Gillies Bay
Shelter Point Regional Park
Long Beach
Harwood Pt.
Dick I.
Mouat Cr.
Mouat Is.
Mouat Bay
(Hydro lines)
Mount Grant
Bob's L.
Davie Bay
Mount Davies
Shingle Beach

Miles
Km
4
4
8

Davis Bay and the mountainous south (covered above). These can make circumnavigating the island a rewarding experience, though you should expect long stretches of unchanging features along the northeast shore. Endangered creatures to watch for on Texada are marbled murrelet, peregrine falcon, short-tailed albatross and western screech-owl. Osprey can also be found across the island, and sea lions are found at numerous locations year-round.

The descriptions below run clockwise from Davie Bay.

Place names: Jose Maria Narvaez, commander of *Santa Saturnina*, named this island in 1791 after Felix de Tejada, a Spanish rear admiral. It was first anglicized as "Favada" by Captain Vancouver in 1792.

Davie Bay

Between Mouat Bay and Cook Bay the Texada Island shoreline is wonderfully scenic. Davie Bay is a highlight, with numerous islands, reefs, headlands and beaches to explore. A few homes and a log dump behind an islet dot this stretch of private property. It's unfortunate—this should be a provincial park.

Camping: There are numerous level upland clearings at Davie Bay, but most areas are privately owned. For an emergency haulout, there are clear areas around the hydro transmission station at the end of the overland transmission cables.

N49°34.74' W124°20.16'. Shingle Beach is a managed forest recreation site with no fees. It's accessible from the water as well as by gravel road from Gillies Bay.

Gillies Bay

This bay is easily identified by a radio tower and the white patch on the north entrance point. Inside is a village centre with a store, post office (V0N 1W0), restaurant, farmers' market, medical centre and RCMP. Oddly, there is no wharf access. Southeast of Gillies Bay is Mouat Bay, which has log dumps and a breakwater south of Harwood Point. Dick Island, south of Harwood Point, is private.

There are some good sandy beaches immediately northwest of Gillies Bay that make excellent kayak stops, though the upland is likely private property (one is N49°40.77' W124°30.58').

Camping: N49°39.40' W124°28.05'. Shelter Point Regional Park extends around both sides of Harwood Point. The best kayak access to the campsites is north of the point on the extensive cobble beach within Gillies Bay. Picnic areas are located closest to the beach; campsites are located a bit farther inland. In all there are 40 sites. Flushing toilets are provided. A caretaker's residence is located within the park.

A view toward Comox from north Texada.

Launches: N49°39.27' W124°28.08'. A concrete ramp for boat launching is located on the south end of the park near Harwood Point.

Welcome Bay

Between Gillies Bay and Favada Point are numerous indentations, with two named as bays—Welcome and Davis. Welcome Bay stands out for the large quarry operation, which includes an orange loading conveyor used by Ideal Cement. Watch for sea lions on the offshore rocks at Welcome Bay. This stretch is also notable for the number of eagles and falcons.

Northwest Texada

Favada Point is a picturesque rock bluff with sea lions year-round. To the north of the point are two bays. Crescent Bay has a few homes scattered on the bluffs, with beaches from the centre northward. Limekiln Bay, farther north, is backed by views of the quarry operating at Blubber Bay.

Camping: N49°43.79' W124°37.50'. While the beaches at Crescent Bay are appealing, they are adjacent to residences. A beach in an unoccupied cove can be found in the first bay southeast of Favada Point. It is rock at lower tides and gravel at higher levels, with neap tide clearance on the beach among the drift logs. For spring tide

Grilse Point.

clearance, the bluffs to the immediate south of the beach have level areas for a tent or two. A rough trail leads to the clearing.

Blubber Bay

This bay houses the terminal for the ferry service from Powell River. The bay's history includes a Sliammon village on the shore, Tah lahk nahtch, and a whaling station in the 1880s–90s, part of a short-lived history of commercial whaling in the Strait of Georgia. Today the upland is a busy quarry area, which dominates the viewscape. A ruined wharf once used for explosives is on the east side. The community at Blubber Bay includes a post office (V0N 1E0). Small cottages dot the west shore but the east to Grilse Point is uninhabited. The shoreline around Grilse Point is a complex karst formation, including a small potentially paddle-in cave just south of the point. A cobble beach just west of the point allows kayakers to explore the area by foot.

Van Anda

This small community hugs two connected coves. A government wharf dominates the much smaller Van Anda Cove to the east and houses line the shore. To the west is Sturt Bay, which is home to a marina, boat ramp and a barge loading facility for the gravel quarry on the bay's southeast. Facilities here include a hotel, restaurant and bank. Cliffs and a beach line the south end of the bay.

Ecological oddities: Van Anda Creek is home to two very rare species of stickleback: the benthic Van Anda Creek stickleback and limnetic Van Anda Creek stickleback.

Place names: The Van Anda Copper and Gold Mining Company owned 340 ha (840 acres) on the northeast side of the island. The company president, Edward Blewitt of Seattle, named both his son and his mining company after his friend Carl Van Anda, a popular New York City journalist in the 1870s.

Spratt Bay

East of Van Anda, between Van Anda Cove and Butterfly Point, is a large quarry operation. Another limestone quarry is located in Spratt Bay. The piles at the waterfront are a landmark visible for miles.

Pocahontas Bay

Pocahontas Bay is one of two significant bays in the stretch between Van Anda and Northeast Point. Just west of Northeast Point is Northeast Bay, where there are several beaches. Pocahontas Bay has a nice grassy upland area that is private property.

Camping: N49°43.40' W124°24.76'. The best beach in the area by far is immediately east of Pocahontas Bay. Behind the gravel beach are clear areas in the alder forest.

Place names: The first merchant vessel to enter Port Alberni in 1861 was *Pocahontas*.

Long Beach

The northeast side of Texada from Northeast Point to Anderson Bay is a mixture of unremarkable rock shoreline and rocky beach. The mountainous backdrop is less rugged, the shore monotonous and the beaches poor. The section known as Long Beach is several miles of poor-quality beach characterized by large rocks at all but the high tide line.

Camping: N49°37.82' W124°16.83'. If you are in need of a campsite along this stretch, aim for the power lines, visible from a distance. Here the beach is gently sloping cobble and rock. To the immediate southeast of the hydro right-of-way is a copse of alder trees clear of undergrowth. Look for a grassy bank as well. This is my choice for the best site in a poor area for camping.

Malaspina Strait

This strait separating Texada Island from the mainland has weak currents that rarely exceed a knot. The ridge of Texada acts as a windbreak from westerlies, but in southeasterlies conditions can become very poor. The water is prone to chop, particularly near Cape Cockburn and Quarry Bay on the mainland side.

Scotch Fir Point

This is where waters from Jervis Inlet meet Malaspina Strait, and the result is currents and rips. Northwest of the point is McRae Islet, a granite island remarkable for its breeding population of glaucous-winged gull. Pelagic cormorant, pigeon guillemot and black oyster-catcher also nest here. Surf scoter, western grebe and Barrow's goldeneye visit in high numbers between October and March.

Stillwater Bay, to the northwest of McRae Islet, is a log booming ground. A hydroelectric plant on the north shore of the bay is conspicuous, as is an inland water tower.

Grief Point

Grief Point, at the south end of the municipal limits of Powell River, is low, grassy and fronted by a sandy beach. A marina for a resort hotel and breakwater are southeast of the point. A beach adjacent to the marina could be used as a kayak launch (N49°48.08' W124°31.05').

Westview

This town centre within Powell River is 2.9 km (1.8 miles) north of Grief Point. Two basins in front of Westview have a public wharf between them. The wharf is used mainly for handling petroleum products. A boat harbour used by fishing vessels and sheltered by breakwaters is located south of the wharf, along with a barge-loading wharf. Another boat harbour north of the wharf is a marina run by the municipality. The ferry terminal for service from Vancouver Island is in Westview as well.

Launches: N49°50.29' W124°31.81'. The municipal launch is located just north of the ferry terminal. There is no beach, just the concrete runway. Parking is available nearby.

Powell River

This small city of about 13,000 is the hub for a recreationally diverse area of semi-alpine wilderness, lakes, mountainous vistas and old-growth forests. Its prosperity is tied to the fate of the local pulp mill, the region's largest employer and one of the largest pulp and paper mills in the world. Southeast of the main wharves for the mill a breakwater of floating boat hulks protects a log storage area.

Much of the town's waterfront recreation is focused around Willingdon Beach, which has a trail on an old logging railroad complete with historic logging equipment, a forestry museum and camping.

Powell Hill, northeast of the town, has a bare summit; a red and white striped chimney is a landmark.

Place names: Dr. Israel Wood Powell (1836–1915) was the first McGill graduate in medicine to practise on the West Coast and the first superintendent of Indian Affairs in British Columbia.

Camping: The Willingdon Beach Municipal Campground is located along the waterfront off Highway 101 near central Powell River. It has electricity, grassy tent areas, hot showers, flush toilets, laundry, fire pits, ice, a fishing pier, a playground and even some cable TV sites. There are waterfront locations that would be good for kayaks hoping to stop here, but expect them to be filled first. This would be more convenient as a staging ground. Call **604-485-2242**.

Weather

Powell River	May	June	July	Aug.	Sept.	Dec.	Av./Ttl.
Daily average temp. (C)	12.7	15.6	18.2	18.3	15.5	4.4	10.6
Daily maximum (C)	16.9	19.7	22.7	22.6	19.3	6.5	14.0
Daily minimum (C)	8.5	11.5	13.7	14.1	11.7	2.2	7.2
Precipitation (mm)	70.4	62.5	40.1	47.1	56.9	141.2	1103.7
Days of rainfall + 0.2mm	12.5	11.5	7.5	8.3	10.1	18.3	170.6
Days with rainfall +5mm	4.7	4.1	2.7	3.1	3.8	8.9	72.0
Days with rainfall +10mm	2.2	2.0	1.3	1.7	1.8	4.8	35.7
Days with rainfall +25mm	0.2	0.2	0.13	0.13	0.17	0.9	4.8
Wind speed (km/h)	7.2	7.2	6.9	6.1	5.5	6.5	6.8
Prevailing direction	E	E	W	W	W	E	E
Bright sunshine (hours)	229.3	220.8	280.0	266.6	206.1	35.5	1817.6
% of daylight hours	48.1	45.3	56.9	59.5	54.3	14.0	37.3

The Powell Forest Canoe Circuit

Canoeists will want to head inland in the Powell River area. The Powell Forest Canoe Circuit includes Lois, Horseshoe, Nanton, Ireland, Dodd, Windsor, Beaver, Little Horseshoe and Khartoum lakes, with multiple road acceses, maintained portages and recreation sites. It's not a closed loop—the beginning of the route ends 32 km (20 miles) from the end. A bonus is the possibility of viewing a herd of 130 Roosevelt elk resulting from a reintroduction at the Nanton Lake area.

Harwood Island

This large island is a Sliammon reserve. Prominent white cliffs facing south are a landmark easily visible from Vancouver Island. The north end is a grassy spit. It's a popular recreation destination that makes an ideal campsite for kayakers transiting the region, but only if you don't mind snakes. The island has many, and they tend to be on the large side. Permission from the Sliammon First Nation is required to camp on the island. Call **604-483-9646** and ask for the band administrator.

SECHELT PENINSULA

The community of Sechelt sits on a narrow isthmus at the base of Sechelt Peninsula between the Strait of Georgia and Sechelt Inlet. The peninsula has a convoluted shoreline with numerous island clusters, harbours and coves before opening into Jervis Inlet. The array

Sargeant Bay.

of features and proximity to Vancouver have made it a top boating, fishing, cottaging and even kayaking destination. Highway 101 along the coast provides vehicle access to the various communities that hug the shoreline, ending at Egmont at the confluence of Jervis and Sechelt inlets. There you'll find a ferry link to Powell River.

A distinct downside is the amount of urban development along the outer shoreline, although frequent parks offer pockets of wilderness.

Trail Bay

This bay hugs the south end of the neck of land joining Sechelt Peninsula and the mainland. A portion is backed by the Sechelt First Nation reserve, where a huge quarry feeds gravel via conveyor onto barges in the bay. Immediately west of the reserve is the Sechelt commercial district, with shopping a block from the waterfront. There's an extensive stone and gravel beach along most of the Sechelt waterfront, making kayak launches possible from multiple locations, though it's potentially exposed. The bay is often used as an anchorage. The Trail Islands are private.

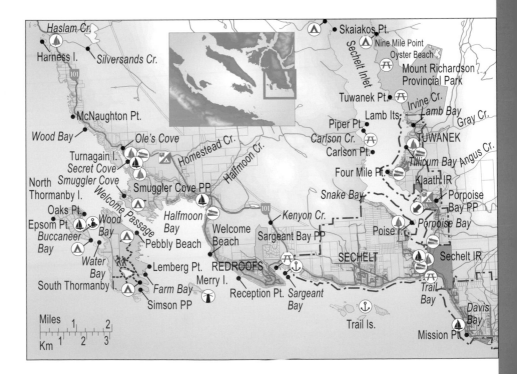

Early morning on Sechelt Inlet.

Sargeant Bay Provincial Park

This day-use park features a grassy area behind a cobble beach with drift logs backed by a wetland. Pit toilets are provided, but camping is prohibited. Trails cross the park, which is bisected by Redrooofs Road. One-third of the park is on the ocean side. The park was logged in the early 1900s when a sawmill was located at the mouth of Colvin Creek. An old steam engine boiler from the sawmill is visible in the mud of a lagoon at low tides. Also, watch for Virginia rails. A trail leads to the creek and is an easy 1-km (0.6-mile) hike. Longer trails lead to Triangle Lake and Trout Lake.

Sargeant Bay

This bay is largely residential except for Sargeant Bay Provincial Park, which protects a cobble day-use beach. The bay is used as an anchorage. Redrooofs, a residential community immediately to the bay's west, is situated above a shoreline cliff.

Halfmoon Bay

This residential area features an expansive pebble beach and a government dock located next to a general store. Kayak rentals are available in the bay.

Launches: N49°30.26' W123°54.55'. A community park with a boat ramp is located at Lyons Cove on the east side of Halfmoon Bay. There is a good beach area for kayakers. This is a good starting point for trips to Thormanby Islands.

Merry Island

This is a private island that's mostly unlogged. A staffed lighthouse on the east end was established in 1902.

Weather

Merry Island	May	June	July	Aug.	Sept.	Dec.	Av./Ttl.
Daily average temp. (C)	12.7	15.4	17.8	18.0	15.0	5.0	10.7
Daily maximum (C)	15.8	18.5	21.0	21.1	17.8	6.6	13.1
Daily minimum (C)	9.6	12.3	14.5	14.8	12.1	3.3	8.2
Precipitation (mm)	60.6	56.5	40.2	35.6	53.3	144.6	1035.1
Days of rainfall + 0.2mm	12.9	11.5	7.0	6.8	9.1	18.6	165.3
Days with rainfall +5mm	4.3	3.9	2.7	2.3	3.6	8.5	69.3
Days with rainfall +10mm	1.7	1.8	1.3	1.0	1.8	4.8	33.6
Days with rainfall +25mm	0.13	0.17	0.17	0.14	0.17	0.7	4.0
Wind speed (km/h)	16.1	15.8	14.4	14.3	14.6	21.4	
Prevailing direction	NW	SE	NW	NW	NW	E	
Bright sunshine (hours)	231.5	217.6	284.1	272.2	213.2	50.9	1890.6
% of daylight hours	48.7	44.8	58.0	60.9	56.2	19.9	39.4

Thormanby Islands

These islands make a great day trip or overnight destination. Glacial sands have contributed to nice beaches on North Thormanby Island; the spit on the southeast tip is protected as Buccaneer Bay Provincial Park. The sandflat with its distinctive sand cliffs protects an anchorage at Buccaneer Bay. The west side of the bay, known as Vaucroft Beach, is backed by mainly summer cottages. The public wharf at the beach is for loading and unloading only.

The white cliffs of North Thormanby's outer shoreline are visible from distant points in the Strait of Georgia. While North Thormanby is flat, South Thormanby has a bare rock summit, Mount Seafield, which is a modest 122 m (400 feet).

Place names: Thormanby was a race horse and winner of the Derby Stakes in 1860. Other names with a racehorse theme here are Buccaneer Bay, Derby Point, Latterham Ridge and Welcome Pass.

Hiking: Overgrown logging roads form routes within Simson Provincial Park, with viewpoints on Spy Glass Hill and Mount Seafield. The trails link Farm Bay and Pebbly Beach but may be poor in places.

Camping: N49°28.55' W123°57.41'. Farm Bay is a narrow, enclosed cove where easterlies and southeasterlies can funnel. The beach is rock with considerable driftwood at the high tide line. The campsite is atop a grass slope in an open, grassy area. This is not a casual kayaking stop. If you land at low tide you'll have to scramble over rocks, driftwood and then a hill before reaching your campsite.

N49°29.81' W123°57.70'. Pebbly Beach is located on the northeast end of South Thormanby facing Welcome Passage. Level, clear areas are in an alder forest directly behind the beach.

N49°29.73' W123°59.45'. The sand beach on the south end of North Thormanby Island in tiny Buccaneer Bay Provincial Park has room for about 10 to 12 tents.

Welcome Passage

Welcome Passage, about 320 m (0.2 miles) wide, separates the Thormanby Islands from Sechelt Peninsula. In the narrowest portion currents of 2–3 knots can be encountered, with the flood setting north and the ebb south. In the southeast end the passage is wider and the current rarely exceeds 2 knots. Note that the flood stream tends to set toward South Thormanby at Lemberg Point, which is strewn with rocks.

Smuggler Cove

This is a popular anchorage known for its scenic, sheltered waters within a maze of islets and reefs. Many of the islets are privately owned and topped by cottages. Much of the inner cove is protected as a provincial park, with beach access at the innermost portion of the cove. A number of the park's islets and headlands are off-limits due to a reclamation effort.

Place names: Larry Kelly came to Canada after fighting with the Confederates in the U.S. Civil War. When the Canadian Pacific Railway was completed, unemployed Chinese workers wanting to head to the United States were denied entry. Kelly helped out in return for a hefty fee. To ensure he wouldn't be captured if U.S.

officials stopped him, Kelly roped the men to a chunk of pig iron; his plan was to throw the pig iron overboard—with the Chinese workers still attached. Or so the story goes. The cove was also used to store liquor made at Cook Bay on Texada Island in the 1920s; from there it was smuggled into the U.S. Other names on Texada, such as Whiskey Still Creek and Rumbottle Creek at Raven Bay, also reflect that history.

Camping: N49°30.73' W123°57.69'. At the southern extent of Smuggler Cove is a small beach area with access to the park's five designated camping sites, which are set along a trail behind the beach. Outhouses are provided. The campsites are about 4 km (2.5 miles) from the parking area off Highway 101 and are accessible by trail, making them popular with backpackers.

Secret Cove

Several marinas are tucked into various arms of Secret Cove. A government dock is in the north arm, plus fuel sales and stores. The cove's Homesite Creek is known for Homesite Cave and Homesite Falls, which are accessible by community trails.

Camping: The Homesite Creek forest recreation site provides upland camping off Highway 101 near Secret Cove. It's often referred to as Secret Cove Forest Recreation Site but isn't accessible from the cove. It may serve as a convenient staging area for trips in the region.

Sechelt Inlet

Sechelt Inlet begins at the junction of Agamemnon Channel and Jervis Inlet and leads about 35 km (22 miles) southeast to Porpoise Bay. It is one of the few B.C. inlets that's a recognized kayaking route. Sechelt Inlets Marine Park provides multiple campsites, a rare established travel corridor that should be a model for elsewhere on the coast.

Simson and Buccaneer Bay provincial parks

Owner Calvert Simson cleared a farm site, which is still visible in a meadow and orchard behind Farm Bay, in 1912. The farm was abandoned in 1948, and only the foundations of the buildings remain. The park was created in 1986 as a result of a donation by the estate of George Simson. It is an area historically popular with hunters. The population of blacktail deer on South Thormanby has been as high as 300; grouse is another preferred quarry. The park protects 461 ha (1,140 acres).

A new park feature is a swampy lake. A beaver moved to the island in 1984, and in 1985 a mate was introduced. Now a dam blocks the old meadow drainage ditch, creating a lake that attracts bird species, including merganser, kingfisher and blue heron.

Buccaneer Bay park protects just a hectare (2.5 acres) of North Thormanby Island, providing day use and camping in a sand dune ecology. The park was established in 1989.

At the campsite, Smuggler Cove.

The inlet is not pristine. Quarries, logging, marine farms, resorts, cottages and shellfish tenures all make use of the northern sections, while the southern extent is residential bordered by communities such as Tuwanek and Sechelt. However, frequent cobble beaches and a mountainous backdrop provide an attractive wilderness setting, with Narrows Inlet the scenic highlight.

The area is prone to winds. Ocean southerlies blow through, and the inlet can create its own inflow winds.

Descriptions and maps for Sechelt Inlet are split among this section and Lower Jervis Inlet, beginning page 287.

Travel notes: During a 16-day tour of this area in May 2006, I saw no other kayakers in Jervis Inlet or its nearby waters (Agamemnon, Hotham Sound, Blind Bay or Thormanby Islands). One group of four kayakers was on a day trip to Merry Island. Meanwhile, about 20 kayakers were in multiple groups in Sechelt Inlet. Clearly, the word has gotten out about Sechelt, but other locations in this region don't share the burden. It's of concern to B.C. Parks that several sites in Sechelt Inlet are nearing capacity.

Porpoise Bay

Porpoise Bay, at the head of Sechelt Inlet, has drying mud flats, residences, log dumps and log booms southeast of Poise Island. A public wharf is west of the mud flats, with marinas on both sides and another west of Poise Island. Look for Sandy beaches at Sandy Hook and pebble beaches at Trail Bay.

Launches: N49°28.91' W123°45.49'. A launch is available at the end of Porpoise Bay by the government dock. Long-term parking is nearby. Launching a kayak is possible at Porpoise Bay Provincial Park, though overnight parking may be an issue.

Camping: N49°30.61' W123°45.26'. Porpoise Bay Provincial Park has 84 vehicle-accessible campsites and accepts reservations (**1-800-689-9025**). Kayakers could conceivably use the "cyclists-only" campsite meant for those arriving by bike or foot; reservations are not required for these pleasant sites. This campsite would also

South Sechelt Inlet from Porpoise Bay Provincial Park.

make a good base for arriving at Sechelt before an excursion up the inlet. Amenities are phones, a playground, showers, toilets and a trail to the Angus Creek estuary.

Tuwanek

A small residential community is established in this area known for its warm water. A marina at Tillicum Bay has a boat launch often used by kayakers entering the inlet as well as a kayak rental outlet. The west shore of the inlet across from Tuwanek is mostly undeveloped. Near Piper Point is a day-use and picnic area that is sometimes used for camping. It has a pit toilet. North of Tuwanek is Mount Richardson Provincial Park, with a backdrop of unlogged forest affected by a forest fire about 80 years ago. The shore of the park is undeveloped, with numerous beaches. The closest beach to Tuwanek is mainly a day-use area with a pit toilet, but there is a tent pad and a few other camping opportunities. A second site, known as Oyster Beach, features a few possible tent sites behind a gravel beach. A pit toilet and group fire ring is provided.

Camping: N49°35.43' W123°47.04', Nine Mile Point. The campsite called Nine Mile Point is actually over a kilometre (0.7 miles) south of the point within Mount Richardson Provincial Park. This is the best of the three options in the park. Camping is possible on both sides of a creek. Two large fire rings with rough benches are provided. Pictographs can be viewed just south of the site.

Porpoise Bay Provincial Park
The Crowston family homesteaded here at the turn of the last century; the land was purchased from the family for a park in 1966. It features open grass areas and sand beaches. It protects 61 ha (150 acres) and is popular in November and December when chum and coho salmon return to Angus Creek to spawn.

LOWER JERVIS INLET

This is cottage country, with Nelson Island, most of the smaller surrounding islands and even some of the mainland peninsulas under private ownership. Some logging and fish farms round out the area's use. These combine to give the Nelson Island area limited recreational appeal, though the channels do have a stunning mountainous backdrop. Expect gravel or rock beaches, as sediment is rare here. Jervis

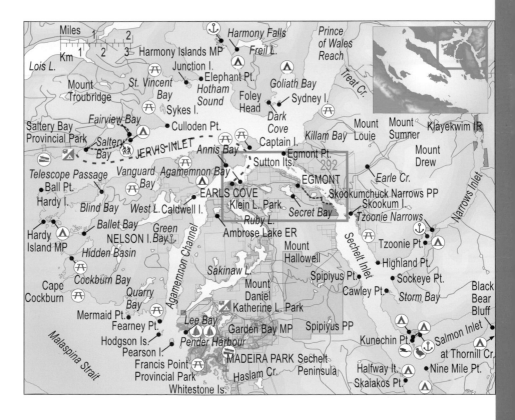

Inlet begins at Scotch Fir Point and the west end of Hardy Island, extending inland for a total of 74 km (46 miles). The north portion past Goliath Bay is covered separately, beginning on page 302. This segment begins with descriptions for the north end of Sechelt Inlet. For descriptions of the southern portion, see page 285.

Place names: Though outnumbered, Rear Admiral Sir John Jervis won a battle over the Spanish in 1797. His victory earned him the title Earl St. Vincent. Vancouver named the inlet prior to that victory in 1792. Galiano and Valdes named it Brazo de Mazarvedo after a naval officer in the Spanish navy who went on to become admiral.

Kunechin Point

Kunechin Point is a bare headland overlooking Kunechin Islets, a pretty cluster of treed and bald rocks that are marine and shorebird nesting habitat and a seal haulout. The outer, bald islet is occasionally used as a campsite but should be avoided, as the natural residents are sensitive to disturbance. Scuba diving is popular at the *Chaudiere*, a former Canadian destroyer that was sunk as an artificial reef.

Camping: N49°37.47' W123°48.37'. The headland at Kunechin Point is the choice location, and it's apt to be full during peak summer periods. A rough beach on the west side of the headland provides access. It tends to disappear at high tides. The designated site is at Kunechin Bay, with two campsites for up to four tents.

N49°35.88' W123°49.17'. A small portion of Sechelt Inlets Marine Park is located almost directly south of Halfway Islet; it's known as Halfway Beach. Sites here are set back in an expansive, clear forest area. It also tends to be busy, as it's midway on a route to Tzoonie Narrows.

Mount Richardson Provincial Park
This park protects 1,000 ha (2,500 acres) in a wilderness setting accessible by water or by land via rough, active logging roads suitable for 4x4s only. Roads or trails lead to Richardson Lake and some old forest recreation campsites. Trails are listed as "bushwhacking" only. Not surprisingly, the park sees few visitors. Flying squirrel, coyote, bobcat, marten, cougar and black bear inhabit the area. The park was established in 1999.

Salmon Inlet

This inlet extends 20 km (12 miles) from Sechelt Inlet into the B.C. interior. It's less scenic than other outer areas, with marine farms, booming grounds and hydro lines. It's also prone to strong winds, which helps keep kayakers away. The inlet ends in Clowhom River, where there is a dam and power plant.

Hotham Sound.

The river leads to Clowhom Lake and a lodge. A portage is possible between the inlet and the lake.

Camping: N49°39.41' W123°36.54'. Thornhill Creek is 14.4 km (9 miles) northeast of Nine Mile Point. It's visited less than the other Sechelt Inlets Marine Park sites in large part due to the difficult winds. There are few options to escape the weather along the way. There are two tent sites and a pit toilet. The beach is stone and rock.

Narrows Inlet

This inlet, backed by mountains such as Mount Drew at 1,887 m (6,191 feet) and Earle Peak at 1,938 m (6,358 feet), is the visual highlight of Sechelt Inlet. The inlet extends 19 km (11.8 miles) in a northeast curve ending at Tzoonie River and the Klayekwin Indian Reserve. There are log booming grounds, marine farms and even resorts along its length, but most of it is pristine. A notable feature is Tzoonie Narrows, where the passage constricts to 90 m (300 feet). Currents can reach 4 knots but it's free from turbulence.

Camping: N49°42.34' W123°46.78'. A campsite is located on the south shore just southwest of the narrowest portion of Tzoonie Narrows. Two rough beaches that tend to disappear at high tides give

The islets off Kunechin Point.

access to flat, clear areas and to trails through the forest to the pit toilet and other clear areas set back in the woods. Remnants of old logging operations abound. This is a large site with many clear areas well suited to groups.

Skookumchuck Narrows

Skookumchuck Narrows lies at the entrance to Sechelt Inlet. Though it's generally referred to as Skookumchuck, it's called Sechelt Rapids in *Canadian Tide and Current Tables, Volume 5.*

The rapids are considered world-class for whitewater kayaking. The peak flow is about 18,000 cubic metres per second reaching 16.5 knots—one of the fastest tidal currents in the world. This creates standing waves of over 3 m (10 feet). The rapids tend to be more confused on the ebb tide; whitewater kayakers favour the flood tide, when suitable waves form.

A park protects the rapids but not the surrounding countryside, which has been heavily logged. A large quarry occupies the shoreline and uplands immediately north of the rapids.

Place names: Skookumchuck means "large current."

Hiking: A trail from just west of Egmont leads through some private land into Skookumchuck Narrows Provincial Park, where there are observation points at Roland and North points. The trail is about an hour one way and passes Brown Lake and a handy café near the parking area.

Camping: Klein Lake Campground is a vehicle-accessible forest recreation site between Earls Cove and Egmont. It has 23 sites available for a fee. It makes a convenient staging area.

Navigating Skookumchuck Narrows: Sea kayakers should have no difficulty if they cross at slack tide. It will also be far safer if the crossing is made when the tide is changing to a favourable direction. I recommend against arriving at the end of a favourable current and trying to cross before the change. The rapids at Skookumchuck can last right until the turn of the tide.

Another suggestion is to arrive a bit early and watch the last of the opposing current. There are good eddies for kayakers along the nearby shoreline so it's possible to get quite close and observe while avoiding the main current. Wind and freshwater runoff can affect when the current turns and it can vary considerably from the time predicted in *Canadian Tide and Current Tables, Volume 5*, so arriving early will ensure you don't miss the slack.

A secondary issue is traffic. Tugboats and recreational boats may converge on the narrows at or near slack tide, causing congestion. Kayakers should keep close to the shoreline to avoid the competition for space.

Egmont

This small community is set in Secret Bay (not to be confused with Secret Cove near Pender Harbour), just northwest of Skookumchuck Narrows. It's a gateway for trips to both Princess Louisa Inlet and Skookumchuck. The Bathgate Marina and a public wharf are on the west shore. The marina has accommodation, a store, liquor sales, a laundromat and showers. There's a launch north of the public dock. A community park with a public toilet is located a block up Egmont

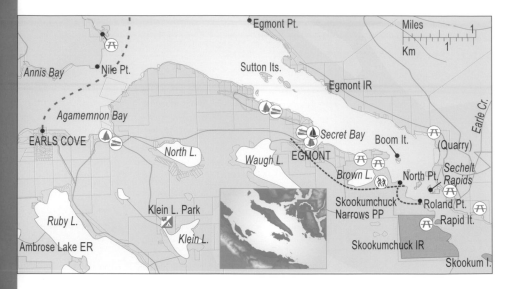

Road (follow the road inland from the wharf). On the far side of the park is the post office (V0N 1N0). Next to the post office is long-term parking that's cheaper than that provided by the marina, closer to the launch. Another block up Egmont Road, past the park, is the trailhead for Skookumchuck Provincial Park. Just inside the trail is a bakery and coffee shop.

A second marina, Egmont, located south of Sutton Islets, has full services, including a launch, showers, laundry, accommodation, kayak rentals and tours. This makes a good staging ground for trips into Jervis Inlet.

Place names: The 74-gun HMS *Egmont* was involved in the battle of Cape St. Vincent in 1797 under the command of Capt. John Sutton. The traditional name for Egmont Point is Quatam-moos, meaning "high face or bluffs."

Agamemnon Bay

Earls Cove, a small community set in Agamemnon Bay, is the ferry terminal for service to Saltery Bay. In the southeast end of the bay is a marina and an associated launch area. To the immediate west is a log dump. The marina and launch are connected with Moccasin Valley, a resort with cabin rentals. The resort has ample parking for those launching from here, making this a good base for ventures into upper Jervis Inlet.

Rapids at Skookumchuck Narrows.

The ferry terminal offers a restaurant, washrooms and a pay telephone. There is no beach access at the terminal; visiting kayakers would have to land near Moccasin Valley and walk the 2 km (1.2 miles).

Pender Harbour

This sheltered anchorage has grown in recent years from a collection of cottages to a thriving tourist and residential community. Three communities—Garden Bay, Madiera Park and Irvines Landing—are known collectively as Pender Harbour.

The harbour is a busy area with numerous marinas located in its multitude of coves: Irvines Landing, Farrington Cove, Duncan Cove, Hospital Bay, Garden Bay, Gerrans Bay and at Madeira Park. Public floats or wharfs are located at Hospital Bay's east side, at the head of Welbourn Cove and at the south end of Gerrans Bay in Whiskey Slough. Anchorages can be found at Welbourn Cove, Gerrans Bay, Garden Bay, Gunboat Bay or west of Garden Peninsula.

Skookumchuk Narrows Provincial Park

This park protects 71 ha (175 acres) on both sides of Sechelt Rapids, as well as an inland lake. Viewpoints give visitors a close-up look at the rapids. The park has a pit toilet, information kiosk and interpretive displays. There is no camping.

The bluffs at Francis Point.

Francis Point Provincial Park

Francis Point was once considered an island, and it was named Beaver Island despite the connection of a drying mud flat in Bargain Narrows. The outer shore of the point was made a park in 2004, one of 37 new parks created that year. It protects 81 ha (200 acres) of steep bluffs and rocky shoreline.

Both Garden Bay and Madeira Park are full-service communities including post offices (V0N 1S0 for Garden Bay and V0N 2H0 for Madeira Park).

Bargain Bay is navigable via Bargain Narrows, often called Canoe Pass. It dries shallow and is usually navigated only at high water. A bridge crosses the narrows, connecting Francis and Sechelt peninsulas. While boaters make good use of the waters here, it has little kayaking appeal.

Launches: N49°37.37' W124°01.54'. Launching is possible at marinas around Pender Habour or the public ramp at Madiera Park (the waypoint). It is a busy tourist area, so parking may be an issue.

Francis Point

This is a new day-use park allowing foot access to the bluffs alongside Francis Point. Middle Bay is a good resting spot for kayakers.

Hiking: The main trail begins at the end of Merrill Road and runs a short distance to Middle Bay. One branch leads north up a steep bluff to a lookout, while a branch south heads along the bluffs to the navigation light on the southern point. This is an exceptional route: it's one of just a few trails on the coast that traverse shoreline bluffs rather than forest.

Garden Bay

This residential bay is backed by a beach protected as a provincial park. A pit toilet is provided. This would make a good kayak haulout and a possible launch site for day trippers. You could unload at the beach, then drive back to the park's main parking area.

Agamemnon Channel

This passage separates Nelson Island and the Sechelt Peninsula in a setting of low, rolling hills and bluffs. The bluffs keep both development and the number of beaches to a minimum. The result is a scattering of dwellings centred in locations like Green Bay and Earls Cove. Otherwise there are just a few fish farms, log dumps and the occasional home in the middle of nowhere. For kayakers it's a pleasant 15-km (9-mile) route from Pender Harbour to Jervis Inlet. Currents are mild in the channel, usually just 1–2 knots, with a flood setting north. Watch for eddies near Fearney Point on spring tides.

Place names: The 64-gun *Agamemnon* was the first battleship commanded by Admiral Nelson. Launched in 1781, she was lost running aground at Rio de la Plata in 1809.

Ecological oddities: Agamemnon Channel is known for its gorgonian corals and cloud sponges. This and deep walls make it a notable dive site.

Camping: N49°45.08' W124°02.32'. There is little to recommend as a suitable kayaking stop along this channel, but the best prospect appears to be a beach north of Caldwell Island and northeast of a hydro transmission line that crosses the channel.

Cape Cockburn

Cape Cockburn is the southwest corner of Nelson Island, distinctive for its white granite bluffs. The bay immediately to the east has a gravel operation in its centre with a noticeable loading conveyor. Fittingly, the bay has several nice gravel beaches—about the best in the area—to the west of the conveyor. Backing the last beach is an abandoned cottage. This is potentially a good low-tide camping area. To the north of the cape is Hidden Basin, which has an islet at the entrance that contributes to a reversing tidal waterfall. A headland overlooking views of the rapids can be reached from a beach to the south. The headland is private property.

To the east of Cape Cockburn is Quarry Bay. It is surrounded by cottages.

Garden Bay Marine Park

This park includes 200 m (656 feet) of shoreline and a backdrop that extends to the summit of Mount Daniel. It's a culturally rich area with burial markers of a First Nation graveyard near the park's dock and moon rings at the mountain summit. The rings of stones were part of a rite of passage. Girls entering puberty were sent to the mountain for four months, during which time they'd construct stone rings, with the stones representing the moon. The mountain was also a defensive site for the Sechelt.

The park protects 163 ha (402 acres) and is accessible by boat (moorage at the public dock) and by road. Trails throughout the park include a route to the Mount Daniel summit. Camping is not permitted.

Place names: Admiral Sir George Cockburn was captain of the frigate *Minerve* in Commodore Nelson's fleet. He joined Sir John Jervis for the battle of St. Vincent. In 1813 he was part of a joint force that captured the city of Washington and destroyed government stores. In 1815 he transported Napoleon to exile at St. Helena.

Blind Bay

Hardy Island is the largest of a cluster of islands that sit off the west side of Nelson Island. Together Hardy and Nelson islands create a sheltered waterway called Blind Bay. While appealing as an intricate archipelago, most of the islands are private. A quarry occupies the hillside north of Hardy Island Marine Park. At the north end of Blind Bay the space between the islands constricts to create Telescope Passage, a route into Jervis Inlet with drying rocks mid-channel. It's advised for small boats only. Watch for the fish weir here.

Camping: N49°43.64' W124°12.85'. The high percentage of private property in Blind Bay means the best option for camping is at Musket Island in the provincial park. Musket Island is connected at most tide levels to Hardy Island by a low ridge of rocks. The best landing opportunity is on the inside of the bay created by the island and the rocky ridge. At higher tides the beach will be rocky; at lower tides a muddy and rocky shellfish bed will emerge. Camping is atop the bluff on Musket Island. Level areas are at a premium, but it could accommodate a group if necessary. Note the rocks leading to the bluff can be slippery when wet. Unfortunately, designated options are few

Ruby-Sakinaw-Agamemnon Circuit

It's possible to complete a lake circuit through Sechelt Peninsula that begins at the top of Ruby Lake. You can reach the lake from a trail that runs along the power lines 4 km (2.5 miles) from Ruby Lake Resort. At the southwest corner of the lake, a portage of almost a kilometre (0.6 mile) is needed to get to Sakinaw Lake. Paddling the length of Sakinaw Lake leads to a short portage to Agamemnon Channel. The circuit ends at Earls Cove, about a kilometre (0.6 mile) from the starting point.

in this area. Some campers will prefer low-tide beach camping at the areas mentioned above.

Place names: Vice Admiral Sir Thomas Masterman Hardy was Lord Nelson's captain in the *Victory* at the Battle of Trafalgar. Blind Bay and Telescope Passage are references to the Battle of Copenhagen, when Nelson put his blind eye to his telescope, allowing him to ignore his commander-in-chief's signal of recall. The traditional name is Atsilatl, meaning "nice calm water."

Travel notes: Under the right conditions, at night at high tide, water rushes over the rock ledge between Musket and Nelson islands, and phosphorescence in the water creates a mesmerizing light show well worth the midnight vigil.

Vanguard Bay

This deep bay has a large shellfish farm on the south end, but an inviting beach south of the west entrance. Two ruined boats lie atop the beach. Some houses are in the area, which is only marginally suited to camping.

Saltery Bay

This busy bay has a government marina, ferry terminal, log dump, booming ground and float-plane terminal. The ferry terminal is in the southwest entrance to the bay, while the public wharf is to the east. The nearby provincial park is located off Highway 101. The campground in the park's east parcel is not marine-accessible. There's a small beach at Mermaid Cove to use as a rest area.

Place names: The bay is named for the fish saltery located here in the early 1900s.

Launches: N49°46.93' W124°13.07'. There's a boat ramp with a good beach adjacent in the day-use parcel of the park.

Camping: Saltery Bay Provincial Park has a vehicle-accessible campground with 42 campsites and pit toilets. Reservations are taken May

Ambrose Lake Ecological Reserve
This reserve, created in 1971 to protect a small lake and bogland, also includes the adjacent forest and a substantial shoreline of inaccessible rock bluff along Agamemnon Channel—228 ha (563 acres) in total. Access is not allowed.

Across Blind Bay.

to September. Convenient to the Saltery Bay ferry, this would be a good staging ground in the area.

Fairview Bay

This small bay east of Saltery Bay has a float in the middle and beaches to the west and north ends. The north end of the west beach gives access to the Sunshine Coast Trail (see page 324). This provides paddlers a chance for a day hike to Rainy Day Lake or, for the more ambitious, a viewpoint on Mount Troubridge.

Camping: N49°47.37' W124°07.27'. If you land at the west beach, look for a short trail on the north end leading to a pleasant clearing in the forest complete with a stout picnic table. There is no view, but this site does provide high tide protection. At neap tides beach camping is a possibility, with good views north to Princes of Wales Reach.

Captain Island

This island has rock shoreline and is heavily treed and undeveloped. The only beach access is a small stone site on the south end. It's separated from Nelson Island by Agnew Passage, which is generally

Musket Island, Hardy Island Marine Park.

Hardy Island Marine Park

This park protects the upland of Hardy Island surrounding an anchorage, with shelter courtesy diminutive Musket Island. A bench on the bluff of Musket Island provides a place to enjoy the view toward Texada Island. It's the park's only amenity.

The park was formerly known as Musket Island Marine Park, a name still proclaimed on the sign at the park. The Council of BC Yacht Clubs petitioned the name change to reflect the anchorage, known as Hardy Island Anchorage. The change was made in 2004. The park was created in 1992 and protects 16.8 ha (41.5 acres).

protected from the wind, even when a westerly is blowing down Jervis Inlet. The difficulty is the Saltery Bay–Earls Cove ferry route through this narrow passage. Sightlines are poor, a problem that extends into both Jervis Inlet and Agamemnon Bay. Use caution when crossing the area.

Between St. Vincent Bay, Captain Island and Hotham Sound is a rarely used Canadian Forces exercise area for torpedo firing and air-to-surface missiles.

The islet on the north tip of Nelson Island is a pleasant place to visit. It's connected to Nelson Island by a gravel and clamshell bar. This is a popular recreation area with an established campsite on the islet, though the uplands on both sides are private property. Low-tide camping is possible on the gravel bar.

Mermaid Cove, Saltery Bay.

Saltery Bay Provincial Park

This park is divided into two distinct sites. The western portion is a day-use area with a rocky beach popular for swimming and picnicking, plus a boat launch. The eastern portion is a campground, complete with showers and a change room, in a forest setting with beach access at Mermaid Cove. A unique feature popular with divers is a 3-m (9-foot) bronze statue of a mermaid at 10 fathoms in the cove. The park is completely wheelchair-accessible, including the change room, showers, toilet and even the access ramp for scuba diving (best used at high tides). The park was created in 1966 and protects 69 ha (170 acres).

Place names: Captain Island was named after HMS *Captain*, 74 guns, built on the Thames in 1787. At the battle of St. Vincent in 1797 Commodore Nelson ordered the ship to turn out of the line of battle, the famous move that prevented the Spanish fleet from escaping.

St. Vincent Bay

Long beaches line the southwest and northwest shores of this large bay. Otherwise it's relatively featureless; there are shellfish farms at Sykes and Junction islands and homes dot the area.

Hotham Sound

This sound extends 10 km (6 miles) north and its impressive mountainous backdrop rivals Prince of Wales Reach. It ends in a marine farm. The main attraction is Harmony Falls, locally known as Freil Falls, which cascades down 450 m (1,400 feet) in several tiers. Slightly to the north is Harmony Islands Marine Park. The park protects the southernmost of the three islands that make up the island group. The other two are private.

Looking toward Captain Island from the islet at north Nelson Island.

Granville Bay, to the south of Harmony Falls, is a log dump with a few houses, some in ruins. Logging is extensive on the hillside. Foley Head is the south end of a peninsula that divides Hotham Sound and upper Jervis Inlet. It is steep and rocky.

The two mooring buoys southwest of Syren Point are reserved for the navy.

Place names: Admiral William Hotham (1736–1813) was rear admiral of the Princess Royal in the Nootka controversy in 1790.

Camping: N49°51.15' W124°00.17'. Immediately south of Harmony Falls is a small rock beach with a clear section behind it—a good base for exploring Hotham Sound and Harmony Falls.

Goliath Bay
This bay has limited development in the south end, with two houses in Dark Cove and a marine farm off Sydney Island. North of a prominent headland is the ruin of a single house. The rest of the bay is undeveloped.

Camping: N49°50.34' W123°56.55'. On the north end of Goliath Bay is a rock beach west of a creek with bald bluffs on both sides. A good upland clearing is available for a tent or two. A bonus is the creek, which is likely to provide good water during most seasons.

Jervis Inlet is 74 km (46 miles) from the entrance at Malaspina Strait to the tip at Skwawka River. Most visitors never reach the end, however, and instead turn off through Malibu Rapids into Princess Louisa Inlet. There are many adjectives to describe the inlet. Perhaps the most glowing tribute I've heard is "life-altering." Princess Louisa Inlet has grown to become one of the top cruising destinations in North America, and a regular stream of boat traffic makes its way up and down Jervis Inlet daily. Day tours and water taxis are available from Egmont, making the beauty accessible to people who would otherwise not be able to experience it.

It's rarely described, though, as a kayaking destination. Jervis Inlet's reputation as being steep-shored and inhospitable is unfounded; river deltas and low-elevation forest areas provide camping opportunities at strategic points. And while many portions are steep and the distance is long, it's a manageable and leisurely two-day paddle up the inlet from a launch near Egmont.

Jervis Inlet has a long history of First Nations use, reflected in several dozen pictographs that can be seen along its length, from the start of Agamemnon Channel to Patrick Point. Look for the dull ochre impressions under slight overhangs where the exposure to weather is lessened. Good locations to see them are Vancouver Bay, Smanit Creek and Patrick Point.

Tidal currents are generally weak in the inlet; wind is likely to be a larger factor. Lower Jervis Inlet (see page 287) is prone to westerlies, but weather from the Strait of Georgia, particularly westerlies, tends to die off at Goliath Bay, after which Jervis Inlet begins its own wind and weather pattern. This may be inflow or outflow winds. The weather is likely to include cloud and rain, far more so than nearby coastal locations. If the weather is partly cloudy elsewhere, Princess Louisa can be socked in for days. However, even in low cloud cover the steep, waterfall-studded mountainsides provide striking views. Just be aware that if it's wet, it will likely be very wet. Plan accordingly.

Prince of Wales Reach

This reach encompasses the lower two legs of Jervis Inlet north of Sechelt Inlet. The first portion is about 10 km (6 miles) northeast to Saumarez Bluff, the second about 13 km (8 miles) northwest to Moorsam Bluff. The lower portion is rolling hills, rocky crags and

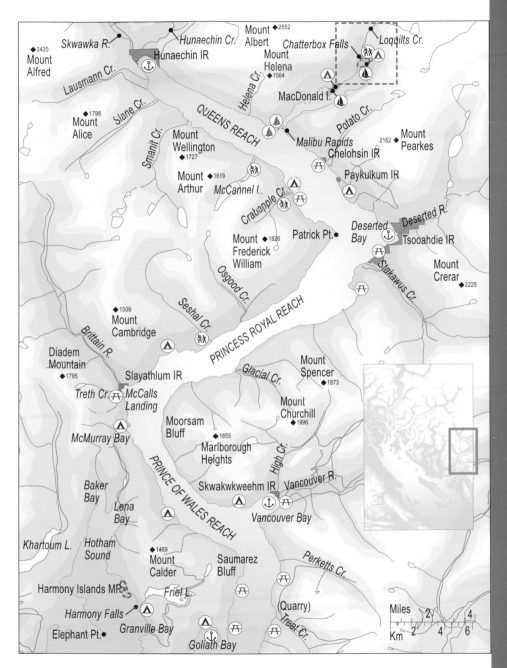

a few bays. At Treat Creek a large quarry operation has turned the valley front into sand bluffs and the creek area into a loading facility. At Saumarez Bluff the intrusion of civilization melts away and the height of the surrounding mountains grows to 1,855 m (6,085 feet) at Marlborough Peak, the highest of the range called Marlborough Heights. Vancouver Bay is at the base of a deep valley. It has pictographs and a beach at the head, but it's too short to allow the mountain viewscape to change, making it a low-priority destination.

Place names: King Edward VII was Prince of Wales when this inlet was named in 1859. Edward succeeded to the throne in 1901 upon the death of Queen Victoria.

Camping: There are numerous beaches along Prince of Wales Reach. Most are rock, but a few are more forgiving stones or pebbles. Landing options are better at higher tides. The problem with most beaches, though, is the upland is steep, heavily forested and overgrown with scrub. Some exceptions are listed below.

N49°55.04' W123°55.45'. The north entrance to Vancouver Bay is a curve of shore with a rough but extensive beach. The upland is low-elevation, level forest. You may need to bushwhack to create a clearing.

N49°54.83' W123°58.13'. Look for a pleasant beach mid-channel on the south shore west of Vancouver Bay. It's backed by low-lying forest. A collapsed cabin occupies one level area in the upland, and at present is a hazard. Immediately southeast is a flat area that, with a bit of work, would make a good camping area. Note this location makes the chance of paddling in one day to Malibu Rapids questionable.

N49°58.23' W124°00.56'. McMurray Bay is easily identified by the pronounced headland. Tucked into the headland is a good gravel beach. In the upland is a trail that leads to a ruined cabin and shelter. Clear, level areas can be found around the cabin. Some might like to set a tent on the mossy rock immediately to the north of the beach. The beach is also fairly high-backed and would be a nice place to camp during lower tide levels. This is the maximum recommended distance from Malibu Rapids if you want to make the rapids in a single day of paddling.

Heading up Jervis Inlet.

Princess Royal Reach

Princess Royal Reach begins at Brittain River and McCalls Landing. The estuary at Brittain River is sand, with private property and reserve land around the area. Watch for ruins of old buildings and jetties. The reach continues about 16 km (10 miles) northeast to Patrick Point, with a usual width of about 1.6 km (1 mile). At the northeast extent is Deserted Bay, which is surrounded by nice beaches and an old collection of homes near Stakawus Creek. Logging is active in the area, and there's a log dump in the northwest corner.

Place names: Empress Frederick of Germany and Princess Royal of England (1840–1901) married Frederick, Crown Prince of Prussia, soon to be German Emperor, in 1858.

Camping: N50°01.18' W123°57.91'. About 4 km (2.5 miles) northeast of Brittain River is a rough stone and rock beach. Here you'll find another ruined cabin in the woods. There are a few clear areas along the beach at the high tide level, though you might have to remove some brambles. This is a good site for reaching Malibu Rapids the next day.

Hiking: Logging roads at Seshal Creek lead to a collection of sub-alpine lakes and eventually a pass into Smanit Creek.

Queens Reach

Queens Reach, the final leg of Jervis Inlet, runs 16 km (10 miles) northwest to end at marshy ground that soars to Mount Victoria at 2,088 m (6,850 feet). Beaches line the approach to Malibu Rapids. On the north shore they're likely reserve property, while on the south shore the first main beach is private property backed by a conspicuous cabin. To wait out a tide change, pull in to Crabapple Creek, where there's a better beach and remnants of past logging.

Hiking: A route from Crabapple Creek leads to Mount Frederick William, the nearby ridge and an adjacent lake. Another option is a trip to McCannel Lake via an old logging road from the north-east. Bring a rod—it's a good trout lake, complete with a dock. Float planes are the usual method of arrival. Note these trails are not official routes and may be overgrown.

Camping: N50°07.26' W123°47.76'. Crabapple Creek may be a necessary stop if you miss a tide change at Malibu Rapids. Or look for a beach on the north shore to the south of Paykulkum reserve. These are my choices for the two best options outside the reserves. Be prepared for a bit of site development, as these are not established campsites.

Malibu Rapids

This is a narrow channel further constricted by rocks and islets. Currents can reach 9 knots, with dangerous rips, eddies and standing waves. Conditions are generally worse at low water. The current at low tide turns 35 minutes after the tide change at Point Atkinson, and the change at high tide 25 minutes after. If in doubt, stop at the Malibu Club to check out the current before entering. There's a nice beach outside the northwest entrance to the rapids behind the navigation light rock. Club staff are generally amenable to visitors.

The Malibu Club dominates the headland around Malibu Rapids with cottages, lodges, docks, an extensive boardwalk around the outer point and groomed grounds that include a golf course. Trails used by the club, a private camp run by the Christian ministry Young Life, lead to various local peaks. To find out more about the club, visit **sites.younglife.org/camps/MalibuClub/default.aspx**.

Near McMurray Bay, looking up Princess Royal Reach.

Princess Louisa Inlet

This inlet is impressive in part because it's so narrow—as little as 800 m (half a mile) wide—and because the neighbouring mountains are so high, soaring to 2,552 m (8,372 feet) at Mount Albert. The scenery at Chatterbox Falls is also renowned. Just outside the falls there's a long boat dock associated with the park, plus outhouses, trails, picnic tables and a gazebo with a central fire pit.

Place names: Princess Louisa Inlet was known as Suivoolot, or "sunny and warm" to the Sechelt.

Hiking: A loop trail leads from the dock through the picnic area to Chatterbox Falls and back. A more strenuous hike is to Trapper's Cabin. The unmaintained trail leads from the loop trail up into the alpine region behind Princess Louisa Inlet. It's about two hours one way to the cabin. From there it's possible to traverse the glaciers in a route exiting at the Sims Creek valley near Squamish. According to the staff at the Malibu Club, a pair of men did the route from Squamish to the inlet, then floated down Jervis Inlet in an inflatable kayak in the dark. And, yes, it did spring a leak.

Camping: N50°11.26' W123°48.21'. One of the two provincial park campgrounds in Princess Louisa Inlet is located behind MacDonald

At Patrick Point.

Island, 4.2 km (2.6 miles) from Malibu Rapids. A dock and rough beaches give access to several forested sites with picnic tables. Adjacent to the park campground is a dock and an outstation for the Malibu Club. You'll likely see the outstation dock before the park dock, which can be hidden by MacDonald Island.

N50°12.31' W123°46.15'. The inner provincial park campsite is immediately to the east of Chatterbox Falls. You can land at the dock or the sand beach in front of the sites. These have the advantage of views and fire pits, as well as access to the gazebo. They are along a trail used by sightseers and are prone to foot traffic. They are also likely the first to be nabbed during the summer season.

Kayaking to Princess Louisa Inlet: Despite its reputation to the contrary, reaching Princess Louisa Inlet can be achieved easily in a two-day paddle from Egmont or Earls Cove. The return would be one or two days, depending on conditions. It's probably best to plan for at least five days, or better yet a week, which would give you time to explore the inlet.

The best time to depart is early morning, preferably with a low tide. Leave an hour or two before low tide when the adverse current is minimal, then benefit from the assistance of the flood tide for the following six hours or so. Don't take your lunch break during the middle two hours of the flood; that's when you'll get the full

The lodge at Malibu Rapids.

Chatterbox Falls.

Princess Louisa Marine Park

Princess Louisa Inlet was transferred from private hands to a non-profit society in 1953 and made a provincial park in 1965. James 'Mac' Macdonald purchased the head of the inlet in 1927 after first visiting in 1919. He built a lodge that burned down in 1940, then turned the property over to the Princess Louisa International Society to hold for all in perpetuity. The transfer to a provincial park was made with his blessing. The park, meanwhile, is a small portion of the 964 ha (2,382 acres) in the Princess Louisa Inlet Conservation Area. The conservation area was made possible by a donation from the Tula Foundation and Weyerhaeuser. This protects the area from shoreline to alpine.

benefit of the current. Hopefully the tide will turn at about the same time the afternoon outflow winds (if any) begin. Morning outflow winds could be a trip spoiler. Either way, try to end your first day somewhere no farther away from Malibu Rapids than McMurray Bay. From there it's about 32 km (20 miles), or a good six to eight hours of favourable paddling conditions, to the rapids.

On the second day repeat the strategy of the first day—depart before the change to low tide and before the winds begin. If all goes according to plan you'll arrive at Malibu Rapids at about high tide in the early afternoon, hopefully riding the last of the falling current into Princess Louisa Inlet.

The return journey will be much simpler. If you spend several days in Princess Louisa, the tide will start to change from a morning low (assuming you left with that) to a morning high. This is desirable, as you can pass Malibu Rapids at or near high slack, then get a boost from the ebb flow the whole morning. The assistance will be stronger than the flood due to the freshwater runoff. The only thing that might stop you is an inflow wind. If that doesn't occur, paddlers should be able to return to Egmont in a day. Plan the trip for May or early June to avoid crowds and to see snow on the peaks and more and stronger waterfalls. Plan for August if you want a better chance at sunshine.

One of the numerous waterfalls in Princess Louisa Inlet.

Roscoe Inlet.

Desolation

CHAPTER SIX

CAPT. GEORGE VANCOUVER MAY HAVE NAMED DESOLATION SOUND IN disappointment for what he found here, but the name, ironically, now evokes images of a place that is rugged, grand, imposing and wildly beautiful. It's a magnet for boaters and kayakers alike, who are drawn to the warm waters and intricate coastline.

Desolation Sound is just a small portion of this highly varied region that encompasses several large islands and a huge mainland fiord—Toba Inlet. Many of the smaller neighbouring islands, like Kinghorn and Martin, are part of the main Desolation Sound kayaking network, but to the north the number of visitors falls off sharply. While kayaking campsites like Curme Islands are near capacity during peak summer periods, Pryce Channel is rarely visited. Cortes Island offers another secondary route, with its many bays, off-lying island clusters and provincial parks.

The most adventurous will want to head deep into Toba Inlet, where some peaks tower to over 2 km in height (about 7,000 feet).

Exploring by kayak

Most kayakers, and even boaters, tend to cluster along the established areas of Desolation Sound Provincial Park and the immediate adjacent waterways. The most popular areas for kayakers are Copeland and Curme islands. One of the unique features of this region is the number of level, mossy or grassy headlands perfect for a tent. The hitch is getting to them. Desolation Sound has a lack of kayak-friendly beaches. Sediment is almost non-existent, so many of the popular sites require rock-ledge landings (see page 15). This hasn't thwarted kayakers, though. Because access to the campsites tends to

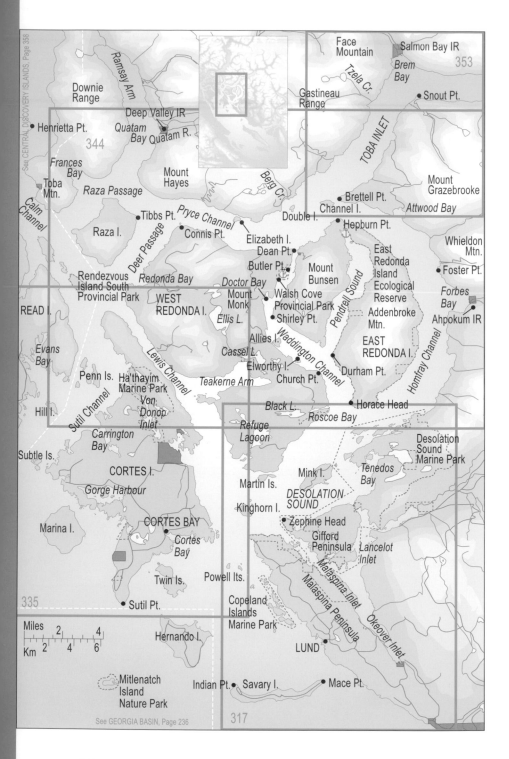

See CENTRAL DISCOVERY ISLANDS, Page 358

Downie Range

Ramsay Arm

Face Mountain

Salmon Bay IR

353

Tzela Cr.

Brem Bay

Snout Pt.

Gastineau Range

Deep Valley IR

Quatam Bay

Henrietta Pt.

Quatam R.

344

TOBA INLET

Frances Bay

Mount Grazebrooke

Toba Mtn.

Mount Hayes

Raza Passage

Berg Cr.

Brettell Pt.

Channel I.

Attwood Bay

Calm Channel

Tibbs Pt.

Pryce Channel

Double I.

Hepburn Pt.

Raza I.

Connis Pt.

Elizabeth I.

Whieldon Mtn.

Deer Passage

Dean Pt.

East Redonda Island Ecological Reserve

Foster Pt.

Rendezvous Island South Provincial Park

Redonda Bay

Butler Pt.

Mount Bunsen

Pendrell Sound

Forbes Bay

WEST REDONDA I.

Doctor Bay

Mount Monk

Walsh Cove Provincial Park

Addenbroke Mtn.

Ahpokum IR

READ I.

Ellis L.

Shirley Pt.

EAST REDONDA I.

Homfray Channel

Evans Bay

Allies I.

Waddington Channel

Cassel L.

Penn Is.

Lewis Channel

Elworthy I.

Durham Pt.

Ha'thayim Marine Park

Teakerne Arm

Church Pt.

Hill I.

Von Donop Inlet

Sutil Channel

Black L.

Horace Head

Roscoe Bay

Subtle Is.

Carrington Bay

Refuge Lagoon

Desolation Sound Marine Park

CORTES I.

Mink I.

Tenedos Bay

Gorge Harbour

Martin Is.

DESOLATION SOUND

Marina I.

Kinghorn I.

Zephine Head

CORTES BAY

Gifford Peninsula

Lancelot Inlet

Cortes Bay

Malaspina Inlet

Twin Is.

Powell Its.

335

Sutil Pt.

Copeland Islands Marine Park

Malaspina Peninsula

Okeover Inlet

Miles 2   4

Km 2   4   6

Hernando I.

LUND

Mitlenatch Island Nature Park

Indian Pt.

Savary I.

Mace Pt.

See GEORGIA BASIN, Page 236

317

be difficult and good sites snapped up quickly, kayakers usually find a comfortable place to establish a base camp. To avoid crowds, plan to visit in May, June and September, when the weather is still generally favourable and the visitors far fewer.

Away from Desolation Sound there's much less competition for sites, even though the camping areas can actually be better. Oddly, the best beach in the region is in Toba Inlet (odd because inlets are notorious for poor camping opportunities). Together these secondary campsites create a network that takes in some fabulous mountain scenery and explores beautiful passages such as north Waddington Channel, well away from the main crowds.

Recommended kayaking trips

- *If you have a day:* For those travelling the BC Ferries' circle route (see page 226), Desolation Sound lends itself well to day trips; possibilities include a circumnavigation of Savary Island from Lund, a trip to Copeland Islands from Lund or an exploration of Okeover Arm and Malaspina Inlet from the launch at Okeover. If you are on Cortes Island and are looking to paddle for a day, consider a launch from Cortes Bay and a paddle around the nearby headlands and the Twin Islands area. Another good option is from Mansons Landing around Marina Island or up Sutil Channel.

- *If you have two days:* A good overnight destination is the Copeland Islands from Lund; overnighting at Feather Cove, Galley Bay, Kinghorn or Martin islands is possible from Lund or the Okeover Arm launch. Just be sure of your tide times if you're travelling through Malaspina Inlet. From Cortes, an overnight trip from Manson Landing to Penn Islands or Von Donop Inlet would be interesting.

- *If you have three days:* Because of the slim number of launch sites, triangle routes are difficult to create. I suggest establishing a base camp anywhere convenient in Desolation Sound and spending the middle day exploring the area. Consider the Copeland Islands with a day trip to Tenedos Bay. On Cortes, stay two nights at Penn Islands and explore Von Donop Inlet the middle day, or vice versa.

- *If you have five days:* Most people who travel the distance to Desolation Sound will likely plan on a minimum stay of five days. Base-camp exploration is the norm, but some pleasant circuits are possible, such as a circumnavigation of Cortes Island. For this I suggest Lund, Twin Islands, Ha'thayim Marine Park, Teakerne Arm, Copeland Islands and back. Advanced kayakers could reach Toba Inlet. A suggested itinerary is Lund, Curme Islands, Toba Inlet entrance, a day trip into Toba Inlet, Roscoe Bay, then back to Lund.

- *If you have a week:* With this much time, a circuit of the area is possible. An itinerary might be a launch from Lund, Copeland Islands, Roscoe Bay, Attwood Bay, Deer Passage, Teakerne Arm, Kinghorn Island and back to the launch site. It could easily be extended with various side trips, such as Toba Inlet or the west side of Cortes Island.

- *The ideal trip:* The most idyllic area is Desolation Sound Marine Park, so it pays to spend at least a few days here before exploring the wider region. My ideal trip would probably be a stay at Curme Islands with a few days based there exploring the region; a day at Roscoe Inlet with perhaps an extra day spent on the hikes; a trip to Toba Inlet, then west to Deer Passage, with a stay at South Rendezvous Island; a night at Penn Islands with maybe a side trip into Von Donop Inlet; a stay at Marina Island; and finally Copeland Islands, then home. This could be accomplished in 10 days or even less, but would be best as a two-week trip. There are many options for side trips, such as to Teakerne Arm, or shortening the trip by staying to the east side of Cortes Island instead of visiting Penn and Marina islands. However you finally arrange it, this area makes an exceptional kayaking holiday.

DESOLATION SOUND

Desolation Sound is a relatively placid area, without the strong rapids that exist between some of the nearby islands (with the exception of Malaspina Inlet). The flood streams from Queen Charlotte Strait and Juan de Fuca Strait meet here, creating generally weak currents usually below 2 knots. They can also be irregular and prone to wind influence. The flood flows north along the west side of Kinghorn Island and east along the north side, then northeast through Desolation

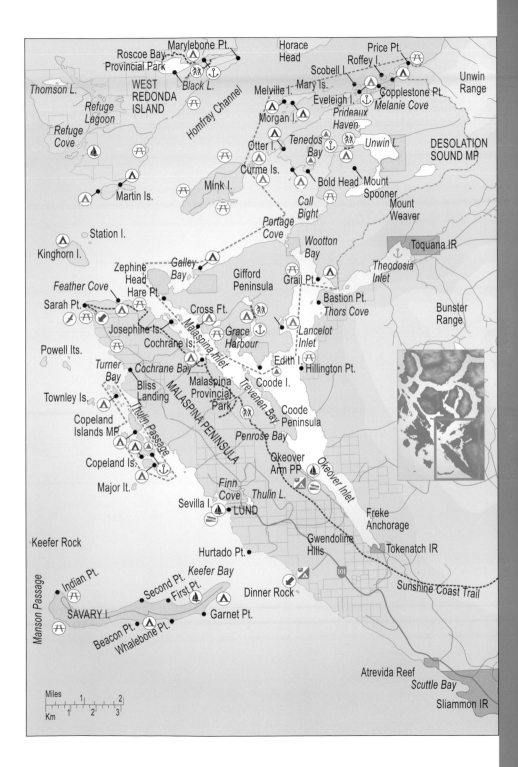

Thomson L.

WEST
REDONDA
ISLAND

Refuge
Lagoon

Refuge
Cove

Roscoe Bay
Provincial Park

Marylebone Pt.

Black L.

Homfray Channel

Martin Is.

Mink Is.

Melville I.

Morgan I.

Otter I.

Curme Is.

Portage
Cove

Horace
Head

Mary Is.
Scobell I.

Melville I.

Eveleigh I.

Tenedos
Bay

Bold Head

Call
Bight

Price Pt.
Roffey I.

Copplestone Pt.

Melanie Cove

Prideaux
Haven

Unwin L.

Mount
Spooner

Unwin
Range

DESOLATION
SOUND MP

Mount
Weaver

Station I.

Kinghorn I.

Zephine
Head
Hare Pt.

Feather Cove

Sarah Pt.

Josephine Is.

Powell Its.

Galley
Bay

Cross Ft.

Cochrane Is.

Gifford
Peninsula

Grail Pt.

Grace
Harbour

Wootton
Bay

Bastion Pt.
Thors Cove

Lancelot
Inlet

Theodosia
Inlet

Toquana IR

Bunster
Range

Turner
Bay

Cochrane Bay

Bliss
Landing

Malaspina
Provincial
Park

Edith I.

Coode I.

Hillington Pt.

Townley Is.

Copeland
Islands MP

Copeland Is.

Major It.

Thulin Passage

MALASPINA PENINSULA

Coode
Peninsula

Penrose Bay

Okeover
Arm PP

Okeover Inlet

Freke
Anchorage

Tokenatch IR

Sevilla I.

LUND

Finn
Cove

Thulin L.

Keefer Rock

Hurtado Pt.

Gwendoline
Hills

Manson Passage

Indian Pt.

SAVARY I.

Second Pt.

First Pt.

Beacon Pt.

Whalebone Pt.

Garnet Pt.

Keefer Bay

Dinner Rock

Sunshine Coast Trail

Atrevida Reef

Scuttle Bay

Sliammon IR

Miles
Km

A small island near Preedy Harbour.

Sound. The two conflicting flood streams can meet at Squirrel Cove on Cortes Island, but in bad weather—southeast winds—can shift as far north as the north end of Lewis Channel.

Ecological oddities: An estimated 10 percent of the Canadian population of marbled murrelet can be found in Desolation Sound during summer. Eighty-five nests have been indentified in the nearby forests by using radio collars, but much of murrelet behaviour remains a mystery, including the number of breeding birds in this region. Rare creatures to watch for in the sound include short-tailed albatross, western screech-owl, coast tailed frog and northern abalone.

Place names: Capt. George Vancouver named this sound based on his appraisal of the region. He wrote in June 1792: "Our residence here was truly forlorn; an awful silence pervaded the gloomy forests, whilst animated nature seemed to have deserted the neighbouring country, whose soil afforded only a few small onions, some samphire and here and there bushes bearing a scanty crop of indifferent berries. Nor was the sea more favourable to our wants, the steep rocky shores prevented the use of the seine, and not a fish at the bottom could be tempted to take the hook."

Savary Island

This island is almost completely fringed with sandy beach. At Second Point it extends almost a kilometre (0.6 miles) at low tide. The gently sloping north side is highly residential, with the village centre concentrated around the government wharf on the north side of the island in Keefer Bay. Blame pioneer developers for the current concentration of homes, as they subdivided the island into small lots in 1910. The south side of the island has numerous sandy cliffs as high as 84 m (275 feet). Extensive pockets of offshore boulders lie in the shallow water off the south and west shores, particularly south of Indian Point. This can make kayak navigation a

Typical sandy bluffs on the south shore of Savary Island.

challenge, especially as Indian Point is prone to turbulence. Keep an eye open for submerged rocks. The last ice age created the unusual composition of the island. Streams of melting water in advance of the glaciers deposited the sand about 20,000 years ago. The glaciers followed, depositing the boulders. Rare plants to be found here include contorted-pod evening-primrose and redstem springbeauty.

Savary Island is about 7.6 km (4.7 miles) in length and about 450 m (1,500 feet) wide at its narrowest. A circumnavigation is about 18.6 km (11.5 miles). The current year-round population is about 90; in summer it burgeons to about 2,000.

Place names: Captain Vancouver named it Savary's Island in 1792; the reference is a mystery. It is Áyhus, or "double-headed serpent" in Sliammon, thought to be a reference to the island's shape. In Sliammon legend, the Transformer spied a double-headed serpent on its way back to its cave at Hurtado Point and changed it into the island.

Looking out from the south Copeland Island.

Camping: N49°56.20' W124°48.14'. Camping is possible anywhere below the high tide line around the island; this is attractive to back-packers and unpopular with residents. The beach northeast of Garnet Point is a key location for tenters. Here the homes are high above a sandy bluff, minimizing conflict. However, I recommend the beach between Beacon and Whalebone points. The upland is backed by the island's airstrip, keeping it free from residences—probably the only beach location on the island where homes can't be seen.

Lund

This small community centres on a cove with a government wharf and boat ramp. Services are clustered around the area and include a store, liquor sales, a post office (V0N 2G0), restaurants, a pub, showers, laundry, water, a water taxi and a hotel. To the south is Dinner Rock, a small islet with nearby waters prone to turbulence. Notable is a large cross on the rock. It was erected in 1998 in memory of five people who died in 1947 when the *Gulf Stream* struck the rock with 41 people aboard. Three children died, including an 18-month-old girl whose father erected a cross on the islet. Fifty years after the accident a more permanent cross was erected during a memorial service. The original cross is now in the Powell River Museum.

Launches: N49°58.92' W124°45.69'. A twin boat ramp is located next to the government dock. The ramps are concrete and there's no beach. Kayakers should use the inside ramp; the outer ramp is deeper and used by larger boats and barges, and kayakers are liable to be ushered aside to make way. It's a busy area. Parking is available in a private lot nearby or for free alongside various roads outside the core area. A steep car-top boat launch is located at the Dinner Rock campground, 4 km (2.5 miles) south of Lund.

Camping: N49°57.07' W124°43.43'. A good staging area is at the Dinner Rock campground, 4 km (2.5 miles) south of Lund. It's ac-cessible by a rough logging road and is also marine-accessible, should you be paddling by. It's located about half a kilometre (500 yards) north of Dinner Rock. The campground offers washrooms and water. Call **604-483-2435**.

Copeland Islands

These islands are popular for the bays, islets and nooks, as well as close proximity to the launch at Lund. The islands are separated from Malaspina Peninsula by Thulin Passage, which is used by recreational and commercial traffic.

Place names: Joe Copeland was a pioneer who apparently rowed to Theodosia Arm from the United States at the turn of the last century. He became a well-known logger and trapper, his fame stemming largely from greeting visiting steamboats dressed in a full Confederate uniform. Legend has it he was a stagecoach robber who fled to Canada. Or so the story goes.

Camping: There are four main campsites (three official, with pit toilets) in the Copeland Islands. The names given below are based on the assumption there are four main islands (an arguable premise, as the north island is actually split in two). The descriptions run south to north.

N49°59.90' W124°48.21', South Island. A rock beach on the central northeast side of the southern island has a kayak skid cleared. Above are two wooden tent pads with additional flat areas for another four tents or so. For a quaint alternative, look for a tiny, drying cove just to the southeast of the main camp (N49°59.90' W124°48.01'). The flat headland is suitable for a tent, though access might be difficult at some tide levels.

N50°00.11' W124°48.57', Second Island. The first cove on the southeast side of the second island is a popular anchorage. The cove to the west of the anchorage has a flat headland used for camping. I found the access dubious, though, with little in the way of a beach. A second, smaller site is hidden up the west headland of the anchorage cove.

N50°00.74' W124°48.85', Third Island. This site can be reached from beaches to both the east and west, with the best access from the west. The bay to the east is a well-used anchorage. In the forest upland are clear tent areas and a trail across the island that connects the two beaches. Some campers may also find rock ledge camping on the nearby islets favourable.

N50°01.54' W124°49.44', North Island. What may appear to be a single island on the north end of the marine park is really two, with a channel running east-west. The camping area can be approached from beaches to either the north or south. The north beach has a kayak skid. In the forested upland are tent clearings and a pit toilet.

Bliss Landing

This small community at Turner Bay has a private marina and homes on the bay and surrounding headlands. To the immediate north is a small bay with a good beach for a break.

Sarah Point

This very pretty point is accessible by the Sunshine Coast Trail. The trailhead is at a beach south of the point, where a wooden sign is visible from the water. Landing at the beach and walking to the point makes a good break. It's a key bird area, used by marbled murrelet, cormorant, surf scoter and western grebe. Camping options are poor at the beach.

Launches: N50°03.54' W124°50.21'. A forestry road from Lund ends at the beach to the south of Sarah Point, from which a car-top boat or kayak could be launched. Just be cautioned that the road from Lund is extremely poor and deteriorates substantially after Bliss Landing. A 4x4 would be a necessity and even then it may be tough.

Place names: Sarah was the wife of Roderick Finlayson, chief factor of the Hudson's Bay Company in 1859.

Camping: N50°03.80' W124°49.28'. Feather Cove, east of Sarah Point, is a key kayaking campsite for Desolation Sound Marine Park. It can be reached on foot by the Sunshine Coast Trail and consequently is used by both kayakers and backpackers. Sites are located in a forest clearing at the midpoint of the beach. The most favourable sites are two tent clearings on the headland to the east of the beach.

Kinghorn Island

This is a large Crown island north of Malaspina Peninsula with a cliffy south shoreline and rough beaches among rocky headlands on the north side. It's outside the Desolation Sound Marine Park boundaries but, like nearby Martin Islands, is well used recreationally.

The trailhead sign at Sarah Point.

Travel notes: There's a humorous commemorative plaque on the west shore of the island. I won't give away the punchline. It's worth the paddle just to read it.

Camping: N50°05.17' W124°51.15'. On the north side of Kinghorn there are two main beaches divided by a rock bluff. Look for a rough kayak skid just west of the bluff. The skid leads to a clear, forested area hidden behind a huge drift log. Inside are tent clearings, benches and a fire pit.

Malaspina Inlet

This waterway connects Okeover Inlet to Desolation Sound. Cochrane Islands, the eastern Josephine Island and Cross Island are protected as parkland; the western Josephine Islands are privately owned, as are some holdings on the southwest shore of the inlet. Shellfish farms are conspicuous, particularly in Trevenen Bay, which has eight along its length.

Malaspina Inlet is prone to strong currents, which run as high as 4 knots in the narrowest portions. Light rips and turbulence may be encountered through the inlet and at the entrance to Grace Harbour.

Sunshine Coast Trail

This challenging trail runs from the tip of Malaspina Peninsula at Sarah Point through the mountains and forests of the Sunshine Coast to end 180 km (112 miles) away at Saltery Bay, south of Powell River. The northern portion is protected within Malaspina Provincial Park, but only a few portions—Sarah Point, Feather Cove and Cochrane Bay—reach salt water due to the steep and rugged shore along most of its length.

Access to Sarah Point is difficult, and water taxi is a common way to get to the trailhead. It can also be reached by vehicle via the rough forestry road from Lund. Other accesses within Desolation Sound Marine Park are from the Malaspina Peninsula Forest Service Road to Wednesday Lake or Manzanita Bluffs.

A short loop, the Ann Gustafson Way trail, circles Wednesday Lake.

Complete information on the trail is available from the Powell River Visitors Centre at **604-485-4701**.

Paddling Malaspina Inlet.

Place names: Galiano and Valdes named the inlet Brazo de Malaspina in 1792 after Capt. Alexandro Malaspina (1754–1809). Capt. Trevenen Penrose Coode commanded HMS *Sutlej*, Rear Admiral Joseph Denman's flagship 1864–66.

Camping: N50°02.46' W124°46.73', Cochrane Bay. Camping is limited to the north end of the bay; the south portion is closed to protect marine habitat. The designated site is used mainly by hikers of the Sunshine Coast Trail. It's a possibility for kayakers, but it's not recommended as it has a rough beach and sites are set back from the beach within a forest. The best beach access is a designated picnic site just south of the camping area. A creek may provide water.

N50°03.24' W124°46.63', Cross Island. This pretty islet east of the Josephine Islands features an expansive clear, mossy area in the north-central portion of the island. Access is via a beach with narrow strips of stone beach between boulders that can be reached at most tide levels.

Grace Harbour

This pretty, sheltered harbour ends in twin coves. From the north cove a trailhead leads to a nearby lake and beyond, though portions of the trail are rough and muddy. If you take the trail, keep your eye open for the first bypass around a muddy area. An old

Malaspina Provincial Park

This park is one of four in the region that fall under the Desolation Sound Marine Park umbrella; the others are Copeland Islands and Okeover Arm. The park was created in 2001 and occupies the west shore of Malaspina Inlet. The park is not directly accessible by road; visitors use boats or the hiking trail, which can be reached from the forest service road that runs adjacent to the park. Wednesday Lake, within the park boundaries, is popular for swimming.

Hunting is allowed within the park; harvested species include black-tailed deer, black bear, wolf, coyote, racoon, skunk, snowshoe hare, bobcat, cougar, upland game birds and waterfowl.

forestry tractor is visible in the trees to the right. Follow a side trail to the tractor, then go past it down an embankment to a creek and beach. At a small waterfall a simple mechanism has been built using hoses and old milk jugs. A constant stream of fresh water flows from the jugs above head height—a perfect place for a shower. Campers will appreciate this after a few days in the wild.

Note that there is a sizable holding of private property on the south entrance to the harbour and a cluster of cottages on the property.

Camping: N50°03.27' W124°44.79'. The northern head of Grace Harbour features a rock beach with a clearing for dinghies and kayaks. A grassy slope leads to an outhouse with a tent pad nearby. Two more pads are on the adjacent bluffs. Kayakers occasionally use the bluffs at the entrance near the park sign.

Okeover Inlet

This inlet, together with Lancelot Inlet, makes for a tranquil adjunct to Desolation Sound. The warm, sheltered water creates ideal nutrient-rich oyster habitat—evident in the numerous oyster farms and leases that line the shores. The high concentration of commercial and recreational use has led to conflict, particularly over human waste. For this reason management planning for Desolation Sound Marine Park has focused on steering recreational activity, and particularly camping, away from here to the outer waters of the park.

Road access runs along the east shore from Okeover Arm Provincial Park to Penrose Bay, leading to numerous cottages, resorts and kayak rental operations along this stretch. A boat launch and a government dock at Okeover Arm Provincial Park are both heavily used, including the loading and unloading of commercial boats and trucks to and from the various aquaculture operations. The resort closest to the launch has a phone, small store and restaurant. Southeast of the wharf is Sliammon Indian Seafoods Co., with a ramp, floats and building.

Launches: N49°59.50' W124°42.63'. The boat ramp at Okeover Arm Provincial Park is a key access point to Desolation Sound. The ramp is located immediately south of the government wharf and is accessible by good paved road from Highway 101, with the turnoff just south of Lund. The launch is from a wide rock beach. There's a large parking lot up the hill from the launch.

Camping: Okeover Arm Provincial Park has a small vehicle-accessible campsite with an open area for RVs and more secluded sites scattered throughout a pleasant forest setting. Amenities include a pit toilet, water pump, picnic tables, garbage disposal, fire pits and a trail to the beach.

Tux'wnech Okeover Arm Provincial Park

This tiny park on the west shore of Okeover Inlet protects just 4 ha (10 acres) but plays a vital role in the area due to its wharf, launch and campsite. It's an ideal staging point for marine visitors to Desolation Sound. Its Sliammon heritage is reflected in the traditional name, Tux'wnech, and in the park's archaeological sites that include a midden and fish trap.

The park was created in 1979.

Lancelot Inlet

This arm leads northward from Okeover Inlet, creating one side of Gilford Peninsula. Shellfish farms line the east shores. The west shore of the inlet is protected as part of Desolation Sound Marine Park. The inlet ends in Wootton Bay, which has pretty bluffs on the east side and a private holding at the head. Theodosia Inlet extends another 3.6 km (2.2 miles) northeast through a narrow opening near Bastion Point. Tidal currents may be strong at the opening. Theodosia has a shellfish farm and some development at its mouth and a sizable logging operation on its south end. Considerable logging means the backdrop is less than pristine.

Camping: N50°03.36' W124°43.71', Isabel Bay. At the north end of the bay is a rough beach with a flat, clear area above. While camping is possible on the peninsula, a better option is the off-lying islet. It has no beach, just gently sloping rock ledges with level areas on the rock at the top.

N50°04.35' W124°42.27', Grail Point. Just east of this point on the north end of Lancelot Inlet is an oyster beach blessed with some sandy sediment (one of the few sandy spots in Desolation Sound). Up from the beach a level grassy area can be used for camping but it may be overgrown, as it does not see a great deal of use.

Sunshine breaks through at Lancelot Inlet.

Place names: Henry Wootton was second officer aboard the Hudson's Bay Company steamer *Labouchere* in 1859 when it arrived in Victoria. Galiano and Valdes named the bay Brazo de Bustamente after Josef Bustamente, captain of the *Atrevida*, one of Malaspina's two ships.

Galley Bay

This bay is an anchorage fringed by private land and some limited cottage development. Zephine Head, a stunning bluff, is also private.

Camping: N50°04.57' W124°46.52'. The headland to the immediate northeast of Galley Bay has a level area facing northeast to Tenedos Bay. Access is a rough beach just south of the headland. This pleasant site is easily overlooked.

Portage Cove and Call Bight

Portage Cove is private property owned by the University of British Columbia. It was a traditional Sliammon portage called Kigiyin, meaning "short cross-over from one bay to another."

Rough beaches line Call Bight. On the northeast beach a rough clear area in the upland is suitable for camping but isn't recommended.

Bold Head.

Tenedos Bay

This sheltered anchorage is well used, particularly on the north and west sides of a substantial island tucked into the bay. It's arguably one of Desolation Sound's prettiest places, in part due to the sizable cliffs of Bold Head. A short (five-minute) trail runs from a beach at the entrance of Unwin Creek to Unwin Lake, where it's possible to have a swim. An access point to the creek near the beach makes an ideal place for a quick wash. In the creek is a log flume, one of several reminders of settlement in the area that include farms, homesteads and logging equipment. An unoffical trail leads from the bay to Bold Head; another leads from Unwin Lake to Melanie Cove.

Camping: N50°07.44' W124°41.41', Unwin Creek. A designated camping area is at the entrance to Unwin Creek. The site includes two wooden tent platforms, other clear areas appropriate for tents, and a pit toilet. Several bluffs within the bay are also suitable for camping; access is by tricky rock ledge or rough oyster beach only.

N50°06.97' W124°43.24', Bold Head. Two prominent headlands at Bold Head just west of the entrance to Tenedos Bay have established camping areas suitable for small groups on clear, level areas overlooking Homfray Channel. Access is via rock platform only, and it's tricky. The GPS waypoint is for the most accessible of the two options; the other is to the immediate southeast.

Curme Islands.

Curme Islands

This minor archipelago plays a major role as a campsite for kayakers in Desolation Sound. There are two independent clusters. The north group of three main islands form a rough triangle with a common cove in the centre. The cove tends to run dry with numerous rocks and rock ledges. There is no beach as such.

The southern island sits well apart from its cousins. It becomes separated into two islands by a channel at high tides. The island is very pretty, with numerous mossy headlands topped with scrubby arbutus and pine trees.

Place names: Capt. Charles Thomas Curme of the battleship *Repulse* served on the B.C. coast in 1873.

Camping: Curme Islands is probably the most heavily used camping location in Desolation Sound. It's a beautiful place, but capacity is an issue. There are no beaches at most tide levels and no pit toilets.

N50°06.87' W124°44.54', North Islands. The main cluster of Curme Islands has a common central cove. From it rocky beach or rock shelving provides access to numerous clear areas widely dispersed among the various bluffs of the different islands. Several choice sites look south, while difficult-to-access sites can be found on the northwest island. It pays to explore the islands before deciding on a spot. Access options differ with the tide levels. The northwest site can be difficult to reach at low tide.

N50°06.87' W124°44.54', South Island. The southernmost island of the group is dotted with level tent clearings on the various headlands. Some of the sites are exceptional. The difficulty is the main beach is a narrow channel of rock suitable for unloading or loading a single kayak at a time during lower tide levels. The access channel is located on the east side of the island, and it widens slightly into small stones at mid-tide, then divides the islands at higher tides. Be aware of this when you stash your kayaks for the day—don't locate them across the channel from your campsite, especially if you're stowing gear in the kayak. Note the southwest end of the island is an oystercatcher nesting site and should be left alone.

Otter Island

This island off the northwest end of Bold Head is inaccessible but for a boulder beach on the east side. Tall cliffs line the south shore, along with some steep and impressive bluffs. The channel between Otter Island and the mainland is peaceful and sheltered.

Camping: N50°07.43' W124°43.60'. On the mainland across from Otter Island, a north-facing rock beach has a kayak clearing. A trail leads over the headland to a nice bluff facing southwest toward Curme Islands. There is room for a tent or two. This is a pretty spot that may be missed by kayakers flocking to Curme Islands.

Melville Island

This long, narrow island has several beaches on the south side. Nearby Morgan is mainly cliffy shoreline.

Camping: N50°08.58' W124°43.57'. The western extent of Melville Island is connected to a small islet by a rock bar. On the bar is a kayak skid; up from this is a small area on the tip of Melville Island suitable for a tent or two, with views to both sides of Homfray Channel.

N50°08.48' W124°43.29'. A beach in the middle of the southeast side of Melville Island has a kayak skid cleared of rock. In the forest area behind the skid a large clear area is suitable for a group.

Prideaux Haven.

Desolation Sound Marine Park
This park protects more than 60 km (37 miles) of shore and 8,500 ha (33 square miles) of land dotted with camping, anchorages and trails that have gained world-class status among both boaters and kayakers. Expect shores with rugged bedrock outcrops and a few rough beaches along the way. No portion is accessible by road. The many bluffs make it an exceptional place for nook-and-cranny camping. The park was created in 1973.

Prideaux Haven

A collection of small islands has created a cove considered ideal for an anchorage. It's also a great place to explore by kayak, as the island cluster is complex and the intertidal life rich. Look for the sand dollar beach in the drying flat south of Copplestone Island.

Camping: N50°08.72' W124°40.79', William Islands. Camping is possible on the headlands around Prideaux Haven, but beach access is poor. The best option is the south end of William Islands (it's not named on the regional map but it does have a brown tent icon; consult a chart). A portion of the rough, south-facing beach has been cleared of rocks, giving access to a dubiously level headland. Given its proximity to the anchorage, this site is probably best used as overflow camping for boaters anchoring here.

Melanie Cove

This pleasant cove runs east from Prideaux Haven and is used as an anchorage. The head is an oyster beach that dries extensively at low tide.

Hiking: It's possible to hike to Tenedos Bay via Unwin Lake. The trailhead is N50°08.44' W124°40.64'. Another shorter trail leads from the head of Melanie Cove at N50°08.56' W124°40.16' to Laura Cove.

Camping: N50°09.06' W124°39.62'. Behind Roffey Island is a rough beach with access to a clear area suitable for a group. There is no view, however, and the beach dries extensively at low tide.

Refuge Cove

This cove on the southwest extent of West Redonda Island is a good resupply location for boaters and campers in Desolation Sound. It offers a public wharf, fuel, a store, a hamburger stand, a post office

The east campsite at Martin Islands.

(V0P 1P0), garbage disposal, laundry, washrooms and showers.

Martin Islands

Southeast of Refuge Cove, off the south end of West Redonda Island, are the Martin Islands, a pretty pair of islands used mainly for camping.

Camping: N50°06.47' W124°49.94', West Martin. The west side of the west Martin Island has a prominent headland with a number of fairly level areas that could host a group. Benches and a fire pit have been created. The difficulty is access. It is by rock ledge only, albeit gently sloping ledges, with rough beach areas only at certain tides.

N50°06.62' W124°49.32', East Martin. Beaches to the north and south allow access to this site on the eastern of the two islands. Up from the beach is a clear, grassy, level area on the beachfront and clear, forested areas farther upland. Benches and a fire pit have been created.

ne of the more remote residential islands serviced by BC
equires two links—first to Quadra, then Cortes. Most of the
1,000 residents live in the lower half of the island, which has a preferable climate and receives less rain. Village centres are located at
Whaletown (where the ferry lands), Mansons Landing and Squirrel
Cove. Squirrel Cove is also home to a Klahoose First Nation village.

Visitors enjoying Cortes by land will find a vehicle-accessible
campground at Smelt Bay and trails in the region of Carrington Bay,
Von Donop Inlet, Squirrel Cove and Hague Lake at Kw'as Park. Other
parts of the island can be explored by old logging roads or, more
recently, constructed trails, as residents continue to build a network
of routes. Boaters make use of anchorages at Mansons Landing,
Squirrel Cove, Von Donop Inlet, Cortes Bay and Gorge Harbour.
Two large parks—Carrington Bay, a regional park, and Ha'thayim
Marine Park—are located on the less developed northern end of the
island. Mansons Landing Provincial Park protects a waterfront area
and tidal lagoon, as well as a sand beach at Hague Lake.

Cortes Island is 25 km (15.5 miles) from Sutil Point to Bullock
Bluff, and 15 km (9.3 miles) wide from Plunger Pass to Mary Point.
A circumnavigation is approximately 67 km (41.6 miles).

Place names: Hernando Cortes (1485–1547) was the famed con-
queror of Mexico, reaching the throne of Montezuma in 1520 (thus
also Hernando Island).

Weather

Cortes Island	May	June	July	Aug.	Sept.	Dec.	Av./Ttl.
Daily average temp. (C)	12.7	15.4	17.9	17.9	14.8	3.7	10.2
Daily maximum (C)	16.6	19.2	22.1	21.9	18.3	5.5	13.2
Daily minimum (C)	8.8	11.5	13.6	13.8	11.1	1.8	7.0
Precipitation (mm)	70.2	65.1	50.5	58.8	71.7	187.7	1378.6
Days of rainfall + 0.2mm	13.7	12.6	8.6	9.2	10.2	18.5	
Days with rainfall +5mm	5.2	4.2	3.3	3.5	4.5	10.0	
Days with rainfall +10mm	1.9	2.2	1.6	1.8	2.5	6.1	
Days with rainfall +25mm	0.2	0.08	0.33	0.46	0.46	1.4	

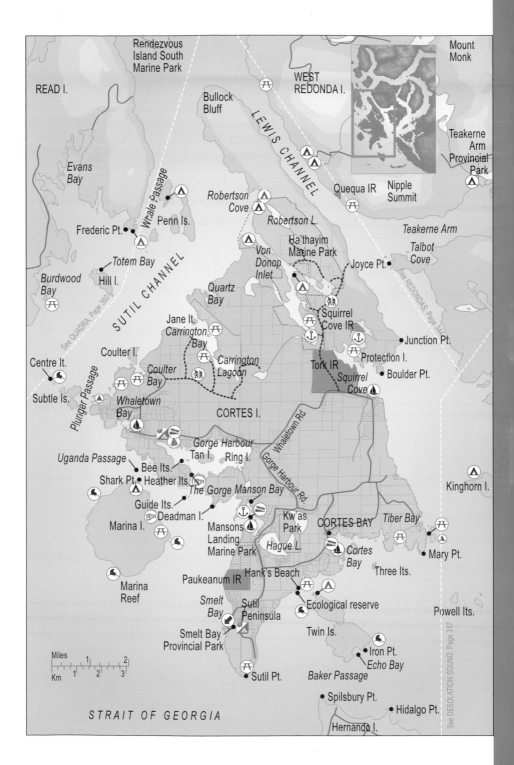

READ I.

Rendezvous
Island South
Marine Park

Mount
Monk

WEST
REDONDA I.

Bullock
Bluff

LEWIS CHANNEL

Teakerne
Arm
Provincial
Park

Quequa IR   Nipple
Summit

*Evans
Bay*

Whale Passage

Penn Is.

Frederic Pt.

*Robertson
Cove*

Robertson L.

Teakerne Arm

*Talbot
Cove*

Totem Bay

Hill I.

*Von
Donop
Inlet*

Ha'thayim
Marine Park

Joyce Pt.

*Burdwood
Bay*

SUTIL CHANNEL

*Quartz
Bay*

Squirrel
Cove IR

Junction Pt.

Centre It.

Jane It.
*Carrington
Bay*

*Carrington
Lagoon*

Tork IR

*Squirrel
Cove*

Protection I.

Boulder Pt.

Coulter I.

*Coulter
Bay*

Subtle Is.

Plunger Passage

*Whaletown
Bay*

CORTES I.

Whaletown Rd.

Gorge Harbour

Tan I.   Ring I.

Gorge Harbour Rd.

Kinghorn I.

Uganda Passage

Bee Its.

Shark Pt. Heather Its.

Guide Its.

The Gorge Manson Bay

Kw'as
Park

CORTES BAY

Tiber Bay

Deadman I.

Marina I.

Mansons
Landing
Marine Park

Hague L.

*Cortes
Bay*

Mary Pt.

Three Its.

Marina
Reef

Paukeanum IR

Hank's Beach

Ecological reserve

Powell Its.

*Smelt
Bay*

Sutil
Peninsula

Twin Is.

Smelt Bay
Provincial Park

Iron Pt.

Echo Bay

Miles
Km

Sutil Pt.

Baker Passage

Spilsbury Pt.

Hidalgo Pt.

STRAIT OF GEORGIA

Hernando I.

Hernando Island

This private island lies in a remote area northwest of Savary Island and south of Cortes. It is low-lying and heavily forested, with sandy cliffs on the southwest. Tidal streams between Savary and Hernando islands can reach 2 knots.

Ecological oddities: Hernando Island is home to B.C.'s largest aspen (the trembling variety). It can be seen at Ashworth Point on the island's southeast end.

Sutil Peninsula

This residential southern arm of Cortes Island is low, treed and fronted by mainly rock beaches. From Sutil Point on the west side to Smelt Bay, the nearshore waters are shallow and pocked by boulders, which can make navigation dangerous for kayakers when there are wind waves. Stay out of the green water. Smelt Bay Provincial Park has camping, but not within easy access of the beach for kayaks. A parking lot is adjacent to a cobble beach; there's water and garbage disposal in the vicinity of the beach, but no pit toilet.

The rest of Smelt Bay is residential.

Launches: The gravel boat launch within Smelt Bay Provincial Park is best used at higher tides. Kayaks or smaller boats can be launched on the gravel beach.

Camping: The campground at Smelt Bay Provincial Park is open all year; fees are charged May 15 to Sept. 30. Reservations are accepted at **1-800-689-9025.**

Manson Bay

This is a popular anchorage and boating area with a government wharf and floats at Mansons Landing Marine Park. The wharf is usually busy enough to require rafting. The south approach to the bay is a long stone and cobble beach with some sandy portions. It ends in a sandy spit that forms a drying lagoon behind the landing. There are no services within the park beyond a telephone at the top of the government wharf and a picnic table. A road leads through the park, south of which you can find a café, post office (V0P 1K0) and bank. The north side of the bay and many of the islands are residential.

Hiking: Two trails lead through the park—one from the government wharf along the lagoon to Hague Lake and another along the seashore, which ends at the local school not far from the park. It was created as part of a school-to-sea project.

Launches: N50°04.34' W124°58.93'. A natural boat ramp within the provincial park is located at the northwest side of the spit between the bay and the lagoon.

Place names: Michael Manson was an immigrant who arrived from Scotland in 1880 and built a trading post where the park is located, running it until 1896. Eventually a small general store was built on the trading post site, and in 1995 it was moved next to the community centre south of the park. It's now a museum.

Gorge Harbour

Gorge Harbour is a mixed-use area with numerous shellfish farms, oyster beaches and some limited log handling alongside homes and a marina. The Gorge Harbour Marina is a focal point for boaters, offering RV and tent sites, a restaurant, showers, laundry, a store, liquor, a boat launch and car and scooter rentals. A public dock is east of the marina. The entrance to the harbour is via a narrow opening, the Gorge. Currents can go above 4 knots. Watch for a pictograph of a stick man on the west side as you enter the harbour.

Marina Island

This sandy island is largely fringed by boulders. A superb area of sand is located at Shark Point, where a long, sandy spit extends far enough to almost close off Uganda Passage. Boaters have to be wary of following the navigation markers to clear the narrow opening. The spit presents a wonderful opportunity to stroll. Be sure to look for sand dollars. This is a recreational hub, with an established camping area on the point at the edge of the tree cover. It's a private island, but the owners don't discourage its use. A sign asks simply that you don't have fires.

The beach and anchorage at Manson Bay.

Manson Landing Provincial Park

This day-use park protects a lagoon rich with marine and coastal birds, including a great blue heron nesting site. Small boats can enter the lagoon at high tide. Watch for moon snails and nudibranchs. Parking is available at the government wharf. The park extends to Hague Lake, which offers freshwater swimming and cutthroat trout fishing. There is no camping. The park protects 100 ha (250 acres) and was established in 1974.

The island is used by migratory birds, seals, sea lions and herring that spawn on the south end. It was once a large Sliammon village that extended along the northeast side of the island.

Place names: Galiano and Valdes named this island in 1792 after the woman Hernando Cortes obtained at San Juan de Ulloa along with other captives in 1519. She became Cortes's mistress, interpreter and guide. She is credited with counselling the Spanish during attacks on Mexico.

Whaletown Bay

The dominant feature of this residential bay is the ferry terminal for service to Quadra Island. The community, on the south shore, has a store, phone and post office (V0P 1Z0). The public wharf is used by seaplanes.

Sutil Channel

Sutil Channel runs the west side of Cortes Island, from Subtle Islands to Bullock Bluff. The tide splits at roughly Penn Islands, with the flood setting north in the south, and south in the north.

Most of the islands along the Cortes side of Sutil Channel—those being Subtle Islands, Coulter Island and Jane Island—are privately owned. Some of the unnamed Crown islets have headlands that might be suitable for camping. Beaches on Cortes along the channel are generally rough and would make poor camping. Coulter Bay dries extensively and is residential.

Travel notes: *Sailing Directions* describes the currents in this channel as "weak, rarely exceeding 2 knots." I found this was representative of considerable understating of the currents in this region. In my experience, currents ran at several knots during most tide times through Lewis Channel, Calm Channel and others in the area. This discrepancy is significant, as you may be tempted to disregard the effect of tides in this region. I recall being swept past Rendezvous Islands into Lewis Channel at a considerable speed, and I pulled out rather than fight the tide in Deer Passage. A trip through this region will be much simpler if travel is timed for a favourable tide.

Carrington Bay

This bay is known as an anchorage and for its shellfish; there are four active shellfish leases in the bay. A regional park fronts the north side of the bay. Most beaches are rough rock or even boulders; the sandiest beach appears to be directly north of an islet set back in the bay next to an anchorage. It's marked on the map with a picnic icon.

Penn Islands

These four islands are mainly rock shoreline. All are undeveloped Crown land. An aquaculture operation is to the south of the northernmost island.

Camping: N50°11.84' W125°01.47'. The northern island has a rock beach on its east side that faces south; look for the boat skid cleared among the rocks. To the north of the beach is a prominent headland. Behind the beach is a clear, level area used for camping. A path leads to the headland, which features more clear areas—a wonderful camping opportunity. The site has been well used, probably as a fishing camp, and there's a multitude of benches and other clutter. A unique touch is the large, hollow tree trunk reinvented as an outhouse.

Von Donop Inlet

This is a pretty location that's popular as an anchorage, but it's also a good place to meander by kayak. The convoluted shoreline splits into a deeper inlet and a lagoon. Combined with hikes and the opportunity to walk from Robertson Cove to a lake for a dip, several days could be spent exploring the area and the nearby islands.

Hiking: Trails lead from various access points along the inlet to Lewis Channel and Squirrel Cove.

The campsite at Penn Islands.

Camping: N50°10.90' W124°58.95'. As you enter the inlet, the first beach on the right (south) is good gravel beach; unfortunately a fallen tree blocks most of the beach at lower tides. In the forest are clear areas for tents. This is a good site if you are simply passing through the region, as it's close to the inlet's entrance, but it's not particularly pretty.

N50°10.04' W124°57.38'. On the headland between the lagoon and where the inlet turns south is a rough beach with a cleared kayak skid. Clear areas in the upland forest are large enough for several groups. A picnic table is pleasantly located next to the waterfront.

Robertson Cove

A salmon farm occupies the northwest corner of the cove; two main beaches are to the southeast. From the southernmost of the two there's a trailhead for a rough path to Robertson Lake.

Camping: N50°11.63' W124°58.55'. The beach at the south end of Robertson Cove is backed by a clear area in the upland forest. Another site is to the north between two bluffs at N50°11.76' W124°58.45', but access is a difficult rock and boulder beach. (I wouldn't have considered it based on the beach, but there were five kayaks hauled up onto the rocks when I passed, so it must have its appeal.)

Looking out Von Donop Inlet.

Lewis Channel

This channel separates Cortes and West Redonda islands between Junction Point and Calm Channel. The northern portion is narrow, with relatively strong tidal currents. It is also prone to wind flow from Bute Inlet.

North of Teakerne Arm, the best beaches are on the West Redonda (east) side. The channel is a thoroughfare for recreational boats.

Place names: Capt. Herbert George Lewis served the Hudson's Bay Company from 1846 to 1870 and commanded vessels such as the *Otter, Beaver, Labouchere* and *Enterprise.*

Camping: N50°12.86' W124°57.14', Lewis Channel north, and N50°12.61' W124°56.91', Lewis Channel south. There are two similar gravel beaches oriented northward immediately north and south of a conspicuous log dump. The northernmost beach has a clear area in the forest upland suitable for a tent or two. The southern option has a path leading from the beach to a flat headland with benches, a fire pit and grassy areas for a tent or two, as well as nice views along the channel. The two sites are 0.5 km apart (0.3 miles). My advice: take the south site.

Ha'thayim Marine Park

This undeveloped park incorporates lakes, a saltwater lagoon and an old-growth forest known as Ha'thayim in Coast Salish. Traditional Klahoose use includes spiritual and burial sites. Traces of its mining and logging past also dot the area. The park is popular as an anchorage and for wilderness camping. Unusual denizens here are flying squirrels and Douglas squirrels. It protects 1,277 ha (3,155 acres) and was created in 1993.

Squirrel Cove

This is a community centre, with a government wharf, general store, phone, laundry, craft store and restaurant all in close proximity at the south entrance to the cove. On the west side is a Klahoose settlement, conspicuous by the church. The north end of the cove, north of Protection Island, is a popular anchorage. Protection Island is fringed with boulders and rock shoreline, making it far from ideal for camping. A wreck lies just north of Protection Island.

Cortes Bay

This is a boating centre with a boat launch and government wharf on the southwest side. It's also an outstation for the Seattle Yacht Club, which broadcasts broadband wireless Internet through most of the bay. Expect the possibility of seaplanes landing. The bay and surrounding shorelines are dotted with homes. Toward Mary Point there are wonderful cliff headlands and coves with rock or gravel beaches. This area would make a nice day trip out of Cortes Bay. North of Mary Point is Tiber Bay, a residential area. Just off the bay are several islets connected to Cortes by a sandy bar used for shellfish farming. The islets make a nice place to visit, with rugged camping possibilities. The best landing is to the north.

Twin Islands

These large, privately owned islands are most famous for having hosted Queen Elizabeth and Prince Philip during royal tours of Canada. The Queen has visited the islands twice: with Princess Anne in 1971 and with Prince Philip in 1994. The original lodge was built in the 1930s as a getaway for a Vancouver businessman. The islands were purchased by Margrav Maximillian Von Baden of Baden, Germany, in the 1950s as a summer retreat. It later became Ulloa Resort.

Islets lie off the northwest corner of the Twin Islands. Tucked in behind the islets is a small shellfish operation. Along the Cortes Island shore northwest of the Twin Islands is a series of pleasant beaches on either side of an unnamed point capped by a rock bluff. Some wonderful sandy portions can be found on the beaches south of the point. The beaches closest to the point are part of a locally managed ecological reserve. Trails lead through the reserve and the immediate area. The beach to the immediate north of the ecological reserve is called Hank's Beach. It is currently private property, though there is a move afoot to make it a public day-use area.

Camping: N50°02.59' W124°56.81'. To the immediate northwest of Twin Islands is a cluster of Crown islets and rocks. You can gain access via rough oyster beaches or rock ledges. A variety of level clearings are suitable for camping; the best is the south centre of the main islet, though access is difficult. A bench has been constructed.

THE REDONDAS

Homfray Channel, Pryce Channel and Deer Passage separate the two Redonda islands from the B.C. mainland, while Waddington Channel separates them from each other. All are minor secondary routes compared to the traffic in nearby Desolation Sound, despite good campsites and wonderful views into Toba Inlet and up Homfray Channel.

Place names: Galiano and Valdes named the Redondas Isla Redonda, presumably for the rotund shape.

Teakerne Arm

The highlight of this pretty bay is Cassel Falls, protected as part of Teakerne Arm Provincial Park. The area around the falls is a popular anchorage, while aquaculture is prevalent elsewhere in the arm. Cassel Falls is located at the head of a small canyon, with a dinghy dock on the north headland and a rough rock trail leading to Cassel Lake alongside the falls. Look for remnants of old logging operations along the trail. The lake is cold but good for a swim.

Camping: N50°11.85' W124°51.22'. West of Cassel Falls is a stretch of gently sloping grassy bluffs. Look for a rock spit with level areas perfect for camping.

Roscoe Bay

This anchorage is protected as a provincial park. The north bank of the inlet is quite cliffy at points. The bay extends about 1.7 km (about a mile) to end in a river that flows from Black Lake. A clam beach blocks the inner portion of the bay at low tide.

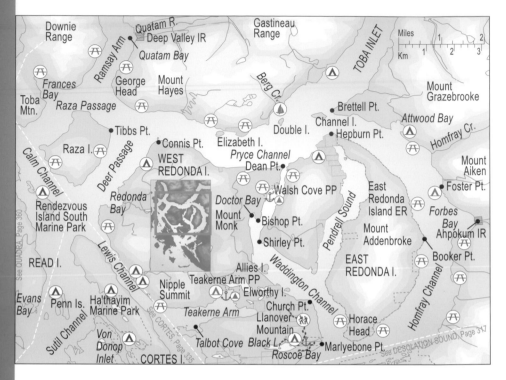

Ecological oddities: Roscoe Bay is known for its annual bloom of moon jellies. Hundreds of thousands stay in the bay each year, avoiding being swept away in the falling tide by dropping below the fastest surface current during an ebb tide. Moon jellies have short tentacles ringing a bell-shaped body, and their sting is less venomous than other jellyfish. Look for a comprehensive and updated information board on the status of the jellies at the trailhead for the Llanover Mountain trail.

Hiking: There are three trailheads at Roscoe Bay. The most basic leads a short distance from the head of the bay to Black Lake. From there the trail continues around the lake's north shore along an old logging road. It ends at a mossy ledge and a viewpoint over the lake. Expect the hike to take two to three hours return. From a creek to the northwest of the head of the bay, at N50°09.66' W124°46.22', is the trailhead to Llanover Mountain. It leads 6 km (almost 4 miles) along an old logging road then through dense forest to end at a sweeping view of the surrounding countryside. The elevation gain is 700 m (2,300 feet) and it's listed as a three- to five-hour hike. Another trail

Looking east toward Desolation Sound from the islet off Twin Islands.

leads from the southeast side of the bay. Called the South Ridge Trail, it's 3 km (almost 2 miles) along a rough trail that follows a ridge west with views along Homfray Channel. The elevation gain is 250 m (820 feet), with a return time of about three hours. Flags on the south shore of the inlet mark the trailhead.

Camping: N50°09.49' W124°46.48'. At the head of Roscoe Bay is a large clear area for tents, a rustic picnic table and an outhouse adjacent to the river. A nearby alternative is to the northeast, just east of a creek and the trailhead to Llanover Mountain. Look for a rough beach and a grassy area next to some impressive bluffs. A short, steep trail leads alongside the bluffs to a viewpoint.

Teakerne Arm Provincial Park
This park protects a picturesque waterfall that cascades from Cassel Lake directly into the ocean. Teakerne Arm offers a protected anchorage and access to a freshwater lake for swimming or fishing, accessible by a 1-km (half-mile) trail. It includes 128 ha (316 acres) and was made a park in 1989.

Waddington Channel

This channel separates East and West Redonda islands, narrowing considerably toward the north, where the currents are apt to be strongest. Elsewhere they rarely go above 1 knot. Doctor Bay is developed with a salmon farm, and there's a shellfish farm on the east shore

Roscoe Bay.

Derelict logging equipment at Teakerne Arm.

opposite Walsh Cove. Beaches are common, especially in the narrow northern portion, but they're generally rocky and the uplands overgrown. If camping is necessary here, consider the bluffs on the island creating Walsh Cove or directly across the channel, just north of the aquaculture. There are numerous pretty, flat areas, but access is rock ledge only.

Roscoe Bay Provincial Park
This small fiord in West Redonda Island is a good anchorage and offers hiking and swimming at Black Lake. It protects 247 ha (610 acres) and was created in 1971.

Place names: Victoria pioneer Alfred Waddington began constructing a wagon road from the head of Bute Inlet to Fort Alexandria in 1862. In 1864 the Chilcotin Indians killed 14 of his 17 road builders, ending the project.

Pendrell Sound

Pendrell Sound extends 10 km (6 miles) north into East Redonda Island. The east shore is an ecological reserve. The sound is most notable for its unusually warm waters, which makes it ideal for the collection of oyster spat—one of two inlets on the B.C. coast where this takes place, usually in July. (The other is Pipestem Inlet on the west coast of Vancouver Island.) A trail at the head leads to views of Homfray Channel above Hepburn Point. Look for the trailhead east of the rock bluff. Also, watch for pictographs along the cliffs.

Homfray Channel

This channel runs 20 km (12 miles) between East Redonda Island and the mainland, with depths up to an impressive 730 m (2,400 feet). Tidal currents are generally weak, with the flood flowing south except in the south, where it floods north. Mount Grazebrook rises to 1,700 m (5,577 feet) and Mount Aiken to 1,830 m (6,000 feet), making this an impressive place to visit. Horace Head or even Forbes Bay would make great day trips from some of the Desolation Sound campsites.

The East Redonda Island shore is generally steep and inaccessible. The borders of two private holdings within the reserve are easily identified by younger forests recovering from logging.

The bluffs south of Forbes Bay are impressive granite cliffs. Look for petroglyphs at Forbes Bay.

Attwood Bay has several good beaches and a log dump at its head. Toward Brettell Point the shore is rocky. Channel Island has no beaches, which is unfortunate, as the views down Homfray Channel and up Toba Inlet from the Channel Island shore are among the best in British Columbia.

Camping: N50°15.78' W124°37.25', Foster Point. South of Foster Point is a low headland with a level rock ledge and a mossy clearing. It's undeveloped and far from a perfect campsite, but I'd recommend it over pushing back into forests behind beaches elsewhere in the area.

N50°18.58' W124°39.69', Attwood Bay. The south beach in Attwood Bay is mainly rock, but some strips with small stones are suitable for kayak landings. There are a number of clearings for camps in the upland, but in 2006 they were neglected and becoming overgrown. This has the potential to be a prime camping location, with a good beach and good views.

Pryce Channel

Pryce Channel leads 12 km (7 miles) along the north shore of the Redonda Islands, connecting Homfray Channel and Toba Inlet to Deer and Raza passages. The Redonda Islands along Pryce are steep,

Looking north toward Walsh Cove.

with few beaches. The north side and the nearby island, particularly around Elizabeth Island, have boulder beaches only and the uplands are heavily overgrown. Look for a gravel beach at a creek west of Elizabeth Island for a break. North of Double Island, at Berg Creek, is a small marina with moorage, ice and showers.

Walsh Cove Provincial Park
This small park protects an anchorage in a scenic cove of steep bluffs and rocky islets. There are no facilities or development of any kind. Look for pictographs on the cliffs next to the anchorage. The 85-ha (210-acre) park was created in 1989.

Camping: N50°17.74' W124°45.24', North Redonda. Just west of a conspicuous log dump is an above-average stone beach. A trail leads to several clear areas in the upland forest. This is a strategic site for circumnavigation of East Redonda Island.

Deer Passage
Deer Passage separates Raza and West Redonda islands. A public wharf and cannery were located in Redonda Bay, but they were demolished and only a few pilings remain. The bay now has a log dump, boom, shellfish aquaculture and more construction underway. Raza Island is steep and has only rough beaches.

East Redonda Island Ecological Reserve

At 6,212 ha (24 square miles) this is one of the province's largest coastal reserves. It encompasses almost the entire east side of the island, including impressive Addenbroke Mountain, 1,590 m (5,216 feet). The reserve was established in 1971 to protect an extensive coastal ecosystem for forestry research and for its second-growth forest stands. It contains marbled murrelet nesting sites plus pictographs and petroglyphs.

Camping: N50°17.48' W124°55.91'. Just south of Connis Point on West Redonda Island are two creeks. Between them is a gravel beach with access to a clear forest floor suitable for up to perhaps three tents.

Travel notes: If you do stop at this campsite, be sure to take a look at the southern of the two creeks. If you break through the tree cover you'll find a natural archway made by a huge fallen tree. Beyond this arch there's a 2.5-m (8-foot) waterfall into a natural cavern walled almost entirely with tree roots. It's topped with fallen logs, creating the feeling of a woody cave. The waterfall is the ideal size for a shower, but be warned—the water is chillingly cold.

Raza Passage

Raza Passage connects Calm Channel to Ramsay Arm and Pryce Channel. It's not particularly pretty: Raza Island is visibly logged and Frances Bay has a log dump. The peaks of Toba Mountain and the Downie Range are wonderfully bold, though, and there's a good beach immediately east of the log dump.

Ramsay Arm

This inlet cuts about 12 km (7 miles) into the mainland with heavily forested mountains on both sides. Logging is heavy, especially on Mount Hayes. The shoreline is mostly unremarkable. Quatam Bay is reserve land, with a lengthy beach.

TOBA INLET

This inlet extends 33 km (20 miles) into the B.C. mainland with a backdrop of magnificent mountain scenery. Visitors need not venture far to appreciate it—the view is magnificent from the entrance at Brettell Point. This would be the undisputed highlight of a circumnavigation of East Redonda Island. There are three main portions of Toba Inlet—the first leg to Brem Bay and Snout Point, a second leg to the end of the bay past Alpine Creek and the final stretch to Toba River.

Pryce Channel.

Place names: Galiano and Valdes named the inlet Canal de la Tabla in 1792 for their discovery of a strange wooden table carved with native images. Due to an engraving error on the map, Tabla became Toba, and the error has never been corrected.

Snout Point

This is arguably the most scenic leg of the inlet, with a superb waterfall along the northwest shore and the craggy peaks of Mount Grazebrook and the Gastineau Range as a backdrop. An old logging road east of Snout Point provides an opportunity for hikers to reach the alpine levels of Mount Grazebrook. A small beach is located near the log dump.

Camping: N50°21.07' W124°44.79'. A wide beach with a grassy mid-section lies directly north of Brettell Point. The west portion of the beach is fine gravel—better than any of the Desolation Sound beaches. Camping on the beach is possible for most tide levels. East of the unnamed river that cuts through the beach is a small strip of gravel. A clear area in the forest behind could accommodate a small group of tents, if need be. This beach has more afternoon sun than the west beach.

Alpine Creek

The second leg of Toba Inlet is narrower and relatively straight, hemmed in with tight clusters of mountains. Racine Creek has a prominent waterfall. In this stretch the water becomes a milky green from glacier runoff. It's almost saltless to the taste.

Camping: N50°25.01' W124°30.51'. There are very few beaches along this stretch. An islet on the east end of a large unnamed bay has no beach, just gently sloping rock ledge on the southeast side. Be aware the rock is extremely slippery when wet. Atop the islet is a grassy bank suitable for a tent, or perhaps two in a squeeze. This would make a good base camp for a day trip to the head of the inlet for grizzly watching, rather than setting up camp near the estuary.

Toba River

The final leg of the inlet is not quite as scenic along most of its length, as the mountains become more dispersed and less craggy. The gentler slopes also tend to reveal the logging. Beaches are rare until the estuary. At the end is Toba River, a good place to view grizzly bear among the Sitka spruce and salmonberry. You'll also find a log

Toba Inlet.

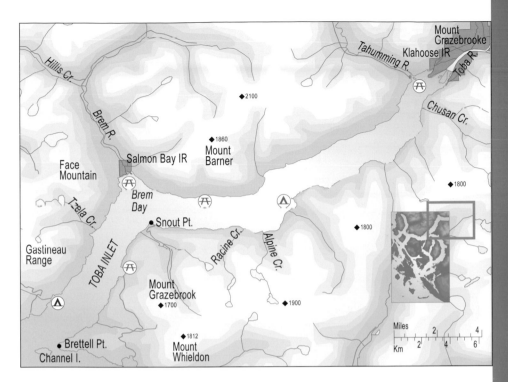

dump and booming grounds. Logging roads provide access through the uplands. The mouth of Toba River is a Klahoose reserve with an old cemetery. A 120MW hydroelectric project is planned for the East Toba River, with production slated for 2008. The Klahoose are opposed.

Hiking: The road at the head of Toba Inlet crosses the estuary of the Tahumming River before continuing for several miles up the Toba Valley. This is a recreational paradise for those who like alpine as much as maritime. The Tahumming Range is popular for both hikers and climbers. The Southgate Toba Divide is also a ski mountaineering destination.

Kayaking Toba Inlet: Any exploration of the inlet involves about a week from a launch at Lund or Okeover. Expect a day to Roscoe Inlet, a day to the entrance of the inlet, at least a day paddling up the inlet and equal time in return. Since most of the best mountain scenery is near the entrance, a day trip from a base camp into the inlet is probably sufficiently rewarding with the least effort.

Waterfall, Toba Inlet.

Toba Inlet.

However, for those determined to complete the inlet, expect few suitable beaches for breaks and the possibility of strong inflow and/or outflow winds. The Toba River estuary is grizzly territory, so consider staying at the islet mid-way or at a camp near the estuary and making the final leg a day trip. The adventurers, though, will want to travel up Toba River, something that should be particularly appealing to canoeists. Be warned: the downstream current will be strong. As with many of these inlets, a water taxi to the head and a one-way return journey could be the best use of time and energy. As currents are stronger on the outward journey, the main barrier will be the possibility of inflow winds. (As a footnote, an inflow wind was the bane on my return journey. It ran down Brem Bay, hitting Snout Point and turning east. West of Snout Point it was calm.)

Taking a break in Bute Inlet.

Central Discovery Islands

CHAPTER SEVEN

QUADRA IS THE LARGEST OF THE DISCOVERY ISLANDS, A VARIED GEOGRAPH-ical grouping that includes East and West Thurlow islands, Sonora, Maurelle, Read, the Rendezvous Islands, Cortes, Stuart and East and West Redonda islands. Cortes and the Redondas are covered in Chapter 6; West Thurlow is covered in Chapter 8.

These are working islands. Logging, fish farming, commercial shellfish harvesting, fishing, resorts—it's not entirely wilderness out there. Logging is ubiquitous. With the current political wisdom favouring smaller cutblocks, the mountainsides are turning into patchwork quilts of differing tree ages. In many areas, especially the north Discovery Islands, people earning a living fishing, logging or fish farming will outnumber tourists.

Hurdles to exploring this region are the rapids. A few are quite famous; others are little known. Seymour Narrows, on the main route through the region, is transited daily by freighters, barges, cruise ships and log booms, despite currents of up to 16 knots. Surge Narrows, on the other hand, has become a tourist attraction, particularly of late among kayakers. Yuculta Rapids, Dent Rapids and Arran Rapids guard the resort haven of Big Bay on Stuart Island. And yet more rapids block the north end of Okisollo Channel.

Most kayak exploration tends to focus on the south end of Quadra Island and its nearby islands. Heriot Bay on Quadra is a staging ground, especially for day trips. Okisollo and Cordero channels are used mainly by boaters looking for an alternative to Seymour Narrows. What they will find is some incredible scenery in Cordero Channel and Bute Inlet, picturesque island groups and narrow, meandering wilderness passages.

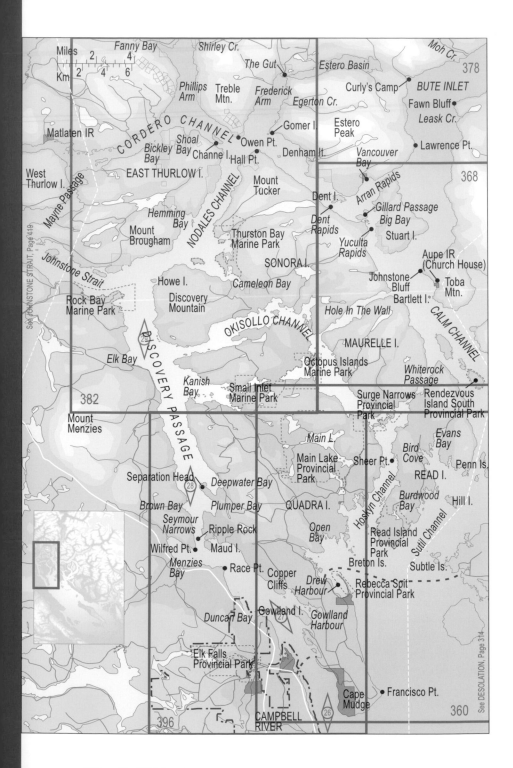

Miles

Fanny Bay

Shirley Cr.

The Gut

Estero Basin

Moh Cr.

378

Km

Phillips Arm

Treble Mtn.

Frederick Arm

Egerton Cr.

Curly's Camp

BUTE INLET

Fawn Bluff

Leask Cr.

CORDERO CHANNEL

Gomer I.

Estero Peak

Matlaten IR

Bickley Bay

Shoal Bay

Channe l.

Owen Pt.

Denham lt.

Vancouver Bay

Lawrence Pt.

Hall Pt.

West Thurlow I.

EAST THURLOW I.

368

Mayne Passage

Mount Tucker

Dent I.

Arran Rapids

NODALES CHANNEL

Gillard Passage

Big Bay

See JOHNSTONE STRAIT, Page 419

Hemming Bay

Dent Rapids

Stuart I.

Mount Brougham

Thurston Bay Marine Park

Yuculta Rapids

Aupe IR (Church House)

Johnstone Strait

SONORA I.

Johnstone Bluff

Toba Mtn.

Howe I.

Cameleon Bay

Bartlett I.

Rock Bay Marine Park

Discovery Mountain

Hole In The Wall

CALM CHANNEL

OKISOLLO CHANNEL

MAURELLE I.

382

Elk Bay

DISCOVERY PASSAGE

Kanish Bay

Small Inlet Marine Park

Octopus Islands Marine Park

Whiterock Passage

Mount Menzies

Surge Narrows Provincial Park

Rendezvous Island South Provincial Park

Main L.

Evans Bay

Main Lake Provincial Park

Sheer Pt.

Bird Cove

Penn Is.

Separation Head

28

Deepwater Bay

READ I.

Burdwood Bay

Hill I.

Brown Bay

Plumper Bay

QUADRA I.

Hoskyn Channel

Sutil Channel

Seymour Narrows

Ripple Rock

Open Bay

Read Island Provincial Park

Subtle Is.

Wilfred Pt.

Maud I.

Breton Is.

Menzies Bay

Race Pt.

Copper Cliffs

Drew Harbour

Rebecca Spit Provincial Park

Duncan Bay

Gowlland I.

Gowlland Harbour

See DESOLATION, Page 314

Elk Falls Provincial Park

Cape Mudge

Francisco Pt.

396

CAMPBELL RIVER

26

360

Exploring by kayak

The main kayaking areas are generally limited to Hoskyn Channel, Sutil Channel and the south end of Calm Channel. I found it interesting that just about all the main kayak-friendly beaches I visited along Okisollo, Nodales and Cordero channels had no developed campsites. This tells me there are no established kayaking routes through these areas, most likely due to the numerous rapids. Properly planned, they are part of the attraction, and good kayaking opportunities can be found throughout this area.

Frederick Arm.

Recommended kayaking trips

- *If you have a day:* Beginner kayakers will have a wonderful time launching from Heriot Bay on Quadra and exploring the bluffs and coves around Open Bay and the beach at Rebecca Spit. More confident paddlers may want to put in near Surge Narrows and explore that area, possibly lunching at Octopus Islands.

- *If you have two days:* If you launch from Heriot Bay, you can explore into Hoskyn Channel up to Surge Narrows or Sutil Channel to Penn Islands.

- *If you have three days:* Consider a circumnavigation of Read Island. By launching from Heriot Bay you could travel to Surge Narrows, up Whiterock Passage and around the north end of Read Island to Penn Islands, then return home. Another possibility is running Surge Narrows to stay at Octopus Islands. You can hike the trails the middle day.

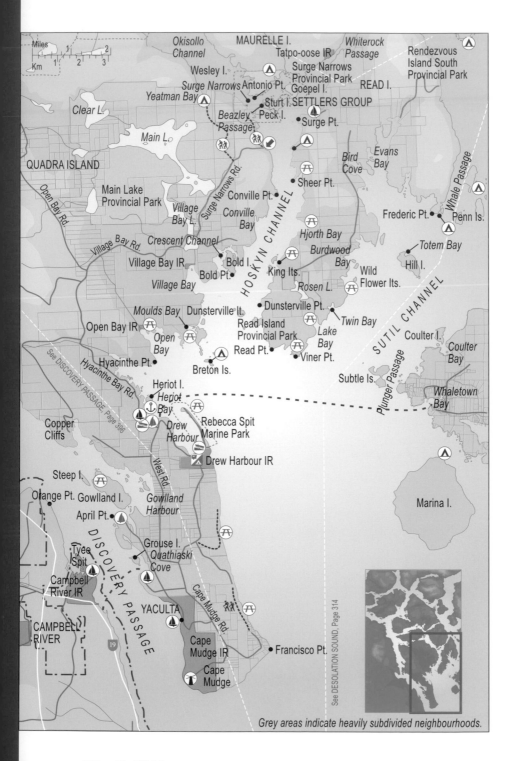

Miles
Km

Okisollo
Channel

MAURELLE I.

Whiterock
Passage

Rendezvous
Island South
Provincial Park

Wesley I.

Tatpo-oose IR

Surge Narrows
Provincial Park

Surge Narrows Antonio Pt.
Goepel I.

READ I.

Yeatman Bay

Sturt I. SETTLERS GROUP

Clear L.

Beazley
Passage

Peck I.

Surge Pt.

Main L.

QUADRA ISLAND

Bird
Cove

Evans
Bay

Sheer Pt.

Whale Passage

Main Lake
Provincial Park

Conville Pt.

Village
Bay L.

Conville
Bay

Hjorth Bay

Frederic Pt.

Penn Is.

Crescent Channel

Burdwood
Bay

Totem Bay

Village Bay Rd.

Bold I.

King Its.

Hill I.

Village Bay IR

Bold Pt.

Wild
Flower Its.

Village Bay

Rosen L.

Dunsterville It.

Dunsterville Pt.

Moulds Bay

Twin Bay

SUTIL CHANNEL

Coulter I.

Open Bay IR

Open
Bay

Read Island
Provincial Park

Lake
Bay

Coulter
Bay

Hyacinthe Pt.

Read Pt.

Viner Pt.

Plunger Passage

Breton Is.

Subtle Is.

Whaletown
Bay

Heriot I.

Heriot
Bay

Copper
Cliffs

Drew
Harbour

Rebecca Spit
Marine Park

Drew Harbour IR

Marina I.

Steep I.

Orange Pt. Gowlland I.

Gowlland
Harbour

April Pt.

Grouse I.

Quathiaski
Cove

Tyee
Spit

Campbell
River IR

CAMPBELL
RIVER

YACULTA

Cape
Mudge IR

Francisco Pt.

See DESOLATION SOUND, Page 314

Cape
Mudge

Grey areas indicate heavily subdivided neighbourhoods.

HOSKYN CHANNEL

Open Bay Rd.

Surge Narrows Rd.

Village Bay Rd.

See DISCOVERY PASSAGE, Page 306

Hyacinthe Bay Rd.

West Rd.

Cape Mudge Rd.

DISCOVERY PASSAGE

19

Breton Islands.

- *If you have five days:* Adventurous paddlers may want to try this
  agenda: launch from Heriot Bay, run Surge Narrows to Octopus
  Islands, run Hole In the Wall to as far as Moh Creek in Bute Inlet,
  explore Bute Inlet for a day, return via Calm Channel to South
  Rendezvous Islands Marine Park and then Sutil Channel.

- *If you have a week:* A circuit through the area is possible in a week.
  Less advanced paddlers will probably want a simpler agenda
  through Surge Narrows and Octopus Islands, perhaps as far as
  Moh Creek in Bute Inlet before returning via Calm Channel (a
  slower version of the agenda above). Advanced paddlers could
  try this: launch at south Campbell River; round Cape Mudge to
  Breton Islands; explore Octopus Islands via Surge Narrows; paddle Hole In the Wall to Moh Creek in Bute Inlet; run Arran and
  Dent rapids into Okisollo Channel; then take either route along
  East Thurlow Island (Cordero or Nodales channels) for a return
  down Discovery Passage through Seymour Narrows. A simpler
  route would be to stay out of Discovery Passage, instead doing a
  circuit around Sonora Island.

• *The ideal trip:* It would be a shame to design a wish-list agenda and not include Desolation Sound. I'd consider a circuit including Desolation Sound; Homfray Channel; a nose into Toba Inlet; a run along Pryce Channel and Deer Passage into Calm Channel with a stay at South Rendezvous Island; a trip down Hole in the Wall to Octopus Islands; a run through Surge Narrows and around Read Island to Marina Island; then back to Desolation Sound and home. This could be expanded to include Cordero Channel and south Johnstone Strait to see killer whales. The latter, in my opinion, closes in on a world-class kayaking itinerary, even though many portions are not even part of an established kayaking circuit.

SOUTHEAST QUADRA

Surge Narrows is the central feature in this area, though Heriot Bay is popular with boaters and as a staging ground for kayak groups. Recreational boaters heading up the Inside Passage tend to favour Hoskyn Channel, taking Whiterock Passage or Cordero Channel before reaching Johnstone Strait or Okisollo Channel.

Francisco Point

This point is cliffy, with drying rocks extending well offshore. Look for four granite boulders with petroglyphs at the beach. Four other petroglyph sites are located around Cape Mudge. North of the point heavy residential stretches are interspersed with undeveloped portions. Kayakers transiting the region should have no problem finding rest spots along the beaches here.

Rebecca Spit

This long, thin neck of land is treed and fringed by sand beaches. Mounds are believed to be the remains of Coast Salish fortifications used to defend against the Kwakwa'wakw several hundred years ago. The spit shelters Drew Harbour, a popular anchorage. Walking trails line both sides of the spit. There is a large picnic area with tables, a playing field, pit toilets and fresh water.

Place names: The British schooner *Rebecca* traded on the B.C. coast for several years in the 1860s.

Launches: A boat launch is located on the west side of the spit near the park entrance.

Camping: Adjacent to the park is the private We-Wai-Kai Campground operated by the We Wai Kai First Nation. This would make a useful staging ground for a trip from Quadra Island. Call **250-285-3111**.

Heriot Bay

This is a village centre for Quadra Island, with a busy government wharf, the ferry terminal to Cortes Island, a marina, hotel, restaurant and a water-accessible commercial (RV-oriented) campsite all within close proximity. The public wharf has garbage disposal, a phone, washrooms and a launch ramp. Up the hill—ask directions from any local at the dock, and that's the answer you'll get, "it's up the hill"—is a well-stocked grocery store, liquor store and post office (V0P 1H0). It's behind the Heriott Bay Inn, up from the same road the ferry terminal is on. And it's only a small hill.

Heriot Bay is part of a large indentation into Quadra Island shared by Open Bay, Hyacinthe Bay and Drew Harbour. The whole area is lightly residential. Beaches are common; the nicest, at Open Bay, is often used as a group campsite for kayaking tours. Islands dot the area, making this a good place to explore.

Camping: N50°07.54' W125°10.85', Breton Islands. The main Breton Island has a level central portion with bluffs to the north and south; the best beach is on the southwest facing Heriot Bay. The beach is rock, cobble and some pebble. The upland has a selection of clear areas, with three fire pits that, unfortunately, take up much of the level space that could be used for tents. This is a pretty location and strategic for trips through the area. It and most of the other islands in this region are Crown land.

Hoskyn Channel

This passage extends 10 km (6 miles) between Quadra and Read islands to Okisollo Channel. There are numerous beaches in the Village Bay area, but the number drops off once north of the bay. Fish farms are numerous, with several along the northwest edge of Read Island Provincial Park and more along Quadra Island at Conville Bay and Conville Point. The flood runs south and the ebb north at 1–2 knots.

Hoskyn Channel.

Wind may be more of a trip spoiler. If a northwesterly is blowing in Johnstone Strait, it can run down Hoskyn Channel as a northerly.

Launches: Quick access to Surge Narrows is possible from the end of Surge Narrows Road.

Camping: N50°12.62' W125°07.83'. North of Sheer Point is a prominent headland with a beach to the south. A strip has been cleared of rocks for a kayak skid. Tour groups frequently use the headland and adjacent forest area. A variety of camping optionsinclude the headland, a forest clearing or a gravel strip along the top of the high-backed beach.

Surge Narrows

Surge Narrows is one of a number of hurdles you'll need to pass in order to transit this area. Flood tides set southeast at as much as 12 knots and ebb northwest at up to 10 knots. The period of slack varies from 5 to 11 minutes. Most boats use Beazley Passage as the only rock-free route to the narrows. As the rapids are centred in Beazley Passage, paddlers are advised to pick another route. The turbulence in the north or south passages will be a fraction of the rapids in Beazley Passage.

The Settlers Group is a liberal sprinkling of islands southeast of the entrance to Surge Narrows. The currents between these islands can be strong, making casual paddling difficult. The central island, Sturt Island, is private and developed; the other islands and the south end of Maurelle Island are protected as part of Surge Narrows Provincial Park.

Across from the narrows east of Surge Point is the community centre for Read Island, with a government wharf, store and post office (V0P 1W0). Float planes land here. Housing is sporadic along both the Read and Maurelle island shores outside the provincial park boundaries. Dispersed camping is allowed within the provincial park. Goepel Island has some nice headlands on the southwest side, but access is difficult. If you do intend to camp here, take a look at the westernmost of three small coves on south Maurelle Island north of Goepel Island (N50°14.24' W125°08.49'). There's a large grass clearing between the beach and forest.

Surge Narrows Provincial Park

Surge Narrows Provincial Park is notable for its rich marine life. Sea urchin, sea cucumber, sea star, rockfish, prawn and anemone all thrive in the strong tidal waters. All five species of salmon pass through the narrows. The park is undeveloped and has no facilities. It was established in 1996 and protects 488 ha (1,205 acres).

Kayaking Surge Narrows: Surge Narrows is a much simpler route than Seymour Narrows because the rapids are quite localized. By steering clear of Beazley Passage and entering via the north or south channels, kayakers can avoid the worst of the rapids. I would recommend the north channel. Travel is best timed for slack tide, naturally, and approaching the narrows on the last of the opposing current can be easy due to the many countercurrents.

Travel notes: On a trip to Surge Narrows I decided to head south from the Octopus Islands to play in the opposing rapids during the peak ebb current for that tide, making the current about 5.5 knots. I approached along the northeast shore of Okisollo Channel using the countercurrents. At the narrows there was very little turbulence. I scooted into the tiny cove north of Antonio Point, saw no rapids, then rounded the point to come out into the waters by the Settlers Group. Much to my surprise, I encountered barely a ripple. At about the same time another couple of kayakers were crossing with the current from the south passage, and they encountered a similar lack of turbulence. Meanwhile, we could all hear the rapids roaring in Beazley Passage.

The headland at the north entrance to Lake Bay.

Yeatman Bay

Main Lake Provincial Park extends to the shoreline at Yeatman Bay. It's possible to hike from the bay to Main Lake along an old logging road.

Read Island Provincial Park

This park protects the south end of Read Island—an area of prominent granite bluffs, steep shorelines and small coves and bays. It contains some old-growth and second-growth forests and some bog. It's considered high-density bald eagle habitat; look for the nests in tall trees along the shoreline. The park was created in 1996 and protects 639 ha (1,580 acres). It's open for wilderness camping but lacks established sites. Potential sites are Lake Bay or the coves northwest of Viner Point.

Camping: N50°13.94' W125°10.85'. Yeatman Bay is backed by a wide beach that dries extensively. A large clear camping area in the upland could accommodate a group.

Evans and Burdwood bays

Evans Bay, on south Read Island, is surrounded by beaches that appear more appealing from a distance than they really are. The shoreline is dotted with a few homes, as is Burdwood Bay to the south. A cluster of islands, known locally as Wild Flower Islets, are scattered around the south end of Burdwood Bay, with a shellfish operation adjacent. Access to the islands is possible via rough oyster beaches.

South Rendezvous Island looking to Raza Point.

Off-lying Hill Island is private, with a dock in Totem Bay to the north. The Read Island shore becomes steeper to the south of Burdwood Bay, with a pleasant cove in Lake Bay.

Place names: Capt. William Viner Read was a naval assistant for the Hydrographic office of the Admiralty in 1863, as was Staff Commander Frederick John Owen Evans.

Camping: N50°11.08' W125°02.70'. Just north of the entrance to Evans Bay is a cluster of islets joined by rock bars to each other and to Read Island at low tides. The outer two headlands are accessible by a south-facing rock beach. Benches and clear areas on the headlands are suitable for a small group.

CALM CHANNEL

Calm Channel leads about 14 km (9 miles) from Sutil and Lewis channels to Bute Inlet and Cordero Channel. Currents are weak until the northwest portion and the entrance to Yuculta Rapids. A flood current will run hard between Kellsey Point and the bay at Mushkin Indian Reserve before dispersing. This is a pretty area. Numerous

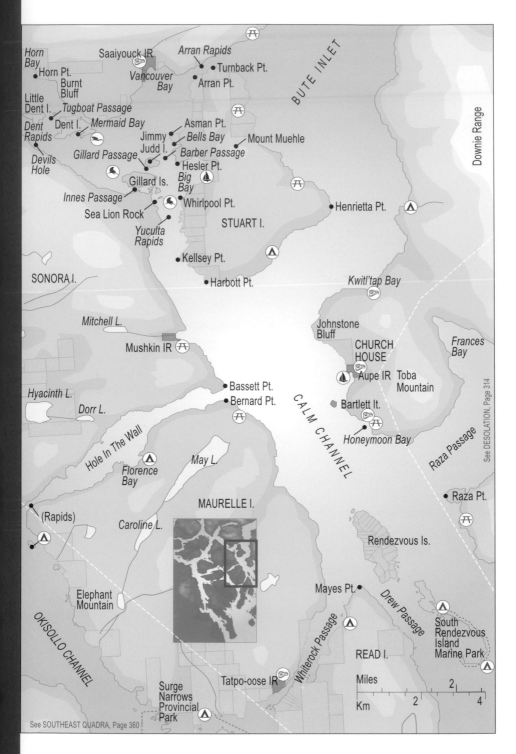

Horn
Bay
• Horn Pt.
Burnt
Bluff

Saaiyouck IR

Arran Rapids
• Turnback Pt.

Vancouver
Bay
• Arran Pt.

BUTE INLET

Downie Range

Little
Dent I.   Tugboat Passage
Dent I. Mermaid Bay
Dent
Rapids

Asman Pt.
Jimmy • Bells Bay
Judd I. Barber Passage
Gillard Passage

Mount Muehle

Devils
Hole

Hesler Pt.
Gillard Is. Big
Bay
Innes Passage

Whirlpool Pt.

• Henrietta Pt.

Sea Lion Rock

STUART I.

Yuculta
Rapids

SONORA I.

• Kellsey Pt.

• Harbott Pt.

Kwitl'tap Bay

Mitchell L.

Johnstone
Bluff

Frances
Bay

Mushkin IR

CHURCH
HOUSE

Aupe IR Toba
Mountain

Hyacinth L.

Dorr L.

• Bassett Pt.
• Bernard Pt.

CALM CHANNEL

• Bartlett It.

Honeymoon Bay

Hole In The Wall

May L.

Florence
Bay

MAURELLE I.

Raza Passage

• Raza Pt.

(Rapids)

Caroline L.

Rendezvous Is.

Elephant
Mountain

Mayes Pt. •

Drew Passage

OKISOLLO CHANNEL

Whiterock Passage

READ I.

South
Rendezvous
Island
Marine Park

Tatpo-oose IR

Surge
Narrows
Provincial
Park

See SOUTHEAST QUADRA, Page 360

Miles

Km

2

2

4

See DESOLATION, Page 314

Looking toward the rocks at the south entrance of Whiterock Passage.

eagles nest in the area and the waters are home to prawn, squid, octopus, sea cucumber, hake and groundfish. The rich marine life makes for good scuba diving at Little John and Dent islands.

Calm Channel is a primary migration route for Pacific herring, and a secondary route for Fraser River salmon. During the salmon runs expect numerous seabirds, particularly cormorant, murre, grebe and marbled murrelet.

Whiterock Passage

Whiterock Passage has been dredged, resulting in a calm passage with maximum currents of about 2 knots. The flood sets north. A beach area on the north shore is the Tatpo-oose Indian Reserve, once a principal village of the Klahoose. Homes are intermittent on the Read Island side.

Camping: N50°15.95' W125°04.94'. South of Mayes Point are two islets; the southern one is connected to a headland at low tide. Beach access to the headland is possible from both sides, with best access from the south. On the headland is a grassy area near debris from an old cabin. Note the beach dries extensively at low tide.

South Rendezvous Island.

Rendezvous Islands

The three Rendezvous Islands lie in the middle of Calm Channel off the northwest tip of Cortes Island. The northern two are private and lightly developed; the southern is a provincial park.

Ecological oddities: The park represents the northern limit of the range of the arbutus tree.

Camping: N50°16.06' W125°02.40'. Dispersed camping is allowed anywhere in the park. Here's my pick. On the north end of the provincial park island are two headlands that shelter a beach that is progressively stone, gravel and large rocks, with the most difficult access at high tide when landing on the large rocks would be required. On the headland east of the beach are a number of flat, grassy spots that would support a small group. Another site, on the south end of the island, was cleared of old buildings early in 2006 and now has room for a large group.

Rendezvous Island South Provincial Park

This park protects an entire island, the southern of the three Rendezvous Islands, at 113 ha (280 acres), plus 51 ha (126 acres) of marine foreshore. The park was created in 1997 as a step in a marine trail system for the province.

Church House

This is part of an area rich in First Nations heritage that begins southeast of Bartlett Island at a place locally called Honeymoon Bay, a traditional village site. It's a good beach for a rest or picnic. North of the bay is a rock formation and a spring considered culturally significant by the Homalco.

Church House is a Homalco reserve, with most homes in ruins. The old church for which the community is named is aging poorly and appears in danger of collapsing. Beside Church House is a rock face known as Raven's Chamber Pot. At Kwitl'tap Bay, 2.1 km (1.3 miles) northeast of Johnstone Bluff, there's a pictograph 4.5 m (15 feet) above the high water mark.

Church House's bay is shared with a large log dump and booming ground on the south side of the bay and a large fish farm on the north end—unfortunate use of such a historic area.

Hole in the Wall

This passage divides Sonora and Maurelle islands, with strong currents at the west entrance where tidal streams can reach 12 knots. The flood sets northeast. On the flood expect rips and turbulence until east of a prominent headland on the north shore, 1.3 km (0.8 miles) from the west entrance light. The rest of the channel is generally placid. The south shore is indented by Florence Cove, which is occasionally used as an anchorage (though the passage doesn't see much traffic). The cove is a traditional deer hunting and clam harvesting area. Cormorant, murrelet and murre frequent the passage in the fall. At low tide watch for spinet pink scallops and urchin beds in the water at the entrance.

Current times have their own entry in *Canadian Tide and Current Tables, Volume 6.*

Camping: N50°18.76' W125°09.82'. The best beach in Hole In the Wall is at Florence Cove on the east side behind a headland. The upland is undeveloped and is thick with wild raspberries, but the beach will support a tent or two during most tide levels. It will take some work, though, to become a group site. Expect to bushwhack. There's another beach with potential to the north, on the other side of the headland.

Sitting in the countercurrent at Kellsey Point.

Stuart Island

This island is extensively developed on the west side, where numerous lodges are located—about 16 in total in this region. Big Bay is the focal point for traffic, due mainly to the government wharf, which is used frequently by float planes. The bay was formerly a service centre with a fuel dock and a store, but both were closed in 2005—a fact that has stranded some boaters expecting fuel. The nearest alternatives are Heriot Bay on Quadra Island to the south or Blind Bay on West Thurlow Island to the west. Given the three rapids that must be transited, the west side of Stuart Island is not recommended for anything less than expert kayakers. The south and east shores of Stuart Island tend to be undeveloped steep rock bluff with occasional boulder beaches and difficult upland access only.

Camping: N50°22.17' W125°06.52'. On the south end of Stuart Island is a rough beach backed by a young alder forest growing over an extensively logged region. This is the best beach in the area. Look for clear, level areas, including one on a small portion of old logging road not far inland. This spot is undeveloped and isn't the prettiest location, but it's strategic for overnighting while waiting for a favourable turn of the tide in Yuculta Rapids.

Yuculta Rapids

This is the southernmost of three rapids that must be crossed to pass from Calm Channel to Cordero Channel. Currents here run as strong as 10 knots, with the flood setting south and the ebb north. The ebb current is usually weaker, reaching a maximum of just 8 knots. The turn to flood is 25 minutes after the turn at Gillard Passage to the north, while the turn to ebb is 5 minutes after.

A flood current creates strong counter-currents west of Harbott Point to Kellsey Point; it's possible for kayakers to nose right up to Kellsey Point and await a change in tide.

Gillard Passage

Gillard Passage lies between Gillard and Jimmy Judd islands west of Stuart Island. As a rapid it has its own entry in *Canadian Tide and Current Tables, Volume 6*. The flood sets east and the ebb west. Velocities reach 11.5 knots on the flood and 9.5 on the ebb. The main trouble spot is east of the Gillard Islands navigation light at the junction of Barber Passage. Expect dangerous whirlpools east of Gillard

Islands two hours after the turn to flood until an hour before the turn to ebb. Ebb currents are generally more friendly than the flood. On the ebb the turbulence is likely north of Jimmy Judd and Gillard Islands; during the flood the turbulence will be to the south.

There are two alternative passages to Gillard: Barber Passage to the north and Innes Passage to the south. Barber Passage is prone to currents of up to 10 knots, with the ebb setting roughly north. Kayakers may be tempted to take Innes Passage, as it's narrow—less than 90 m (300 feet) in portions—and shallow, and is avoided by all but small boats.

Dent Rapids

Dent Rapids, between Dent Islands and Sonora Island, is the northernmost of the three rapids in the area. The flood current runs southeast at up to 11 knots. The worst turbulence will be on the southwest shore, where whirlpools and eddies are likely. Devils Hole is the name for a dangerous tidal whirlpool that forms west of Little Dent Island on large flood tides. This can appear two hours after the turn to flood and last until an hour before the turn to ebb. The ebb sets northwest at a maximum of 9.5 knots and is usually less turbulent than the flood, with trouble limited to near Dent Islands. The ebb current will continue for nearly a kilometre (0.5 miles) along the southwest shore. Slack at Dent Rapids occurs 15 minutes before Gillard Passage on the turn to flood and 25 minutes before the turn to ebb.

An alternative route is Tugboat Passage between Dent Island and Little Dent islands. As the name implies, it's used by tugs, often carrying booms. Most boats avoid it due to the islets, shoals and irregular currents.

Arran Rapids

This is a fourth rapid in the area; it lies north of Stuart Island and links Cordero Channel with Bute Passage. Consequently, for most transits of the area it isn't a factor. Currents set east on the flood at a maximum of 14 knots and west on the ebb at a maximum 12.5 knots. This route is rarely used. The flood current will extend northeast well into Bute Inlet, so boats or kayakers running up the west shore of Bute Inlet may inadvertently find themselves in the rips and turbulence of the main current stream from the rapids as it exits the narrows. The time of slack water is the same as Dent Rapids, with a slack of 4 minutes. The main hazard is a sizable overfall—up to several metres—during peak currents.

At Vancouver Bay is the Saaiyouck reserve, once the principal village site of the Kwiakah described by Captain Vancouver in his journals as "village of the friendly Indians."

Kayaking the triple rapids: Considering there are three rapids that must be crossed over a distance of about 8 km (5 miles), this is a perilous trip for kayaks. It can be avoided by taking Okisollo Channel instead. However, if you wish to transit this area, consider the following.

There is no savings in distance by considering running Arran Rapids instead of Yuculta Rapids and Gillard Passage. The distance from Turnback Point to the far end of Little Dent Island is 7 km (4.4 miles), the same distance as Kellsey Point to Little Dent Island.

A run on the ebb is arguably better due to the reduced turbulence. If you choose to run south to north at Yuculta Rapids at the slack you will pass Dent Rapids as a current is building—a bad thing—but it will be on an ebb current, which means less turbulence and no whirlpool at Devils Hole. However, keep in mind all three currents change directions at different times, and in this direction those changes will work against you, as slack at Dent Rapids is a half-hour before slack at Yuculta on the change to ebb. This means if you take an hour to reach Dent Rapids after slack at Yuculta you will be running Dent with current levels for 1.5 hours after slack. In other words, you lose a half hour out of the gate to beat the growing turbulence at Dent Rapids.

If you run the rapids north to south, you will be doing it on a flood current, which is more turbulent. The good news is you can run Dent Rapids at slack, avoiding any dangers there. Since the turn to ebb is 15 minutes before Gillard Passage, the change works in your favour. However, it's still likely you'll reach Yuculta with some current, and this at a lower tide when turbulence will be worse. Considering you gain 20 minutes on the change this route, you are likely to pass within the first hour of the change of current when turbulence will be minimal, so your risk is (in theory) not great. If planned well you should get no more than a gentle current-aided ride through Yuculta. A kayaker could conceivably run Arran Rapids the same way to get to Bute Inlet.

Another option for a north-to-south trip is to run the rapids at the end of the flood tide—say an hour before the turn to flood at Dent Rapids. The advantage of doing this is you'll be running all three rapids at a higher tide, meaning less turbulence, plus the variation in the change of times to ebb among the three rapids will work in your favour. When Dent is slack, you'll still have 25 minutes of extra flood tide at Gillard Passage, and another five minutes of flood time in Yuculta Rapids. This considerably reduces the risk of the current changing before you can clear the rapids.

(The reverse, trying to run the rapids south to north at the end of an ebb tide would be foolhardy, as the variations in current changes will work against you.)

No matter the route you take, this is not a casual trip. Traffic tends to bottleneck waiting for favourable tides. Pleasure craft generally won't be a problem beyond a wake, but you may encounter tugs pulling barges or log booms. They will take right-of-way and it would be unfortunate to be delayed by a slow-moving tug at a time when the current is building in danger. Note also that many of these vessels may not be in complete control due to the currents.

Always remember you can pull into Big Bay or Vancouver Bay and wait for more favourable conditions after the peak tide if you get delayed or find the rapids building too quickly for your liking.

The final and perhaps biggest consideration is that not all tides are equal. At 3:10 p.m. on August 10, 2006, Gillard Passage was running at its peak for that current at 10.7 knots. On August 30 at 12:48 p.m. it was running at a peak for that current of 3.8 knots. By choosing the right time of the month, and even the right tide for that day, you can reduce your risk considerably.

BUTE INLET

This inlet extends about 75 km (47 miles) north into the mountainous interior of the B.C. mainland. It's known for its deep, milky-green water, glaciated mountains, grizzly habitat and high winds. Expect a constant ebb flood of a knot or so during the summer due to the freshwater runoff. This and Bute Inlet's famous katabatic and outflow winds can make an inbound journey difficult. Owen Lange, in his book *The Wind Came All Ways*, offers these remarks about the inlet: "If you hear a roar up the mountains, you have four hours to get out of the inlet. The winds are so strong that you cannot cross the mouth of Bute during an outflow. Bute winds are very vicious. You need to respect them."

Toba Inlet.

Place names: Captain Vancouver named the inlet in 1792 after John Stuart (1713–92), third Earl of Bute.

Lower Bute Inlet

Bute Inlet begins as a wide fiord with steep shores at Johnstone Bluff at the junction of Calm Channel. The cove at Leask Creek, often referred to by boaters and locals as Fawn Bluff, is a traditional anchorage and campsite that has recently been sold and is now being heavily developed right down to the beach, known locally as Freddie's Beach. A road is also being blasted to the waterfront. The status of a trail to nearby Leask Lake is in limbo. A lot of the recreational traffic is shifting to Moh Creek, as has the shared-use cabin previously located at Fawn Bluff.

At the first sharp turn of the inlet is a bay known locally as Curly's Camp. An old log dump has altered the rough beachfront here, which is the starting point of a traditional First Nations trail that leads to Estero Basin (see page 392).

Just west of Moh Creek a beautiful gravel beach is separated into two parts by a headland. This is an anchorage with upland access. Look for eagle nests near here; they are numerous.

Camping: N50°30.87' W125°02.80'. The beach southwest of Moh Creek is a private upland available for public use. A sign reads,

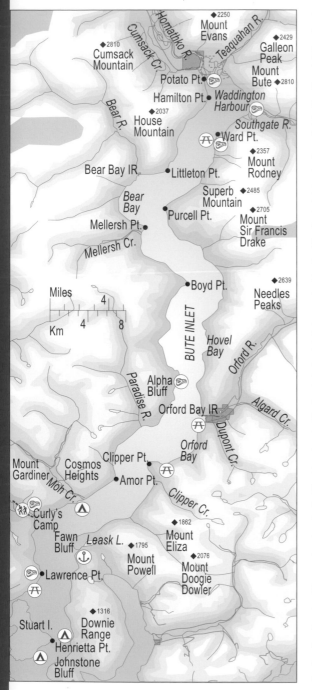

"Greetings! In the interest of the campers who follow you, please: take all your garbage with you, put out your fire/avoid fires when it's dry, and please don't leave any food for wildlife. Thanks! The Owners." On the property is a well-built shared-use cabin moved from Fawn Bluff. East of the cabin is a level grassy area suitable for camping. This is a beautiful spot with beautiful views, and the owners deserve much credit for sharing this wonderful place.

N50°22.97' W125°03.27'. East of Stuart Island's Henrietta Point, on the east side of Bute Inlet, 4.6 km (3 miles) northeast of Johnstone Bluff, is a good stone and rock beach next to a creek. Flat areas at the top of the beach will survive most tide levels and there's good potential for site development behind the beach. This is a pretty location with water from the creek through most of the year.

Upper Bute Inlet

Orford Bay is tucked into the east side of Bute Inlet, with a drying flat at its head and a ruined pier on the south end. This is an occasional anchorage. Watch for both

The view at the beach near Moh Creek.

black and grizzly bear in the intertidal areas in spring and during berry crops and salmon runs.

A traditional canoe landing spot is at the first bay east of Clipper Point. A distinctive rock crevice at the creek north of Alpha Bluff resembles overturned canoes and is a part of Xwémalhkwu (Homalco) mythology. It is one of a number of legendary sites in this area; there are 28 protected cultural sites in total. Crevices were often burial sites and pictographs can be found along the northern shoreline of Alpha Bluff. About 4.4 km (2.7 miles) north of the bluff is a natural corral at the base of the mountain, which was used for hunting mountain goat.

At the head of Bute Inlet is Waddington Harbour. It's a difficult anchorage but used heavily as a booming ground. Flowing into the harbour is the Homathko River, which even in August flows out at a speed of about 5 knots. The seawater is pale green due to minerals from the Homathko Icefield, 8 km (5 miles) to the northeast.

The Southgate River also flows into the head of the inlet. A permanent Xwémalhkwu village was once located here. Look for the stone fish traps and the burial ground at Potato Point. South of the point is a spring accessible from the shore. This was the site of a traditional village and, in later years, a cannery. At Ward Point is a former seasonal village site. There's a safe landing for canoes

The view of Philips Arm from Shoal Bay.

and kayaks on the small point to the south, possibly a good base for exploring the head of the inlet. Southgate River is an important chum river; the salmon make their way up 35 km (20 miles) of the river to spawn. This makes it prime grizzly habitat.

South of Purcell Point is an old steam donkey.

Place names: James Johnson Southgate was a ship's master in Victoria 1859–65.

Hiking: The Homathko River originates in the Chilcotin. Back in 1862–64 a wagon trail was built along the river to link the Chilcotin with the coast; parts of it can still be found. The logging roads from Orford Bay can be hiked, as can the roads near the Homathko River. The latter can give access to the Homathko Icefield, one of the largest icefields in B.C. It's surrounded by Cambridge (2,704 m/8,871 feet), Howard (2,575 m/8,448 feet) and Plateau (2,545 m/8,350 feet) mountains. This is for serious mountaineers only.

Kayaking Bute Inlet: This is a long and difficult stretch of water that will appeal to a select few. Due to the difficulties of the ebb current and outflow winds, taking a water taxi to the head and paddling back down would make for a simpler and more enjoyable trip. This would also eliminate doubling up your route, and you'll get a good idea of the landing opportunities and possible campsites on your trip up. Water taxis are available from Lund, Campbell River or Quadra Island.

The Octopus Islands from the campsite at Francisco Island.

CORDERO-NODALES-OKISOLLO

This is one of those B.C. regions that has escaped the kayaking radar. All three channels here lack a network of established campsites once outside Octopus Islands. Meanwhile, the area is heavily used by recreational boats travelling the Inside Passage, particularly Cordero Passage, which tends to escape most of the winds that can plague Johnstone Strait.

Octopus Islands

This is an archipelago of two main islands and a scattering of islets. It's a popular anchorage. Kayakers generally use it as the northern end of a route between Surge Narrows and South Rendezvous Islands. The north and south entrances to Waiatt Bay and many of the nearby islets are protected in Octopus Islands Marine Park. Unfortunately, the two largest islands are private. The waters around Francisco Island are prone to eddies and turbulence.

Camping: None of the islands within the marine park have beaches. Kayakers have no option but to scramble up bedrock to reach otherwise pleasant, level headlands. The only established island campsite and the

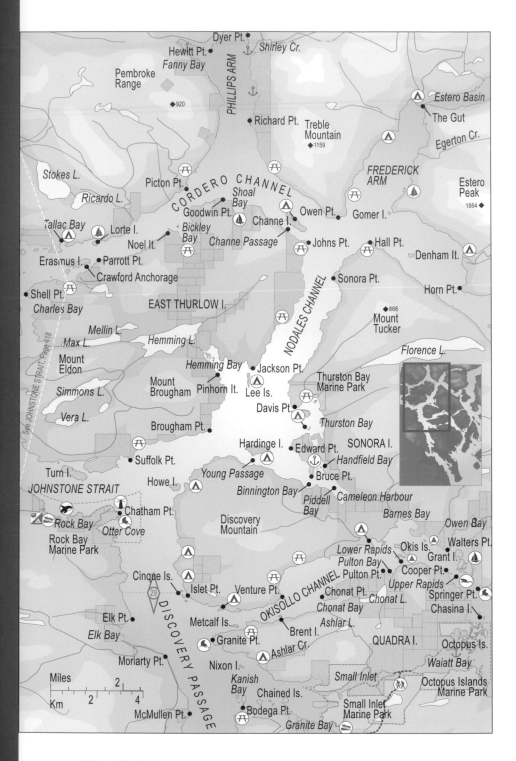

Dyer Pt.

Shirley Cr.

Hewitt Pt.
Fanny Bay

PHILLIPS ARM

Pembroke
Range

◆920

Richard Pt.

Treble
Mountain

◆1159

Estero Basin

The Gut

Egerton Cr.

**FREDERICK
ARM**

Estero
Peak

1664◆

Stokes L.

Ricardo L.

Picton Pt.

C O R D E R O   C H A N N E L

Shoal
Bay

Owen Pt.

Gomer I.

Tallac Bay

Lorte I.

Goodwin Pt.

*Bickley
Bay*

Channe I.

Johns Pt.

Hall Pt.

Denham It.

Noel It.

Channe Passage

Sonora Pt.

Horn Pt.

Erasmus I.

Parrott Pt.

Crawford Anchorage

Shell Pt.

Charles Bay

EAST THURLOW I.

NODALES CHANNEL

◆866

Mount
Tucker

Florence L.

Mellin L.

Max L.

Mount
Eldon

Hemming L.

Simmons L.

Hemming Bay

Mount
Brougham

Pinhorn It.

Jackson Pt.

Lee Is.

Davis Pt.

Thurston Bay
Marine Park

Vera L.

Brougham Pt.

Thurston Bay

SONORA I.

Suffolk Pt.

Hardinge I.

Edward Pt.

Handfield Bay

Turn I.

Howe I.

Young Passage

Bruce Pt.

JOHNSTONE STRAIT

Binnington Bay

Piddell
Bay

Cameleon Harbour

Barnes Bay

Owen Bay

Chatham Pt.

Otter Cove

Discovery
Mountain

Lower Rapids

Okis Is.

Walters Pt.

Rock Bay

Rock Bay
Marine Park

Pulton Bay
Pulton Pt.

Grant I.

Cooper Pt.

Upper Rapids

Springer Pt.

Chasina I.

Cinque Is.

Islet Pt.

Venture Pt.

OKISOLLO CHANNEL

Chonat Pt.

Chonat Bay

Chonat L.

Elk Bay

Elk Pt.

Metcalf Is.

Brent I.

Ashlar L.

QUADRA I.

Octopus Is.

Granite Pt.

Ashlar Cr.

Moriarty Pt.

Nixon I.

Waiatt Bay

Octopus Islands
Marine Park

Miles

2

*Kanish
Bay*

Small Inlet

Km

2   4

Chained Is.

Small Inlet
Marine Park

McMullen Pt.

Bodega Pt.

Granite Bay

D I S C O V E R Y   P A S S A G E

See JOHNSTONE STRAIT, Page 418

only one with a beach is a pretty spot at Francisco Island (N50°17.29' W125°12.51')—which is odd, as it is outside the park and the park was created supposedly as part of a marine trail link. Groups wanting to stay inside the park who aren't deterred by rock ledge camping will probably be most interested in the island nearest the an-

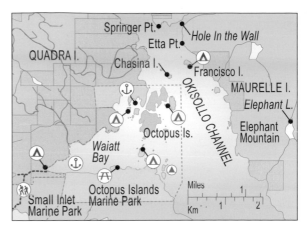

chorage to the west of the largest of the Octopus Islands at N50°16.64' W125°13.86'. Individuals or couples with a single tent will probably prefer the north headland on the island directly south of the main Octopus Islands at N50°16.13' W125°13.61'.

Waiatt Bay

The foreshore of the entire bay is protected within Octopus Islands Marine Park, but portions of the immediate upland to the north are private property. The bay is popular as an anchorage. A clam bed and

Waiatt Bay.

Octopus Islands.

Octopus Islands Marine Park
This group of small islands protects a key anchorage for boaters travelling the Inside Passage. The park was created in 1974 and protects 760 ha (1,878 acres), most of which is foreshore. The name is derived from the high number of octopus in the waters here.

the trailhead to Small Inlet are at the head of the bay. This is a traditional portage route that's still occasionally used for that purpose.

Hiking: A short, 1.5-km (1-mile) trail connects Waiatt Bay and the head of Small Inlet. A branch leads to Newton Lake, a popular swimming area. The turnoff is not marked; it's next to the easternmost section of log walkway. The walk to Newton Lake is about a mile, with some difficult uphill portions. The lake, though, is refreshing. From the lake another leg leads 3 km (2 miles) to Granite Bay.

Camping: N50°15.81' W125°15.56'. There are clam beaches along much of Waiatt Bay, but the best option is at the head of the bay by the trailhead. The upland is clear and grassy.

Upper Rapids

These rapids lie in Okisollo Channel just north of Hole in the Wall. They are prone to a maximum of 11 knots on both ebb and flood and are known for their overfalls and eddies. Flood tides set south and the ebb north. Current times are listed in *Canadian Tide and Current Tables, Volume 6* as a secondary station to Seymour Narrows. This is unnecessarily complicated, as Hole in the Wall has its own entry, and the current times for Hole in the Wall and Upper Rapids are almost simultaneous. Flood currents will run south through the Upper Rapids, with a portion entering Hole in the Wall. On the ebb the current from Okisollo Channel will be joined with the rush from Hole in the Wall as it constricts at the Upper Rapids. Owen Bay is a residential area with a public wharf on the east shore; there are no services. Look for the petroglyphs in Owen Bay if you visit. This is also a geological site of note—a meteor struck here. The bay is one of two safe anchorages in the area; the other is Barnes Bay.

Lower Rapids

This set of rapids is northwest of the Upper Rapids in Okisollo Channel, and it turns at approximately the same time as the Upper Rapids. The maximum current is about 6 knots. The rapids can be avoided by going north of Okis Island, although the current will still be strong. Numerous islets sit off the southwest end of the main Okis Island. Those and other nearby islets toward Owen Bay may be of interest to hardy campers for the pleasant mossy headlands. Don't expect beaches, though.

Camping: N50°18.89' W125°17.78'. Two km (1.2 miles) west of Okis Islands is probably the best beach in the channel not adjacent to a fish farm. It's gravel and grit and faces east in the cover of a small bay, providing a sheltered pullout. It is currently undeveloped, with an upland of heavy scrub. It needs work but is strategically significant.

Kayaking the Okisollo rapids: If you approach on the change of tide, you're unlikely to have a problem. Since there is also Surge Narrows to consider, you may be best off planning your trip to end one day crossing Surge Narrows, overnighting at Octopus Islands, then running the Upper and Lower Rapids the next day. If you're heading north from the Octopus Islands, leave your campsite before high tide slack. There are eddies on the west shore to aid your approach. If timed correctly you'll likely be well past Okis Islands before any rapids appear at the Lower Rapids.

If you're approaching from Hole In the Wall rather than Surge Narrows, you could easily run all three rapids in one day (Hole in the Wall and Upper and Lower). Approach near high tide slack, overnighting at Florence Cove if necessary. By crossing Hole in the

The view from the headland at Okisollo entrance.

Wall at slack you'll have lots of time to clear Lower Rapids, or simply stay north of Okis Islands. The same principles apply for a run south through the rapids. I'd suggest doing your best against the last of the ebb current to get to Owen Bay by hugging the north shore and using countercurrents. If you're near Grant Island at slack, you should have no problem making Hole in the Wall before a current builds.

North Okisollo Entrance
West of Lower Rapids, Okisollo Channel becomes a mix of logged hillsides and fish farms. The low, rolling topography is one of the less scenic on the coast; the highlight will be views of the mountains to the east.

Camping: N50°17.47' W125°22.71'. North of Metcalf Islands a long, thin headland creates a bay to the north; it's easily identified by the wreck of an old boat at the high tide line. South of the wreck is a second, smaller, wedge-shaped sand beach. At the top of the beach a clear area on the headland is currently suitable for just one tent, though more sites could be developed. This is a very pretty spot with views into both Discovery Channel and the entrance of Okisollo Channel.

The lighthouse buildings at Chatham Point.

Kanish Bay

This bay is the entrance to Small Inlet Marine Park. It's dotted with undeveloped islands, with a concentration of residential development squeezed into Granite Bay.

Camping: N50°16.03' W125°21.37'. At the north entrance to the bay, 2.2 km (1.4 miles) southeast of Granite Point, is a rough rock beach at Ashlar Creek. An open area of young forest, perfect for a group camp, is to the right of the creek.

Small Inlet Marine Park

This park on the north end of Quadra island protects an anchorage and Newton Lake, a swimming lake accessible by trail from both Small Inlet and Waiatt Bay on the east end of Quadra Island (see page 384). The park protects 487 ha (1,203 acres) and was created in 1996. There are more than 10 archaeological sites in the park, including the traditional portage to Waiatt Bay, plus evidence of early logging and mining.

North Discovery Passage

South of Chatham Point the winds that funnel down Johnstone Strait will begin to disperse, as will the worst of the currents that stream through the south strait. The Vancouver Island shoreline is a mix of heavily logged hillsides and scatterings of private holdings. Most kayakers will probably want to stay close to the more scenic Quadra and Sonora shorelines during this stretch, particularly around Cinque

Islands and Kanish Bay. Chatham Point and Otter Cove, where the Vancouver Island shoreline is convoluted and rocky, with lots to see, are exceptions. Several prominent buildings on the point and a radio tower are connected with the former lighthouse at Chatham Point, now a manned weather station. This was one of the later lighthouses on the B.C. coast, established in 1959.

The Cinque Islands light is a Vessel Traffic Services call-in point. It will be most useful to those transiting Seymour Narrows. See page 397 for details.

Weather

Chatham Point	May	June	July	Aug.	Sept.	Dec.	Av./Ttl.
Daily average temp. (C)	11.4	13.7	15.8	15.8	13.1	3.4	9.1
Daily maximum (C)	15.1	17.4	19.8	19.5	16.2	4.9	11.8
Daily minimum (C)	7.7	10.0	11.8	12.0	10.0	1.9	6.4
Precipitation (mm)	126.2	129.2	78.7	98.4	112.3	285.4	2274.7
Days of rainfall + 0.2mm	15.5	14.2	9.5	10.0	12.4	20.3	195.7
Days with rainfall +5mm	7.3	6.8	4	4.7	5.5	13.6	112
Days with rainfall +10mm	4.4	4.4	2.4	2.9	3.5	9.8	75.7
Days with rainfall +25mm	1.0	1.2	1.0	1.1	1.3	3.2	24.7
Wind speed (km/h)	15.6	17.2	19.4	17.6	14.1	13.3	14.4
Prevailing direction	W	W	W	W	W	SE	W

Camping: N50°18.16' W125°24.02'. Half a kilometre (0.3 miles) north of Cinque Islands a sand and gravel beach provides a good patch of sand high enough to survive most tide levels. This is an undeveloped site.

N50°18.90' W125°24.12'. In the middle of the deepest bay on the west side of Sonora Island, a derelict old cottage sits on an expansive grassy bank that is suitable for camping.

Travel notes: Seeing nature at work close-up is one of the advantages of kayaking, and one of the oddest encounters I witnessed occurred along the west shore of Sonora Island. Hearing an unusual squawk, I turned to see an eagle land on the beach next to a mink at the water-line. The message from the eagle was clear: "I've got you, now let's see what you're going to do." The mink, not the brightest of creatures, rather than making one last mad dash for survival, ran in front of the eagle, jumped onto a large rock beside the bird, leaned out as far as it could and sniffed the eagle's head. I'm sure if the eagle could have, it would have rolled its eyes. The eagle waited a few moments, almost as if it was tolerating the mink's attention, then in a flash it was gone and flying away, the mink hanging limply in its claws, proving Darwin's theory correct once again.

Rock Bay

Rock Bay is at the southeast entrance to Johnstone Strait, an area known for strong currents and rips. The bay is connected to the Vancouver Island highway via Rock Bay Road. The foreshore is private, with an RV campground on the upland. Launching would be possible from here.

Rock Bay Marine Park

This is an unusual park, consisting of foreshore only, plus a few rocky islets. The land behind the park is entirely private property and there is no land access to the park, though there is a private campground, a dock, walking trails and a boat launch. The park protects 525 ha (1,300 acres) and was created in 1995. It's a popular marine destination with a sheltered anchorage at Otter Cove.

Nodales Channel

This is a scenic route between Discovery Passage and Cordero Channel, particularly on a clear day when the snow-capped mainland mountains are in view. It's clear from the lack of campsites at ideal beaches that this is not part of an established kayak route, which is astounding considering the many attractions, particularly the island clusters off Hemming Bay and in Thurston Bay.

Tidal currents within the channel can reach 3 knots, with the flood setting northeast. Fish farms dot the channel, which is otherwise largely undeveloped. On the north end of the channel the shore becomes steeper, with some impressive headlands around Thurston Bay. Some good beaches can be found on the southwest entrance near Howe Island and Suffolk Point.

Hemming Bay and Chameleon Harbour are salmon streams, with a fishway in Hemming Bay Creek. This is an orca migration route and habitat for the California gull, loon, marbled murrelet, common murre and western grebe. Look for eagle nests at Lee Islands and Brougham Point. Hall Point on the north entrance is a popular sports fishing area; in season dozens of boats may be trolling the area

Nodales Channel.

Place names: Galiano and Valdes named Nodales Channel in 1792. The significance was not recorded.

Camping: N50°20.65' W125°23.77', South Nodales Entrance. East of Howe Island is a pair of wide rock beaches. The south beach has two strips of gravel for landing. In the forest there's a developed tent clearing. The beach to the immediate north has more sediment and better campsite potential due to its spacious alder forest and sparse undergrowth, but it's undeveloped. The waypoint is for this beach, as it will make a superior site once it's developed.

N50°23.12' W125°21.55', Lee Islands. On the southeast end facing Thurston Bay is a rock beach with access to a choice of undeveloped sites with great potential—either behind a bedrock mound in the middle of the beach or the north headland. Both have small existing areas for tents; more sites could be developed by cutting back the undergrowth.

Thurston Bay

This is a deep and convoluted area with portions protected by parkland. Anchorages can be found in Thurston Bay and Handfield Bay to the south. The southern portion, to Cameleon Harbour, is used for salmon farming. Islets dot Thurston Bay, with some limited potential for camping.

Hiking: Ruins of a forestry station are located on the north end of the bay. An old logging road leads to Florence Lake, but the trail is not maintained and is likely to be in poor condition. Look for the trailhead by the creek. Another logging road heads up Mount Tucker to an old forestry lookout. Again, the trail is likely in poor shape.

Camping: N50°21.46' W125°20.90', Hardinge Island. This is a large, undeveloped island with the best stone and gravel beach on the southeast side. Behind is a pleasantly sparse old forest free of undergrowth. The site is undeveloped but there are clear, level areas.

Denham Islet

This rocky islet sits north of Sonora Island in a relatively placid portion of Cordero Channel northwest of Dent Rapids, though currents can reach 4 knots near the island. The channel widens considerably north of Horn Point. Beaches are non-existent on the Sonora Island side but are numerous on the mainland side under the cover of Estero Peak, distinctive for the massive landslide down the south face. This area is prone to considerable boating traffic shortly after the turn to ebb at Dent Rapids.

Camping: N50°26.44' W125°13.49'. In the large bay below Estero Peak a set of creeks exit along a stone beach. North of the creeks is a strip of gravel, above which is a clear area for camping under the cover of a big old maple tree. This is a strategic site for crossing Dent and Yuculta rapids, and it has the advantage of access to fresh water.

"The Gut" into Estero Basin.

Thurston Bay Marine Park
This park protects an anchorage in a strategic location on the northwest side of Sonora Island. The upland is split into two portions—one on the north end of Thurston Bay and another on the north side of Handfield and Piddell bays. The park is undeveloped, although wilderness camping is allowed. The 389-ha (960-acre) park was created in 1970.

Frederick Arm

This inlet extends 5 km (3 miles) into the B.C. mainland. It's hardly pristine: there are two log dumps, fish farms and even a restaurant behind the islets about a kilometre (half a mile) north of the east entrance. The restaurant, Oleo's, has moorage for a few boats. The arm is used commercially for troll fishing and a spot

The view from Channe Island.

prawn fishery, plus commercial bear hunting. It shoals toward the head, where a river drains Estero Basin. Expect extensive flats at low tide. Kayakers may want to use the arm for access to Estero Basin, which is secluded thanks mostly to its inaccessibility. The current on the connecting river can be strong. For this reason a visit to the basin is recommended as a day trip when the kayak is empty. This way you can portage along the shoreline, or even walk your kayak up the waterway. This channel is known as "The Gut." The basin itself tends to be placid.

Channe Island

This island lies in Cordero Channel between Frederick and Phillips arms. Johns Point at the northwest entrance to Nodales Channel has a wonderful beach. It's used as an outstation for barbecues by a resort.

Camping: N50°27.33' W125°19.92'. The northeast side of Channe Island has two coves; the southern of the two is a rock beach with a strip of small stones down the middle. A clear area in the forest has a rudimentary sleeping bench and tarp frame that appears long abandoned. The forest is open and mature, but level areas are hard to find.

Phillips Arm

This arm extends about 8 km (5 miles) north to end in a drying flat. It and Fanny Bay are used heavily for log handling and fish farming.

Phillips Arm.

A fish farm blocks the southeast entrance, and during a July 2006 visit two helicopter logging operations were active. The head of the arm is a major wetland and prime sockeye habitat, which translates into excellent grizzly viewing. The estuary is a protected area; archaeological sites include middens and a fish weir.

Ecological oddities: The Phillips River is home to red-fleshed, six-year chinook. Most other mainland chinook are white-fleshed. The Phillips chinook also turn purple during spawning.

Shoal Bay

A large public wharf dominates the centre of this bay. Houses line either side of a resort. The main lodge burned down in 2000, but instead of rebuilding it the new owners have started small, beginning with a pub (drinks only; no food) and a cottage. There are also showers and laundry. Future plans include rebuilding the lodge.

Shoal Bay was once a sizable mining town, part of a gold rush in 1898. Like most boomtowns, though, it declined and was virtually abandoned by the 1950s. Most relics of the boomtown days are gone, except for a few gold mines up the hillside and the old store at the foot of the government dock. It is closed and will be torn down.

Bickley Bay, west of Shoal Bay, has a large clearcut on its west shore. It's surrounded by private land.

The government dock at Shoal Bay, along with the old store that won't be around much longer.

Hiking: Shoal Bay presents a unique opportunity to visit an abandoned gold mine and a lookout over Phillips Arm. The trailhead is just east of the government wharf and immediately east of a creek. Look for the flag at the trailhead. The trail follows an old logging road that's well marked. In about an hour it emerges at a lookout, then continues for another 10 minutes uphill to an old gold mine entrance. Bring a flashlight. The mine is open, but watch for open vertical shafts near the entrance. It's possible to get past them to explore deeper into the mine, but I chickened out. Other old gold mines are in the area.

Erasmus Island

This island sits in Cordero Channel near the junction of Mayne Passage and Greene Point Rapids—see page 426 for the latter. The island is private; a huge log dump and log sort occupy the unnamed bay south of Erasmus, between Shell and Parrot points on East Thurlow Island. Lorte Island, to the north of Erasmus, shelters a small bay backed by Cordero Lodge; moorage is available for access to a restaurant. Float planes use this small bay.

Camping: N50°26.74' W125°28.38'. Tallac Bay has the undisputed best beach in the area, with the disadvantage that the bay is shallow and dries extensively at low tides. The beach is backed by tall intertidal grass, then a sparsely treed forest that is currently

Seymour Narrows.

overgrown with scrub. This could be a great group camping area, but it's currently undeveloped. For an alternative on this side of Greene Point Rapids, look to Cordero Islands (see page 426) or Charles Bay (page 425).

SOUTH DISCOVERY PASSAGE

Discovery Passage separates Vancouver Island from Quadra and Sonora islands. It and Johnstone Strait form the main shipping channel north of the Strait of Georgia. Discovery Passage runs 41 km (25 miles) from Cape Mudge to Chatham Point; the northern extent is covered beginning page 387. Seymour Narrows is the main hurdle to navigating this stretch, but problems with currents extend beyond the narrows to south of Cape Mudge. The visual highlight is Mount Menzies on Vancouver Island, at 1,239 m (4,065 feet), though pronounced bluffs through the narrows and on Quadra Island are quite scenic. Look for a petroglyph on a large boulder near the stream at McMullen Point, 10 km (6 miles) north of Seymour Narrows.

Call-in points: The public can monitor the progress of commercial traffic on Channel 71. This is advised for kayakers or those in small boats. Boats with small engines or paddlers may not be in complete control of their vessels, and faster barges and freighters can sneak up suddenly as they roar through the main tidal stream.

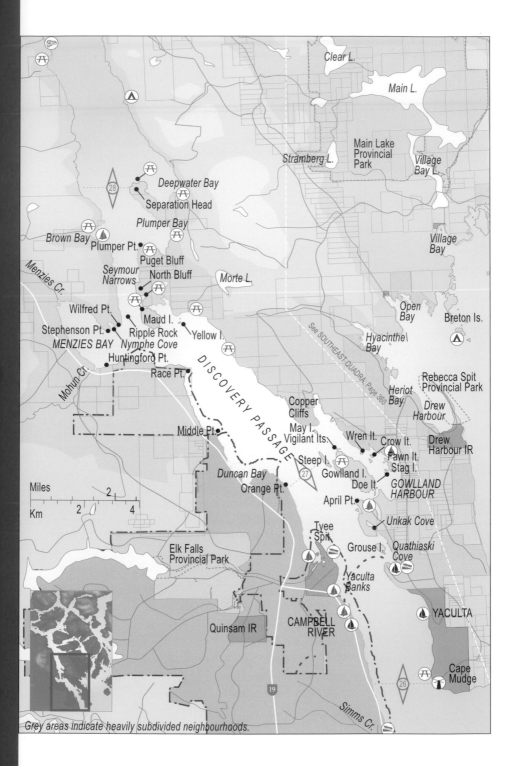

Clear L.

Main L.

Main Lake
Provincial
Park

Stramberg L.

Village
Bay L.

Deepwater Bay

Separation Head

Plumper Bay

Village
Bay

Brown Bay

Plumper Pt.

Puget Bluff

Seymour
Narrows

North Bluff

Morte L.

Open
Bay

Breton Is.

Menzies Cr.

Wilfred Pt.

Maud I.

Yellow I.

Hyacinthe
Bay

Stephenson Pt.

Ripple Rock

MENZIES BAY

Nymphe Cove

Huntingford Pt.

Race Pt.

Rebecca Spit
Provincial Park

Heriot
Bay

Drew
Harbour

Mohun Cr.

DISCOVERY PASSAGE

See SOUTHEAST QUADRA Page 360

Copper
Cliffs

May I.

Middle Pt.

Vigilant Its.

Wren It.

Crow It.

Drew
Harbour IR

Fawn It.
Stag I.

Steep I.

Gowlland I.

Doe It.

GOWLLAND
HARBOUR

Miles

2

Duncan Bay

Orange Pt.

April Pt.

Unkak Cove

Km

2

4

Elk Falls
Provincial Park

Tyee
Spit

Grouse I.

Quathiaski
Cove

Yaculta
Banks

Quinsam IR

CAMPBELL
RIVER

YACULTA

19

Cape
Mudge

26

Simms Cr.

Grey areas indicate heavily subdivided neighbourhoods.

- *26, Cape Mudge:* Vessels will call in at a line running east-west through the Cape Mudge lighthouse. Northbound vessels will report their estimated arrival time for Steep Island and the Maud Island light. Maud Island is located at the south entrance to the narrows.

- *27, Steep Island:* This is a line that runs 50°–230° degrees through Steep Island. Northbound vessels will report their estimated time for reaching Separation Head and update their estimate for reaching Maud Island, if necessary.

- *28, Separation Head:* This point runs east-west through the Separation Head navigation light. Southbound vessels will report an estimated time for reaching Steep Island, and update their Maud Island arrival time, if necessary.

- *29, Cinque Islands:* This line runs east-west through the Cinque Islands navigation light in north Discovery Passage; see page 382 to locate it on a map. Southbound vessels will report an estimated time for reaching both the Separation Head and Maud Island lights.

Place names: Captain Vancouver named the passage in 1792 after his ship. The *Discovery* was built on the Thames River in 1789 and between 1792 and 1794 examined and charted the coast from 30°N to 60°N, aided by the *Chatham*.

Cape Mudge

From the water Cape Mudge stands out, with tall, south-facing yellow-earth cliffs and a lighthouse on the southwest corner. Tidal streams and rips are strong through the area.

The main tidal stream for Discovery Passage runs mid-channel west of Cape Mudge; it can reach 9 knots but will average a maximum of 5–6 knots—still substantial. The flood is south and the ebb north. On the flood expect a series of rips from Cape Mudge extending south well into the Strait of Georgia as far as Shelter Point, southeast of Campbell River.

A strong countercurrent along southern Cape Mudge will extend to approximately the lighthouse. On the ebb a countercurrent will run between the lighthouse and Yaculta village. Currents will turn 30 minutes after high or low water on the shore.

The lighthouse at Cape Mudge.

The Cape Mudge Lighthouse is a staffed station with a home and associated buildings.

Place names: Zachary Mudge (1770–1852) was first lieutenant of the *Discovery*. Vancouver named the cape in 1792.

Weather

Cape Mudge	May	June	July	Aug.	Sept.	Dec.	Av./Ttl.
Daily average temp. (C)	12.1	14.7	17.0	17.0	14.1	3.5	9.7
Daily maximum (C)	16.4	19.0	21.8	21.7	18.5	5.9	13.4
Daily minimum (C)	7.8	10.3	12.1	12.2	9.7	1.1	6.0
Precipitation (mm)	69.3	66.1	43.1	47.3	55.2	221.0	1486.3
Days of rainfall + 0.2mm	14.6	14.0	9.1	8.6	9.1	19.9	185.8
Days with rainfall +5mm	4.9	4.6	2.7	2.9	3.5	11.9	85.4
Days with rainfall +10mm	1.9	2.1	1.2	1.5	1.7	7.4	48.8
Days with rainfall +25mm	0.1	0.05	0.14	0.18	0.3	2.0	11.5
Wind speed (km/h)	9.7	9.5	9.6	8.6	8.0	10.4	9.7
Prevailing direction	SE	NW	NW	NW	NW	SE	NW

From Gowlland Island looking toward the Copper Cliffs.

Yaculta

This is a village of the Wei Wai Kum First Nation. Homes line the waterfront behind an expansive beach with a public wharf. On the reserve is the Tsa-Kwa-Luten Lodge, a band-run facility with ocean views, traditional architecture and an RV park. Visit **www. capemudgeresort.bc.ca** or call **1-800-665-7745**.

Quathiaski Cove

This cove faces Campbell River. The main settlement in the south-east corner has a ferry dock and government wharf. There is also a fish processing plant, shipyard and fuel floats. Up from the wharf are stores and a post office (V0P 1N0). A launching ramp is immediately north of the ferry wharf.

Place names: Quathiaski means "small item in large mouth," referring to Grouse Island's location in the middle of the cove.

Gowlland Harbour

Residences and marinas surround this harbour, which is dotted with numerous islands and islets. Among those is Steep Island, named for

The waterfront in south Campbell River.

its cliffs on the south-west side. It's private and developed with cottages. The four Vigilant Islets lie off the north end of Gowlland Island, a private island with some wonderful beaches on the north and west shores. Note that currents can be very strong along the harbour, up to 5 knots, with eddies off the Vigilant Islets and Steep Island. There's a prominent resort at April Point. Copper Cliffs to the north are named for the traces of copper ore.

Place names: John Thomas Gowlland, second mate of HMS *Plumper* and *Hecate*, surveyed the coast 1857–62.

Campbell River

A full-service pulp mill and resort community, Campbell River is located on the west shore of south Discovery Passage, on Vancouver Island. This is a busy commercial and recreational area. Most of the marine activity is based out of Tyee Spit, where you'll find a government wharf, the ferry terminal to Quadra Island, Fisherman's Wharf, a customs office, a cruise ship terminal and several private marinas. Tyee Spit shelters Campbell River, which is blocked by drying bars and log booms. On the spit is Discovery Terminal, where ore is loaded into deep-sea vessels. To the north at Orange Point, named for its earthy, reddish cliffs, is an oil delivery wharf. Nearby Duncan Bay is the site of a large pulp and paper operation served by bulk freighters, barges and tugs. Considering the marine traffic, this is probably an area best avoided by small, slow-moving and difficult-to-see kayaks. Should you need to visit, the public wharf, located 0.5 km (0.2 miles) south of the ferry terminal, has washrooms, showers and laundry. Otherwise, you're well advised to travel on the Quadra Island side.

Launches: There are a good number of potential launch sites in Campbell River, including six boat ramps. Here are two options.

N50°02.67' W125°15.00', Tyee Spit. Find your way to Highway 19A through Campbell River and turn north onto Spit Road behind Canadian Tire just northwest of the Discovery Harbour Centre. A good launch site off the spit is just past Argonaut wharf, an area with big industrial buildings and a fancy metal fence in front, about three blocks from the highway. This launch would be convenient for a quick crossing to Quadra, but it potentially puts you in strong currents.

N49°57.88' W125°12.50'. South of Willow Point, 2 km (1.2 miles) south of Simms Creek, is a good beach and launch site for getting to Cape Mudge. It's adjacent to a waterfront park and seawalk, and it's far enough south to avoid most of the commercial traffic and the strong currents associated with Discovery Passage. Sightlines are good for crossings to Cape Mudge. It's in south Campbell River across from a Rona store. To get here from the Island Highway, take the Jubilee Parkway to its end and turn left. The launch is just past the waterfront gazebo, a little over 2 km (1.2 miles) from the parkway.

Weather

Campbell River	May	June	July	Aug.	Sept.	Dec.	Av./Ttl.
Daily average temp. (C)	11.2	14.2	16.9	16.9	13.4	1.7	8.6
Daily maximum (C)	16.8	19.7	23.0	23.1	19.5	4.8	13.5
Daily minimum (C)	5.6	8.7	10.8	10.7	7.3	-1.4	3.8
Precipitation (mm)	61.3	56.7	40.8	43.6	53.9	221.5	1452.9
Days of rainfall + 0.2mm	13.8	13.4	8.4	7.9	9.4	17.5	176
Days with rainfall +5mm	4.1	4.0	2.8	3.0	3.7	10.5	79.1
Days with rainfall +10mm	1.7	1.7	1.3	1.4	1.6	7.3	46.6
Days with rainfall +25mm	0.05	0.0	0.12	0.28	0.17	2.4	12.8

Race Point

The current from Seymour Narrows runs past this rocky bluff at up to 10 knots, with the flood setting at 105°, then gradually turning south along the east side of Discovery Passage toward Copper Cliffs. Rips and whirlpools can be expected near the point and as far as 1.3 km (0.8 miles) east. This sets the stage for a countercurrent south of Race Point to Middle Point.

The ebb current will pass Race Point at 3–6 knots at 322°, then quickly shift west and strengthen until Maud Island. Maud is connected to Quadra via a dam. On strong ebbs, watch for overfalls near the southeast of Maud Island. East of Maud Island diving buoys mark where the wreck of the HMCS *Columbia* was sunk as an artificial reef.

Menzies Bay

This is an industrial area with a large booming ground, dryland log sort facility and a barge-loading ramp at Huntingford Point. A strong countercurrent develops in the bay. That and the industrial traffic are good reasons for kayakers and small boats to transit the Quadra Island shore instead.

Seymour Narrows

The narrowest portion of Discovery Passage is about 3 km (2 miles) long and bordered by rugged bluffs. Ripple Rock, in the centre of the channel, is the source of a great deal of turbulence, and the narrows has a history of fatalities. Boats should avoid the west shore during flood currents. Currents can run as high as 16 knots, with the flood setting south and the ebb north.

On the flood (southerly) stream, eddies and rips will start opposite North Bluff. There are conspicuous power cables; watch for strong upwellings in their vicinity and along the west shore. Keep in mind the maximum turbulence on a flood is actually beyond Race Point, past the narrows.

On the ebb, the water is generally smoother until North Bluff. Here rips form, along with whirlpools and eddies. The turbulence will continue to Puget Bluff, then drop off at Separation Head. One hour after maximum ebb current the turbulence will diminish greatly, making for a much safer ride.

Place names: Sir George Seymour was commander of the Pacific station of the Royal Navy 1844–48.

Navigating Seymour Narrows by kayak: This isn't generally advised,

The bluffs in Seymour Narrows.

but it's possible, though not without difficulty. I recommend staying to the Quadra Island side on both directions to avoid the Campbell River commercial and industrial traffic, the turbulence of the flood current and the countercurrent around Menzies Bay. There are also more safe pockets to dip into on the east side.

On a run from north to south, approach at the end of an ebb current. Advantage can be taken of the countercurrents along Discovery Passage to reach Deepwater Bay, just north of Separation Head. Watch for turbulence in the bay. As the current diminishes you should be able to get around Separation Point into Plumper Bay and watch for conditions in Seymour Narrows, entering when you believe it to be safe and navigable with the current still against you. There are a good number of pullouts along the way, if need be, but you should be able to make it as far as Maud Island against the last of the ebb. You won't get much farther until slack tide, however, as the current runs strong right against the south end of Maud Island. Once the current is in your favour you will get a good push down the passage to Gowlland Harbour. Dilly-dally at your peril, as the journey isn't over. It's 22.5 km (14 miles) from Seymour Narrows to the Cape Mudge lighthouse. Even at a good, current-aided speed, this will bring you to Cape Mudge at a time approaching peak current.

If you're continuing south and are unafraid of rips you can ride the main current well beyond Quadra Island. Beware of commercial traffic, however, also running the current. Because of the speeds involved you are unlikely to be fully in control, and because of the noise of the rushing water and the fact you are concentrating on kayaking, large and much faster ships can sneak up on you. This can include freighters and cruise ships, so it pays to look back every so often or to monitor VHF Channel 71 for traffic locations.

It's worth noting the main stream is narrow and it's easy to be turned aside; chances are you'll be thrown out once or twice on a run whether you want to leave the current or not. This can place you into countercurrents that you'll likely want to avoid.

If you're planning on turning off and around Cape Mudge, or are crossing to Cape Mudge from a launch, be prepared for strong countercurrents that could stop you dead near the lighthouse. If this is the case, it may be worth a break at the beach near the lighthouse to await a drop in the current before continuing.

On an ebb run—south to north—try to run the countercurrents alongside Yaculta and duck into Quathiaski Cove, then Gowlland Harbour at Copper Cliffs on the last of the flood. Even if you reach that far it's still 11.5 km (7 miles) to Plumper Point, so expect a good current by the time you reach Seymour Narrows, along with some turbulence. If you find conditions unfavourable on a run, there are two safety pullouts just north of Maud Island. These are always an option as the main turbulence doesn't appear until North Bluff, so you should be able to see it as you approach and have time to avoid it. Just be sure to stay near the shore so you aren't swept past the pullouts.

As always, your risk is lessened by travelling on days with a reduced current. For instance, on August 10, 2006, the peak afternoon current was 14.2 knots. On August 29 it was 5.5 knots.

Naturally, any run of the narrows is for advanced kayakers only who are comfortable with—or better yet, enjoy—rips and turbulence.

Separation Head

This cliffy neck of land separates Plumper and Deepwater bays. Plumper Bay is located just north of Seymour Narrows and is often used by boats awaiting favourable tides in the narrows. It's fringed with beach and would make a pleasant kayak haulout and a camp, if necessary, before or after a crossing. Across the narrows is Brown Bay, conspicuous for its RV park, marina, launching ramp and breakwater of old tank cars. Deepwater Bay, to the north of Separation Head, also has beaches suitable for a haulout. Both Deepwater and Plumper bays are prone to turbulence and countercurrents. Rips can be encountered north of Separation Point on an ebb.

Camping: N50°12.75' W125°21.39'. A stone beach with a gravel strip is 3.25 km (2 miles) north of Separation Point. Above the beach is a grassy clearing in front of forest cover. This is a good group site in a strategic location for beginning or ending a run of Seymour Narrows.

Wonderfully rugged islands face Queen Charlotte Strait in the Broughton Archipelago.

PART THREE

The North Island Straits

THIS PORTION OF THE BOOK COVERS THE NORTHERN COAST AND ADJACENT waterways of Vancouver Island along Johnstone Strait and Queen Charlotte Strait to Port McNeill. The western extent, from Port Hardy around Vancouver Island to Cape Scott, is covered in *The Wild Coast, Volume 1*. Queen Charlotte Strait from Port Hardy on Vancouver Island and Shelter Bay on the mainland to Cape Caution—the approach to the central coast—is covered in *The Wild Coast, Volume 2*. The main transit route through the region is via Johnstone Strait, but the North Island coast is convoluted, with features ranging from the hundreds of low-lying islands and islets in Broughton Archipelago Marine Park to the huge icefield-fed fiords of Kingcome, Loughborough and Knight inlets.

GETTING HERE

By road

The mountainous and fractured coast has made road building almost impossible through the mainland north of Lund, so all road access to this region must originate from Vancouver Island. Even then, access to the coast is limited, as the Island Highway turns inland between Campbell River and Port McNeill. This limits paved road access in this region to Sayward, Telegraph Cove and Port McNeill. A few other access points are possible by logging road: Little Bear Bay, Adam River and Naka Creek. More specific directions on reaching these locations are described under those headings.

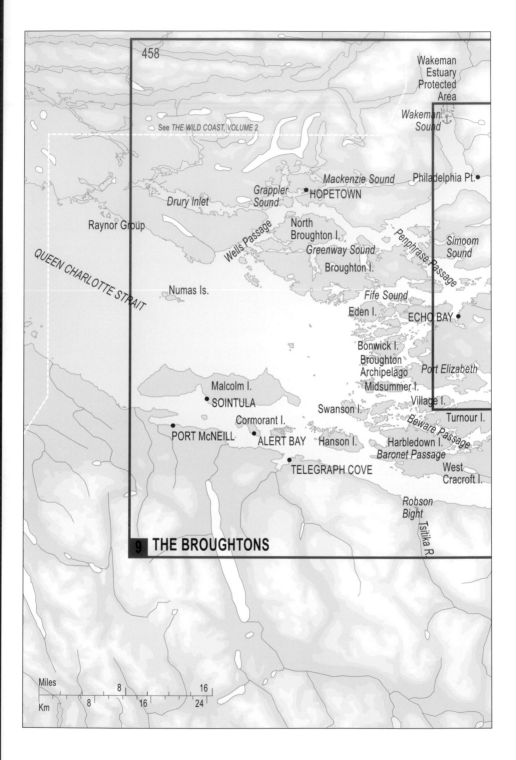

458

Wakeman
Estuary
Protected
Area

*Wakeman
Sound*

See THE WILD COAST, VOLUME 2

Mackenzie Sound

Philadelphia Pt.•

*Grappler
Sound*

•HOPETOWN

Drury Inlet

Raynor Group

North
Broughton I.

*Simoom
Sound*

Wells Passage

Greenway Sound

Penphrase Passage

Broughton I.

QUEEN CHARLOTTE STRAIT

Numas Is.

Fife Sound

Eden I.

ECHO BAY •

Bonwick I.

Broughton
Archipelago

Port Elizabeth

Malcolm I.

Midsummer I.

•SOINTULA

Swanson I.

Village I.

Turnour I.

Cormorant I.

Beware Passage

PORT McNEILL

ALERT BAY

Hanson I.

Harbledown I.

Baronet Passage

West
Cracroft I.

•TELEGRAPH COVE

*Robson
Bight*

Tsitika R.

9 THE BROUGHTONS

Miles

8

16

Km

8

16

24

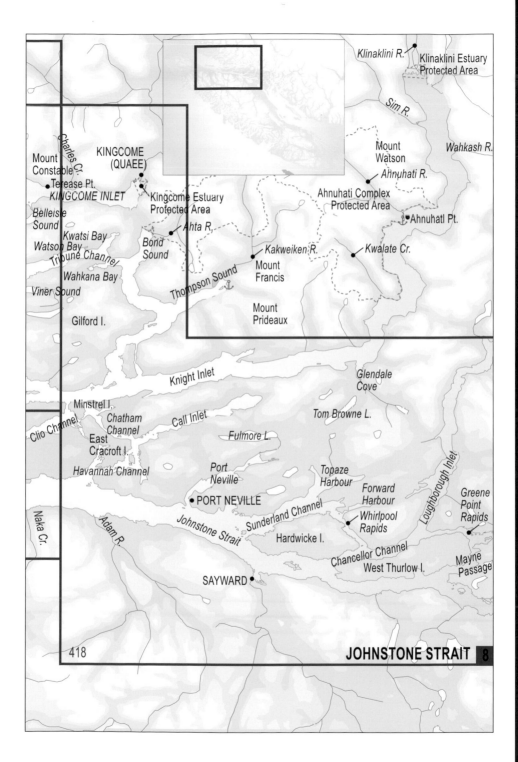

Klinaklini R.

Klinaklini Estuary
Protected Area

Sim R.

Wahkash R.

Mount
Watson

Ahnuhati R.

Ahnuhati Complex
Protected Area

Ahnuhatl Pt.

Charles Cr.

KINGCOME
(QUAEE)

Mount
Constable

Terease Pt.

KINGCOME INLET

Kingcome Estuary
Protected Area

Belleisle
Sound

Ahta R.

Kwatsi Bay

Kakweiken R.

Kwalate Cr.

Watson Bay

Bond
Sound

Mount
Francis

Tribune Channel

Wahkana Bay

Thompson Sound

Viner Sound

Mount
Prideaux

Gilford I.

Knight Inlet

Glendale
Cove

Minstrel I.

Chatham
Channel

Call Inlet

Tom Browne L.

Clio Channel

Fulmore L.

East
Cracroft I.

Port
Neville

Topaze
Harbour

Forward
Harbour

Havannah Channel

Loughborough Inlet

Greene
Point
Rapids

Naka Cr.

PORT NEVILLE

Whirlpool
Rapids

Adam R.

Johnstone Strait

Sunderland Channel

Hardwicke I.

Chancellor Channel

West Thurlow I.

Mayne
Passage

SAYWARD

418

JOHNSTONE STRAIT 8

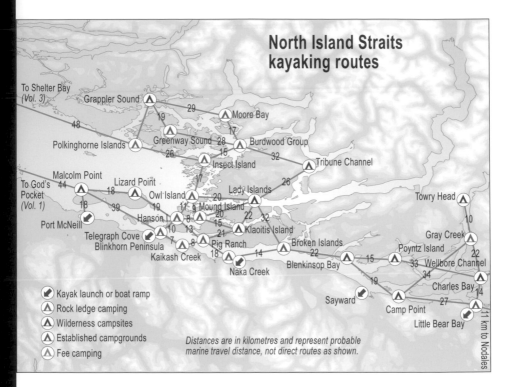

North Island Straits kayaking routes

To Shelter Bay (Vol. 3)
Grappler Sound
Moore Bay
29
19
17
48
Polkinghorne Islands
Greenway Sound 28
Burdwood Group
26
15
32
Insect Island
Tribune Channel
Malcolm Point
Lizard Point
To God's 44
18
17
26
Pocket
Owl Island
Lady Islands
Towry Head
(Vol. 1)
18
19
11
Mound Island
10
39
20
Port McNeill
Hanson I.
8
15
22
32
10
13
21
Klaoitis Island
Gray Creek
Telegraph Cove
7
8
Pig Ranch
Broken Islands
Poyntz Island
22
Blinkhorn Peninsula
18
14
22
33 Wellbore Channel
Kaikash Creek
Blenkinsop Bay
15
34
Naka Creek
19
Charles Bay 14
Sayward
27
Camp Point
14
Little Bear Bay

Kayak launch or boat ramp
Rock ledge camping
Wilderness campsites
Established campgrounds
Fee camping

Distances are in kilometres and represent probable marine travel distance, not direct routes as shown.

11 km to Nodales

By ferry

The only ferry service in this region is to Sointula and Alert Bay. Ferries depart from Port McNeill. Water taxis are a popular alternative and can be chartered from Telegraph Cove, Port McNeill and Campbell River.

By kayak

The summer migration of killer whales has given this region its status as a kayaking destination. Kayakers congregate in high numbers around Johnstone Strait near Telegraph Cove, Hanson Island, the Indian Group and the southern islands in the Broughton Archipelago. Naturally, close proximity to the launch sites makes these locations ideal—if you don't mind crowds. Essentially ignored are those areas farther afield: Tribune Channel, Grappler Sound, Malcolm Island and Kingcome Inlet. Kayakers need stray only a few miles from the established areas to avoid a crowd; a little farther beyond that will take you to places rarely explored.

Arrow Passage, Broughton Archipelago.

GEOLOGY AND ECOLOGY

Vancouver Island tends to go through a transformation as you head northwest. The mountains in this region reach their highest elevation along the coast with Mount Palmerston at 1,765 m (5,790 feet). The mountains push up the moisture-laden Pacific air, causing rain and making the Vancouver Island coast a wet environment suitable for a western hemlock forest. Northwest of Telegraph Cove the mountains become lower and transform into the gently rolling hills of the Nahwitti Lowlands.

The mountain ranges on the mainland tend to be rugged and are often topped with glaciers. Along Knight Inlet, for instance, a parade of mountains is crowned by Mount Stanton at 2,870 m (9,415 feet). The forests here are mainly Sitka spruce, mountain hemlock and amabalis fir, with western hemlock at lower elevations. Their inacessibility helps keep them free from development. Some areas, such as Bond Sound,

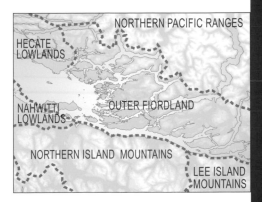

Many of the Broughton Archipelago islands are formed of tonalite, an igneous plutonic rock dating to the late Jurassic or early Cretaceous period.

have never been logged. These remote watersheds provide prime salmon and grizzly habitat.

Between the two mountain groups are the sounds, islands, peninsulas and inlets that form a rugged, low-lying fiordland ecology. Strong currents wash in nutrients that create a productive marine environment.

Johnstone Strait and Blackfish Sound are renowned for the summer migration of killer whales—Robson Bight is one of the most important killer whale sites in the world. Both transient and resident populations pass through Queen Charlotte Strait and Blackfish Sound to Johnstone Strait each summer, making the area around Hanson Island an excellent location for whale watching.

FIRST NATIONS OVERVIEW

This is the land of the Kwakwaka'wakw, often referred to as the Kwakiutl, who resided in about 30 tribes that occupied traditional territories throughout northern Vancouver Island, Queen Charlotte Strait and as far south as the north end of the Strait of Georgia. They are united by their use of the Kwak'wala language, which in turn is part of the Wakashan language family shared by the Haisla and Heiltsuk of central B.C.

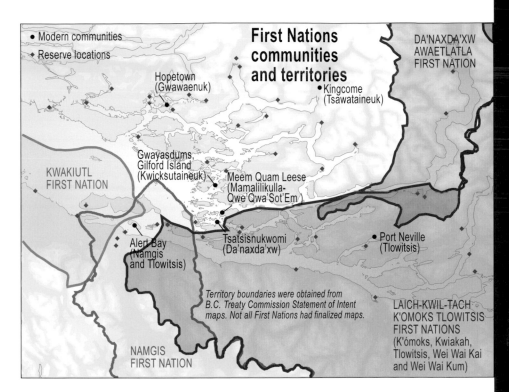

Map legend:
- Modern communities
- Reserve locations

First Nations communities and territories

DA'NAXDA'XW AWAETLATLA FIRST NATION

Hopetown (Gwawaenuk)

Kingcome (Tsawataineuk)

KWAKIUTL FIRST NATION

Gwayasdums, Gilford Island (Kwicksutaineuk)

Meem Quam Leese (Mamalilikulla-Qwe'Qwa'Sot'Em)

Alert Bay (Namgis and Tlowitsis)

Tsatsisnukwomi (Da'naxda'xw)

Port Neville (Tlowitsis)

Territory boundaries were obtained from B.C. Treaty Commission Statement of Intent maps. Not all First Nations had finalized maps.

LAICH-KWIL-TACH K'OMOKS TLOWITSIS FIRST NATIONS (K'ómoks, Kwiakah, Tlowitsis, Wei Wai Kai and Wei Wai Kum)

NAMGIS FIRST NATION

The Kwakwaka'wakw are renowned for their crafts, artwork and potlatches. The culture is seeing a resurgence and being revitalized today, with bands like the Da'naxda'xw Awaetlala (page 480) and Mamalilikulla-Qwe'Qwa'Sot'Em (page 479) leading the way in cultural tourism.

Tlowitsis: The Tlowitsis First Nation was known as the Turnour Indian Band until 1983. The band numbers 349, with the residents split largely between Alert Bay and Campbell River. Only a few (about 28) live on traditional land, with the main reserve community at Port Neville. The band holds 12 reserves totalling 201 ha (497 acres). A large community abandoned in recent history is Karlukwees on the southwest side of Turnour Island facing Beware Passage (see page 470). The Tlowitsis traditional territory includes Turnour Island and areas near Johnstone Strait.

Namgis: The Namgis traditionally centred their lives around the Gwa'ni River, which was incorrectly interpreted by Capt. George Vancouver as the Nimpkish River when he visited in 1792. The name is derived from a mythical monster resembling a halibut that's large enough to submerge canoes and cause tide rips off the Nimpkish River. In Vancouver's time the population was estimated to be between 8,000 and 10,000. Today it is 1,557.

After the late 19th century the population shifted from Nimpkish River to Alert Bay on Cormorant Island. There the band maintains a community health centre, a drug and alcohol recovery home and the U'Mista Cultural Centre (see page 495). Other services include a longhouse, administration office, a fishing net loft building and a funeral home.

Da'naxda'xw Awaetlala (Tanakteuk): The Da'naxda'xw Awaetlala First Nation is an amalgamation of the two tribes of Knight Inlet. The main village of the Da'naxda'xw, Tsatsisnukwomi, is located on Harbledown Island at Dead Point and is currently being repopulated after being vacant for many years. The traditional territories include the lands surrounding Knight Inlet and its watersheds, including the Klinaklini River. The southern boundary is Protection Point and Hoeye Head. Today the band numbers about 153.

The Da'naxda'xw is taking a leadership role in cultural heritage tourism with cultural tours and a campground, with performances of traditional songs and dances, plus a salmon barbecue at Tsatsisnukwomi. See page 480.

Mamalilikulla-Qwe'Qwa'Sot'Em: Once the Village Island Indian Band, the Mamalilikulla First Nation is repatriating its main village, which was abandoned in the 1970s in favour of better access to government services at Whe-la-la-U in Alert Bay. The band hosted the famous potlatch of 1921 that resulted in a court case and seizure of artifacts (see page 479). Many of the artifacts have been recovered and are on display at the U'Mista Cultural Centre in Alert Bay.

Mamalilikulla is believed to mean "seen to be swimming."

Kwicksutaineuk-Ah Kwaw-ah-mish: Once the Gilford Island Indian Band, about 50 of the 238 band members still reside on Gilford Island at Gwayasdums, a community of about 22 homes with a band office, long house and community hall. Other traditional sites were the Ah Kwaw-ah-mish summer home of A-tl-al-to at the head of Wakeman Sound.

Gwawaenuk (Kwa-wa-aineuk): This band is centred out of a small community on Watson Island called Hopetown. Currently about 19 people live on the reserve; another 21 live off the reserve. Few services are available within the community—just the band office and a workshop. In all, the Gwawaenuk have 10 reserves through Grappler Sound, Mackenzie Sound and Drury Inlet.

Tsawataineuk: Also known as the Kingcome Inlet Indian Band, the main community is on the Quaee reserve about 7 km (4.5 miles) upriver from Kingcome Inlet. Facilities there include a band office, community hall, school, a longhouse and a church. The band numbers about 448, with about 150 living at Quaee. A major development for the community is the possibility of constructing a road from the village to Kingcome Inlet to provide all-season access.

Kwakiutl: Formerly the Fort Rupert Band, this group is centred out of Port Hardy (see *Volume 1*). Their traditional territory extends as far east as Malcolm Island.

The campsite at the entrance to Simoom Sound at Deep Sea Bluff.

Johnstone Strait

CHAPTER EIGHT

LOTS OF WILDLIFE AND LOTS OF PEOPLE—I HEARD THAT DESCRIPTION OF Johnstone Strait once and it has stuck with me, because it rings so true. This chapter covers Johnstone Strait east of West Cracroft Island—the area of the strait that *isn't* a kayaking destination. It's not for a lack of wildlife. On a visit here from Sunderland Channel, I was in Johnstone Strait for perhaps 10 minutes when a pod of killer whales passed by McLeod Bay. Before I could reach Ransom Point, just a few miles away, more orcas passed.

One reason to avoid this area is the wind. South Johnstone Strait is probably second only to Juan de Fuca Strait for wind speeds on the south B.C. coast, and it's not unusual to have gales continue unabated for days. I have travelled many nearby routes in calm conditions while listening to Chatham Point report wind velocities of 20–30 knots—or more. Coupled with strong ebb currents, which the strait favours, the resulting sharp wind waves can make travelling miserable. The best way to avoid the worst winds is to travel the north route through the more sheltered Cordero, Chancellor and Sunderland channels.

Another reason to avoid the area is the tidal currents, which from Sayward east to the junction with Discovery Passage are as strong as many south coast narrows. Travellers should be strongly cautioned that these two features can be trip killers for casual or unprepared visitors, and it's not uncommon to see boaters or paddlers hunkered down in Sayward for several unplanned days.

The countryside here is typically gently rolling and heavily forested, with some areas denuded by logging. Fish farms are also common along channels or hidden away in coves. You may be the

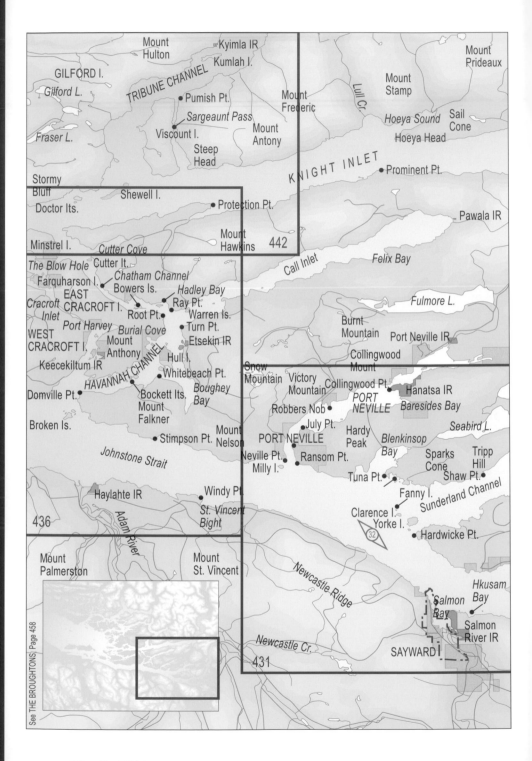

Mount Hulton
Kyimla IR
Kumlah I.
Mount Prideaux

GILFORD I.
Gilford L.
TRIBUNE CHANNEL
Pumish Pt.
Mount Frederic
Mount Stamp
Hoeya Sound
Sail Cone

Fraser L.
Sargeaunt Pass
Mount Antony
Hoeya Head

Viscount I.
Steep Head
KNIGHT INLET
Prominent Pt.

Stormy Bluff
Shewell I.
Protection Pt.
Pawala IR

Doctor Its.
Minstrel I.
Cutter Cove
Mount Hawkins
442
Felix Bay
Call Inlet

The Blow Hole
Cutter It.
Chatham Channel
Fulmore L.

Farquharson I.
Bowers Is.
Hadley Bay
EAST CRACROFT I.
Ray Pt.
Burnt Mountain
Port Neville IR

Cracroft Inlet
Root Pt.
Warren Is.
Collingwood Mount

WEST CRACROFT I.
Port Harvey
Burial Cove
Turn Pt.
Etsekin IR
Snow Mountain
Victory Mountain
Collingwood Pt.
Hanatsa IR

Mount Anthony
Hull I.
Whitebeach Pt.
PORT NEVILLE
Baresides Bay

Keecekiltum IR
HAVANNAH CHANNEL
Robbers Nob
Seabird L.

Domville Pt.
Bockett Its.
Mount Falkner
Boughey Bay
July Pt.
Hardy Peak
Blenkinsop Bay
Sparks Cone
Tripp Hill

Broken Is.
Mount Nelson
PORT NEVILLE
Shaw Pt.

Stimpson Pt.
Neville Pt.
Ransom Pt.
Tuna Pt.
Fanny I.
Sunderland Channel

Johnstone Strait
Milly I.
Clarence I.
Yorke I.
32
Hardwicke Pt.

Haylahte IR
Windy Pt.
St. Vincent Bight

436
Adam River
Mount St. Vincent
Hkusam Bay
Salmon Bay

Mount Palmerston
Newcastle Ridge
Salmon River IR

See THE BROUGHTONS, Page 458
Newcastle Cr.
431
SAYWARD

418   The Wild Coast

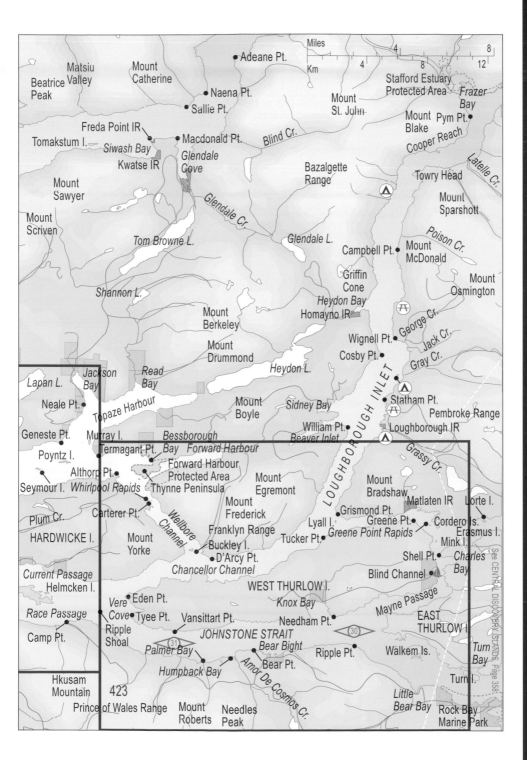

Miles
4   8
Km
4   8   12

Matsiu Valley
Beatrice Peak
Mount Catherine
Adeane Pt.
Naena Pt.
Sallie Pt.
Mount St. John
Stafford Estuary Protected Area
Frazer Bay
Mount Blake
Pym Pt.
Freda Point IR
Tomakstum I.
Siwash Bay
Macdonald Pt.
Blind Cr.
Cooper Reach
Latelle Cr.
Kwatse IR
Glendale Cove
Mount Sawyer
Glendale Cr.
Bazalgette Range
Towry Head
Mount Sparshott
Mount Scriven
Tom Browne L.
Glendale L.
Campbell Pt.
Mount McDonald
Poison Cr.
Mount Osmington
Shannon L.
Griffin Cone
Heydon Bay
Homayno IR
Mount Berkeley
Wignell Pt.
George Cr.
Jack Cr.
Mount Drummond
Cosby Pt.
Gray Cr.
Heydon L.
Jackson Bay
Read Bay
Mount Boyle
Sidney Bay
Statham Pt.
Lapan L.
Neale Pt.
Topaze Harbour
William Pt.
Beaver Inlet
Pembroke Range
Loughborough IR
Geneste Pt.
Murray I.
Bessborough Bay
Forward Harbour
Grassy Cr.
Poyntz I.
Termagant Pt.
Forward Harbour Protected Area
Mount Egremont
Mount Bradshaw
Matlaten IR
Lorte I.
Althorp Pt.
Thynne Peninsula
Grismond Pt.
Greene Pt.
Cordero Is.
Seymour I.
Whirlpool Rapids
Mount Frederick
Lyall I.
Greene Point Rapids
Erasmus I.
Plum Cr.
Carterer Pt.
Wellbore Channel
Franklin Range
Tucker Pt.
Mink I.
HARDWICKE I.
Mount Yorke
Buckley I.
Shell Pt.
Charles Bay
D'Arcy Pt.
Blind Channel
Current Passage
Helmcken I.
Chancellor Channel
WEST THURLOW I.
Knox Bay
Mayne Passage
EAST THURLOW I.
Race Passage
Vere Cove
Eden Pt.
Tyee Pt.
Vansittart Pt.
Needham Pt.
Turn Bay
Camp Pt.
Ripple Shoal
JOHNSTONE STRAIT
Bear Bight
Ripple Pt.
Walkem Is.
Turn I.
Palmer Bay
Bear Pt.
Hkusam Mountain
423
Humpback Bay
Amor De Cosmos Cr.
Little Bear Bay
Rock Bay Marine Park
Prince of Wales Range
Mount Roberts
Needles Peak

See CENTRAL DISCOVERY ISLANDS, Page 358

only kayaker, but you won't be alone, as commercial and industrial activity is never far away.

Place names: James Johnstone was master of the armed tender *Chatham*. The cutter was exploring this region in July 1792 with Vancouver when they discovered this passage linking the Gulf of Georgia (as it was then known) with Queen Charlotte Strait. Johnstone became a captain in the Royal Navy in 1806 and later a commissioner in Bombay. Spanish explorers Galiano and Valdes sailed this strait about the same time as Vancouver and named it Canal de Descubierta (Discovery Strait).

Exploring by kayak

Many people will use this area as a transit corridor, linking an exploration of the Discovery Islands with the Broughtons, perhaps, or running the Vancouver Island coast. If you're travelling northwest, the outer channels are preferable for avoiding the worst of the prevailing northwesterlies in Johnstone Strait. Both routes have their attractions, so a circle tour of the area would not be time wasted.

Recommended kayaking trips

- *If you have a day:* From Sayward, head to Yorke Island to explore the old fort, and maybe travel as far as Blenkinsop Bay for lunch. Or, with the right currents, explore Helmcken Island. From Little Bear Bay explore Walkem Islands and the shoreline around Rock Bay Marine Park. Just be sure to time your visit for sympathetic or low currents, or your trip could go astray.

- *If you have two days:* From Sayward a good overnight trip would be to Poyntz Island, circumnavigating Hardwicke Island via both Sunderland and Wellbore channels.

- *If you have three days:* A modest trip would be a circumnavigation of West Thurlow Island. From Little Bear Bay take Mayne Passage to Charles Bay, then Chancellor Channel, returning via Johnstone Strait on the third day.

- *If you have five days:* A visit to Loughborough Inlet is possible with this much time. On the first day travel the 40 km (25 miles) from Sayward to Charles Bay (made simple with favourable tide and wind), then run Greene Point Rapids in the morning to get you well up Loughborough Inlet on the second day. Camp at the islet at Gray Creek, then on day three use that as a base camp to explore up the inlet. On day four return directly via Chancellor Channel or head up Wellbore Channel to Poyntz Island via Whirlpool Rapids. On the final day visit the military ruins on Yorke Island and return to Sayward.

- *If you have a week*: You could use the agenda above and spend an extra two days exploring. I recommend an extra day in Loughborough Inlet watching grizzlies and/or extending your westerly meanderings into Johnstone Strait to see some killer whales. This trip combines a good range of widlife viewing—grizzlies and killer whales—along with some first-class mountain scenery, rapid traverses and idyllic campsites. And to think it's not even a kayaking destination!

- *The ideal trip:* The trip above is pretty darn good, but here's an alternative, focusing on the west side and features covered in Chapter 9 by circumnavigating Gilford Island. From Naka Creek head around East Cracroft Island then take Tribune Channel around Gilford Island, coming out at the Burdwood Group for a return via Broughton Archipelago. This trip combines rarely explored areas with the standard Johnstone Strait attractions.

Call-in points: There are three Vessel Traffic Service call-in points along south and central Johnstone Strait. This is a good way for kayakers to ensure they aren't broadsided by a tug or cruise ship during a crossing or transit of the area.

- *30, Ripple Point:* This is a line running north-south through the Ripple Point light. Ripple Point is on Vancouver Island opposite the entrance to Mayne Passage.

- *31, Vansittart Point:* This is a line running north-south through the Vansittart Point light. Vansittart Point is located on the southwest of West Thurlow Island.

- *32, Fanny Island:* This is a line running 45°–225° through the Fanny Island light. Fanny Island is located northwest of Yorke Island.

Rock ledge camping at Cordero Islands.

WEST THURLOW ISLAND

Two distinct routes lead around West Thurlow Island. Johnstone Strait is the most common and is used by shipping traffic. It has strong tidal currents, up to 6 knots near Ripple Point, including rips and turbulence. Chancellor and Cordero channels, meanwhile, form a less common route to the north, popular with recreational boaters escaping Johnstone Strait. Strong currents are confined mainly to Greene Point Rapids and Whirlpool Rapids along this portion.

The view from the forest recreation site at Little Bear Bay.

Little Bear Bay

A vehicle-accessible forest recreation campground shares the bay with log booms and a salmon hatchery. This is a good wildlife viewing area, with a killer whale rubbing beach adjacent to the bay—one of just a few of these on the B.C. coast. A short trail leads from the forest recreation site to a waterfall and some old-growth firs.

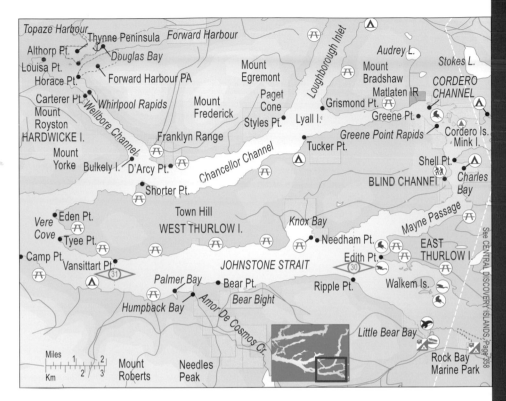

Launches: The rough boat launch at the forest recreation site is accessible by logging road from Highway 19 north of Campbell River. The turnoff, the Rock Bay forest service road, is marked from the highway but it's still easy to miss. It's the next west after the Pye logging road. If you can navigate by GPS, the turn is at approximately N50°15.23' W125°25.38'.

Camping: N50°20.25' W125°31.08'. A forest recreation site along the shoreline at the east end of Little Bear Bay has 15 sites, many open to the shoreline, with picnic tables and fire pits.

Walkem Islands

This pretty group of islets makes for exceptional kayaking. The surrounding shoreline of East Thurlow Island is mainly good sand beach, and any beach is a potential wilderness campsite. Currents can be strong through all the islands; watch for rips on the far sides of island groups. Seals and sea lions haul out here and eagles nest throughout the area.

Seals make the most of submerged rocks, Walkem Islands.

Knox Bay

This bay has a long history as a pioneer logging camp that was once served by steamboat. One of the province's earliest forest plantations, dating to 1932, is here. Today the bay is used as a log dump and booming ground. Logging operations are also obvious at Bear Bight, across Johnstone Strait.

Ripple Point

Turbulence can be expected here—hence the name. The flood sets east at 2–3 knots; the strongest currents, 2–5 knots, can be expected on the ebb. Rips can be encountered off both Needham and Ripple points. The current station for this area, listed in *Canadian Tide and Current Tables, Volume 6*, is Bear Point near the mouth of Amor De Cosmos Creek, 7 km (4.3 miles) west of Ripple Point. Ripple Point is a Vessel Traffic Services call-in point; another is 11.5 km (7.1 miles) to the west at Vansittart Point.

Camping: N50°21.78' W125°46.22'. Southwest of Vansittart Point across Johnstone Strait on Vancouver Island is a prominent headland surrounded by a stone and gravel beach. There's a young alder forest with a large, flat, clear area with lots of foxglove among the alders.

This would make a good group site. The best access is just west of the point.

Mayne Passage

Currents can run as high as 5 knots, particularly around Shell Point, where the flood current from Greene Point Rapids will race into Charles Bay before dispersing. Expect westerlies to diminish once out of Johnstone Strait.

Most activity in the passage focuses on Blind Channel, a small community on the east side of West Thurlow Island. Blind Channel began as a sawmill at the turn of the last century and by 1918 had grown into a fair-sized community with a cannery, shingle mill

Typical scenery—and weather—on South Johnstone Strait, near Knox Bay.

and two dance halls. Today the bay has several homes and a marina, Blind Channel Resort, which has a lodge, restaurant, store, laundry, showers, Interac access, a post office (V0P 1B0), moorage and fuel.

Place names: Richard Charles Mayne was lieutenant on the surveying vessels *Plumper* and *Hecate* 1857–61. He retired as rear admiral in 1879.

Hiking: Forest trails start near the wharf, one heading to a viewpoint and a huge old-growth western redcedar believed to be about 800 years old.

Camping: N50°25.15' W125°29.39', Eclipse Islet. In Charles Bay is tiny Eclipse Islet, surrounded by a pleasant gravel beach. Areas of grass and scrub are suitable for campsite development. This would make an exceptional kayaking stop with potential as a key stopover for the area.

Greene Point Rapids

This is the fourth set of rapids along Cordero Channel, with a maximum current of 7 knots. The flood sets southeast and the ebb northwest. On the flood the rapids will affect Mayne Passage along Mink Island and Shell Point.

Bear watching, Loughborough Inlet.

The rapids are created in part by the Cordero Islands to the east. These islands make for an interesting area to explore, with the option of some bluff camping. The passage between the mainland and the westernmost of the Cordero Islands is blocked on a low tide, helping create a sheltered anchorage. Much of the upland surrounding the rapids is privately owned, with some development on the north shore adjacent to the Matlaten reserve.

Kayaking Greene Point Rapids: These rapids have the advantage of being fairly localized. If you wait for slack you should have no difficulty. At high tide a run from the Cordero Islands will give you a favourable tide for the next six hours or so west down Chancellor Channel. If you plan it properly you can use the tail end of the same ebb tide to run Whirlpool Rapids in Wellbore Channel, 22 km (14 miles) to the west. This could plonk you at Poyntz Island at the end of the favourable tide, or vice versa. The shoreline tends to be shallow with good countercurrents along the south shore, so it's possible to beat a moderate opposing current at Greene Point if you arrive before slack.

Place names: Molesworth Greene Jackson was lieutenant aboard the HMS *Topaze*.

Loughborough Inlet

This inlet is a poor cousin to the more famous and more frequently visited inlets of the south B.C. coast. There is a reason. The entrance to the inlet is unspectacular: low, rolling, heavily forested mountains. The best mountains—the snow-capped, craggy peaks—don't really appear until Towry Head. The lack of popularity has its advantages. Traffic is almost non-existent, except for the occasional curious pleasure boat or workboat serving logging camps. For kayakers, a rare feature is a good selection of beaches—wonderful stretches with sand, something not often found in B.C.'s inlets. And lastly, it has grizzly bears. Lots of them. Grizzly estuaries are at Grassy Creek, Gray Creek, Jack Creek, George Creek, Stafford River, Apple River, Heydon Bay and Beaver Inlet Creek. This makes it one of the better potential grizzly viewing areas.

At Gray Creek look for the petroglyph along the beach near an old sawmill site. It will be covered at high tide.

Tidal currents are low in Loughborough, rarely exceeding 2 knots. Freshwater runoff can create a constant ebb tide. Be prepared for cold water. Logging is extensive. There are bound to be several active logging camps, with the most recent focused on the east shores on mounts Sparshoff and Osmington.

Wind can be a problem. The lower portion of the inlet is prone to channelling westerlies turning northward from Chancellor Channel. If travelling south against the wind down the inlet, hug the west shoreline to avoid the worst.

Most beaches are on the east side of the inlet, and there are many to choose from. If you don't see grizzlies, you'll probably see black bears foraging among the rocks.

Both Beaver Inlet and Sidney Bay have private land holdings and some houses. Towry Head is a prominent bluff occasionally used as an anchorage. South of Poison Creek is a second creek often used as a water supply point. And no, it's not poisoned.

The waters here are ecologically rich, with groundfish including yellow eye, black cod and skatela; there are also various shrimp, crab, hake, perch, dogfish, wolf eel, octopus, red and green urchin and sea cucumber. The assortment is rich enough to support commercial fisheries for crab, prawn, octopus and dogfish.

The Stafford River estuary, part of a new protected area, has never been logged, providing a good opportunity to see an estuary in its natural state. Rare plants in the estuary include smooth willowherb and Payson's sedge.

Place names: In 1792 Capt. George Vancouver named the inlet after Alexander Wedderburn, the first lord Loughborough, Earl of Rosslyn and Lord High Chancellor of England 1733–1805.

Chancellor Channel.

Camping: There are numerous good camping beaches in Loughborough Inlet, but here are four good options. As always, camping is not recommended in the main estuaries—especially at Stafford and Apple rivers—to avoid grizzly bear conflict and to protect sensitive habitat. See the main chapter map on page 419 for locating place names, and the icons for campsite locations.

N50°28.39' W125°34.62', Loughborough east entrance. Two beaches are located 2.8 km (1.8 miles) north of Grismond Point. The northern of the two has a better beach, better high tide clearance and better potential for campsite development.

N50°29.94' W125°33.14', Grassy Creek. A beautiful sand and gravel beach is just south of Grassy Creek near the pilings. There are no developed campsites, but lots of potential, plus good beach height for most tide levels. This is certainly the best and prettiest beach in the area, but be aware it's in close proximity to grizzly habitat at Grassy Creek. Another option is the three coves south of Statham Point. The middle cove has a good gravel beach with some level upland areas outside the tree line.

N50°32.16' W125°32.19', Gray Creek. Off the Gray Creek estuary are two islets connected by a drying clam beach with rough rock patches. Up from this bar on the south islet is an expansive, flat headland with a grassy top. This is an ideal campsite except for three warnings. First, watch for natural drainage ditches hidden among the grass on the headland. Second, the drainage ditches are there because most of the headland extends only as high as the high tide level, so seek the highest ground near a maximum tide. Third, at high tide you might be required to make a rock-ledge landing. Otherwise this is a wonderful spot with a view over the grizzly delta at Gray Creek as well as the full extent of the inlet. The photo on the acknowledgements page is taken from this site.

N50°39.31' W125°32.34', Towry Head. Southwest of Towry Head, across the inlet, a good gravel and stone beach faces south. The upland is heavily overgrown with scrub, but this is an ideal base for day trips to the head of the inlet.

Chancellor Channel

This narrow and relatively sheltered route connects Johnstone Strait to Cordero Channel, a distance of about 15 km (9 miles). Currents rarely exceed 2 knots, and wind tends to channel less violently here than in Johnstone Strait, making it a good route for leisurely travel. Expect log handling and fish farms.

Place names: Vancouver named the Thurlow islands in 1792 after Lord Chancellor Thurlow (1732–1806). Chancellor Channel was named in 1869 because it separates two features named by Vancouver that relate to British chancellors.

Camping: N50°25.68' W125°36.76'. Southwest of Tucker Point is a mixed beach of gravel, stones and rock. At the top of the beach is access to an open and airy forest with level areas that would suit a dispersed group.

Wellbore Channel

This is a pretty area with Whirlpool Rapids to contend with at Carterer Point. Recreational traffic uses this channel to avoid Race or Current passages in Johnstone Strait and for the anchorage at Forward Harbour. For kayakers, there are rough beaches along most of the channel's length, so pullouts are not a problem. Wortley Creek at the head of Forward Harbour has chum and coho salmon populations that in turn support grizzlies. A fishing lodge is located near Wortley Creek. Look for the petroglyphs near the head of the harbour. They are on three boulders at the mid-tide line.

Helmcken Island.

Place names: John Wellbore Sunderland Spencer was captain aboard the *Topaze* 1860–63. The gunboat HMS *Forward* was used on the Vancouver Island coast in the 1860s. It was later sold to the Mexican government, only to be seized by revolutionaries and burned.

Whirlpool Rapids

This rapid twists its way past Carterer Point in Wellbore Channel. The maximum velocity is 7 knots, with the flood current setting south. Slack lasts about 6 minutes. During fast currents expect turbulence south of Carterer Point on the flood; on the ebb, turbulence will be to the north. It's not particularly difficult to transit, as there are good countercurrents along the shore to approach against the tide. I ran it against the current along the east shore and had little trouble except for a short portion of fast paddling around a rocky point north of Carterer Point. Otherwise I was making as good time as the motorized yachts bucking the current in the centre of the channel.

SAYWARD

This portion represents the western extent of the Discovery Islands. Kayakers who wish to travel Johnstone Strait at this point will have to deal with the rapids at Current or Race passages, while Sunderland Channel is relatively benign. Lots of islands and some good beaches make this a good potential kayaking area.

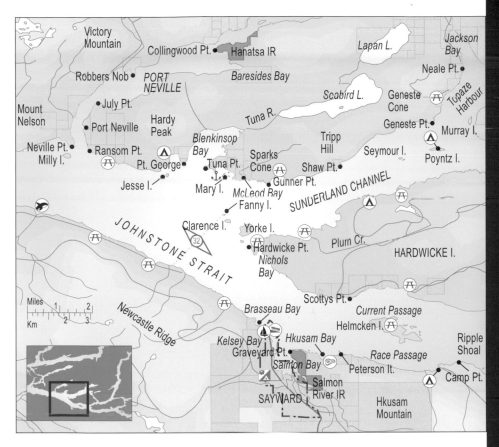

Race and Current passages

Helmcken, a forested, heavily indented island augmented by several islets, divides Johnstone Strait. The currents in the neighbouring passages run as high as 5 knots, with the flood setting east and the ebb west. Expect strong eddies. Note that the turn to flood is simultaneous in both passages, but the turn to ebb in Race Passage toward Camp Point occurs 1 hour and 15 minutes after the turn to ebb in Current Passage. The difference in the two passages is reflected in *Canadian Tide and Current Tables, Volume 6.* Only Current Passage is listed as a secondary station; for Race Passage use Camp Point.

These passages are on a main shipping route used by tugs, barges, freighters and cruise ships. Westbound traffic runs north of Ripple Shoal through Current Passage; eastbound traffic heads south through Race Passage. It's possible for ships to be unable to make the turn at Ripple Shoal, requiring them to use Race Passage heading west. Call-in points at Fanny Island to the west and Vansittart Point to the east are used to regulate traffic.

The tidal streams will be strong around Camp Point, where maximum currents average 5 knots. Eddies and rips can also be encountered around Ripple Shoal.

Due to the strong currents kayakers probably won't want to linger, which is unfortunate. There are good beaches on all sides, including some rough ones in the coves on Helmcken Island. Any could make a good emergency haulout.

Next to Ripple Shoal is a submerged orca rubbing area. Sea lions may be hauled out on a number of rocks in the area (Camp Point, Helmcken Island and Graveyard Point). Also, look for eagle nests on Helmcken.

Camping: N50°22.97' W125°50.69', Camp Point. A west-facing stone beach is backed by a grassy upland about a kilometre (just over a half a mile) west of the point. There is good group potential here, with the advantage of access to a creek.

Salmon Bay

This is a large, deep and industrial bay backed by the community of Sayward. The northwest portion, Kelsey Bay, houses the government dock and a marina (mainly commercial). Five ship hulks protect the marina—the Union Steamship *Cardena*; three Second World War frigates, HMCS *Runneymede*, HMCS *Longueil* and HMCS *Lasalle*; plus one unknown ship. Road access from the government wharf leads to Sayward, a community of about 1,000. It's about a 20-minute walk from the wharf to the well-stocked grocery store. Sayward also has a hotel, post office (V0P 1R0) and restaurant. Services at the government wharf are currently (2006) limited to a burger stand and gift shop. Neighbouring the wharf is a community-run RV park.

South of Kelsey Bay, in Salmon Bay, there's a large log sorting facility and a number of abandoned or decrepit industrial buildings. The bay continues south to a large estuary and wetland.

East of Salmon Bay is Hkusam Bay, the location of a former First Nations village.

Launches: N50°23.88' W125°57.73'. Adjacent to the government wharf is a boat ramp run by the local Community Futures organization.

Camping: The Village Centre Campground in Sayward is a good staging area for kayak launches. It's located next to a pond in the downtown area and has toilets and water. It's not marine-accessible. RV-style camping is possible next to the boat ramp at Salmon Bay.

Yorke Island

This island off the west end of Hardwicke Island, at the entrance to Sunderland Channel, was an artillery site in the Second World War. The gun battery housed two 4.7-inch guns installed in 1938, and was upgraded to two 6-inch guns in 1942. Remains of the fort can be seen in the pilings on the west side of the island and two buildings on the southwest side. The gun placement is the most easily seen. This was the principal gun deployment in Johnstone Strait, created to thwart a surprise attack on Vancouver from the north. If you want to explore the ruins, there's a gravel beach on the east side and a stone beach on the west side near the gun placement. Look for eagle nests on the island and possibly sea lions on the nearby rocks.

The gun placement at Yorke Island.

The currents in Johnstone Strait tend to be lower west of Yorke Island and pick up speed east of it and south of Hardwicke Island.

Place names: Philip Yorke was third earl of Hardwicke and son of Lord Chancellor Yorke in 1770.

Sunderland Channel

This channel divides Hardwicke Island from the mainland. The west entrance has the strongest currents; they can reach 4 knots and create rips. There will be no flood current when high water at Alert Bay is predicted at below 3.7 m (12.1 feet).

The shoreline is mostly steep and rocky, with a few good beaches scattered about. The channel is rich in prawns and octopus and home to the brown eel (wattled eelpout). Pigeon guillemot nest on the cliffs midway along the south shore. Salmon farms are on the north and south shores.

Camping: N50°28.99' W125°50.57', Poyntz Island. This is really two islands connected by a rocky spit. The spit is best approached from the east. It's level, with some clear areas, but most of it is overgrown with scrub—a sign it's seldom used. It's a great spot, though, in a strategic location, and it should evolve into a key kayaking camp. It's very pretty.

N50°27.73' W125°53.49'. Numerous beaches along the Sunderland Channel shores are suitable for camping, but this one is good for its access to an open and spacious forest, even if the beach is a second-rate mix of gravel and rock. It's located on Hardwick Island, 6.4 km (4 miles) from Hardwicke Point. In the forest there's room for a dispersed group seeking protection from strong westerlies that can plague Poyntz Island.

Topaze Harbour

This is a shallow bay with rock cliff and gravelly beaches backed by the dramatic cliff faces of Mount Drummond. Prawn, crab and octopus are harvested here. Jackson and Read bays lead north from the harbour (see the main chapter map on page 419). A large log sorting facility is in Jackson Bay. The estuaries of Read and Jackson bays and the small creek at the head of Topaze Harbour are used by grizzly bears.

Ecological oddities: Watch for cockles in Jackson and Read bays, but please don't pick them. Cockle beaches are easily denuded.

Place names: The gunboat HMS *Topaze* served on the B.C. coast 1859–63 and again 1866–96. Its captain was John Wellbore Sunderland Spencer. Spencer Mountain north of Topaze Harbour is named after him, as well as Sunderland Channel.

Hiking: At the head of Topaze Harbour is a traditional Xwémalhkwu trail to Heydon Bay that can still be walked.

Blenkinsop Bay

This bay is surrounded by good beach. An extensively drying eelgrass estuary at the head is a grizzly feeding area. Dungeness crab is abundant. Neighbouring McLeod Bay is a boat haven.

Place names: George Blenkinsop (1822–1904) was second in command for the Hudson's Bay Company at Fort Rupert and chief trader of Fort Colville.

Camping: N50°28.95' W126°01.64'. West of George Point on the west entrance to Blenkinsop Bay is a small cove with a sweeping, white sand beach. The nicest portion is the northwest corner. Camping is possible on the beach or in the open forest. The best upland access is about 30 m (100 feet) left of the fallen tree lying across the beach.

Port Neville

This inlet leads about 14 km (9 miles) northeast into the B.C. mainland. A government wharf about a kilometre (0.6 miles) north of Ransom Point is used by a small community and served by a post office (V0P 1M0). The inlet is mainly low, rolling forest with the exception of the picturesque bluffs of Mount Nelson. There's a nice cobble spit at Neville Point. The upland is private, as is Milly Island. Logging is extensive in the area.

Tidal streams at the entrance to the inlet can reach 3 knots. The inlet ends at Fulmore River, a salmon stream and once the site of a large Tlowitsis village. Be sure to look for the petroglyphs at Robbers Nob, a conspicuous scrub-covered rock over a grassy point, and eagle nests east of Ransom Point. Another petroglyph is at Collingwood Point.

Ecological oddities: On the south side of Johnstone Strait, across from Port Neville in an unnamed bay between St. Vincent Bight and Hickey Point, is a killer whale rubbing beach, one of those rare spots ideal for the orcas to rub themselves on the pebbles.

HAVANNAH-CHATHAM

This section covers a small portion of Johnstone Strait and two interesting channels that join Johnstone Strait to Knight Inlet. Cruising boats seeking anchorages or the marina near Minstrel Island travel

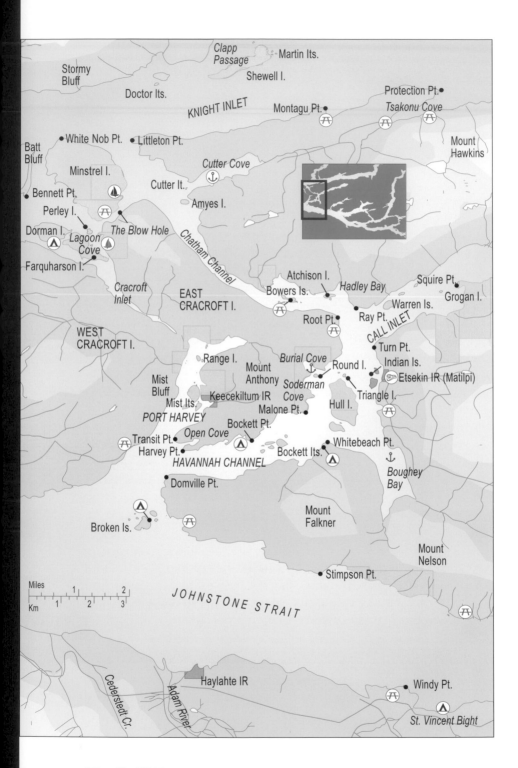

Clapp Passage

Martin Its.

Stormy Bluff

Shewell I.

Doctor Its.

KNIGHT INLET

Montagu Pt.

Protection Pt.

Tsakonu Cove

Mount Hawkins

White Nob Pt.

Littleton Pt.

Batt Bluff

Minstrel I.

Cutter Cove

Cutter It.

Amyes I.

Bennett Pt.

Perley I.

Dorman I.

The Blow Hole

Lagoon Cove

Farquharson I.

Chatham Channel

Cracroft Inlet

EAST CRACROFT I.

Atchison I.

Bowers Is.

Hadley Bay

Squire Pt.

Grogan I.

Warren Is.

Root Pt.

Ray Pt.

CALL INLET

WEST CRACROFT I.

Range I.

Mount Anthony

Burial Cove

Round I.

Turn Pt.

Indian Is.

Etsekin IR (Matilpi)

Mist Bluff

Keecekiltum IR

Soderman Cove

Triangle I.

Mist Its.

Malone Pt.

Hull I.

PORT HARVEY

Bockett Pt.

Transit Pt.

Open Cove

Harvey Pt.

Bockett Its.

Whitebeach Pt.

Boughey Bay

HAVANNAH CHANNEL

Domville Pt.

Mount Falkner

Broken Is.

Mount Nelson

Stimpson Pt.

Miles

1

2

Km

1

2

3

JOHNSTONE STRAIT

Haylahte IR

Windy Pt.

Cedarstedt Cr.

Adam River

St. Vincent Bight

this corridor, but it's rarely used by kayakers, despite numerous appealing beaches, island groups to explore and a long and sometimes still visible First Nations history.

St. Vincent Bight

This bight on the south shore of Johnstone Strait sits under the cover of Mount St. Vincent, contributing to the condi-

The campsite at Dorman Island.

tions at aptly named Windy Point. The point itself is part of a long, convoluted and magnificently cliffy headland that is broken by occasional beaches and one camp with cabins. Windy Point was a forward observation point for the military installation at Yorke Island during the Second World War. It's also part of the old telegraph line trail along the Vancouver Island coast and portions are still visible along the bluff and near the shore of the bight.

Camping: N50°27.30' W126°09.57'. The beach in the centre of the bight provides good access to a relatively clear forest. Drift logs seem to be less numerous here than at some of the other beaches in the bight.

Adam River

Adam River is a major estuary currently used as a log sorting facility and booming ground protected by a breakwater. The log dump and upland logging camp is leased to the Tlowitsis for development. The area includes a private dock and boat ramp. A small, seven-site forest recreation camp is located upland from the logging property, but it's not marine accessible.

The estuary is a drying mud flat used by migratory birds.

Launches: Adam River has traditionally been used as a kayak staging area, but since the area is under a private lease the access is in question and signs currently prohibit trespassing. One option is to phone the Tlowitsis First Nation at **250-830-1708** to seek permission. Otherwise continue on the same logging road west to Naka Creek.

Broken Islands

This small group of islands is located in Johnstone Strait at the entrance to Havannah Channel. Kelp beds, clam beaches and seal and sea lion haulouts can be found here; the most imperilled resident is the red-listed *Tayloriella divaricata* algae in the subtidal waters.

The area between Broken Islands and Domville Point is filled with reefs. Bear frequent the beaches south of Domville Point.

Camping: N50°30.83' W126°17.56'. A rough beach with an established camp in the forest cover is on the northeast side of the largest of the Broken Islands.

Port Harvey

This inlet is surrounded by considerable private land; there are anchorages at Mist Islets and north of Range Island, plus commercial uses that include a log dump on the west shore, a boom ground at the head and two towboat reserves. This is Tlowitsis traditional territory with three cultural sites along the east side of the port. Two houses and ruins of a public wharf are at the head of the port. Kayakers may be tempted to try the channel between Port Harvey and Cracroft Inlet at high tide. It runs dry at lower tides and is pocked with boulders.

Near Bocket Point, Havannah Channel.

Place names: Thomas Harvey was captain of *Havannah*, which assisted the *Plumper* in surveying the coast.

Havannah Channel

Havannah Channel, together with Chatham Channel, links Johnstone Strait to Knight Inlet. It's a low-current waterway known for its warm waters and frequent plankton blooms. There's a delightful mixture of islands and coves, with some limited development at private land holdings around Soderman Cove and Hull Island. You can avoid the marina, anchorage, towboat reserve and commercial wharf by going east of Hull Island.

Matilpi, an abandoned First Nations village, is flanked by Indian Islands. Whatever remains of the village is hidden in the dense scrub behind; until a few years ago some ruins were visible. The former village site is fronted by a white clamshell beach.

Place names: *Havannah* served on the B.C. coast 1855–59. It was built in Liverpool in 1811 and had 19 guns.

Ecological oddities: The Pealie peregrine falcon is normally a resident of the Queen Charlotte Islands. It can be found in small numbers on the lowlands of northern Vancouver Island and one area in this region: Havannah Channel and East Cracroft Island.

Camping: N50°32.40' W126°14.95', Bockett Point. West of Bockett Point is a cove with a rough beach and some sand or gravel areas leading to a grassy clearing suitable for camping.

N50°32.23' W126°12.85', Whitebeach Point. This point, on the south shore of the channel west of Boughey Bay, is named for the crushed clamshell at the high tide line. Limited camping is possible at the high tide line, and there's ample space in the forest behind. Access is not well established, though, forcing a rough climb up a short embankment—at least until it's developed.

Call Inlet

This deep inlet runs almost 20 km (12 miles) northeast from Havannah Channel. The sides are steep and cliffy, and the mountain backdrop rises to 1,445 m (4,740 feet) on the north side. It ends in an extensive, swampy mud flat. It's not often visited as it doesn't have a secure anchorage and is known for funnelling wind. It is, however, well used for log handling, with four log dumps, four log storage areas and a barge ramp. Kayakers will find regular places to stop at the inlet's nine clam and one oyster beach.

Place names: Sir John Call (1732–1801) was a military engineer for the East India Company.

Chatham Channel

This narrow channel connects Havannah Channel with Knight Inlet. It's prone to high currents, with the flood setting southeast. The strongest currents are around Bowers Island toward Root Point, where they can reach 5 knots. Kayakers can beat moderate opposing tides by sticking to the shallows out of the main tidal stream. A good place to wait out the tide is Bowers Island, which has good beaches above a light forest, with good possibility for a campsite. A lodge midway along the northeast shore of the channel has a gift shop and post office (V0P 1L0). A boat haven is located in Cutter Cove, while a towboat reserve for tugs awaiting a favourable tide is at the cove's entrance.

Place names: HMS *Chatham* was the small consort of Capt. George Vancouver's *Discovery*, at the time commanded by Lieutenant Commander Broughton. John Pitt was second earl of Chatham and First Lord of the Admiralty 1788–94.

Minstrel Island

This island has a long history as a regional centre, in part due to a popular pub that was a watering hole for the Knight Inlet region for several generations. Other services were a repair shop, hotel, school and a dance hall that was torn down in 1990. In 2005 the island was essentially abandoned, with the closing of the marina. It was sold in 2006, so expect it to reopen in some capacity. In the meantime the government wharf remains in place, giving access to trails that cross the island. The north and west sides of the island are steep and cliffy.

The community at Minstrel Island.

South of the island is a passage known as The Blow Hole. It's a difficult transit for boats, but kayaks will have no problem. The best beach in the area is on the Minstrel Island side. The upland is private.

Kingcome Inlet.

Place names: Local legend tells of a "minstrel boat" arriving here when a survey crew was working in the area. That boat is believed to be HMS *Amethyst*, which took Governor General Frederick Temple and his wife on a cruise to Metlakatla in 1867. The boat apparently had minstrels aboard. Both Mr. Bones and Sambo (Bones Bay and Sambo Point) were characters in minstrel shows popular at that time. It's likely a performance took place here.

Cracroft Inlet/Lagoon Cove

A floating lodge is on the east side of Lagoon Cove, along with numerous floating cabins toward Farquharson Island. The area is a popular anchorage. Services at the marina include showers, laundry and a store. Note that Farquharson and Dorman islands are linked via a clam bar.

Place names: Sophia Cracroft was niece of Sir John Franklin, the Arctic explorer who died in the infamous 1847 expedition. Sophia and Lady Franklin visited the B.C. coast in 1861. Note also Sophia Islets and the Franklin Range.

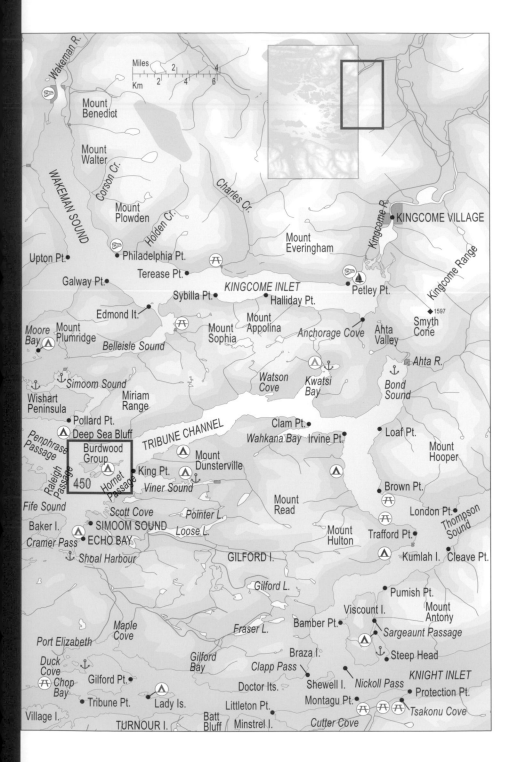

Camping: N50°35.96' W126°20.07'. Kayakers wanting to stay out of dark forested areas here could set up on some of the rock bluffs around south Farquharson Island. For those seeking a traditional beach, the most accessible is on the southeast end of Dorman Island, west of the bar between Dorman and Farquharson islands. It's grassy at the high tide line, with various access points into the forest. Level areas could accommodate several tents. It's well protected if not overly pretty. Groups may want to try the high ground on the grassy bar between the islands, but I found it grubby and unwelcoming.

GILFORD

This portion represents the little-travelled north and east sides of Gilford Island, including two major inlets: Knight and Kingcome. None of these areas, with the exception of the western end toward the Burdwood Group and Echo Bay, are part of any established kayaking route and they're rarely paddled. Knight Inlet continues both west and east of the regional map; the western entrance is covered in Chapter 9, beginning page 457. The eastern extent is shown on the regional map on page 418–19.

Port Elizabeth

This deep port is on the south end of Gilford Island. Commercial use of the port includes two log dumps, two log handling facilities, heli-logging and an upland logging camp.

Chop Bay, to the west of Port Elizabeth, is the most kayak-friendly of the outer beaches; the rest are all quite poor, including the four beaches on the east side of Village Island that from a distance seem quite appealing. Most kayakers will want to head to Lady Islands, the highlight of the area with some pleasant areas to explore.

The currents tend to run at several knots along this stretch of Knight Inlet, with the main stream curving southwest around Village Island past Tribune Point. If you're trying to take advantage of the tide, watch that you don't get caught in one of the many countercurrents that flow through this area. Note that the current tends to turn from flood to ebb long before high tide. The ebb will generally be stronger than the flood due to freshwater runoff.

Place names: In association with Port Elizabeth, the Lady Islands were named during the 1867 survey for Lady Elizabeth, wife of Lord Gilford.

Lady Islands.

Knight Inlet behind Rest Islets.

Camping: N50°38.53' W126°25.88', Lady Islands. The eastern and smallest of the two main Lady Islands has a small islet on the southwest end. The two are connected by a clam bed and rock ledge. On the islet are two separate, mossy, level clearings. Together they could easily house a group of four to five tents. This is a wonderfully pretty site, though the first few steps to the mossy clearing up the embankment might be tricky for some. A short rope is in place to help.

Upper Knight Inlet

Knight Inlet holds the title for longest inlet on the B.C. coast. Do not confuse that with being the prettiest. While some summits along the later portions adjacent to the shoreline do reach 1,500 m (4,921 feet), most of the lower extent is simply rolling forested slopes very similar in appearance to Johnstone Strait. The last turnoff is at Sargeaunt Passage at Viscount Island. Consider taking it; after that the inlet continues 37 km (23 miles) east then turns north for another 43 km (27 miles).

There are logging camps but no communities or marinas along its length. Currents will run at several knots, stronger on the ebb, but wind is more likely to plague a trip. The steep shoreline tends to funnel the westerlies from Queen Charlotte Strait, plus you also

A view toward the Miriam Range from Gilford Island.

have to contend with inflow or outflow winds.

For all the distance there really is no scenic highlight. Remnants of past activity can be seen in places like Hoeya Sound, where there's a logging camp at the head, or Glendale Cove, where there's a ruin of a cannery. The site of a former logging camp is now the Knight Inlet Lodge, which offers eco-tours but no services to visitors.

Place names: Valdes and Galiano named it Braza de Vernaci after the lieutenant of the *Mexicana*. Commander Broughton visited here in 1792. He named it after Sir John Knight.

Kayaking Knight Inlet: Given the lack of features, the length and the potential for troublesome winds, Knight is probably the inlet least suited to kayaking on the B.C. coast. Even if you take a water taxi to the head your return trip could see you paddling for 37 km (23 miles) against the same westerlies that plague Johnstone Strait, without the advantage of frequent side-channels to use as escapes.

Ahnuhati Estuary Protected Area
Ahnuhati Point is the only safe anchorage in the upper portion of Knight Inlet. The head of the inlet is a mud flat with a marshy upland. It's a major coastal wetland, with the Klinaklini river supporting

black bear, mountain goat, moose, deer and wolf. The Ahnuhati Complex encompasses three rivers—the Ahnuhati, Kwalate and Ahta. They represent three of the last four undeveloped watersheds over 5,000 ha (19.3 square miles) in size on the central coast. The area is home to about 60 grizzly bears; that may sound like a lot but it's below the estimated miminum population of 90 needed for the grizzlies to remain viable in the region. Large salmon runs have historically supported the population.

Sargeaunt Passage

This is a very quiet and exceptionally pretty stretch of narrow water. A fish farm operates at the south entrance. North of it the passage narrows at several gravelly shoals. There are stunning bluffs on Viscount Island overlooking the passage. A private dock is located near the north end of the passage. Steep Head is a cormorant roosting site. Nearby Shewell Island is private property.

Camping: N50°41.19' W126°11.83'. The passage shoals at three points on the east side. The southernmost shoal has a creek running through a rough rock, stone and clamshell beach. Camping is possible on the upland, but it's currently overgrown with scrub. Beach camping is possible at some tide levels. This is a very screne spot, but it needs development.

Tribune Channel

Tribune Channel curves around Gilford Island from Knight Inlet, eventually joining with Fife Sound, a distance of about 45 km (28 miles). Tidal currents run below 2 knots, and turbulence will be limited to wind waves, if any. Most beaches are on the south end of the channel below Irvine Point. The worst winds have a tendency to funnel along the north leg; on the south leg they will be intermittent, occasionally coming off the mountainsides and channelling into Thompson Sound, for instance. Some of the surrounding mountains are quite striking, particularly toward the Miriam Range in the channel's north end.

Place names: Richard James Meade was Viscount Gilford and captain of HMS *Tribune* on the B.C. coast 1862–64. He served as Admiral of the Fleet 1895–1902.

Camping: N50°44.34' W126°10.90', Kumlah Island. West of Kumlah Island is a wide bay with an east-facing beach. It provides access to an undeveloped but level, spacious forest area. This is by far the best kayaking campsite in the region; unfortunately, there's a possibility for conflict as a commercial tenure exists for this location. As of 2006 no access restrictions were posted.

N50°47.85' W126°13.76', East Gilford. Three km (1.8 miles) south of Irvine Point is a creek. North of the creek is a good beach of sediment and gravel at higher levels, with stone at lower tide levels. The beach provides access to an undeveloped but open forest with several existing flat areas.

N50°49.18' W126°21.41', North Tribune. Beaches are almost non-existent on the north leg of Tribune Channel. If you're unable to finish the leg to the Burdwood Group, consider a rough rock beach at a creek on the south shore 6.6 km (4 miles) northeast of King Point. Look for clear areas in a young alder forest on an eroding bank, being sure to stay away from the muddy creek floodplain that crosses the embankment.

Thompson Sound

This long, steep-sided inlet is heavily used for log handling. A dozen salmon streams here help attract a rich selection of waterfowl. The sound is a minke whale feeding area in the summer. Human use includes a sport fishery; commercial harvesting of prawn, shrimp and crab; salmon trolling, gillnetting and seine fishing; a dozen log handling and storage sites; a heli-logging site; industrial storage tanks and a private moorage. A safe anchorage is located at Sackville Island.

Bond Sound

Bond Sound extends north from Tribune Channel and supports numerous salmon streams with the pristine landscape of the Ahta River, which has never been logged. To fully enjoy it, a recreational trail leads from the estuary to the alpine level. Waterfalls and pictographs round out the attractions. The Ahta River flowing into the head of Bond Sound is a grizzly viewing area in the fall.

The sound is used for log handling, storage, heli-logging and camp tie-ups.

Kwatsi Bay

This is a deep, curving inlet known for its three waterfalls hemmed in by steep mountains. The bay has a safe anchorage and a marina with moorage, trails to the waterfalls, a gift shop and showers. The marina can also serve as an emergency haulout for kayakers needing a place to camp. Watson Cove, to the west, is also known for its waterfalls.

Viner Sound

This inlet extends 6 km (3.8 miles) east into Gilford Island from King Point near the west entrance to Tribune Channel; the last 1.5 km (almost a mile) is a drying mud flat. Murre nest on the pleasant cliffs at the north entrance. The south side is heavily logged. Halfway along its length the sound narrows to a thin inlet. A cove to the north, just west of the limit of the mud flat, is a nicely protected anchorage with a forest recreation site.

Travel notes: A resident humpback in the sound has been joined in recent years by its baby. One or the other or both can often be seen cavorting at the entrance to Tribune Channel or in Penphrase Passage near Simoon Sound.

Place names: Capt. William Viner Read was a surveying officer who served in the Hydrographic Office.

Camping: N50°47.28' W126°23.19'. The forest recreation site in Viner Sound has a clam beach backed by a level area with a picnic table, bench, fire pit and an outhouse. It's set into the west entrance of the cove that serves as the anchorage near the head of the sound. The beach leading to the site faces north, so you must enter the cove and look back to see it.

Burdwood Group

This is an exceptional island cluster made all the better by a smattering of kayak-friendly clamshell beaches. Elsewhere the shoreline is rugged and rocky. A fish farm on the west end of the largest island is the only development. It is traditional Tsawataineuk and Kwicksutaineuk-Ah Kwaw-ah-mish land, with nine identified cultural and archaeological sites in the group, including about six village sites and a former defensive site.

The entrance to Simoom Sound.

Camping: N50°47.83' W126°28.09', main camp. Between the two larger eastern islands is a smaller island with rock outcrops guarding a beautiful white clamshell beach. The best low-tide access is from the south. The upland is a well-developed campsite with benches and a fire pit in a forest setting with views clear down Tribune Channel and Viner Sound. It is exceptionally pretty.

N50°47.63' W126°28.32', islet hideaway. The southeast island has a small, rocky islet on its west side connected via rocks and a clam bed beach. The beach gives access to a site that is flat and clear though well hidden by tree cover. This is a great honeymoon site for those who want seclusion.

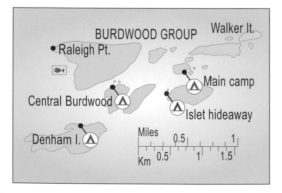

N50°47.67' W126°29.09', central Burdwood. A good clamshell beach faces northwest toward the largest island. The forest is less developed and views poorer than the main site. It would accommodate a couple of tents in its current state.

N50°47.32' W126°29.50', Denham Island. The south-

Echo Bay.

west island has a clamshell beach facing north toward the main island. The forest has level, clear space for a few tents, though the site is poorly developed.

Simoom Sound

This waterway extends northeast with views to rugged Bald Mountain and the scoop-of-mashed-potato shapes of the north side of the Miriam Range peaks. The rest of the land-scapes are low, rolling and heavily logged. An island cluster toward the central anchorage adds some appeal. Beaches tend to be rough along most of the length. A fish farm is located in the bay near the north entrance. Pigeon guillemot nest on Deep Sea Bluff.

Echo Bay Marine Park

This small grassy park on the upland backing Echo Bay covers just 1.5 ha (3.7 acres). A long history of First Nations use is reflected in the midden here. It originally served as a forest ranger station in the 1950s and was made a park in 1971. It's home to a great blue heron rookery.

Camping: N50°49.11' W126°30.45'. A beautiful crushed shell beach is at the south entrance to the sound on the west limit of Deep Sea Bluff. Camping is on the beach at lower tide levels. A portion will survive an unadjusted 4.1-m (13.5-foot) Alert Bay high tide, but not much above that. The upland is accessible, but unfortunately it's a rough scramble up a tall dirt embankment; carrying gear would be next to impossible unless you rig a line to haul it up. If tide levels do allow you to camp, there are numerous rocks off the point that are exceptional for watching the marine wildlife pass by.

Travel notes: I heard there was a super-pod of dolphins in the area, and I finally ran into them at the dogleg in Simoom Sound. Dozens were putting on a show chasing their dinner, which I suspect was a herring ball. A humpback would later join the hunt; it wasn't a good day to be a herring. The humpback also put on quite a show for the Deep Sea Bluff campsite, and it was difficult to go to sleep knowing there was a whale out there still jumping about. This was, as you can imagine, a great place to stay. Time your visit for a neap tide to enjoy it.

Place names: The eight-gun troopship HM *Simoom* was commanded in 1853 by Capt. John Kingcome.

Scott Cove
This cove, once a village site, has a recent history as a logging camp and booming ground. Pierre's Bay Lodge and Marina on the west shore provides dining, a bakery, accommodation, laundry, showers, water and Internet access. Look for an old steam donkey near the dock.

Echo Bay
This small community and regional centre is largely on floats. You'll find a marina, wharf and private moorage. Kayakers often pick Echo Bay for a drop-off or pickup by water taxi. Services include a post office (V0P 1S0), telephone, fuel, grocery store, washrooms, showers, laundry and an art gallery. Float plane service from Echo Bay is available to Seattle, Campbell River and Port McNeill. On shore is a level, grassy field—Echo Bay Marine Park—backed by a community centre and the one-room schoolhouse.

Simoom Sound, to the north, is an abandoned settlement. Shoal Harbour to the south is a boat haven. History buffs will want to be sure to visit Bill Proctor's museum of local fishing, logging and trapping artifacts. It's located in the small bay just south of Echo Bay, along with a dock, sawmill and marine railway haulout. A good source of local history and anecdotes is Proctor's book *Full Moon Flood Tide* (Harbour Publishing, 2003).

Camping: N50°45.04' W126°29.65'. A small grassy field at the Echo Bay Marine Park provides a level camping area near the community centre. No camping fee is charged. It will probably not appeal to those seeking a wilderness setting.

Kingcome Inlet

This coastal fiord extends from the junction of Sutlej Channel and Penphrase Passage 30 km (18 miles) east into the mainland. It's deep, with no all-weather anchorages and just as few good beaches along its length. Probably the best is at Charles Creek, which is reserve land and a culturally significant area. Just west of the reserve are the ruins of an old logging camp along the shore. Also, watch for a memorial on the rock nearby.

Pictographs dot the area. Look for an interesting one at Philadelphia Point. A unique aspect of the inlet is the presence of a few latter-day rock paintings. The largest is a huge design on the rock face north of Petley Point. Other more modern pictographs dot the area. Look for one near Terease Point.

Place names: Rear Admiral Sir John Kingcome was commander in chief on the B.C. coast 1863–64. The Kwak'wala name is Gwa'yi.

Travel notes: A sign on the float at Petley Point states visitors should respect the Tsawataineuk traditional territory. Illustrating the disrespect, the rocks behind have been spray-painted with the names and crew of visiting yachts over past years, as well as childish attempts to mimic pictographs. It's a defacement unworthy of a highway underpass, yet some seem to think it

Modern rock painting at Petley Point.

appropriate for a historic wilderness area. It seems to manifest itself at select coastal locations.

Kingcome Inlet village (Quaee)

A First Nations community is located along the Kingcome River north of the head of Kingcome Inlet. A rarely used government dock north of Petley Point isn't connected to the shore; it's simply a float beneath an exposed cliff. For shore access you have to find your way to a dock up the Kingcome River, and deep-keeled boats need not apply. At the community is a dock served regularly by float plane. Farther up the river there's a small store and post office (V0N 2B0).

To get to the village you must pass through the estuary, which is low, marshy and dotted with low-level grassy flats that create a maze of waterways at high tide. To enter Kingcome River, head north along the cliffside at Petley Point, continuing to a barge landing with some clutter and a shed. Look to your right (east) at the landing. You should see a series of three orange markers—two on wooden posts and one on a tree. Follow the markers by keeping them to your right. The passage will turn left (north) and lead straight to Kingcome village. To get lost, continue north at the barge ramp through the opening beyond the dyke. Inside the tide has eroded numerous channels, creating a maze that will confound and eventually defeat you, as all channels lead nowhere.

Kayaking Kingcome Inlet: Kingcome is shorter than many other major coastal inlets and this makes it a manageable place to explore, but there are slim pickings for campsites. At the head you can pull out on the grassy flats in the estuary—not necessarily a great location, but it's a possibility. Another option is the dock at Petley Point. It's rarely used and large enough to support a group, though it tends to rock and creak loudly when the wind is blowing (which is most often). You may also want to check for beaches at Anchorage Cove south of the head, though this is decidedly out of the way for a trip to the village. The best beaches are at the reserve at Charles Creek, though what appears to be dark dirt is actually a horrid, black, decomposing, seaweed muck. If you can't make it to the forest recreation campsite at Moore Bay, consider the beach in Belleisle Sound. A great way to explore this region would be to take a water taxi to the head of Kingcome and paddle your way back.

The intertidal mouth of the Kingcome River.

Wakeman Sound

This short sound extends 10 km (6 miles) north to end in the Wakeman River estuary. It's a heavily used logging area with a dozen log handling and storage tenures. Boaters will find a safe anchorage at the head of the sound.

The Wakeman River flows for 50 km (31 miles) through a valley supporting salmon as well as grizzly.

Belleisle Sound

This well-protected inlet extends south then west from Kingcome Inlet for a distance of about 7 km (4.4 miles). It's used for forestry, a commercial prawn fishery and a safe anchorage. A Tsawataineuk reserve near the east entrance is part of an extensive beach with ruins of a sawmill and logging camps. The beach is probably the best potential camping spot in the region.

Place names: HMS *Belleisle* was under the command of Commander John Kingcome when it was a troop ship in China in 1842.

Morning in Greenway Sound.

The Broughtons

CHAPTER NINE

THIS IS COUNTRY MADE FOR KAYAKING.

Daily during the summer dozens of kayakers head out from Telegraph Cove, filling the beaches along Johstone Strait and into the Broughton Archipelago. Whale watching is the focus, especially around Robson Bight Ecological Reserve in Johnstone Strait, the only killer whale reserve in Canada. But stray from the key areas and once again the number of kayakers diminishes rapidly. Very few will explore as far as the Broughton Islands and its intricate waterways, rich wildlife and more varied and interesting scenery.

The Broughton Archipelago, protected as a provincial park, is growing in reputation to rival the Broken Group west of Vancouver Island as a top kayaking destination. One of the key attractions in the region is Meem Quam Leese, otherwise known as *Mamalilaculla* or more simply Village Island, an abandoned native village returning to life through tours offered by the Mamalilikulla-Qwe'Qwa'Sot'Em First Nation. Add to this the chance to see killer whales, humpbacks, dolphins and an array of other marine life amid hundreds of islands and islets. There is nowhere else quite like it on the coast.

Exploring by kayak

Most kayakers tend to cluster in Johstone Strait in the numerous campsites between Telegraph Cove and Robson Bight, or in the Village Island area and the south end of the Broughton Archipelago. About the best thing to be said about large crowds of kayakers is the great number of campsites that evolve, so Johnstone has many to choose from. The options decline outside the main kayaking routes, though forest recreation sites provide a good backbone through the north end

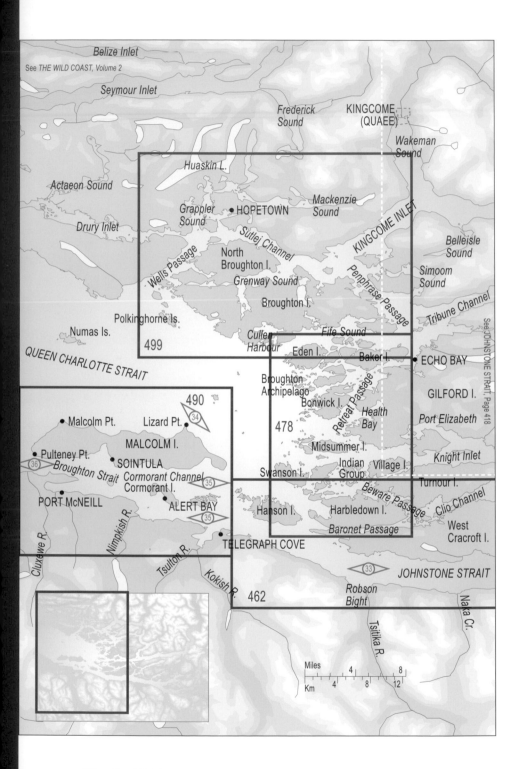

See *THE WILD COAST*, Volume 2

Belize Inlet

Seymour Inlet

Frederick
Sound

KINGCOME
(QUAEE)

Wakeman
Sound

Huaskin L.

Actaeon Sound

Mackenzie
Sound

Grappler
Sound

HOPETOWN

Drury Inlet

KINGCOME INLET

Sutlej Channel

North
Broughton I.

Belleisle
Sound

Wells Passage

Grenway Sound

Penphrase Passage

Simoom
Sound

Broughton I.

Tribune Channel

Polkinghorne Is.

Fife Sound

Numas Is.

Cullen
Harbour

499

Eden I.

Baker I.

ECHO BAY

QUEEN CHARLOTTE STRAIT

Broughton
Archipelago

Bonwick I.

Retreat Passage

Health
Bay

GILFORD I.

490

34

Port Elizabeth

Malcolm Pt.

Lizard Pt.

478

Midsummer I.

36

MALCOLM I.

Indian
Group

Village I.

Knight Inlet

Pulteney Pt.

SOINTULA

Cormorant Channel

Swanson I.

35

Beware Passage

Turnour I.

Cormorant I.

Clio Channel

PORT McNEILL

ALERT BAY

35

Hanson I.

Harbledown I.

West
Cracroft I.

TELEGRAPH COVE

Baronet Passage

462

33

JOHNSTONE STRAIT

Robson
Bight

Miles

4   8

Km   4   8   12

See JOHNSTONE STRAIT, Page 418

At home atop a rock in the Polkinghorne Islands.

of the Broughton Islands. To really stray from the crowds, consider trips around Malcolm Island or to the Grappler Sound area. Both are well suited for a paddling trip, particularly the Polkinghornes, but don't see many kayakers.

Recommended kayaking trips

- *If you have a day:* A good area for a day trip is from Naka Creek. You can stay at the forest recreation site and launch from it. This is a good option for families, for instance, which may have logistical problems with overnight kayaking trips but want to paddle with the orcas. From Port McNeill, a good trip would be to Pulteney Point on Malcolm Island, or perhaps as far as Malcolm Point for lunch before returning.

- *If you have two days:* A good overnight trip from Telegraph Cove might be to Hanson Island, or along the Johnstone Strait shoreline to any of the many campsites near Robson Bight. The closest is Blinkhorn Peninsula.

- *If you have three days:* Most kayakers will probably want to stay around Johnstone Strait for a chance to see killer whales. An unusual adventure would be a circumnavigation of Malcolm

Island from a launch at Port McNeill. You can overnight at just about any of the cobble beaches on the outside of the island. To make it a leisurely four-day trip, consider stops at Malcolm Point, Lizard Point and Pearse Islands.

- *If you have five days:* This is probably the minimum amount of time you'll want to invest to more fully explore the region. A good relaxing trip is from Telegraph Cove through the Broughton Archipelago, up Retreat Passage, then down the Queen Charlotte Strait side. A full itinerary might be Mound Island, the Fox Group, the Burdwood Group, Hanson Island and home. A relaxed itinerary would be Hanson Island, Mound Island, Owl Island, Swanson Island and back.

- *If you have a week:* The most varied trip would be an exploration of the Broughton Archipelago with a few days of whale watching on Johnstone Strait. Consider heading up Baronet Passage, staying at Lady Islands, exploring Meem Quam Leese with a stay at Mound Island, heading up Retreat Passage to the Fox Group, exploring the Broughton Archipelago with a stay at Insect and/or Owl island, and a return to your launch site at Telegraph Cove.

- *The ideal trip:* From Telegraph Cove, head up Baronet Passage, then up Beware Passage for a visit to Meem Quam Leese. Then head up Knight Inlet into Tribune Channel for a circumnavigation of Gilford Island (see Chapter 8 for the details on this area). Stay at the Burdwood Group, then head up Penphrase Passage and Sutlej Channel with a trip into Turnbull Cove, perhaps Mackenzie Sound and down through Grappler Sound and Wells Passage. Be sure to stay at the Polkinghornes. Head back through the Broughton Archipelago, spending what time you feel is necessary, with a stay at White Cliff Islets and maybe a day or two in Johnstone Strait to watch whales. This trip includes whale watching, a venture into mountainous channels, an exploration of isolated northern routes and all the classic attractions of the Broughton Archipelago. This rivals the Desolation Sound region for the best two-week trip on the south coast.

Call-in points: Vessel Traffic Services call-in points for traffic through this region include two in Broughton Strait and one for Queen Charlotte Strait. Another is near the west end of Johnstone Strait

A cloudy crossing of Johnstone Strait.

at Boat Bay. These are useful for kayaks or slow boats in the area of Hanson and West Cracroft islands where sightlines are poor, especially for ships using Blackney Passage.

- *33, Boat Bay:* This is a line running north-south through the Boat Bay navigation light at Swaine Point north of Robson Bight near the west end of Johnstone Strait.

- *34, Lizard Point:* This is a line running 45°–225° through the Lizard Point light at the northeast extremity of Malcolm Island.

- *35, Lewis Point:* This is a line that runs north from the Lewis Point light at the west entrance to Beaver Harbour. This call-in point applies in both Broughton Strait and Cormorant Channel and is divided by Cormorant Island (Alert Bay).

- *36, Pulteney Point:* Vessels entering a three-mile radius centred on the Pulteney Point light on the southwest end of Malcolm Island are required to call in.

NORTH JOHNSTONE STRAIT

This stretch is one of the most-visited whale watching areas on the British Columbia coast, with a correspondingly high number of

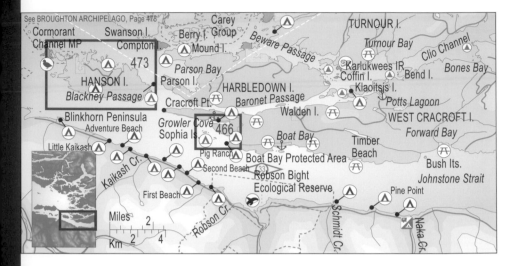

See BROUGHTON ARCHIPELAGO, Page 478

Cormorant
Channel MP
Swanson I.
Compton I.
473
HANSON I.
Blackney Passage
Blinkhorn Peninsula
Adventure Beach
Little Kaikash
Kaikash Cr.
First Beach
Miles
Km

Carey
Berry I. Group
Mound I.
Parson Bay
Parson I.
Cracroft Pt.
Growler Cove
Sophia Is.
Pig Ranch
Second Beach
Robson Bight
Ecological Reserve
Robson Cr.

Beware Passage
HARBLEDOWN I.
Baronet Passage
466
Boat Bay
Boat Bay Protected Area

Walden I.

TURNOUR I.
Turnour Bay
Karlukwees IR
Coffin I.
Klaoitsis I.
Bend I.
Clio Channel
Bones Bay
Potts Lagoon

WEST CRACROFT I.
Forward Bay
Timber
Beach
Bush Its.
Johnstone Strait
Pine Point
Schmidt Cr.
Naka Cr.

kayakers and kayaking-accessible campsites—the highest on the coast outside the Gulf Islands. A growing concern is the competition for space between the commercial operators and private campers. Despite the high number of tent icons on the map, not all sites may be accessible.

The strait is a key migration route for Fraser River salmon, the largest salmon run in the world. This means it's a key fishing area during the commercial fishing season. The most popular location for fishing vessels is along the south shoreline of Johstone Strait, and dozens can be working here. This has the potential for clashing with kayakers, especially since the large seiners often use the shoreline for securing their nets. The vessel noses into the shore, a skiff is used to tie the line to shore, and the large fishing vessel does a quick turn away from the shore to lay out the net. This means kayakers might be in the way whether they're along the shore or by passing around the fishing boat. Since kayakers can interfere with the path of a working fishing vessel, many operators are not sympathetic to the slower speeds and vulnerability of kayaks. You could be casually paddling by the shoreline, then find yourself blasted with an airhorn and yelled at for reasons that, for you, may be incomprehensible. Troll, gillnet and prawn fisheries also operate here.

Johnstone Strait is the major transportation route for barges and cruise ships. Most use Blackney Passage to enter the strait, as it offers the deepest route. This means poor sightlines for kayakers crossing anywhere nearby. Kayakers can reduce the risk by monitoring Channel 71 for oncoming traffic.

Gravel shoals at Naka Creek.

This area is also the migration route and summer resting area for both resident and transient killer whales. If you visit during the summer, your chances of seeing a killer whale are very high—one notch short of being assured.

For all its popularity, this portion of Johnstone Strait can be a difficult area to paddle. Currents are not extreme, usually only a knot or so west of Hardwicke Island, but they can be complicated by the wind opposing the current, creating the sharp, choppy wind waves for which Johnstone Strait is famous. Kayakers may also be in for a surprise at places like Cracroft Point and the Plumper Islands, where currents can reach river-like speeds.

Forward Bay
This stretch of the south shore of West Cracroft Island lies outside the main kayaking route for the area. It's an occasional anchorage with a beach usable for a break. Bush Islets are part of a string of reefs that extends well out from the west side of the bay. Camping potential is low; look for a rough spot at Timber Beach.

Naka Creek
This is an intensive logging area with a log dump and a prominent logging camp. At a managed forest recreation site within the camp, the shoreline is good beach, with potential wilderness camping sites

to both the east and west of the established location. The recreation site can be reached by logging road. To get here from Highway 19, take the East Main logging road north along the Eve River, turning west at the Naka Main. Portions are steep and may be difficult for some cars. If you can use your GPS in the car, the turnoff from Highway 19 is approximately N50°19.49' W126°12.67'.

Launches: N50°28.67' W126°25.63'. A launch onto a gravel beach is adjacent to the recreation site at Naka Creek. The gravel may be difficult for heavy boats on trailers. In 2006 a fee is charged for overnight parking, though camping is free.

Camping: The forest recreation site has seven vehicle-accessible sites with picnic tables and access to fresh water and an outhouse. The site is managed by caretakers-in-residence. This is a good staging ground for kayaking trips into Johnstone Strait, while those passing through the area would probably prefer wilderness sites such as Pine Point. Camping trailers may be available for rent.

Schmidt Creek

This creek is the last accessible point of land before the east border of Robson Bight Ecological Reserve. Public access within the reserve is restricted to 1 km (0.6 miles) from the shoreline, with the eastern border at W126°30.25' extending north. Schmidt Creek has a rock beach where an established commercial camp is based (Coastal Spirits).

Camping: N50°28.93' W126°27.97', Pine Point. Rather than the commercial site or its periphery, kayakers will probably prefer Pine Point, the local name for the headland between Schmidt and Naka creeks. On the headland is a developed clear area with what appears to be a hammock made of fishing net, among other driftwood furniture. The best access is the pebble beach on the west side of the headland.

Robson Bight

Now an area protected for the near-exclusive use of orcas, the bight was once a village site whose ownership shifted between the Matilpi and Tlowitsis as the boundary changed. Now it's a protected reserve, though don't be surprised to see commercial fishing boats entering the restricted waters. They are exempt. Other vessels straying into

The ecological reserve staff campsite at Boat Bay.

the water are likely to be directed away by the reserve warden or a volunteer. The off-limit portion covers 9 km (5.6 miles) of shoreline.

Place names: Lt. Commander Charles Rufus Robson commanded the gunboat *Forward*. He died in 1861 by falling from his horse in Esquimalt. He's credited with aiding the American brig *Consort* when it wrecked in San Josef Bay on northwest Vancouver Island in 1860. The traditional name for the bight is Usaw, meaning "grey haired," a reference to the poor state of the trees in the area.

Robson Bight (Michael Bigg) Ecological Reserve

This sanctuary for whales protects 1,248 ha (4.8 square miles) of Johnstone Strait plus 505 ha (2 square miles) of the surrounding forest. The intent is to give the killer whales an area free from harassment; the main feature is the rubbing beach, one of only a few beaches used for this purpose on the B.C. coast. This is the only one with protection for the whales.

While killer whales are the focus, the reserve also protects a portion of the turn-of-the-century Vancouver Island telegraph trail, a First Nations village site, shell middens and a stone fish weir.

This newly protected area will likely soon have park status, as it's a key area for viewing killer whales at Robson Bight without disturbing the whales. Other species of note include eagle, marbled murrelet and a high population of phalarope.

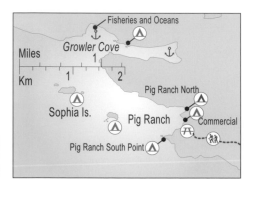

Boat Bay

On the point at the west end of the bay is a collection of tents on platforms and other structures for the ecological reserve warden and volunteers. A beach north of the campsite provides access to a trail that leads to the Eagle Eye Bluff whale research station and beyond to Pig Ranch. Otherwise the bay is used mainly as an anchorage that's strategic for northwest gales in Johnstone Strait. It's also the closest anchorage to Robson Bight and will be well used by commercial fishing boats during fishing season.

The east point of the bay is a beautiful rocky headland used as a commercial base camp (Spirit of the West). Other beaches around the bay offer marginal opportunities.

Pig Ranch

This is the colloquial name for the bay facing Sophia Islets south of Growler Cove on West Cracroft Island. The camping area is well used by kayakers and people associated with the Eagle Eye Bluff whale observation station. A vandal spray-painted the phrase "Pig Ranch" on a rock and the name has since stuck.

Hiking: N50°31.72' W126°36.56'. A trail leads from the beach up the hill to Eagle Eye Bluff, the whale research observation point. It's about one hour one way. Researchers here monitor killer whale movements with telescopes. Commercial tour groups often take lunch breaks at the trailhead.

Camping: N50°31.65' W126°36.85', Pig Ranch South Point. At this large and popular location, the choice sites are on platforms on a bluff overlooking Johnstone Strait (be sure to check their stability before using them). A small beach is located on the northwest side of the point. The central beach at Pig Ranch (N50°31.75' W126°36.58') is a commercial base camp (Out For Adventure).

N50°31.93' W126°36.55', Pig Ranch North. There's a large clearing in the trees to the west of the beach in the north cove of Pig Ranch.

Sophia Islands

These two islands, surrounded by several smaller islands and drying rocks, are a good place to kayak and an interesting camping option. The main northern island has a tiny beach on the east side giving access to bluffs that will accommodate a tent on a slope. There's also a possibility on the west side. It looks dubious but after seeing tents here with views clear along the main orca migration route, they appear to be wonderful places to camp—once you're set up.

The eastern of the two islands is a commercial base camp (Discovery Expeditions) and is highly modified for its use.

Place names: Sophia Cracroft was the niece of Sir John Franklin Cracroft.

Growler Cove

This is a strategic harbour during southeast gales. Fisheries and Oceans Canada maintains a monitoring base at the float at the north entrance to the cove.

Camping: N50°32.51' W126°37.33'. On the mid-north shore of the bay, a prominent point with a rough beach has a good, level clear area suitable for group use.

Cracroft Point

This is the west end of West Cracroft Island at the end of a long peninsula separating Baronet Passage and Johnstone Strait. Use caution when kayaking this area. Three waterways with strong currents meet here—Blackney Passage, Baronet Passage and Johnstone Strait. The flood flows south through Blackney Passage, east through Johnstone Strait and west through Baronet Passage—all opposing directions. On a flood this creates a large counter-clockwise circulation of the water.

The worst clash tends to be west and north of Cracroft Point toward Hanson Island. Rips and whirlpools will appear and you can actually see where the Blackney and Baronet waters meet at peak current in a clash of white water. Also, be aware of the possibility

The crushed shell beach at Klaoitsis Island.

of cruise ships entering Blackney Passage. Due to the currents at Cracroft Point you may not be in full control of a kayak (or even a small motorized boat) when a cruise ship suddenly appears. The line of travel of cruise ships is in close proximity to the point, just outside the worst of the turbulence. It's a good idea to monitor Channel 71 for ships passing the nearby call-in points before and during a crossing.

Baronet Passage

This is a narrow, interesting route along the south shore of Harbledown Island. Boaters avoid it because of the numerous rocks and shallows. The current can run about 3 knots, with turbulence possible around Walden Island and at a prominent point on the south shore about halfway along its length. Watch for some ruins along the south shore and scenic bluffs on Harbledown.

The flood current runs west through the passage. This is counter-intuitive, as Johnstone Strait floods east. The turn to flood is 5 minutes before Seymour Narrows and the turn to ebb 5 minutes after. This is at odds with the change at Blackney Passage, which is about an hour before Baronet Passage—another complication

Deteriorating buildings at Karlukwees.

in trying to figure out what kind of conditions you might find at Cracroft Point, if you're heading in that direction. Given all the potential difficulties, novice kayakers should avoid this area.

Klaoitsis Island

This is the main island in an attractive collection of islands, islets and reefs at the south confluence of Beware Passage, Baronet Passage and Clio Channel. Hidden behind it is Potts Lagoon, a boat haven. The lagoon is dotted with float homes and private holdings.

Place names: Major General A.E. Potts was a professor of agriculture at the University of Saskatchewan who led the Canadian Forces in the raid on Spitzbergen to destroy enemy installations.

Camping: N50°33.81' W126°29.19'. On the west end of Klaoitsis Island is a beautiful white clamshell beach. Above it a lightly vegetated spot could be a campsite. Otherwise, a short trail leads to a clear, forested space suitable for a group. This is a pretty area with the potential for some rock bluff campsites elsewhere among the group.

The first fishing boats arrive to anchor at Blinkhorn Peninsula at the end of the day.

Clio Channel

This channel continues along the south end of Turnour Island, connecting at the northeast with Lagoon Cove, Minstrel Island and eventually either Chatham Channel or Knight Inlet (see Chapter 8). It's a route that's well used as a sheltered alternative to Johnstone Strait. Currents are low, about 1 knot, with the flood setting to the west.

The visual highlight is bluffs on the northern extent of Turnour Island above a fish farm. Two bays, Turnour and Bones, indent the shoreline. A cannery operated until the early 1940s at Bones Bay. The remains are at the head of the bay, with a sports fishing camp to the southwest.

Place names: Capt. Nicholas E.B. Turnour was in command of HMS *Clio* on her second mission to the B.C. coast 1864–68. The 22-gun vessel was built in Sheerness in 1857.

Beware Passage

This is an interesting waterway dotted with rocks and islets. For kayakers it's ideal, with rock-ledge camping possibilities in many areas, particularly the double island in the centre of the passage west of the

Karlukwees reserve. The reserve is the site of a former village active until the 1950s; now the scrub has claimed most of what remains except for the deteriorating wharf and a few waterfront shacks. The village was exceptional; its carvings and art were the subject of works by famous Canadian artists Emily Carr and W.J. Phillips. It's worth looking up these works before visiting so you can appreciate what it was once like. A small island of graves was located opposite the village.

In the northwest entrance a bay south of Dead Point is backed by private land. A historic remnant is the wall and arch of a trading post built in the late 1800s.

Blinkhorn Peninsula

This peninsula is essentially an island joined to a headland by a narrow rocky bar. It shelters an expansive stone beach on the east side. A forest recreation site is set on the upland. The bay is occasionally used as an anchorage. During the commercial fishing season it will be a floating village of boats in the evening.

Place names: Thomas Blinkhorn and his wife, Anne, came in 1851 in the barque *Tory*; they were some of the first settlers not associated with the Hudson's Bay Company to arrive on Vancouver Island.

Camping: N50°32.48' W126°47.04'. The forest recreation site has several access points to clearings in the forest; a couple have picnic tables. Toward the spit is a clear gravel area outside the forest cover. Seek high ground, though, on a spring tide. A few portions of the gravel won't survive a high tide, and water will seep in despite the grassy embankment surrounding the site.

Travel notes: I spent a night here on the gravel embankment during a full moon, which may explain the behaviour of the mice. The creatures spent most of the night scrambling up and down my tent and climbing over the mesh. Eventually I felt a mouse run across my sleeping bag. Turning on a light I found one had chewed through the mesh on the tent door. After an aborted attempt to close the hole by pushing a pack up against it and having to chase another mouse from the tent, at 3 a.m. I found myself duct-taping the hole shut. The mice continued to scramble up the tent for several hours afterward. Sleeping was not an option.

Dozens of kayaks at Kaikash Creek—the odd combination of congestion and wilderness.

Kaikash Creek

This is the largest of several creeks along the south shore of Johnstone Strait between Blinkhorn Peninsula and Robson Bight. Just about every beach along this stretch is a kayaking camp of some sort, though many are undeveloped and require beach camping. The site at Kaikash Creek is almost certainly the busiest. The attraction, of course, is the killer whales transiting Johnstone Strait. Otherwise the waterfront is fairly unremarkable—rock shoreline with frequent grubby beaches fronted by kelp. The beaches can also become quite rocky and difficult to use at lower tide levels.

Camping: While there are many nice cobble beaches for camping, be sure of your tide clearance. Cruise ships passing in the middle of the night create surf, so be sure you have sufficient clearance for a 60- to 90-cm (2- to 3-foot) wake. Names of some campsites have been added to the regional map on page 462.

N50°31.46' W126°43.16', Little Kaikash. This site has a rock beach; a site on the point has a great view and there are several more sites back in the trees. There is room for several groups in the two sites here. It can be a popular place.

N50°31.27' W126°42.66', Adventure Beach. A rough trail up the west side of the beach leads to a clearing on the headland best suited to one tent. Access is difficult, but it's nice once you get here, so it suits a long-term camp rather than an overnight stay. The beach immediately to the northwest, known as Spy Hop Beach, is used exclusively by a commercial operation (Pacific Northwest).

N50°31.09' W126°41.97', Kaikash Creek. This is a large forest recreation site capable of accommodating multiple large groups, which happens quite often since commercial operators make regular use of it. This is apt to be the busiest site, with several dozen people any given night during the summer. The next beach to the east, 1.5 km away (about a mile) at N50°30.78' W126°40.42', is a quieter alternative with camping on the high-clearance cobble beach. There is no upland development. A slightly larger cobble beach, capable of supporting a small group, is located another kilometre (0.6 miles) southeast at N50°30.55' W126°39.61'.

N50°30.34' W126°39.32', Second Beach. There are two clear spots in the upland for camping. Otherwise you'll be using the gravel on the beach. The First Beach site to the southeast is a commercial base camp used throughout the summer.

N50°29.79' W126°37.73', Robson Bight border. This is a small but pleasant beach with some limited level areas up from the beach. It's within the ecological reserve boundary, but so close to the border that its use is, quite literally, borderline, and people occasionally try to squeeze in. Be warned you may be ushered away by reserve officials, but I have also witnessed campers staying there without incident.

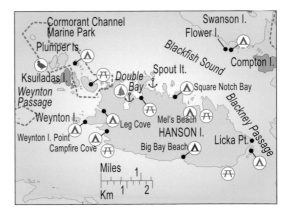

Hanson Island

This island isn't yet a park but is a protected area, except for the private holding at Double Bay, which is dominated by a marina. As part of the land claim negotiations still in progress, the First Nations of Mamalilikulla, Namgis and Tlowitsis have been given a head lease

Leaving Square Notch Bay in the fog.

for the management of the island, which allows them to approve recreation leases and tenures under the banner of the Yukusam Heritage
Society. This gives the island the distinction of private campsites on
otherwise Crown land. It's also home to OrcaLab. Dr. Paul Spong
first began a base for his orca research in a bay on northeast Hanson
Island in 1970, setting up a network of hydrophones for low-impact
monitoring of whale movements. For more information on his work
visit **www.orcalab.org.**

Anchorages are at Double Bay and behind Spout Island.

Ecological oddities: The north shore of Hanson Island has the highest
density of marbled murrelet in Queen Charlotte and Johnstone
straits. Rhinoceros aucklet is also common here in the summer.

Place names: James Hanson was lieutenant of the armed vessel
Chatham 1791–92.

Camping: Hanson Island has numerous campsites (though some are
of dubious quality), plus several commercial sites. Here are a few
choice locations.

N50°34.66' W126°43.73', Mel's Beach. This site on the north end of Hanson Island gets its name from the fellow who has camped here for more than 25 years. Behind the bay is a long and pleasant beach with numerous clear areas in the forest. The downside is an old vehicle and a huge low-bed truck trailer rusting near the shore.

N50°34.91' W126°44.22', Square Notch Bay. This is a pleasant cove on the central north end of the island; two rock ledges bracket the beach and extend outward into the bay. The ledges, particularly the west one, make great day-use destinations in an area where afternoon sunshine is otherwise blocked by trees.

N50°34.59' W126°46.66', Leg Cove. This deep cove northeast of Weynton Island has a good developed group site in the open forest alongside a gravel beach.

N50°34.32' W126°47.19', Weynton Island Point. The peninsula on Hanson Island facing Weynton Island is a commercial base camp (Kingfisher Adventures), which has been extensively developed. Four tent pads have been put aside for public use.

N50°34.08' W126°46.46', Campfire Cove. This cove southeast of Weynton Island is a developed site with benches and tables, but the sloping forest makes level areas hard to find. It could be a dispersed group site, with some spots well back in the forest.

N50°33.53' W126°43.90', Big Bay Beach. A rock beach gives access to an undeveloped and enclosed forest. This is the trailhead to a lookout, a large cedar tree (estimated to be about 1,200 years old) and OrcaLab. The neighbouring headland to the east of Big Bay is a tenured commercial base camp (Northern Lights) with no provisions for public camping.

N50°33.66' W126°41.66', Blackney Passage. South of Licka Point on the east side of Hanson Island are two islands. The largest island to the north has a rocky area on the south end that gives access to grassy, level bluffs. This is a pretty site, in large part due to a dwarf pine tree on the bluff. It's also right on the orca migration route through Blackney Passage.

Blackney Passage

This passage leads between the east side of Hanson Island and Parson Islands, joining Blackfish Sound with Baronet Passage and Johnstone Strait. It's prone to strong tidal currents, a maximum of about 5 knots, with the flood setting south. Beware of turbulence around Cracroft Point (see page 467). On the flood current, the flow

Waiting out the current on Plumper Islands.

split by Hanson Island meets near the south end of Blackney Passage, forming a race in mid-channel.

Place names: William Blackney was the Royal Navy paymaster on the B.C. coast 1863–65.

Plumper Islands

These islands extending northwest from Hanson Island are part of Cormorant Channel Marine Park, a network of islands, islets and rocks complicated by strong tidal currents. The currents within the islands can be quite perplexing, including the possibility of tidal rapids between Ksuiladas Island and the two most northerly islands. It's interesting, though, that while currents may be impassable or

Cormorant Channel Marine Park

This park encompasses three separate island clusters: the Pearse Islands, Plumper Islands and Stephenson Islet. It was established in 1992 to protect the rich marine environment, which is fed by cold, swift currents. This makes it ideal habitat for high populations of sea anemones, urchins, sponges, worms, and hydroids. Rare species are the northern abalone, pomegranate aeolid and raspberry hydroid. Bird species that make use of these islands include red-necked phalarope, marbled murrelet, auklet, petrel, shearwater, albatross and oystercatcher. Notable is the population of rockfish. The park protects 743 ha (1,836 acres).

Paddling the Broughtons.

even dangerous at that spot, the currents to the south of Ksuiladas Island will be relatively benign. Anyone wanting to avoid the worst of the currents can simply keep to the Hanson Island shore.

Plumper Islands and nearby Stephenson Islet, also part of the park, shelter breeding populations of pigeon guillemot, black oystercatcher and glaucous-winged gull.

Place names: The *Plumper* was an auxiliary steam sloop launched at Portsmouth in 1848. It served on the B.C. coast 1857–61 as a survey vessel.

BROUGHTON ARCHIPELAGO MARINE PARK

Broughton Archipelago is a kayaking wonderland of forested islands, rocky islets and kelp waterways in close proximity to two major marine thoroughfares—Queen Charlotte and Johnstone straits. Its main drawback is repetitious scenery of rocky and generally inaccessible shoreline. Sand beaches are almost non-existent. However, most areas do have their charm, particularly the outer (western) islands. The beaches are few and campsites even more rare. The best ones are the many pocket crushed clamshell beaches at the north end of the archipelago, but most are undeveloped—more proof most

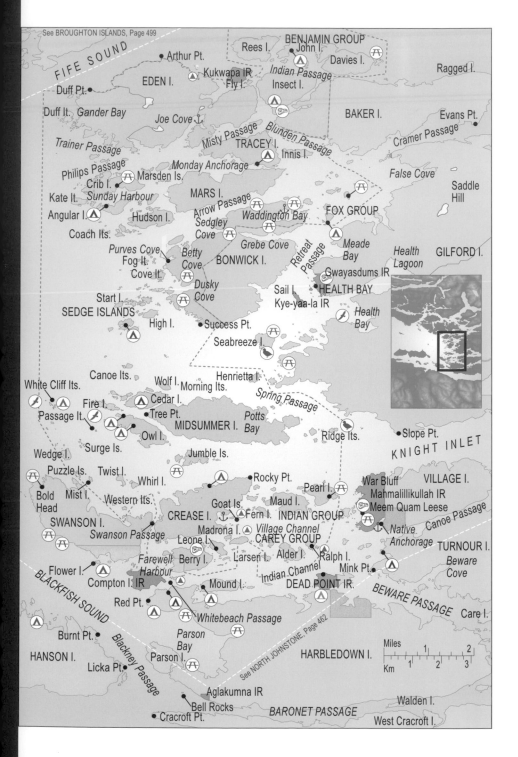

FIFE SOUND

BENJAMIN GROUP

Rees I.   John I.

Arthur Pt.   Davies I.   Ragged I.

EDEN I.   Kukwapa IR   Indian Passage

Duff Pt.   Fly I.   Insect I.   BAKER I.   Evans Pt.

Duff It. Gander Bay

Joe Cove   Misty Passage   Blunden Passage   Cramer Passage

Trainer Passage   TRACEY I.

Innis I.   False Cove   Saddle Hill

Philips Passage   Marsden Is.   Monday Anchorage

Crib I.   MARS I.   FOX GROUP

Kate It. Sunday Harbour   Arrow Passage   Waddington Bay   Meade Bay   Health Lagoon   GILFORD I.

Angular I.   Hudson I.   Sedgley Cove   Grebe Cove   Gwayasdums IR

Coach Its.   Purves Cove   Betty Cove   BONWICK I.   Retreat Passage   HEALTH BAY

Fog It.   Sail I.

Cove It.   Dusky Cove   Kye-yaa-la IR   Health Bay

Start I.   SEDGE ISLANDS   High I.   Success Pt.

Seabreeze I.

Canoe Its.   Wolf I.   Henrietta I.   Morning Its.   Spring Passage

White Cliff Its.   Cedar I.

Fire I.   Tree Pt.   Potts Bay

Passage It.   MIDSUMMER I.

Owl I.   Surge Is.   Jumble Is.   Ridge Its.   Slope Pt.   KNIGHT INLET

Wedge I.   Puzzle Is.   Twist I.   Whirl I.   Rocky Pt.   War Bluff   VILLAGE I.

Bold Head   Mist I.   Western Its.   Pearl I.   Mahmalillikullah IR

Goat Is.   Maud I.   Meem Quam Leese

SWANSON I.   CREASE I.   Fern I.   INDIAN GROUP

Swanson Passage   Madrona I.   Village Channel   Native Anchorage   Canoe Passage   TURNOUR I.

Leone I.   CAREY GROUP   Beware Cove

Flower I.   Farewell Harbour   Berry I.   Larsen I.   Alder I.   Ralph I.   Mink Pt.

Compton I. IR   Indian Channel   DEAD POINT IR   BEWARE PASSAGE   Care I.

Red Pt.   Mound I.

BLACKFISH SOUND   Whitebeach Passage

Burnt Pt.   Parson Bay

HANSON I.   Parson I.   HARBLEDOWN I.

Licka Pt.   Blackney Passage

Aglakumna IR

Bell Rocks   Walden I.

Cracroft Pt.   BARONET PASSAGE   West Cracroft I.

See NORTH JOHNSTONE, Page 462

Miles
1   2
Km
1   2   3

people don't venture far from Johnstone Strait.

Place names: Capt. George Vancouver named Broughton Strait, Broughton Island and Broughton Archipelago in 1792 after Lt. Commander William Robert Broughton, captain of *Chatham*. He was in command of the sloop *Providence* when it arrived in Nootka in 1796.

A collapsed totem at Meem Quam Leese.

Travel notes: Some interpretations define the Broughton Archipelago as only those islands south of Fife Sound—essentially the islands within the park. Officially, the name encompasses all the islands and islets within the border of Wells Passage, Patrick Passage, Sutlej Channel, Pasley Passage, Penphrase Passage, Tribune Channel, Nickoll Passage, Chatham Channel, Johnstone Strait, Weynton Passage and Nowell Channel. This includes the Broughton Islands and Gilford Island. However, the islands protected by the provincial park are geographically distinct, so most references to the Broughton Archipelago in this book refer to the smaller park cluster. The area to the north is referred to as either Broughton Islands or Grappler Sound.

Village Island

The shoreline of Village Island along Knight Inlet and Canoe Passage is mainly rugged rock with little more than rubble beaches. The west end, however, is marked by long stretches of good beach, behind which is the abandoned village of Meem Quam Leese (*Mamalilaculla*). It was inhabited until the 1960s, when the village was relocated to Alert Bay to centralize medical and other services. The result is a collection of abandoned buildings and even totems that are still accessible. The village is most famous for the raid on a potlatch in 1921. Forty-five people were charged with offences such as dancing and carrying gifts to recipients. Twenty-two people received sentences of two to six months in prison. Many ceremonial items, such as masks and coppers, were seized and distributed to both museums

Camping on a rock bluff in the Indian Group.

and private collections. Fortunately many pieces have been recovered and are on display at the U'Mista Cultural Centre in Alert Bay.

Today the village of Meem Quam Leese is open to the public through interpretive tours. A dock is located on the north side of the point for boat access, while kayakers may wish to stop at the expansive beach to the south directly in front of the village.

If you wish access to the island but do not wish a tour, permission is required from the band at **250-287-2955**. A fee applies.

On the south of Village Island is Native Anchorage. A private holding on the east side of the cove has an old cabin, remnants of a pioneer farm.

Indian and Carey groups

Two clusters of islands west of Village Island are bordered by Harbledown, Crease and Berry islands and Knight Inlet. They are separated by Village Channel. The island clusters are generally joined by foul ground, making them unnavigable by boat but perfect for kayaking. Most of the islands are within Broughton Archipelago Marine Park, but an exception is Alder Island, which is privately owned. Off the west end of Larsen Island is a large fish farm that degrades the appeal of the surrounding island cluster. On the north end of Harbledown Island is a reserve, the Da'naxda'xw ancestral home, Tsatsisnukwomi, abandoned for many years. It's now returning to life with a flurry of construction, much of it aimed at tourism. A program of a salmon barbecue, Da'naxda'xw legends and dance is offered weekly. Camping is also available, with kayak-friendly beaches. Visit **www.danaxdaxw.com**. The Da'naxda'xw heritage is also evident at Mound Island, where depressions indicate the location of 14 ancient big houses.

Camping: Rock bluff camping is a possibility throughout the islets in this area, but be warned: several near Meem Quam Leese and one south of Ralph Island in the Carey Group are historic First Nations burial islands. The remains have since been re-interred in concrete housings, but the islands should still be left undisturbed.

N50°35.49' W126°39.34', Mound Island. On the southwest corner of the island a wonderful white clamshell beach gives access to an expansive clear forest area. Choice but exposed campsites are either next to the beach or on the level portion of a connected islet. Many more sites are within the forest. A second group campsite is on the same side of Mound Island slightly to the north at a rougher beach, with upland access via a wooden ladder.

N50°35.48' W126°40.36', Whitebeach Passage. West of Mound Island on Harbledown Island is a bit of a bay with a rough beach that provides access to the forest. This is a good potential overflow site for Mound Island.

Parson Bay

This bay indents the west side of Harbledown Island and appears huge from the entrance, but it really isn't, extending just 3 km (under 2 miles) from Red Point to the head. The bay isn't often visited because there isn't much to see—the shoreline is unremarkable rolling hills. There are many beaches, but most would make dubious campsites. Parson Island is located off the south peninsula of the bay, creating a narrow but navigable channel.

Camping: N50°35.15' W126°40.74', Red Point. This site just southeast of Red Point is a popular location with an upper and lower site in the woods. Be sure to look for the fossils at the beach.

Blackfish Sound

This waterway lies between Swanson Island to the north and Hanson and Plumper islands to the south. Migrating killer whales often enter Robson Bight by travelling north around Malcolm Island, then through Blackfish Sound and Blackney Passage into Johnstone Strait. There are also large populations of migratory and other birds in the sound, including marbled murrelet, bald eagle, mew gull, rhinoceros auklet, common murre, phalarope and sooty shearwater. This is part of the traditional territory of the Mamalilikulla-Qwe'Qwa'Sot'Em and Namgis, with a reserve at Compton Island.

Blackfish Sound is one of those areas that can be remarkably gentle or notoriously turbulent, to the point of being dangerous. During spring tides whirlpools and eddies can appear. Currents run as high as 3 knots, but will usually be much less.

Place names: Blackfish is an alternative name for killer whales.

Crease and Swanson islands

These two islands join together in a sort of wing shape, separated by Swanson Passage. The lower portion of Swanson Island at Freshwater Bay is private property. It began as a store and fish-buying camp in 1914. An ABC Packing Company saltery followed in 1919. Today you'll find a commercial camp at the bay and accommodation just to the west at Hemlock House Lodge. This is worth knowing about if you're in the area during several days of rain and need somewhere to dry out.

A fish farm dominates the north side of Swanson Island.

The bay on the south side of Crease Island near Fern Island is a popular anchorage, while the southwest side of Berry Island, south of Crease Island, is the Farewell Harbour Yacht Club. It has washrooms, showers and a store with snacks. Trails lead from the yacht club around Berry Island.

A main petroglyph in the Broughton Archipelago is located on the rock face on the north side of Berry Island. Near it is a natural rock basin that fills at high tide, known as the Chief's Bathtub. Legend tells of the local chief bathing in the basin, the water warmed with stones heated in a nearby fire.

Place names: Henry Pering Pellew Crease (1823–95) was a judge for the Supreme Court of Canada 1870–95. Farewell Harbour was the last place Pender surveyed aboard the *Beaver* in 1870—the name being a farewell to the coast.

White Cliff Islets.

Camping: There are rough beaches along the southwest side of Swanson Island facing Blackfish Sound. While any could possibly be used as a campsite, none are really worth mentioning, as other better alternatives are so close by.

N50°36.03' W126°42.33', Flower Island. On the east side of the island is a good gravel beach with five spacious and private sites facing the waterfront. This is an exceptionally pretty site.

N50°37.58' W126°39.09', North Crease Island. Just under a mile (1.5 km) west of Rocky Point on the north side of Crease Island is a fine sand and pebble beach. Neap tide camping is possible on the sand at the top of the east end of the beach. Otherwise several access points lead into the forest, with some rough clearings for campsites and even an outhouse. Considering the quality of the beach and the potential for good sites, this is an oddly underdeveloped and under-utilized spot. For small groups this is a beautiful and, for the time being, secluded location.

Owl and Midsummer islands

Owl and Midsummer islands are the largest of a central cluster between the entrance of Knight Inlet to the south and Spring Passage to the north. The north end of Midsummer Island is dominated by a fish farm adjacent to Cedar Island, with another to the east in Potts Bay.

Knight Inlet can be as moody at the entrance as it is along its length. Currents run as high as 3 knots, and usually more powerfully on the ebb. For kayakers this can mean a jumble of turbulence at the entrance between Fire Island and Swanson Island when all is calm elsewhere. At Owl Island the average peak velocity is about 2.5 knots, with the flood current setting southeast at 120°. Currents will also run strong around Cedar and Wolf islands.

The offshore islands—those farthest west—are conspicuous for the white rocks, particularly White Cliff Islets. The entire area is a good place to see marine birds such as common murre, rhinoceros auklet, fork-tailed storm-petrel and phalarope.

Camping: N50°38.79' W126°41.45', Owl Island South. In the deepest bay facing Knight Inlet is a beach with sand at low and high tides but rocks during most tide levels. A large clear area in the forest is suitable for group camping.

N50°38.97' W126°41.70', Owl Island North. Just east of the north tip of the island behind a bit of a headland is a small cove with a sand and gravel beach. Behind it an open, spacious forest would absorb a huge group of campers. This is a superior site, and correspondingly popular.

N50°39.17' W126°41.25', Cedar Island. On the south end of Cedar Island is a good gravel and sand beach with a spacious clearing in the forest. This is a good alternative to the nearby and potentially busier Owl Island campsite.

N50°39.20' W126°43.80', White Cliff Islets. This may seem like a remote cluster, but it's less than a mile (1.5 km) west of Fire Island. These islands will appeal to rugged campers. The easternmost islet is a low, level mound of bedrock with some grassy or rock areas suitable for tents. Access is by rock ledge. Make sure wherever you land is convenient to the area you want to camp at, as the craggy rocks make access along the entire islet difficult. Probably the best access is on the east side.

Retreat Passage

This is a relatively sheltered waterway leading along the northwest side of Gilford Island, separating it and Bonwick Island. It's a key thoroughfare for marine traffic to Health Bay and Echo Bay. Numerous island clusters and deep bays mean almost unlimited possibilities for exploring the area. Most of the Bonwick Island shoreline is outside the Broughton Archipelago Marine Park boundary, which is reflected in the logging and a log dump in Grebe Cove. Waddington Bay is a popular anchorage.

Health Bay on Gilford Island is Gwayasdums, a Kwicksutaineuk-Ah Kwaw-ah-mish reserve with a restaurant, laundromat, clinic and longhouse. The community of about 54 is served by boat and float plane. Look for the fish traps in Health Lagoon.

Broughton Archipelago Marine Park and extension

The Broughton Archipelago Marine Park plays a central role in the tourist industry of north Vancouver Island, attracting kayakers, boaters, fishermen, divers and whale watchers to the maze of wilderness islands. It also preserves significant First Nations cultural history; the inventory consists of 38 shell middens associated with former village sites, pictographs, fortified refuge sites, stone canoe skids and fish traps. European heritage is evident in a few overgrown homesteads and shipwrecks. The park was established in 1992 and protects 11,679 ha (45 square miles).

In April 2006 the process for expanding the park was moved forward with the protection of the Broughton Extension lands, adding many key islands previously within the park boundaries but excluded from the park. These include Eden Island, Mars Island, the north and west portions of Bonwick Island, Midsummer Island, Crease Island and the north end of Swanson Island. Cullen Harbour is also included, as well as many smaller but previously unprotected islands.

Late afternoon in Cramer Passage.

Note that a magnetic anomaly can knock readings off by as much as 18°, particularly near Meade Bay.

Kayakers will undoubtedly be drawn to the Fox Group, a pretty cluster of islands and islets in the middle of the passage east of Waddington Bay. Another cluster at the south entrance is dominated by Seabreeze Island. It and Ridge Rocks in nearby Spring Passage are nesting sites for black oystercatcher and glaucous-winged gull. Health Bay and Shoal Bay are heavily used by migratory birds. Gull and cormorant also nest on Green Rock, south of Bonwick Island.

Place names: Charles Bonwick was the acting chief engineer aboard HM *Beaver* while it surveyed the coast from 1863 to 1870.

Camping: N50°42.95' W126°35.74', South Fox Group. A good site in the Fox Group is on the southernmost island (marked "66" on chart 3546). A gravel beach on the southwest corner gives access to two distinct clear areas on the south headland facing a connected islet. This could house a small group. Other good beaches can be found in the group and around Seabreeze Island.

Sedge Islands
The Sedge Islands are part of a maze of islets and rocks that lie off the west side of Bonwick Island. It makes for excellent kayaking.

Unfortunately, good beaches are rare. In the event of winds, stay out of Queen Charlotte Strait and in the lee of the islands. Kayakers should be able to find a protected route almost all the way along Bonwick Island. For breaks, good beaches are to the north and south of Dusky Cove. They could serve as campsites in a pinch.

Camping: N50°40.83' W126°41.66'. On the largest of the Sedge Islands ("55" on chart 3546) a narrow, deep bay cuts into the west side. Though it faces the prevailing weather, the bay is protected by an off-lying islet, rocks and kelp. Surf shouldn't be a factor. The beach is rock with cobble at the head. Camping is possible on the grass between the beach and the scrub. There is also rough trail access into the island from here.

Arrow Passage
This waterway separates Mars and Bonwick islands. It's exposed to westerlies but is a good escape route to the Fox Group if you've been exploring the outer islands and the wind picks up. A fish farm is in Betty Cove.

Sunday Harbour
This anchorage is protected by a cluster of islands that, along with the Sedge Islands to the south, make for a great area to kayak. There are rough beaches on both Crib and Angular islands for a break.

Camping: N50°43.18' W126°42.26', Angular Island. For a spot best suited to a single tent, I suggest a clam beach off the northwest end of Angular Island that connects a rocky islet. There is no upland access, but camping is possible at most tide levels on the clamshell bar. The campsite may lack space, but the surrounding cove is certainly unique, with numerous rocky islets and waterways in view in just about every direction. Groups will want to head to the beach at Crib Island.

Monday Anchorage
This anchorage is a bit of a cove between Tracey and Mars islands. It's not for all mariners; there are numerous rocks and hazards to navigate. Kayakers will be most at home here, especially in the pass where it narrows on the east side.

Taking a break on a clamshell beach facing Fife Sound.

Camping: N50°44.03' W126°37.91'. On Tracey Island just west of the narrowest portion of the channel east of Monday Anchorage is a great clamshell beach with a good level area. Camping is safest from high tides off the beach in the forest behind. It could accommodate a group.

Benjamin Group

Baker and Eden islands are separated by the wedge of Insect Island. A long-inhabited village here, Hohopa, at the south end, was used by the Kwicksutaineuk, Tsawataineuk and Gwawaenuk.

The Benjamin Group is a pretty selection of rarely visited islands with numerous clamshell beaches and no developed campsites. Off the east end of Davies Island is a great selection of clamshell beaches for a break. The cove on Eden Island west of Fly Island has a good selection of beaches; camping would be possible on the bedrock outcrop between the two beaches at the head of the cove.

Place names: Charles Eden (1808–1878) was Lord of the Admiralty 1859–60. The origin for the Benjamin Group isn't known. Lt. Baker was keeper of the ship's log for the *Discovery*, which surveyed here in 1792.

Camping: N50°45.23' W126°37.51', Insect Island. A good clamshell beach is just northwest of the south point of Insect Island. A steep trail leads up the dirt bank to the level upland, which is an expansive and developed area suitable for numerous groups. An alternative access point is up the rocks to the south of the beach. This is the key campsite for the north end of Broughton Archipelago Marine Park.

N50°46.35' W126°36.85', John Island. In the middle of the three main islands in the Benjamin Group is a good clamshell beach in the cove facing southeast. It must receive almost no wave action; all the fallen branches and twigs have grown barnacles apparently where they fell, an indication they aren't washed aside in surf. There is no upland access (yet), but there is a good, level bedrock outcrop on the south end of the cove. It could host up to four tents or so.

BROUGHTON STRAIT

Broughton Strait is a continuation of the main marine route west of Johnstone Strait. The northern border is Pearse Islands, Cormorant Island and the west side of Malcolm Island. North of Pearse Islands and Cormorant Island is Cormorant Channel. Both are busy commercial and recreational corridors used by the communities of Telegraph Cove, Port McNeill, Alert Bay on Cormorant Island and Sointula on Malcolm Island. For kayakers it's a gateway to the Broughton Archipelago and whale watching in Johnstone Strait. The main shipping channel is to the south of Cormorant Island. Westbound traffic will divide and head north of Haddington Island. Eastbound traffic will pass to the south. Currents will reach 4 knots, with the potential for strong countercurrents east of Alert Bay.

Telegraph Cove

Telegraph Cove was the end of the telegraph line from Campbell River along the Vancouver Island shore in 1912. It gained new life in the Second World War as a relay station. The boardwalk and many of the historic buildings remain as cottages, art galleries or restaurants. It has evolved into the main staging ground for trips into the Broughton Archipelago and Johnstone Strait. Unfortunately, the original charm of the community has been severely diminished by recent development. Across the cove from the boardwalk community is a new marina completely out of scale with the rest of Telegraph Cove. In addition, the headland has been blasted to make way for a housing development. Services include the store, post office

(V0N 3J0), accommodation, RV camping, showers, washrooms, laundry, dining, phones, rentals and tours.

An alternative staging ground is the Alder Bay Resort, located between the Nimpkish River and Telegraph Cove. The resort has a separate kayak launch from the boat launch, parking, camping, RV camping, laundry, showers and a store. To get there, turn off Highway 19 at Bear Cove Road. Travel east for 6 km (3.7 miles) and turn north onto Alder Bay Road.

Launches: Launching is available at the cove, which is now accessible by a paved road. If your visit is to last more than a week, make sure to check for a weekly parking rate or for different rates among the various lots.

The outer shore of Malcolm Island.

Beaver Cove

Telegraph Cove is a notch off the much larger Beaver Cove, a busy industrial area with a lumber mill, log dump and barge facility to the southeast. It's littered with ruins: a disused ferry slip on the northeast corner where the old Kelsey Bay ferry once berthed, a service that ended in 1979; and the old Nimpkish Iron Mines conveyor to the north of the ferry slip. The east side of the cove is dotted with resorts and boathouses.

Nimpkish River

This large river drains Nimpkish Lake and is blocked from navigation by rapids. Large flats are located on both sides of the river. Good beaches are nearby. Northwest on the headland is the community of Hyde Creek and the start of the development associated with Port McNeill that extends westward.

Place names: Capt. George Vancouver first met the Namgis people at the river, Gwa'ni, in 1792. The name was anglicized into Nimpkish.

Weynton Passage

This passage leads between Pearse and Hanson islands, between Johnstone Strait, Broughton Strait, Blackfish Sound and Cormorant Channel. In addition, the tidal waters from Queen Charlotte Strait enter Weynton Passage as they round Malcolm Island. The convergence of so much water can lead to potentially dangerous conditions. Currents can reach 6 knots, and to help manage them Weynton Passage earns its own current listings in *Canadian Tide and Current Tables, Volume 6*. The flood sets south and the ebb north. Turbulence can be encountered near any of the islands.

Pearse Islands

This is a group of closely associated islands with strong tidal currents through most channels. There are mainly rough pocket beaches. Most islands are protected in Cormorant Island Marine Park, but the west side of the largest island is private property and developed with homes and cottages facing Cormorant Island. Numerous rocks and islets lying off the west end would be suitable for a kayak break.

Place names: Commander William Alfred Rumbulow Pearse commanded HMS *Alert* on the coast 1858–61.

Camping: N50°35.11' W126°51.56'. Two large islands in the middle cluster of the Pearse Islands are joined at low tides. On chart 3546 all islands have an elevation number save one. That one has a good beach to the south and a rough one to the east, facing island "88." It's a bit dubious as a campsite, but usable. Another potential spot is on the southeast of the largest island at a headland that may be difficult to reach from the beach.

Pearse Passage

Pearse Passage is a narrow channel (less than a mile/1.2 km) between Cormorant Island and Pearse Islands. Currents run at a maximum of about 4 knots. There is no current station here; use Weynton Passage. The flood sets south. This can mean tide rips and countercurrents throughout the passage.

Cormorant Island and Alert Bay

This island is fringed mainly by rocky beaches. There is no bedrock on the island; it's a layer of gravel and rock left by glaciers over a ridge of sand. Homes line most of the south and southeast shore. The Namgis reserve to the west is mostly undeveloped. A trail leads through the reserve to a beach on the west shore near Yellow Bluff, the distinct cliff on the southwest end of the island.

The community of Alert Bay occupies the bay of the same name on Cormorant Island. Most of the amenities run north-south along the waterfront. Entering from the east you'll first see the Alert Bay Shipyards. A short distance north is the government wharf, where water and a garbage dropoff are available. Visitors can moor for several hours to visit the town. A boat ramp is immediately north. The ferry slip is about a half-kilometre (0.3 miles) farther along. Regular vehicle ferry service is offered between Alert Bay and Port McNeill. North of the ferry terminal is the Alert Bay Boat Harbour. Various other wharves, including the original BC Packers plant wharf, lie between. The saltery, first

A totem outside the former residential school at Alert Bay.

built in 1870, played a key role in the development of the village, attracting steamship service in 1889. The plant has since closed and the building been removed.

Watch for strong tidal currents in the bay.

Alert Bay is a full-service community with restaurants, stores, a hospital, hotels, pubs, a laundromat and a post office (V0N 1A0). Most services are near the waterfront, which is bordered by a neatly manicured walkway. Alert Bay has embraced its cultural heritage with a strong tourism program that includes a show of traditional dancing at the ceremonial big house on the reserve and the U'Mista Cultural Centre, which displays the potlatch items—and their incredible artistry—seized during the famous 1921 potlatch at Meem Quam Leese (see page 479). Other attractions are the totems of the Namgis burial ground in the downtown and the Alert Bay

Ecological Park, which offers the opportunity for a walk through a boggy setting. Interpretive pamphlets for all the attractions can be picked up at the visitor's centre on the waterfront near the government wharf.

Place names: HM *Alert* was a screw corvette with 17 guns, the first steam vessel to call at Alert Bay. It was built in Pembroke in 1856 and served the B.C. coast 1858–61 and again 1865–69. In 1867 the vessel was used to resurvey Alert Bay. The native village was known as Yeleese, Ilis or Yalis, a word meaning "spreading leg on beach," as in a bay bounded by two narrow points. This was a winter village site for the Mamalilikulla, Tlowitsis, Kwakiutl and Namgis.

Weather

Alert Bay	May	June	July	Aug.	Sept.	Dec.	Av./Ttl.
Daily average temp. (C)	10.1	12.0	14.0	14.3	12.3	3.7	8.5
Daily maximum (C)	14.1	15.7	17.9	18.2	16.1	5.6	11.6
Daily minimum (C)	6.1	8.3	10.0	10.4	8.4	1.7	5.4
Precipitation (mm)	73.7	81.0	50.5	65.4	91.3	209.6	1591.5
Days of rainfall + 0.2mm	17.0	15.6	12.5	12.5	14.5	20.4	205.5
Days with rainfall +5mm	4.8	5.4	3.7	4.3	5.9	11.6	91.9
Days with rainfall +10mm	2.0	2.4	1.4	2.0	3.4	6.6	50.0
Days with rainfall +25mm	0.18	0.22	0.04	0.26	0.57	1.8	10.3

Cormorant Channel

This channel separates Cormorant and Pearse islands from Malcolm Island. Currents can run at several knots and will be strongest near Donegal Head on Malcolm Island. The shoreline of Malcolm Island facing Cormorant Channel is mainly private property. A road runs along the waterfront. Mitchell Bay has a public float to serve a small community that fronts the bay. Kayakers needing a break will find numerous cobble beaches along the south side of Cormorant Island.

Ecological oddities: The channel is habitat for the critically imperilled 20-tentacled sea cucumber (*Thyonidium*).

Place names: The *Cormorant* was a six-gun paddle sloop built in 1842 that was the first naval steam vessel on the B.C. coast. It served 1844–50. Capt. William Mitchell (1802–76) arrived on the B.C. coast in 1837. The nearby points and islands are named after officers of the *Thetis*.

Port McNeill

This is a full-service community of about 2,800. Due to its distance from Johnstone Strait and the Broughton Archipelago, kayakers don't often use it but it would make a good staging ground for trips to Malcolm Island. The port has a busy government wharf, marinas and a boat ramp (N50°35.41'

Character buildings line the Sointula waterfront.

W127°05.36'); long-term pay parking is available. The town has a post office (V0N 2R0), hospital, stores, hotels, restaurants and a laundromat across from the government wharf. Showers are available at the harbour.

Place names: Capt. William Henry McNeill (1803–75) commanded the *Beaver* in 1837.

Sointula

A group of Finns founded Sointula in 1901 as a socialist commune—an attempt to create a Utopia. They built a foundry, sawmill and blacksmith shop, but it lasted only four years before the residents disbanded. The communal principle lives on in the Co-op store founded in 1909, the oldest in the province. It's located near the government wharf north of Dickenson Point that doubles as the ferry dock for service to Port McNeill. A small craft harbour in Rough Bay is protected by a breakwater.

The lighthouse at Pulteney Point.

Place names: Sointula is Finnish for "place of harmony."

Pulteney Point

A lighthouse and weather station for the region sit on the point, which is a long gravel bar topped by the light and associated buildings. The lighthouse was first constructed in 1905.

The area east of Pulteney Point is mainly rock beach with occasional lengths of good cobble. The beach improves considerably around and northwest of Pulteney Point toward Graeme Point, where the shore essentially becomes unbroken cobble until Malcolm Point. Kayakers will enjoy the beaches along this stretch, but kelp grows along the shore almost non-stop between Pulteney and Lizard points. The best place to kayak is the small, clear strip between the shore and the kelp.

Camping: N50°39.10' W127°08.88'. Kayakers wishing to pull out along the southwest shore of Malcolm Island will find a multitude of choices. Be sure to avoid the private property near the point, but otherwise just about any beach is fair game. Most of the beaches have high-backed cobble with drift logs. Find a flat location on the cobble or among the drift logs. Upland clearings are rare.

Malcolm Point

The shore from Graeme Point to Malcolm Point is an almost continuous cobble beach. The Malcolm Point area is accessible by trail from a nearby road. The trailhead is N50°40.00' W127°07.21'.

Camping: An extensive beach means many choices. Kayakers may be tempted to land near the point, but be warned the beach is steep and prone to crashing surf—that is, waves may break onto the cobble. Favour the area closer to the trailhead.

Place names: Sir Pulteney Malcolm (1758–1838) served with Nelson's fleet, but never made the Battle of Trafalgar. He

Cobble and driftwood camping on outer Malcolm Island.

was held up by a refit in Gibraltar. He met Napoleon in 1816, who wrote of the encounter, "I never yet beheld a man of whom I so immediately formed a good opinion of as that fine, soldier-like man."

Bere Point

The beach at Bere Point is one of those rare places on the B.C. coast where the shape of the pebbles and the beach is just right for orcas to visit for a rub. It's a good whale watching location regardless, as it's on the migration route for killer whales entering Johnstone Strait. Bere Point has been used as a whale research campsite for a number of years. Also at the point is the Bere Point Regional Park and Campsite, with 22 sites in the trees near the beach. Picnic tables are offered for day use. There's no running water but there is free firewood. A high-tide boat launch gives the possibility of making this a staging ground for kayak trips. The park is the start of the Beautiful Bay Trail that runs for 2.5 km (1.5 miles) along a ridge west of the park with beach accesses along the way. The beach is almost continuous cobble along this portion of the island.

Lizard Point

This represents the northeast extremity of Malcolm Island and is the tip of a series of generally good to excellent beaches, with some boulder areas. Except for some private property between Bere and Bowlder points, you're welcome to stop where you like. Toward Lizard Point in Trinity Bay, the beach is backed by sand cliffs. A good camping possibility is farther northeast toward Lizard Point. Look for the lone petroglyph on a boulder just below the high tide line at the point. The eastern extent of the island is Donegal Head, notable for its white earth cliff. Currents will be most extreme around the head. Kayakers can take advantage of the current while navigating the north end of the island, but watch for countercurrents in the bays between the various points. Lizard Point is a Vessel Traffic Services call-in point.

Queen Charlotte Strait

This wide body of water separates north Vancouver Island from the mainland between Knight Inlet and Queen Charlotte Sound—essentially an inner water of the Pacific Ocean. It's generally 20 km (12 miles) wide; the shortest point, between Malcolm and Broughton islands, is just 12.5 km (7.8 miles). It's a major transportation route and a major salmon migration route, especially for coho. Killer and minke whales feed here in the summer.

Currents set southeast on the flood and northwest on the ebb, with the strongest ebbs and weakest floods along the north shore due to the influence of fresh water. Currents will run as high as 3 knots in George Passage, which runs between Foster Island and the northeast side of Malcolm Island. The prevailing northwest winds in the summer may strengthen the floods elsewhere in the strait.

Remote island clusters dot the eastern end of Queen Charlotte Strait. Foster Island is conspicuous for its cone-shaped hill on the south end. Twin and Penfold islands are a breeding area for black oystercatcher, glaucous-winged gull and pigeon guillemot. Penfold Islet is a Steller's sea lion haulout.

Between Foster Island and Holford Islets is Salmon Channel, where currents can reach 3 knots. Shoals and drying rocks are sure to keep boats at a distance. Numas Islands are 6 km (3.7 miles) from the mainland shore. They are used by migratory birds, and most notably rhinoceros auklets. About 550 pairs are known to nest here on the edge of all the vegetated islands. Expect dense salal on most upland areas. Beaches are rare on any of these islands, and their remoteness makes them poor candidates for visits by kayak.

Place names: Queen Charlotte was the wife of George III. They married in 1761; she died in 1818.

BROUGHTON ISLANDS

For most kayakers the adventure ends well south of the Broughton Islands. For those who make the journey, the adventure begins. Sutlej Channel and Wells Passage give access to an array of interesting coves

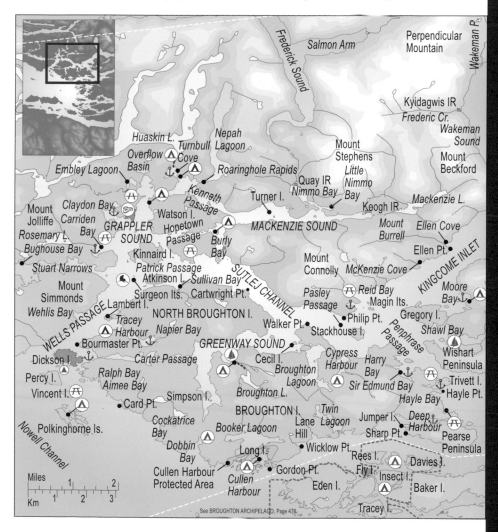

See BROUGHTON ARCHIPELAGO, Page 478.

A pod of dolphins at play, Grappler Sound.

and waterways rich in wildlife. I believe this to be one of the great, underused kayaking destinations on the south coast.

Fife Sound
This waterway separates Broughton Archipelago Marine Park from Broughton Island. Currents are minimal. Development is limited to fish farms at Wicklow Point and Deep Harbour. Migratory birds use most of the sound; common visitors are marbled murrelet, common merganser, gull, common murre, barrow's goldeneye and Pacific loon. Both killer whales and humpbacks can be found here on occasion. The Broughton Island shore is deeply indented, with Twin Lagoon's entrance drying at low tides. During strongest currents it can be a tidal falls.

Place names: James Duff (1729–1809) was the second earl of Fife. Capt. George Vancouver named the sound in 1792.

Penphrase Passage
This passage runs along the east end of Broughton Island. Several bays indent the shores; most can be used as anchorages, and there are boat

havens at Laura Bay and the western end of Trivett Island. The passage between Broughton and Trivett islands dries at lower tides. The clam bed beach at the junction, one of many in the area, can make a good rest spot. Wishart Peninsula on the east shoreline is a prominent cliff —a visual highlight. Expect to see many birds here, including western grebe, common murre, marbled murrelet, goldeneye, gull, grebe and common merganser. In Sir Edmund Bay is an abandoned logging camp and a fish farm. Look for the pictographs on the bluff.

A humpback breaches in Penphrase Passage.

Place names: Sir Edmund Walker Head was governor of the Hudson's Bay Company 1863–68.

Shawl and Moore bays

Shawl Bay is a developed area with a multitude of floathouses and a floating marina. The Shawl Bay Marina welcomes kayakers. It has a kayak area, washrooms, showers, laundry, a store, water, a restaurant, a telephone and Internet access. Cabins can be rented.

Shawl Bay is connected to Moore Bay by a narrow but navigable channel on the east end of Gregory Island. Moore Bay is undeveloped and used as an anchorage.

Camping: N50°52.75' W126°32.36'. On the west end of Moore Bay is a forest recreation campsite. A dock is available, though it's built high and not much use for kayaks. The neighbouring beach is rough and rocky. In the forest are good clear areas with picnic tables, benches, fire pits and an outhouse.

Sutlej Channel

This channel runs along the north end of Broughton and North Broughton islands. It has low currents and few beaches beyond rubble and rocks. This is a migratory route for spring, pink, sockeye and chum salmon. A fish farm is near the entrance of Cypress Harbour.

Place names: HMS *Sutlej*, a 35-gun screw steam frigate, was the flagship of the coast from 1863 to 1869. It was involved in the attack of the *Ahousat* in Clayoquot Sound. Cypress Harbour earned its name in 1865 for being fringed with cypress trees.

Camping: N50°49.62' W126°40.05'. A forest recreation site is located in Stopford Bay in the south end of Cypress Harbour. There are five sites with picnic tables and an outhouse.

Greenway Sound

This is a deep waterway indenting Broughton Island in several legs. Two fish farms are near the entrance along with a few floating homes. Broughton Lagoon is a reversing tidal rapid. In the large cove before the dogleg where the sound turns south is a busy marina, the Greenway Sound Marine Resort. It has a restaurant, washrooms, laundry, garbage drop and store. South of the bay is a dinghy dock that is part of a forest recreation site. This is also the trailhead for a short trail to Broughton Lake. At the lake you'll find a picnic site and float. A branch leads to a smaller lake called Beaver Dam Lake.

Camping: N50°50.19' W126°46.31'. The forest recreation site in Greenway Sound south of the marina has a rough rock beach in front of it. The upland is grassy and clear, with a wooden tent pad and other level areas along with picnic tables, a fire pit and an outhouse. The amount of moss on the pile of firewood indicates this location is probably rarely used.

Patrick Passage

This passage joins Sutlej Channel with Wells Passage south of Kinnaird Island. Kinnaird Island has been heavily logged recently and will take years to recover. Sullivan Bay on the north end of North Broughton Island is a community with a store, post office (V0N 3H0), floating homes, a floating lodge, fuel, washrooms, showers and laundry. Float planes land regularly in the bay.

Grappler Sound

This popular boating area has numerous bays, most of them used as anchorages. Expect mostly rough beaches and little possibility of upland access. A good clam beach is located in Claydon Bay. The north arm of the bay is an anchorage and boat haven. It was once a busy logging camp and steamer landing; in earlier times the north entrance was a village site and the nearby rocky islet a fortified village.

Place names: Sir Harry Verney lived at Claydon House in Buckinghamshire. His eldest son, Lieutenant Edmund Hope Verney, commanded the gunboat *Grappler* 1860–1865. Florence Nightingale was a sister of Sir Harry's second wife, resulting in Sir Harry Range, Verney Mountain, Florence Mountain and Nightingale Mountain. The three-gun *Grappler* served with the *Forward* on the B.C. coast from 1860 until 1868, when it was sold for use as a coastal trader. Fire destroyed it in 1883 near Seymour Narrows. About 72 passengers, mostly Chinese cannery workers, were killed in that incident.

Camping: N50°56.50' W126°51.55'. On the west end of Watson Island south of Watson Point are the ruins of an old sawmill on pilings. South of the sawmill is a good beach—by far the best in the region. Camping is possible on the bank above the beach; there's room for a group in the clear forest area behind the sawmill ruins.

Hopetown Passage

This is a pretty passage leading along the south end of Watson Island between Grappler Sound and Mackenzie Sound. Currents can be strong, especially on spring tides, with the strongest limited to where it narrows on the east end. Countercurrents are prevalent through most of the rest of the passage. There are good sandy beaches on the Watson Island shore, with the best in Hoy Bay at the small First Nation community of Hopetown, the main village for the Gwawaenuk. A few houses are located here.

Mackenzie Sound

This is a surprisingly pretty waterway—surprising because the steep bluffs and mountainous backdrop aren't apparent until you venture inside, at which point you're likely to be momentarily awed. It has low currents and low wave exposure. It's used mainly for log handling and storage, including heli-logging. Prawn and crab are fished commercially; coho spawn in the stream opposite Nimmo Bay and sockeye in Nimmo Bay Creek and Mackenzie River. There's an unusual petroglyph by a creek at the north head of the sound. Look for it on a boulder about 30 m (100 feet) above the water line. Blue tape may mark the site. A trail continues to Mackenzie Lake.

Calm water inside Mackenzie Sound.

The north shore of Little Nimmo Bay is the site of Nimmo Bay Heli Resort, a fishing and helicopter adventure lodge. One specialty trip is being taken by helicopter to the Kinaklini River and rafting 670 m (2,200 feet) down to the head of Knight Inlet.

Beaches are few along Mackenzie Sound's west extent. For a base camp, consider Blair Islet in the entrance to the sound just off Hopetown Passage. Beaches extend along the west shoreline and access to the forest seems good. It is undeveloped.

Place names: Kenneth Mackenzie was in charge of Craigflower, a large farm established by the Puget Sound Agricultural Company near Fort Victoria 1853–66.

Kenneth Passage

This is a pretty area to paddle; boats generally avoid it due to the many rocks that make navigation dangerous. Expect the possibility of strong currents, especially near Kenneth Point on the northern tip of Watson Island. Birds in the area include scoter, goldeneye, gull, grebe and common merganser. The rocks are a major Steller's sea lion haulout.

Roaringhole Rapids

This is the entrance to Nepah Lagoon, a long and narrow waterway with steep shores and few beaches. The rapids live up to their name. On a visit when Kenneth Passage was calm, the rapids here were a tidal chute. The lagoon is rarely visited and is used mainly for log handling. Sea cucumbers are common at the head of the inlet; spring salmon spawn in the upper lagoon.

Turnbull Cove

This is a popular anchorage, and a dozen or so boats will be here at any time during the summer season. It's surrounded by rough beach. On the north end a trail leads over a ridge to Huaskin Lake. The trailhead is N50°57.85' W126°50.13'. At the lake there's a forest recreation campsite, float, picnic table, fire pit and outhouse. The trail is short—about five minutes—making a portage possible.

Place names: Alexander Turnbull was assistant surgeon aboard HMS *Topaze* 1859–63.

Camping: N50°57.42' W126°49.82'. The beaches inside Turnbull Cove aren't really appropriate for camping. On the north entrance point to the cove is a flat grassy area next to a thick forest. There is space for a tent or two above the high tide line. Enter onto the rock outside Turnbull Cove. An unusual feature is three memorial markers. One is engraved and attached to the rocks. The other two are simple markers, apparently for pets that (I'm guessing) expired before finishing a boat trip up the Inside Passage.

Stuart Narrows

Stuart Narrows gives access to Drury Inlet, which continues extensively past the narrows. The current can reach 7 knots at the entrance, and is fastest south of Weld Rock. Use Alert Bay as a reference station; the turn to flood is 5 minutes after low water at Alert Bay and the turn to ebb 10 minutes after high water. Merganser, scoter, scaup, cormorant, loon, grebe, rhinoceros auklet and gull use the entrance.

Drury Inlet

This inlet runs 28 km (17 miles) west, then twists and turns northward for about 15 km (9 miles), first as Actaeon Sound and then

Tsibass Lagoon. Anchorage can be found at Richmond and Sunderland bays. The inlet is dotted with rocks and islets, which might make it ideal for kayaking except the backdrop is unremarkable rolling hills. Beaches are mainly clam beds. The entrance to Tsibass Lagoon is a tidal rapid. High water slack is 2 hours and 20 minutes after high water at Alert Bay. This is when most boats will make the crossing.

Place names: Capt. Byron Drury was commander of the surveying vessel *Pandora* 1850–1856. Features around Drury Inlet are named for the *Pandora* officers master Thomas Kerr (Mount Kerr), surgeon John Jolliffe (Mount Jolliffe) and, of course, Pandora Head for the vessel.

Wells Passage

This passage leads from Queen Charlotte Strait to Grappler Sound. Currents can run as high as 3 knots. Look for sea lions at a colony at Surgeon Islets. Two fish farms are located on the northwest shore below Mount Simmonds and in Wehlis Bay. Tracey Harbour is heavily used for log handling. Napier Bay at the head of Tracey Harbour is a popular boat haven.

Place names: Admiral Sir John Wells (1763–1841) was distinguished for his role in defeating the Dutch fleet in a navy career that lasted 65 years.

Camping: N50°51.31' W126°53.49'. At the south entrance to Tracey Harbour is a small cove with a good beach topped by intertidal grass (it's Cane Point, not marked on the regional map). On the southeast end of the beach is a good clear area above the high tide line, though I found the adjacent rock ledge preferable. This is a pretty spot that could host a small group without being developed.

Travel notes: I was quite sure when I camped here the thick surrounding scrub would ensure no visits by bears. But sure enough, that evening I heard the unmistakable sound of a bear coming my way. After a few whacks of a paddle against the rock, the sound suddenly became that of a bear making its way very quickly in the opposite direction.

The Polkinghorne Islands.

Carter Passage

This narrow passage runs between North Broughton and Broughton islands and is a shortcut to Greenway Sound at high tide only. It dries about 4 km (2.5 miles) east of the west entrance. Complicating any transit are currents that run as high as 7 knots. One possibility for kayakers would be leaving Greenway Sound at high water slack and completing the transit before the worst of the current. The distance is 6.5 km (4 miles), so some current is likely before reaching Wells Passage, but it's unlikely to be hazardous if you don't linger. The west entrance is an anchorage.

Polkinghorne Islands

These islands are part of a string of islets and rocks that begin at Dickson Island and continue through Percy and Vincent islands. This makes it a great kayaking location. Many small islets with grassy bluffs give the opportunity for rock ledge camping, especially on those just south of Dickson Island. Currents are strong through all the islands, with a race and rips northwest of the largest of the Polkinghorne Islands. Beaches are generally rough. The best is in the cove on the north central side of the main Polkinghorne Island.

The process of giving the Polkinghorne Islands protected status has begun. They are winter habitat for humpback whales and minke whales have been observed. It's a good area for rockfish, and harbour porpoises are a likely sight.

Camping: N50°47.93' W126°56.04'. The cove at the middle of the northeast side of the main Polkinghorne Island has good beaches, but no upland for camping. To the north of that bay, around the headland, is a good clam beach with a long rock outcrop extending northwest. The beach can be used for access to the rock during most tide levels. Rock ledge landings may be needed at higher tides, but the rock is gently sloping. The top is expansive and flat and could host a large group above the high tide line. I found this an exceptionally pretty spot and far preferable to a forest location.

Cullen Harbour

This is a newly protected area and part of the extension to Broughton Archipelago Marine Park. It has nine clam beaches and an abalone area on the rocks outside the harbour. It's also a good place to see rhinoceros auklets. The harbour is a popular anchorage, but beaches are poor for kayakers.

At the north end of the harbour is the entrance to Booker Lagoon. The passage is prone to strong currents. There is no current reference for the lagoon entrance, so proceed at your own risk.

Camping: N50°46.34' W126°44.83'. I found Cullen Harbour's beaches rough and not conducive to camping. However, there is a nice rock outcrop in the shallows north of Olden Island, the largest of two connected islands on the central southeast side of Long Island. Camping is possible on the level areas of the rock. Another possibility is at the head of Dobbin Bay; look for the rock outcrop.

Continuing west

To continue along the north Queen Charlotte Strait shoreline for a trip to Cape Caution and other areas along B.C.'s central coast, see *The Wild Coast, Volume 2*. The next camping opportunity west of the Polkinghornes is at Shelter Bay, a distance of about 45 km (28 miles). While that sounds like a long distance, kayakers paddling the central coast need to be prepared for the possibility of 50-km (30-mile) transits, as good all-tide campsites are few and far between. For a break,

Sutlej Passage.

look to Blunden Harbour. Unfortunately, it has a private upland east of Cohoe Bay and is a major log tie-up area. There is no designated campsite, but in calm weather there are good rock platforms in various spots.

To continue west along the Vancouver Island coast toward Cape Scott, see *The Wild Coast, Volume 1*. It is a 37-km trip (23 miles) from the west end of Malcolm Island to a campsite at God's Pocket, the first designated campsite along that route. With volumes 1 and 3, a kayaker could plan a circumnavigation of Vancouver Island.

Epilogue—
Transiting the coast

TOGETHER THE THREE *WILD COAST* KAYAKING GUIDES CREATE A ROUTE from one end of the B.C. coast to the other, from Victoria and Sechelt to the Alaskan border. I'd like to end this series by offering a list of potential campsites along the way through both routes—the Inside Passage and the Outside Passage. Details of these campsites and the hazards along the way are presented in the other volumes, but here is the route I would choose to travel from the south coast to the Alaskan border again. These are not dependent on distance; they are simply places I would choose to stop, but most days are in the range of 35 km (about 20 miles).

THE INSIDE PASSAGE

1. Launch in Vancouver or Howe Sound (a possible camping location in Howe Sound is at Plumper Cove on Keats Island, if necessary). 2. Thormanby Islands. 3. Musket Island. 4. Harwood Island. 5. Kinghorn Island. 6. South Rendezvous Island. 7. Charles Bay. 8. Poyntz Island. 9. Broken Islands. 10. Lady Islands. 11. Tracey Island. 12. Polkinghorne Island. 13. Shelter Bay. 14. Indian Cove. 15. Kelp Head. 16. Penrose Island. 17. Koeye River. 18. Port John. 19. Kynumpt Harbour. 20. Dallas Island. 21. Sarah Island. 22. Flat Point. 23. Redcliff Point. 24. McKay Reach. 25. Union Passage entrance. 26. Nabannah Bay. 27. Stuart Anchorage. 28. Kitson Island. 29. Lucy Islands. 30. Proctor Islands. 31. The Alaskan border and beyond.

An alternative route

1. Launch in Victoria. 2. D'Arcy Island. 3. Portland Island. 4. Wallace Island. 5. Pirates Cove. 6. Newcastle Island. 7. Maude Island. 8. Lasqueti Island. 9. Favada. 10. Harwood Island, then a continuation of the route from Vancouver.

THE OUTSIDE PASSAGE

This supposes a route from the Alaskan border to Victoria via the west coast of Vancouver Island.

1. Proctor Islands. 2. Dundas Island. 3. Melville Island. 4. Phipps Island. 5. Oval Bay. 6. Joachim Spit. 7. Hankin Point. 8. Anger Island. 9. Monckton Inlet. 10. Campania Island. 11. Sagar Islands. 12. Milne Island. 13. Pidwell Reef. 14. Blair Inlet. 15. McMullin Group. 16. Superstition Point. 17. Wolf Beach. 18. Grief Bay. 19. Redsand Beach. 20. Indian Cove. 21. Shelter Bay. 22. Balaclava Island. 23. Cape Sutil. 24. Nissen Bight. 25. Lowrie Bay. 26. Raft Cove. 27. Grant Bay. 28. Lawn Point. 29. The beach near Aster Bay. 30. Nordstrum Creek. 31. Bunsby Islands. 32. Rugged Point. 33. Catala Island. 34. Calvin Falls. 35. Burdwood Point. 36. Hesquiat Harbour. 37. Naxwaqis. 38. Whitesand Cove. 39. Moser Point (Vargas Island). 40. Florencia Islet. 41. Benson Island. 42. Keeha Bay. 43. Clo-oose Bay. 44. Thrasher Cove. 45. China Beach. 46. East Sooke. 47. Victoria.

This, naturally, is the route one might formulate while sitting at home. There are many considerations, and a few I've learned are worth sharing. First, no trip can be planned from the living room. There are days where you will get just a few miles and have to pull out due to the weather. Another day you might encounter superb paddling conditions and simply not want to get out of the water.

This makes keeping friends and family informed difficult. Phones can be hard to find, and cell phone coverage on the coast a few miles outside urban areas is pretty much non-existent. Giving someone a detailed trip plan with the idea that you're going to stick to it—and here I have to go against common wisdom—would only complicate a search and rescue. I find within even a few days I am rarely within a couple of dozen miles of where I intended to be. Sometimes I'm not even within hundreds of miles, as I might change course for weather or for interests only apparent when I arrive. For instance, I might plan several days to explore an archipegalo that I find immediately small and uninteresting, and leave that day; or I might go up an inlet that looks appealing that I had planned on passing. My best advice is to provide a general itinerary, then get to a telephone when you can and give updates on your best guess where and when you can make that next phone call.

Your contact should also realize that a delay of a week or two is not necessarily an indication you are dead or in need of rescue. For instance, I had someone call the Coast Guard on me because I was two days overdue when I had actually phoned and left a message that was apparently lost by an answering machine foul-up. Fortunately, the Coast Guard was cautious in mounting a search, as I was actually at home.

This goes back to my theory (again, an unpopular one) that specific, detailed trip itineraries for longer trips can do more harm in the hands of friends or family than good. Unless your kayak floats away and you are stranded on an island, a rescue will likely only be needed if you somehow end up in the water. If you can't get back in your kayak and require rescue, you will have to get help in the first few minutes. A contact person with an itinerary won't help you here. Flares, a whistle, a mirror and especially a VHF radio will. So will proper clothing, as in a wetsuit. At least that will help delay the onset of hypothermia. For peace of mind, your contact should be prepared for you to be delayed, possibly many days, by foul weather before you can reach a phone. So do leave as detailed a trip itinerary as you can, but explain its shortcomings thoroughly.

For a trip in June, I allow for one of every five days to be foul weather, and one of seven in July and August, but I rarely require them. Kayakers will likely find an evolution in their kayaking that will make keeping to an itinerary difficult, but in a good way. After several weeks of paddling you'll likely be able to far surpass your initial daily estimate of the distance you can travel. I do this regularly by limiting itineraries to 20–30 km, but end up doing as much as 60 km per day for days at a time.

Volume 1 and Volume 2 Addendum/Corrections

IN VOLUME 1, PAGE 135, I SUGGESTED ASTER BAY ON THE NORTH END OF Brooks Peninsula as a campsite for those preparing to head south around the peninsula. I have since heard back that Aster Bay is prone to surf. Instead, a more protected site is located southwest of Aster Bay at a beach behind two islets at approximately N50°11.18' W127°49.76'.

In *Volume 2*, page 227, I suggested a campsite on south Pitt Island facing Otter Channel. I have heard back that this beach has limited potential for site development and as a result I would suggest scrubbing it from the kayaking route list. Instead, the Cherry Islets site in nearby Squally Channel should be favoured, while those wishing to stay on the Outside Passage can go from Monckton Inlet to the beaches near Jewsbury Peninsula without the need of an additional stop.

For more changes and evolutions in the kayaking campsite trail, and to contribute your own experiences and campsite information, visit **www.thewildcoast.ca**.

GPS errata: In *Volume 2*, I began presenting GPS waypoints of campsite locations. This confirmed my suitability for writing rather than mathematics—or anything that lets me near numbers. Three errors crept in.

On page 76, the campsite at Buccleugh Point inadvertently listed the waypoint for outer Fox Island. The waypoint should be N51°05.68' W127°39.93'.

On page 163, Eucott Bay should read N52°27.37' W127°18.73'. The "27" was reversed to a "72", which, of course, is impossible.

The end of a day of kayaking, Sidney Spit.

On page 278, the waypoint for the beach on northeast Banks Island should be N53°37.41' W130°26.01', not "N50" as printed.

Watch **www.thewildcoast.ca** website for additional updates.

Bibliography

Alejandro Malaspina, Portrait of a Visionary, John Kendrick, McGill-Queen's University Press, 1999.

"An amazing, true B.C. fish story," Stephen Hume, *Vancouver Sun,* October 2, 2004.

"Bamberton lands sold: Victoria's Three Point Properties won't rush to develop ill-starred site," Andrew A. Duffy, *Times Colonist,* March 10, 2005.

"The Baynes Sound Coastal Plan for Shellfish Aquaculture," Coast and Marine Planning Branch, Ministry of Sustainable Resource Management, December 2002.

B.C. Treaty Commission Annual Report, 2005.

"Boyle Point Provincial Park Master Plan," B.C. Parks South Coast Region, Ministry of Environment, Lands and Parks, December 1990.

British Columbia Coast Names, Captain John T. Walbran, Douglas and McIntyre, 1971.

"Coastal Zone Strategic Plan, Central Coast Land and Coast Resource Management Plan," Intregrated Land Management Bureau, undated.

"Complexity: Changes In Social Inequality During The Marpole-Late Transition In The Gulf of Georgia Region," Brian Thom, paper presented, Northwest Coast Symposium, 61st Annual Meeting of the Society for American Archaeology, New Orleans, April 10–14, 1996.

"Cortes Island Coastal Plan for Shellfish Aquaculture," July 2003, Ministry of Sustainable Resource Management, Coast & Marine Planning Branch.

"Development Of A Recreation Plan For Coburg Peninsula And Esquimalt Lagoon," prepared for Esquimalt Lagoon Stewardship Initiative, Victoria Esquimalt Harbours Environmental Action Program and Royal Roads University, 2002.

"Drumbeg Provincial Park And Gabriola Sands Provincial Park And Recreation Area Master Plan," Ministry of Environment And Parks, Parks & Outdoor Recreation Division, South Coast Region, August 1987.

"Fillongley, Tribune Bay, Helliwell, Sandy Island Parks Master Plan," Ministry of Environment and Parks, September 1987.

Gabriola: Petroglyph Island, Mary and Ted Bentley, Sono Nis Press, 1998.

"Garden Bay Provincial Park Master Plan," B.C. Parks South Coast Region, Ministry of Environment, Lands and Parks, September 1992.

"Gulf Islands National Park Reserve of Canada Interim Management Guidelines, Draft For Public Review," Parks Canada, undated.

Indian Petroglyphs of the Pacific Northwest, Beth and Ray Hill, Hancock House Publishing, 1974.

"Johnstone-Bute coastal plan," draft, British Columbia, Coast and Marine Planning Branch, September 2004.

Malaspina and Galiano: Spanish Voyages of the Northwest Coast 1791 and 1792, Donald C. Cutter, University of Washington Press, 1991.

"Management Plan, Desolation Sound and Copeland Islands Marine Parks and Tux'wnech Okeover Arm Provincial Park," Ministry of Water, Land and Air Protection, November 2003.

"Management Plan, draft, Malaspina Provincial Park," Environmental Stewardship, Lower Mainland Region, Ministry of Water, Land and Air Protection, November 2003.

"Management Plan, Jedediah Island Marine Park," Ministry of Water, Land and Air Protection, June 2003.

"Management Plan For Pirates Cove Marine Provincial Park," Environmental Stewardship, Vancouver Island Region, April 2004.

"Master Plan For Dionisio Point Provincial Park," Ministry Of Environment, Lands And Parks, May 1995.

"Mothership Meanderings: Estero Basin," Alan Wilson, *Wavelength Magazine*, June/July 2000.

"Newcastle Island Provincial Marine Park Master Plan," BC Parks South Vancouver Island District, April 1995.

"North Island Straits Coastal Plan," Ministry of Sustainable Resource Management Coast & Marine Planning Branch, December 2002.

Notes and Observations on the Kwakiool People of the Northern Points of Vancouver Island and Adjacent Coasts, made during the summer of 1885, George W. Dawson, Royal Society of Canada, 1887.

"Okanagan-Shuswap Land and Resource Management Plan," Okanagan-Shuswap LRMP Process Support Team, April 11, 2001.

"Porpoise Bay Provincial Park Master Plan," Ministry of Water, Land and Air Protection, January 1981.

"Regional District Of Mount Waddington Regional Harbours Initiative Final Report," Mary Murphy, Project Coordinator, March 2005.

"Ruckle Provincial Park Master Plan," J.R. Morris, Ministry Of Lands, Parks And Housing Parks & Outdoor Recreation Division, South Coast Region, May 1986.

"Routes to Jedediah," Bob Schroeder, *Wavelength Magazine*, August/September 1995.

Sailing Directions (Enroute), Ninth Edition, National Geospatial-Intelligence Agency Bethesda, Maryland, United States Government, 2005.

"Sargeant Bay Provincial Park Master Plan," Ministry Of Environment And Parks Parks and Outdoor Recreation Division, South Coast Region February, 1991.

"Savary Island Dune And Shoreline Study Report To The Powell River Regional District," Thurber Engineering Ltd., March 2003.

Senewelets, David V. Burley, Royal British Columbia Museum, 1989.

"Simson Provincial Park Master Plan," Ministry Of Environment And Parks Parks and Outdoor Recreation Division, South Coast Region, April 1987.

"Smelt Bay Provincial Park Master Plan," Ministry Of Environment And Parks Parks and Outdoor Recreation Division, South Coast Region, June 1987.

"Smuggler Cove Provincial Marine Park Master Plan," Ministry Of Environment And Parks Parks and Outdoor Recreation Division, South Coast Region, July 1985.

"Social Inequality, Intensification Of Salmon, And Storage On The Northwest Coast," John Dougherty, Neighbours Community Update, *Timberwest*, June 2002.

Terror of the Coast, Chris Arnett, Talonbooks, 1999.

"Top of the strait—touring northern Georgia Strait," by Robyn Budd, *Wavelength Magazine*, June/July 1995.

"Vancouver Island Region Management Direction Statement for Lower Nimpkish Provincial Park," Ministry of Water, Land and Air Protection Environmental Stewardship, September 2003.

A Voyage of Discovery to the North Pacific Ocean and round the world, in which the coast of north-west America has been carefully examined and accurately surveyed, undertaken by His Majesty's command, principally with a view to ascertain the existence of any navigable communication between the North Pacific and North Atlantic oceans, and performed in the years 1790, 1791, 1792, 1793, 1794 and 1795 in the Discovery, sloop of war, and armed tender Chatam, under the command of Captain George Vancouver, George Vancouver, G.G. and J. Robinson and J. Edwards, London, 1798.

The Wind Came All Ways, Owen S. Lange, Environment Canada, 1998.

Pacific Yachting's Cruising Guide to British Columbia, Vol. III – Sunshine Coast. Fraser Estuary and Vancouver to Jervis Inlet, 1982, Bill Wolferstan.

The following websites were also used in the research for this book:

BC Ferries
www.bcferries.com

B.C. Geographical Names Information Service
www.ilmbwwww.gov.bc.ca

B.C. Parks
www.env.gov.bc.ca/bcparks

B.C. Treaty Commission
www.bctreaty.net/nations_3/councilofchiefs.html

BCGS Geology Map
webmap.em.gov.bc.ca/mapplace/minpot/bcgs.cfm

Canada Post
www.canadapost.ca

Da'naxda'xw/Awaetlala First Nation
www.danaxdaxw.org/about_us.htm

Da'naxda'xw First Nation
www.danaxdaxw.com

Environment Canada weather
www.weatheroffice.ec.gc.ca

Garry oak ecosystems recovery team
www.goert.ca

Islands Trust
www.islandstrust.bc.ca

Lyackson First Nation
www.valdes.ca/lyackson.html

Mount Arrowsmith Biosphere Reserve, South-Eastern Vancouver
Island, British Columbia, Canada
www.mountarrowsmithbiosphere.ca/attributes.htm

Parks Canada
www.pc.gc.ca/pn-np/bc/gulf/carte-map-nfl_e.asp#winter

Regional District of Comox-Strathcona
www.rdcs.bc.ca

Sensitive Ecosystems Inventory
www.env.gov.bc.ca

Songhees First Nation
www.songheesnation.com

The following Purpose Statement and Zoning Plan documents prepared by B.C. Parks' Environmental Stewardship Department were used in the research of this book:

Cormorant Channel Marine Provincial Park Purpose Statement And Zoning Plan, March 2003; Broughton Archipelago Provincial Park Purpose Statement And Zoning Plan, March 2003; East Redonda Island Ecological Reserve Purpose Statement, March 2003; Roscoe Bay Marine Provincial Park Purpose Statement And Zoning Plan March 2003; Walsh Cove Marine Provincial Park Purpose Statement And Zoning Plan, March 2003; Ha'thayim Marine Provincial Park Purpose Statement And Zoning Plan, Feb. 2003; Mansons Landing Provincial Park Purpose Statement And Zoning Plan, Feb. 2003; Rendezvous Island South Provincial Park Purpose Statement And Zoning Plan, Aug. 2003; South Texada Island Provincial Park And Anderson Bay Provincial Park Purpose Statement And Zoning Plan, March 2003; Sabine Channel Marine Provincial Park (Bunny/Jervis Island) Purpose Statement And Zoning Plan, March 2003; Squitty Bay Provincial Park Purpose Statement And Zoning Plan, Dec. 2002; Mount Richardson Provincial Park Purpose Statement And Zoning Plan, March 2003; Ambrose Lake Ecological Reserve Purpose Statement, March 2003; Musket Island Marine Provincial Park Purpose Statement And Zoning Plan, March 2003; Harmony Islands Marine Provincial Park Purpose Statement And Zoning Plan, March 2003; Mitlenatch Island Nature Provincial Park Purpose Statement And Zoning Plan, March 2003; Teakerne Arm Marine Provincial Park Purpose Statement And Zoning Plan, March 2003; Octopus Islands Provincial Park Purpose Statement And Zoning Plan, Feb. 2003; Small Inlet Marine Provincial Park Purpose Statement And Zoning Plan, Aug. 2003; Rock Bay Marine Provincial Park Purpose Statement And Zoning Plan, Aug. 2003; Thurston Bay Marine Provincial Park Purpose Statement And Zoning Plan, Feb. 2003; Robson Bight (Michael Bigg) Ecological Reserve Purpose Statement, March 2003; Echo Bay Marine Provincial Park Purpose Statement And Zoning Plan, March 2003; Princess Louisa Marine Provincial Park Purpose Statement And Zoning Plan, March 2003; Rebecca Spit Provincial Park Purpose Statement And Zoning Plan, Feb. 2003; Surge Narrows Provincial Park Purpose Statement and Zoning Plan, Feb. 2003; Read Island Provincial Park Purpose Statement And Zoning Plan, March 2003; Lasqueti Island Ecological Reserve Purpose Statement, March 2003; Trial Islands Ecological Reserve Purpose

Statement, Sept. 2003; Oak Bay Islands Ecological Reserve Purpose Statement, Oct. 2003; Bellhouse Provincial Park Purpose Statement And Zoning Plan, March 2003; Satellite Channel Ecological Reserve Purpose Statement, Sept. 2003; Mount Tuam Ecological Reserve Purpose Statement, Oct. 2003; Bamberton Provincial Park Purpose Statement And Zoning Plan, March 2003; Ballingall Islets Ecological Reserve Purpose Statement, Sept. 2003; Montague Harbour Marine Provincial Park Purpose Statement And Zoning Plan, March 2003; Bodega Ridge Provincial Park Purpose Statement And Zoning Plan, March 2003; Rose Islets Ecological Reserve Purpose Statement, Sept. 2003; Canoe Islets Ecological Reserve Purpose Statement, Sept. 2003; Whaleboat Island Marine Provincial Park Purpose Statement And Zoning Plan, Aug. 2003; Wakes Cove Provincial Park Purpose Statement And Zoning Plan, March 2003; Sandwell Provincial Park Purpose Statement And Zoning Plan, March 2003; Hudson Rocks Ecological Reserve Purpose Statement, Aug. 2003.

Index

Numbers in italics indicate the best map for locating the entry.

Notes

ABOUT THE AUTHOR

John Kimantas is an editor and writer with 18 years of experience at newspapers in Ontario, Manitoba and British Columbia. His credits include five awards for environmental writing. He is an avid outdoorsman and kayaker. This is his third book. His adventures can be followed at **www.thewildcoast.ca.**

ABOUT THE KAYAK

The kayak used for the 2006 expedition on the south B.C. coast was a Seward Ascente. With a length of 18.5 feet (5.64 m) and a beam of 22.5 inches (57.15 cm), it is a nimbler and more sporty model than many sea kayaks available. The model used was a high volume kayak and could accommodate about four weeks' gear with little difficulty. For more about the Ascente and other Seaward kayaks, see **www.seawardkayaks.com**.